TRAVELS OF
MIRZA ABU TALEB KHAN

broadview editions
series editor: L.W. Conolly

MIRZA ABU TALEB KHAN.

This engraving of Mirza Abu Talib by W. Bond, which served as a frontispiece for both the 1810 and 1814 editions of the Travels, is from a portrait by James Northcote that was painted during his stay in London. See p. 134.

TRAVELS OF
MIRZA ABU TALEB KHAN
in Asia, Africa, and Europe,
during the years 1799, 1800, 1801,
1802, and 1803

Mirza Abu Talib
Translated by Charles Stewart

edited by Daniel O'Quinn

broadview editions

Library and Archives Canada Cataloguing in Publication

Abu Talib Khan, 1752-1806?
   Travels of Mirza Abu Taleb Khan / Mirza Abu Talib ; translated by Charles Stewart ; edited by Daniel O'Quinn.

Translation of: Masir-i Talibi.
Includes bibliographical references.
ISBN 978-1-55111-672-3

   1. Abu Talib Khan, 1752-1806?—Travel.   2. Voyages and travels.
I. Stewart, Charles, 1764-1837.   II. O'Quinn, Daniel, 1962-   III. Title.

G490.A1613   910.4   C2008-905863-1

Broadview Editions

The Broadview Editions series represents the ever-changing canon of literature in English by bringing together texts long regarded as classics with valuable lesser-known works.

Advisory editor for this volume: Michel Pharand

Broadview Press is an independent, international publishing house, incorporated in 1985. Broadview believes in shared ownership, both with its employees and with the general public; since the year 2000 Broadview shares have traded publicly on the Toronto Venture Exchange under the symbol BDP.

We welcome comments and suggestions regarding any aspect of our publications— please feel free to contact us at the addresses below or at broadview@broadviewpress.com.

North America
Post Office Box 1243, Peterborough, Ontario, Canada K9J 7H5
2215 Kenmore Avenue, Buffalo, NY, USA 14207
Tel: (705) 743-8990; Fax: (705) 743-8353;
email: customerservice@broadviewpress.com

UK, Ireland, and continental Europe
NBN International, Estover Road, Plymouth PL6 7PY UK
Tel: 44 (0) 1752 202300   Fax: 44 (0) 1752 202330
email: enquiries@nbninternational.com

Australia and New Zealand
UNIREPS, University of New South Wales
Sydney, NSW, 2052 Australia
Tel: 61 2 9664 0999; Fax: 61 2 9664 5420
email: info.press@unsw.edu.au

www.broadviewpress.com

Broadview Press gratefully acknowledges the financial support of the Government of Canada through the Book Publishing Industry Development Program (BPIDP) for our publishing activities.

This book is printed on paper containing 100% post-consumer fibre.

Typesetting and assembly: True to Type Inc., Claremont, Canada.

PRINTED IN CANADA

Contents

Acknowledgements • 7
Introduction • 9
Mirza Abu Talib and Charles Stewart: A Brief Chronology • 49
A Note on the Text • 53

Travels of Mirza Abu Taleb Khan in Asia, Africa, and Europe, during the years 1799, 1800, 1801, 1802, and 1803 • 55

Appendix A: The Social Context • 371
1. Mirza Abu Talib Khan, "Poem in Praise of Miss Julia Burrell" (1807) • 371
2. The Duchess of Devonshire's Gala Breakfast, *Morning Post and Gazetteer* (7 and 8 July 1800) • 378
3. The Lord Mayor's Feast, *Oracle and Daily Advertiser* (11 November 1800) • 381

Appendix B: Contemporary Reviews • 385
1. *The Quarterly Review* (August 1810) • 385
2. *The Eclectic Review* (August 1811) • 401

Appendix C: Persia: Orientalist Translations and Essays • 404
1. From Sir William Jones, "A Persian Song of Hafiz" (1772) • 404
2. From Sir William Jones, "Essay on the Poetry of the Eastern Nations" (1772) • 406
3. From John Nott, *Select Odes from the Persian Poet Hafez* (1787) • 411
4. Sir Willam Jones, "The Sixth Discourse; on the Persians" (1790) • 419

Appendix D: Comparative Ethnographies • 435
1. From Montesquieu, *Persian Letters* (1762) • 435
2. From Lady Mary Wortley Montagu, *Letters* (1763) • 448
3. From Charles Grant, "Observations on the State of Society among the Asiatic Subjects of Great Britain" (1792) • 451

Select Bibliography • 457

For Eli

Acknowledgements

In a project such as this one accrues many debts. My primary research assistant Laura Stenberg deserves special thanks for her tenacious pursuit of facts and her patience with my errors. Ingrid Mundel helped prepare the text at an early stage. Nigel Leask and Tim Fulford were very supportive from the outset and their suggestions were most valuable. Mohamad Tavakoli-Targhi offered much needed guidance early in the project and his scholarship has been particularly helpful along the way. Thanks to Jane Moody for assistance at the British Library. Teresa Heffernan, Michael J. Franklin, Dan White, and Donna Andrew all read the introduction and provided extremely useful commentary. I am deeply indebted to the legion of scholars who have contributed to the *Oxford Dictionary of National Biography*. Julia Gaunce, Marjorie Mather, Michel Pharand, and Leonard Conolly at Broadview Press were wonderful to work with and they deserve thanks for supporting such an unusual project. Finally, I would like to thank the Social Sciences and Humanities Research Council of Canada for generously supporting my research.

Introduction

When contemplating the complex history of British imperialism in the eighteenth and nineteenth centuries, it is important to remember that the vast archive of official policy documents and published representations of colonial transactions overlays a more diffuse record of the intimate social interactions of people directly and indirectly caught in the web of imperial relations. Take for example the following post script to a letter dated 12 to 17 September 1799 from Capetown's chief hostess, Lady Anne Barnard, to one of Britain's most powerful authorities on Indian affairs, Lord Dundas:

> I have sent a few letters of Introduction with Capt. Richardson & Khan Sayb [Mirza Abu Talib Khan] the first is a man of learning and Intelligence who returns for health chiefly after 20 years spent in India he is much esteemed, & is of the party with Khan Saijb a persian chief, a clever, agreeable & good man, a man of letters also, and far superior to most of the grandees of Indostan—he has the Honor to be a particular friend of Lord Cornwallis & travels chiefly to see the world, possibly he may combine some other motive which he will communicate to Lord Cornwallis but both are worthy of *your* notice I believe—Capt Richardson has translated many things from the persian & in particular part of the asiatic researches—The figurative style of the East breaks forth from the Khan whenever his Imagination is struck—a person remarked to him tother evening at our House, that he was supported by a pretty woman on each side, he smiled and pointing to himself, said in English—"one night–two days—" alluding to his dark complexion of course—[1]

This note captures many of the key questions raised by *The Travels of Mirza Abu Taleb Khan* and can serve as a starting point for considering the demands of this text. Arising from social interactions in Lady Anne's house in Capetown, the letter is a private document that records a fleeting moment in the move-

---

1 Anne Barnard, *The Letters of Lady Anne Barnard to Henry Dundas from the Cape and Elsewhere, 1793-1803 together with her Journal of a Tour into the Interior and Certain Other Letters* ed. A.M. Lewin Robinson (Cape Town: A.A. Balkema, 1973), 199.

ment from India to London of two men. One, Captain David Richardson, is returning after years of service to the East India Company; the other, Mirza Abu Talib, a Persian-speaking poet, historian, and employee of the Company is making his first and only visit to the metropole. Both men are able to operate socially and officially in each other's language and both men seem to embody the charm and responsibility of gentlemanly conduct. It is on the basis of these linguistic and social skills that Lady Anne is recommending both men to Dundas and thus this letter, as innocuous as it seems, is part of the labyrinthine web of personal and official documents through which colonial affairs were managed at the end of the eighteenth century.

But the letter also attempts to characterise Abu Talib's specific difference from his traveling companions and his hosts in terms of a routine orientalist understanding of "the figurative style of the East." The scene of reported self-figuration is understood as a rhetorical flourish typical of what Sir William Jones categorised as the poetry of the Eastern nations (see Appendix C2). Abu Talib seems to perform precisely according to an orientalist script: his remarks are entirely metaphorical, they are preoccupied with sexual desire for his female companions and they ultimately figure forth his ethnic and racial difference. However, we must remember that this performance is both ascribed to him and yet arises out of his own actions. In this space between being scripted and scripting oneself lies a complex set of problems not only for the practice of reading this text, but also for the historical task of understanding imperial relations as a negotiation between metropole and colony. Is Lady Anne constructing Abu Talib according to her own preconceptions of Eastern culture, society, and identity? Or is Abu Talib enacting or mimicking the very stereotypes that attempt to contain everything he says and does in order to emphasise their speciousness? Or does some complex blend of both intercultural transactions infuse this erotic interchange with larger cultural and social significance? These questions demand careful scrutiny of the relationship between text and performance, between East and West, between intention and transmission, and of the foreclosures nascent in each of these terms. Any universal or totalizing definition of these terms will prove to be a serious hindrance to understanding the historical problems posed by this edition of the *Travels of Mirza Abu Taleb Khan*.

The *Travels* is the 1810 translation of a travel narrative written by a Persian-speaking bureaucrat and *littérateur* named Abu Talib from Lucknow who worked first as a revenue officer under Mukhtaru'd-Dawlah, the Nawab of Oudh, and later as an assistant to several East India Company Residents who succeeded the Nawab. He went out of favor with various factions of both the East India Company and the Nawab's court and found himself without official position in Calcutta through much of the late 1780s and early 1790s. Abu Talib was a deeply learned man who was trained by Iranian scholars in the most elite institutions of Lucknow, the center of Persian learning in India at this time. While "unemployed" in Calcutta, he wrote a history of Asafu'd-Dawlah's governance of Oudh,[1] edited a collection of Hafiz's poems, and became an important critic, historian, and poet.

In 1799, Abu Talib undertook an ocean journey from Calcutta to London via Capetown and Dublin, eventually returning to India after a tour through France and the Mediterranean, and an overland journey from Constantinople through present day Iraq. While traveling through Iraq, Abu Talib performed a pilgrimage to Shiite holy sites. This journey became the occasion for a Persian language travel narrative entitled *Masir-i Talibi*, which is the source text for the *Travels*, and a collection of poems based largely on his experiences in London entitled *Diwan-i Talib*. Abu Talib was not the first or the last Persian traveler to London and Europe in the late eighteenth and early nineteenth centuries. He was preceded by I'tisam al-Din, who helped William Jones in his Persian studies at Oxford in 1768, Mir Muhammad Husain, who visited France and England in 1775 to gain knowledge of European scientific and technological discoveries, and the European travels of Mirza Abu al-Hasan in 1809-10 were a *cause célèbre*.[2] But Abu Talib's text is arguably one of the most extensive ethnographic accounts of British and European life by an Indian Muslim. As such, it is a crucial document not only for British social history, but also for the history of Indian and Persian perceptions of the West. Because this edition is designed primarily for students of British imperial culture, this introduction will focus on the text's representation of Britain. As we will see, the text documents the performance of a form of colonial subjectivity that slides between complicity and resistance that perhaps calls into question the very applicability of such terms.

---

1 See p. 66, note 2.
2 See Gulfishan Khan, *Indian Muslim Perceptions of the West During the Eighteenth Century* (Karachi: Oxford UP, 1998), 71-119.

Masir-i Talibi was written in 1803 and circulated widely among Persian readers in manuscript form. The text was brought to England by Lt. Col. Lennon and then translated from Persian by an Irish scholar of Oriental Languages at the East India Company College at Haileybury named Charles Stewart. It is likely that he was assisted in some degree by the first Indian to join the College, Sheth Ghoolam Hyder, who like Abu Talib came to London in search of employment teaching Persian.[1] There are two nineteenth-century English editions of the text from Longman (1810 and 1814), an abridged Persian-language version published by the Hindoostani Press in Calcutta, edited by Abu Talib's sons, and numerous editions of the Persian text throughout the nineteenth and twentieth centuries.[2] Stewart worked for the East India Company, first at the College of Fort William in Calcutta, which was established by the Marquess of Wellesley to train Company bureaucrats in the languages of commerce and government in India, and then at the Company's college in Hertfordshire. Stewart's knowledge of Persian and other Asian languages, like that of many professional orientalists, was derived from Indian scholars who were characterised as *munshis* or servants to their student masters and whose efforts were quickly consigned to oblivion.[3] Thus the translation bears the marks not only of errors in linguistic and cultural interpretation, but also of a systemic derogation of the work of the very scholars who enabled its production. These errors and the disregard which preceded them are part and parcel of the document, and thus inflect any conclusions derived from readings of the *Travels*. Most importantly, Stewart elided most of the poems—various examples of Persian genres such as *qasidah, mathnawi,*

---

1   See Michael H. Fisher, *Counterflows to Colonialism: Indian Travellers and Settlers in Britain, 1600-1857* (Delhi: Permanent Black, 2004), 112-29 for a discussion of Ghoolam Hyder's career and for an account of the derogation of Indian professors by British orientalists at the College.
2   The most recent edition of Stewart's translation is *Westward Bound: Travels of Mirza Abu Taleb* ed. Mushiril Hasan (Delhi: Oxford UP, 2005).
3   See Mohamad Tavakoli-Targhi, *Refashioning Iran: Orientalism, Occidentalism and Historiography* (Houndmills: Palgrave, 2001), 18-34 for a detailed account of how the labor of Persian scholars was subsumed into the "innovations" and "discoveries" of Orientalists such as William Jones. For a detailed discussion of the relationship between munshis and their master/students at the College of Fort William see Sisir Kumar Das, *Sahibs and Munshis: An Account of the College of Fort William* (Calcutta: Orion, 1978).

and *ghazal*—which were embedded in the original and thus brought the text in line with European expectations that travel writing work primarily through factual description.

Both *Masir-i Talibi* and the *Travels* were circulated under the aegis of the East India Company and it is important to recognise the place of these documents in the ongoing debate regarding education and governance in India at the turn of the nineteenth century. The East India Company was chartered in 1600 and over the ensuing 200 years became the most powerful and most vexed commercial operation in the world. Under its direction, an extraordinarily profitable trade in spice and textiles developed that extended not only into India but into China and other Asian principalities. At the height of its operations in the late eighteenth century, its stock ballooned to the point of threatening the autonomy of the British economy.

But it is impossible to talk about the East India Company in purely mercantile terms; with the disintegration of the Mughal empire in the first half of the eighteenth century, the Company's activities became inextricably tied to the complex political dynamics of the Asian sub-continent. When the Mughal empire collapsed in all but name, various regional states such as Oudh, Bengal, and Gujarat became autonomous political entities. In addition, powers that were never fully under Mughal control, such as the Hindu Maratha Confederacy, the Sultanate of Mysore, and the Nizamate of Hyderabad continued as significant political and military presences. This factionalization of India meant that the East India Company and the French *Compagnie des Indes* were either drawn into regional conflicts or played out larger global conflicts between England and France on Indian soil. Between 1744 and 1761, France and England were at war with each other both directly and as allies of rival claimants to the thrones of Arcot and Hyderabad. The French were essentially defeated by the end of this period and aside from momentary attempts to aid rebellious figures such as Tipu Sultan of Mysore in the 1780s and 90s, their influence in the region waned. British influence, however, did not. After a series of key military victories in Bengal against the resistant Nawab Siraj-ud-Daula and his ostensibly pliable replacement Mir Kasim, Robert Clive precipitated formal Mughal recognition of the East India Company as rulers of Bengal. The conferral of the *diwani* meant that the Company was now directly responsible for the civil, judicial, and revenue administration of the province. What had been a trading company now found itself collecting taxes and governing twenty million people. The servants of this new, hybrid entity had to become judges, soldiers, bureaucrats, and interpreters of culture, and naturally they were often ill-suited to the tasks. The militarization of the Company is a crucial component of the transformation because, despite Clive's military and diplomatic victories in the 1750s and 60s, full territorial control did not come until the defeat of Mysore in the 1790s, and the Marathas in the early years of the nineteenth century. In fact, British forces in the region sustained spectacular losses in the early phases of these conflicts, so the consolidation of British power in India was not only haunted by incessant anxiety about prior losses, but also marked by compensatory expressions of triumphalism.[1]

As the East India Company made the difficult transition from a mercantile corporation to a sovereign governmental body responsible for the administration of millions of people and the management of vast amounts of money and resources, the question of how best to regulate its activities became the topic of intense scrutiny and debate. During the 1770s and 80s the Company continued a long-standing policy of non-intervention in the cultural practices and social norms of Hindu and Muslim people in India. Orientalists such as Sir William Jones brought all of their linguistic knowledge to bear on the problem of gaining sufficient fluency in the laws and strictures of the native cultures in order to govern the subject people on their terms. However, with the increasing militarization of Company interests, the expansion of territorial governance under the rule of Hastings, Cornwallis, and Wellesley, and the increasing pressure exerted by evangelical figures such as Charles Grant in the 1790s, came increasing pressure to Anglicise not only legal and governmental institutions, but also the entire educational system. Charles Grant's *Observations on the State of Society among the Asiatic Subjects of Great Britain* (written 1792, published 1813) argued not only that residents of Hindostan "are a people exceedingly depraved," but also that the only hope for such people was to train them in the tenets of Christianity.[2] Crucial to this paternalistic enculturation was the propagation of the English language. Grant's views would eventually reach their most widely known articulation in Thomas Babington

---

1 For a succinct account of these anxieties see Linda Colley, *Captives* (New York: Pantheon, 2002), 269-95 and Kate Teltscher, *India Inscribed: European and British Writing on India 1600-1800* (Delhi: Oxford UP, 1995), 229-58.
2 See Appendix D3.

Macaulay's "Minute on Indian Education" (February 1835) and would become the law following Lord William Bentinck's momentous decision the following month to "promote European science and literature amongst the natives of India" such that "all the funds appropriated for the purposes of education would be best employed in English education."[1] This meant that money previously allotted for orientalist research and publication was immediately terminated and that English became the official lingua franca of the Asian sub-continent.

Prior to this decision European involvement in Asia had generated a wide range of orientalist materials. Orientalist fantasies suffused all forms of cultural production in the eighteenth and early nineteenth centuries. But despite the ubiquity of such fantasies there are important distinctions to be drawn between forms of orientalist discourse. For example, much of the orientalism emerging from France in the mid-eighteenth century explicitly deploys the East as an alternate cultural formation from which to critique European governmental traditions and religious orthodoxy. Montesquieu is perhaps the most obvious case in point. His *Persian Letters* (1721), which makes a fascinating comparison to the *Travels*, works in precisely this way, and his *Spirit of the Laws* (1748) lays out much of the fantasy of Eastern despotism for years to follow. The *Persian Letters'* fictional Persian travelers describe Parisian manners in such a way that allowed Montesquieu ample room not only for an enlightened critique of European institutions, but also for the exploration of alternative social arrangements projected onto Eastern society (see Appendix D1). Similarly, Lady Elizabeth Hamilton's *Translations of the Letters of the Hindoo Rajah* (1796) stages Hindu difference in order to hold the vices and foibles of British society to account.[2] There is also a significant erotic and pornographic archive with ostensibly Eastern themes and scenarios. Often expressions of political critique and sexual desire go hand in hand: in many eighteenth-century texts governmental and sexual perversion are linked precisely through their shared associations with Eastern tropes and figures.

The orientalist activities promulgated by the East India Company take a different approach to Asian cultures. Aside from

---

1   Quoted in Suresh Chandra Ghosh, *The History of Education in Modern India, 1757-1998* (Hyderabad: Orient Longman, 2000), 33.
2   Oliver Goldsmith's *Citizen of the World* (1762) also sits squarely in this tradition.

the relentless categorization of peoples and cultures that infuses most enlightenment contact literature, there is a large body of Company/state sanctioned learning that was propagated through institutions such as the Asiatick Society of Bengal. The journal of the Society, *Asiatick Researches*, and its principal members, Sir William Jones and Nathaniel Halhed, attempted to resolve contemporary problems in governance, such as the ability to adjudicate in legal matters, by learning the ancient texts of Hindu and Muslim culture. As Kate Teltscher, Edward Said, and others have argued, it is extremely difficult to separate the cultural from the administrative in these scholarly enterprises, but one of the most salient issues arising from Jones's work is the way its largely antiquarian impulses effectively ignored contemporary Indian society.[1] Like most enlightenment attempts to characterise cultural difference, much of the research of the Asiatick Society erased contemporary social relations in favor of overwhelming models of tradition. This had the effect of interpreting a living, breathing culture through an antiquarian lens.

By the early nineteenth century, this antiquarian bias was displaced by more utilitarian and proto-sociological knowledge practices. When Abu Talib wrote *Masir-i Talibi* and Stewart translated the text, both men were actively arguing for increased language training for colonial officials. Persian was the language of business, law, and government and thus was a crucial tool for colonial administrators. Abu Talib not only argues that, due to Jones's imperfect efforts, the current state of Persian language training was woeful at best, but also proposes a plan in which he would supervise future instruction in Persian at an institution in England. Likewise, we can understand Stewart's translation and the East India Company College's sponsorship of the text's publication as an implicit argument against Anglicization. In this sense, the publication of the *Travels* is intended as an attempt to counteract or slow down the marginalization of Stewart's philological career and of those who went before him. And yet beyond these directly instrumental ends, the translation makes an eloquent argument of its own regarding the importance of fostering intercultural dialogue and the cost of what amounts to cultural genocide through forced Anglicization.

That argument proceeds subtly in the text. The narrative's account of everyday life in London is extremely detailed and stands as a remarkable document for the analysis of British social

---

1 See Teltscher, 192-228.

history. Abu Talib is fascinated by the space of the city itself and gives careful descriptions of its technological modernity. But the bulk of his discussion of London is divided between disquisitions on British institutions and long accounts of his social interactions with a wide range of notable personages. Abu Talib insinuated himself into the affairs of some of London's most prominent people of fashion. As we will see, these moments of intercultural sociability pose complex challenges not only for reading, but also for the historical evaluation of Abu Talib's observations.

One of the most important things to realise about the *Travels* is that it testifies to a high degree of intercultural dialogism prior to Abu Talib's journey to Europe. It is clear from various references throughout the text that he is proficient in English and that he is well read in European letters.[1] And Abu Talib is careful to emphasise that he does not come to London as a complete stranger. Because the East India Company's tentacles extended throughout imperial society, Abu Talib's prior associations with Company officials gave him entry to a variety of social circles from the highest levels of government and fashionable society to the mercantile houses of the City to the seats of higher learning. When he requests a meeting with Dundas, then the Home Secretary, he is granted access the next day, perhaps because of the aforementioned letter from Lady Barnard, and perhaps because it became known that the object of his journey was not to pass on further complaints about the Company's administration of India (see p. 193-94). These prior associations distinguish him from other notable visitors from distant lands. During his account of his encounters with Sir Joseph Banks, there is an implicit distinction drawn between himself and Mai, or Omai, the native of Raitea who came to London after Cook's second journey to the South Seas and circulated in fashionable circles while under the

---

1   Aside from the skills required to converse in fashionable society, including reading the newspapers, Abu Talib refers to a range of European literature in the text. The bulk of the materials directly cited are British texts of oriental learning by Ouseley, Symes, Sir William Jones, Jonathan Scott and particular numbers of *The Asiatic Annual Register*; but also cited are Goldsmith's *The Hermit* and Edward Young's *Night Thoughts*. There are also indirect references to a variety of European scientific texts and to works of classical history. And there is significant internal evidence that he was familiar not only with the *Letters of the Right Honourable Lady Mary Wortley Montague: written, during her travels in Europe, Asia and Africa* (1763), but also Mary Wollstonecraft's *Vindication of the Rights of Woman*.

care of Banks. Abu Talib tends to counteract any perception of him as a curiosity either with satirical jibes at the sanctioned ignorance of his interlocutors, or with direct assertions of cultural and social complementarity. The most important element of the latter strategy is his careful tallying of the number of people in London with whom he is able to converse in Persian or other Asian languages. This has the effect not only of emphasizing the utility of the kind of language training he wishes to establish in Britain, but also of highlighting the substantial degree of inter-cultural knowledge between some East India Company officials and himself.

Perhaps the most resonant aspect of Abu Talib's account of his social interactions with Europeans is the way in which he counters stereotypical constructions of himself. The most instructive of these occurs prior to his stay in the British Isles when his ship stops over in the newly acquired port of Cape Town. In a gesture that presages much of his writing on London and repeats some elements of Lady Anne's account of his actions, Abu Talib offers a symptomatic assessment of the beauties and accomplishments of the Dutch and English women living at the Cape. This attention to matters of desire is important because it sets up the following scene:

> Although I was ignorant of the Dutch language, and could not converse with the young women, yet in dancing they made use of so many wanton airs, and threw such significant looks towards me, that I was often put to the blush, and obliged to retire to the other side of the room. A party of these girls once attacked me: one of them, who was the handsomest and most forward, snatched away my handkerchief, and offered it to another girl of her own age; upon which they all began to laugh aloud: but as the young lady did not seem inclined to accept the handkerchief, I withdrew it, and said I would only part with it to the *handsomest*. As this circumstance was an allusion to a practice among the rich Turks of Constantinople, who throw their handkerchief to the lady with whom they wish to pass the night, the laugh was turned against my fair antagonist, who blushed, and retreated to some distance. (1.83-4) [85]

Abu Talib's jest turns on the pre-existing stereotypes of Eastern sexuality and despotism among his European interlocutors. What is fascinating is the way in which the stereotypical trope of the sultan choosing his sexual partner from the harem is established, perhaps inadvertently or perhaps not, by the young women at the dance, and then wrested from them by Abu Talib himself. Throughout the eighteenth century, the sexuality of the stereo-typical sultan was consistently ridiculed by Europeans as effeminate by the interposition of masculinised, often European, women in the harem. In passing the handkerchief among themselves, the young women figuratively negate the sexual agency of its owner. Abu Talib's aesthetic judgement interrupts this scene by phantasmatically reasserting the masculine "rights" of the sultan figure to choose his sexual partner, and the scene unfolds at the expense of those who figured him forth as the effeminate despot. Abu Talib's willingness to play out a scene that exists primarily in European fantasies of Eastern sexuality allows him to isolate and ridicule the mediating role played by orientalist desire within European subjectivity.

This scene underlines the ethical complexity of reading this text. Abu Talib enacts the women's misreading of himself in order to critique the knowledge practices through which he is understood. In other words, Abu Talib embraces moments of misreading as an occasion for questioning the social and cultural relationship between himself and his European hosts. I would suggest that this scene offers a theory of reading applicable to this entire text. If we understand misreading to be a contamination of an archive or a text by present desires and concerns, then the resulting foreclosures and disclosures demand that the reader ethically engage with history—literary or otherwise. By actively embracing a tendentious reading practice, one dramatises the indeterminate condition of reading itself and foregrounds the question of a reader's historical responsibility. In the case of the ball scene, one could argue that Abu Talib accepts the women's misreading in order to demonstrate that their ethnocentric addresses are culturally constructed and thus connected to a history of real and imagined domination. In short, the blushes that close the scene may be connected to political as well as sexual shame.

A similar dynamic emerges when we look at Abu Talib's discussion of the social phenomenon of the masquerade in London. As Terry Castle and others have demonstrated, orientalist tropes play a key role in the sexual economy of the masquerade. In *Roxana* (1724), for example, the deployment of "Eastern" costume is crucial to Defoe's exploration of the normative limits of sexuality in British society. Abu Talib's observations are remarkably attentive to the relationship between ethnic and class impersonation:

> The English have an extraordinary kind of amusement, which they call a *Masquerade*. In these assemblies, which consist of several hundred persons of both sexes, every one wears a short veil or mask, made of pasteboard, over the face; and each person dresses according to his or her fancy. Many represent Turks, Persians, Indians, and foreigners of all nations; but the greater number disguise themselves as mechanics or artists, and imitate all their customs or peculiarities with great exactness. Being thus unknown to each other, they speak with great freedom, and exercise their wit and genius.... Several of the ladies of quality permit their acquaintances to come to their houses in masquerade dresses, previous to their going to the public room, where they exhibit their wit and skill at repartee. (1.283-5) [154-55]

Aside from his recognition that the masquerade constitutes a realm of relative social "freedom," Abu Talib emphasises not only that this freedom is grounded on the participants' "fanciful" construction of alterity, but also that this erasure, reduction, and reconstitution of subjects such as himself in order to generate an emergent set of social norms are a regular component of metropolitan life.[1] Otherness in this social situation, whether it is figured in terms of class or ethnicity, is purely instrumental in that it allows for the participants to momentarily inhabit a fiction suited to the fulfillment of their immediate desires. That these desires are sexual is underlined by his suggestion at the close of the passage that the masquerade has private as well as public manifestations.

The emphatic interconnectedness of sexual and imperial fantasy at this moment in British society is perhaps why Abu Talib's text returns again and again to the question of women, desire, and the sexual dynamics of social intercourse. For Abu Talib and other Asiatic travelers such as Mirza Abu al-Hasan, the continuous observation of public intimacy between men and women, not to mention women's sheer visibility, constitutes the most radical difference between sociability in Europe and India.

---

1   See Judith Butler, "Imitation and Gender Insubordination," *inside/out: Lesbian Theories, Gay Theories*, ed. Diana Fuss (New York: Routledge, 1991), 20.

Abu Talib's negotiation with this particular manifestation of cultural and social difference is not only complex, but also deeply ambivalent. This is most forcefully felt in the text's amorous verse, much of which Charles Stewart left untranslated. Weaving in and out of carefully double-voiced descriptions of social gatherings, the text frequently breaks into Hafiz-inspired odes not only on London itself, but also on her many beauties. These two concerns are brought together in the "Ode to London," which figures the metropole as a vast cornucopia of feminine beauty. At one level, the poem hyperbolically constructs London as replete with women who ravish the poet's senses, but such ravishment leads to a crisis of faith, which Abu Talib renders playfully as follows:

If the Shaikh of Mecca is displeased at our conversion, who
    cares?
May the Temple which has conferred such blessings on us,
    and its Priests, flourish!

Fill the goblet with wine! If by this I am prevented from
    returning
To my old religion, I care not; nay, I am the better pleased.

If the prime of my life has been spent in the service of an
    Indian Cupid,
It matters not: I am now rewarded by the smiles of the
    British Fair. (1.219) [130]

It is tempting to read the poem in the tradition of Hafiz's conventional expressions of excessive desire, such that Abu Talib's desire for the women of London operates as an allegory for divine love. As Mohamad Tavakoli-Targhi argues:

Infatuated with the unveiled female beauties witnessed in Europe a few Persian travelers like Mirza Abu al-Hasan and Mirza Abu Talib uttered poems and statements similar to unorthodox utterances, *shathiyat*, of intoxicated Sufis. The classical Sufi poems were basically ambiguous, leaving unspecified the beloved and the nature of the love. Yet in the poetic utterances of *voyeugers*, occasionally heaven is compared with parks, European women with *houris*, and Islam was abandoned in favor of physical love.[1]

---

1 Tavakoli-Targhi, 58–59.

In "Ode to London," the feminine referent remains ambiguous and thus the suggestion that the poet gives up his religious convictions to devote himself to "British fair" can operate both as a trope aimed at indicating the power of his desire, and as a direct recognition of the social dilemma posed by the circulation of women in public for a visitor used to the sequestration of women from view.

The *Masir-i Talibi*, as noted above, is full of highly eroticised verse that Stewart chose not to translate. We can get some sense of the importance of these materials from a translation by George Swinton, a student of Abu Talib's, of the "Poem in Praise of Miss Julia Burrell" (see Appendix A1). The fact that the poem addresses a specific woman verges on the scandalous and probably accounts for why Stewart did not include it in the text. But the following passage from the poem in praise of Miss Burrell's veil indicates the importance of this material:

If he had not concealed the sun of her face by a veil,
The world would have been consumed by the splendor of
    her cheeks.
And although that cloud appears as a shade,
Yet it augments our fever by the desire of seeing through it.
Think not, that under that shade you can enjoy repose;
The very obstacle it opposes to our sight, increases tenfold
    our curiosity.
Like the dew on the rose, it is sometimes of white lace;
And she has chosen it to strain the too[1] powerful odour of
    the rose.
The looks of men, like flies, are in it entangled:
If it be compared to the spiders' web, it deserves it.
It increases her beauty and our raging madness to behold,
As a picture appears to more advantage behind glass.
But should she be acquainted with its effect,
When would she show her face unveiled?
Like a garland of roses, from both sides of her neck;
She has crossed around her waist a silken kerchief.
The white amongst the green appears like the milky way;
Or it is the striped Indian serpent carrying poison in its bag.
If the idols of India had ever beheld it,
They would have cast away their necklaces of pearls and
    emeralds.

---

1 I have corrected this from Swinton's translation, which uses the word "two" here.

At one level, the poem's hyperbole fits nicely within Lady Anne Barnard's ethnocentric notion of Abu Talib's stylistic excess, but careful observation reveals that the hidden beauty of the woman described here is not merely sexually threatening—it has the potential to hold the idols of India in thrall. The serpent metaphor that eventually overtakes the passage has the curious effect of affording Miss Julia Burrell's beauty the ability to extract jewels from the subcontinent. And in that gesture Abu Talib makes an important argument, for the extraction of luxury goods from India was driven by the forces of conspicuous consumption in the metropole. This directly ties the sexual economy of metropolitan life to the imperial economy. That this sudden economic turn is embedded in a poem on the veil, the most clichéd stereotype of Eastern feminine desirability, further heightens the irony. By not translating these poems, Stewart may have been protecting himself from charges of impropriety, but in so doing he suppressed some of the most challenging and provocative elements of the text.

Despite the largely episodic construction of the *Travels* and despite Stewart's suggestion that the work lacks internal coherence (ix-x) [57], events and opinions are disclosed in the narrative according to a larger argument regarding intercultural contact and negotiation. This observation could be made of all travel narratives, but in this particular case the order of entry is extremely significant. Because he moves from Calcutta to Capetown to Dublin to London, Abu Talib is able to explore distinct yet related forms of colonial sociability between India and London. As we will see, this is particularly important with regard to the case of Ireland, but for the moment it is instructive to consider the text's entry into London itself.

Abu Talib's account of life in London opens with a brief itinerary of his places of residence. Unhappy with the initial arrangements made for him, he moves to a neighborhood "where there were both hot and cold baths, and where I enjoyed the luxury of daily ablution" (1. 194) [122]. It is a subtle gesture, but it indicates that his foremost concern upon arrival in London is to secure a place where he can practice his religion. When he is forced to move, he decides to live in a district of London famous for its brothels and prostitutes, and he notes that he "was much gratified by seeing a number of beautiful women" who populated the neighborhood. At one level, his decision declares his voyeuristic pleasure, but when he elaborates on his accommodations he offers a symptomatic analysis of his situation in London itself that trenchantly indicates not only how he figures in the minds of those observing him, but also how those he observes ultimately stand in his moral accounting of the metropole:

A few days after I was settled in my new lodgings, some of my friends called, to remonstrate with me on having taken up my abode in a street, one half of the houses of which were inhabited by courtezans. They assured me that no ladies, or even gentlemen of character, would visit me, in such a place: however, ... I determined to remain where I was; and as my reputation in the minds of the English was as deeply impressed as the carving on a stone, my friends had the condescension and goodness to overlook this indiscretion; and not only was I visited there by the first characters in London, but even ladies of rank, who had never in their lives before passed through this street, used to call in their carriages at my door, and either send up their compliments, or leave their names written on cards. (1.195-6) [122]

Aside from the explicit declaration that the English opinion of him is fixed and largely prefigured by fantasies of oriental otherness, the text leaves the question of his reputation startlingly ambiguous. Do the English overlook his indiscretion because they expect him to be a sensualist, or because they know that his religion and his ostensible class render him uninterested in the temptations around him, or because European fantasies of Oriental masculinity encompass both sensualism and fanaticism? It is left ambiguous in part because ultimately the different possibilities are operative in any external assessment of his "character" and that the internal rules by which his character operates are suspended. By suggesting that both prostitutes and ladies of rank circulate in his neighborhood, Abu Talib not only effaces the difference between the two classes of women, but also demonstrates that "character" or "reputation" are ultimately insufficient limits on social circulation.

This is no small matter because Abu Talib is deeply interested in how these limits are exercised and what they indicate about the moral character of British society. In a very real sense, women become not only the focus of comparative ethnography, but also the test case for the health of metropolitan society. This is most explicitly articulated in his "Vindication of the Liberties of the Asiatic Women" (3.258-83). [361-69] This essay was published while Abu Talib was in England and attempted to intervene in the debate on women's place in public life which was staged largely as a debate on comparative ethnography.[1] In this light, it is helpful to compare it with Lady Mary Wortley Montagu's famous remarks on the liberty of veiled women.[2] As is well known, Lady Mary was quick to recognise that in contrast to veiled Muslim women, women in England, especially women of fashion, were fettered by their sheer visibility and the fact of their public circulation. In a similar vein, Abu Talib argues that the masculinist restraint of female agency that appears manifest in the veil has its counterpart in the European inculcation of restraint through education and the continuous surveillance of reputation. Perhaps against his own intentions, Abu Talib both identifies a shared misogyny across Christian and Islamic cultures and implies that the one practiced in Europe may be more effective because it is more insidious. In a more general sense, Abu Talib's contention concerns whether power is more effective when applied directly in all its visibility, or invisibly through the operation of ideology.

The question of ideology is important because Abu Talib's evaluation of the vices and virtues of the English in Chapters 19 and 20 focuses on questions of "character" in the broadest possible sense. As J.G.A. Pocock has reminded us, arguments over virtue are deeply enmeshed within British attempts to theorise not only governmentality, but also the proper constitution of society:

> From 1688 to 1776 (and after), the central question in Anglophone political theory was not whether a ruler might be resisted for misconduct, but whether a regime founded on patronage, public debt, and professionalization of the armed forces did not corrupt both governors and governed; and corruption was a problem in virtue, not in right, which could never be solved by asserting a right of resistance. Political thought therefore moves decisively, though never irrevocably, out of the law-centered paradigm and into the paradigm of virtue and corruption.[3]

1 See Michael H. Fisher, "Representing 'His' Women: Mirza Abu Talib Khan's 1801 'Vindication of the Liberties of Asiatic Women,'" *Indian Economic and Social History Review* 37.2 (2000): 215-37 for a careful discussion of the text's argument and its circulation as an essay separate from the *Travels*.

2 See Appendix C2. Lady Mary's letter was composed in 1717 but not published until 1763. It was very much a part of late eighteenth-century debates on the place of women in the public sphere both at home and abroad.

3 J.G.A. Pocock, *Virtue, Commerce, and History: Essays on Political Thought and History, Chiefly in the Eighteenth Century* (Cambridge: Cambridge UP, 1985), 48.

Thus for British readers of Abu Talib's catalogue of vices and virtues, the stakes are extraordinarily high: they speak directly to the viability of the state because the nation's management relies on the promulgation of virtue.

This is even more significant if we expand outward to the question of empire. Shortly after the British victory over France in the Seven Years' War, with its clear establishment of Britain's global empire in America and Asia, Edmund Burke's immediate concern was that the acquisition of these vast realms would result in an erosion of governmental and social virtue:

> What, then, will become of us, if Bengal, if the Ganges pour in a new tide of corruption? Should the evil genius of British liberty so ordain it, I fear this House will be so far from removing the corruption of the East, that it will be corrupted by them. I dread more from the infection of that place, than I hope from your virtue. Was it not the sudden plunder of the East that gave the final blow to the freedom of Rome? What reason have we to expect a better fate?[1]

This fear of corruption and the direct comparison to the decline and fall of the Roman empire had extraordinary purchase throughout the late eighteenth century. It was probably most forcefully felt during the impeachment of Warren Hastings in 1787, but it continued to operate in less spectacular, but arguably more pervasive, ways in the actions and policies of the Government and the East India Company. An important corollary to this fear of corruption from the outside was an ongoing anxiety that British society was already in a state of decline. These arguments focused on aristocratic vice and frequently tied the feminisation of aristocratic men to the rise of "nabobry" in England. In a very real sense, the ostensible deterioration of landed society was linked to the corrupting influence of the "East." For many observers at this moment, moral corruption was a symptom of a culture headed for a fall. In this context, Abu Talib's catalogue of the vices and virtues of the British in Chapters 19 and 20 is both aimed at, and would be read as, foretelling the fate of the empire. And it would not have been lost on any of his readers, Persian,

---

1   18 December 1772, *Parliamentary History*, 17:672-73. Quoted in Nancy F. Koehn, *The Power of Commerce: Economy and Governance in the First British Empire* (Ithaca: Cornell UP, 1994), 213.

Indian, or British, that his catalogue points to irrevocable decline.[1]

It is in this context that the Duchess of Devonshire is such an important presence in Abu Talib's narrative. The Duchess was without question the most famous woman of fashion in the late eighteenth century. Beautiful, cultured, and highly influential, she in many ways embodied Islamic constructions of appropriate elite femininity, except that she exercised her charms and her power in a thoroughly public fashion. Her affiliations with Charles James Fox and other prominent Whigs went beyond that of private intimacy to extend into matters of intense public concern. The scandal surrounding the Duchess's participation in the 1784 election indicated that the kind of political subjectivity she was crafting pushed the limits of feminine propriety in England. Abu Talib's political opinions are largely Foxite, so it should come as no surprise that he finds the Duchess's company delightful. But it is important to keep in mind who the Duchess was when Abu Talib tells us that it was at her insistence that he catalogued the vices and virtues of the British nation. It is a crucial distancing gesture, for these all-important chapters in which Abu Talib not only critiques British society, but also predicts the decline and fall of the empire are quite literally produced for the Duchess's benefit. This can be read in two ways. It either casts the Duchess as the symptom of a culture in moral decline and thus in need of instruction, or it depicts her as the ultimate agent of social and cultural self-diagnosis. Or perhaps it works both ways simultaneously: like Oedipus trying to search out the ills of the polis, the Duchess here asks Abu Talib to engage in an ethnographic evaluation of British society that will ultimately recoil on her own gender, race, and class identity.

The Duchess's exemplarity is played out in a different register in Abu Talib's account of the Gala breakfast at Chiswick House on 5 July 1800. The text gives little indication of the significance of this occasion, but it was the culminating event of the fashionable season and received extensive attention in the daily papers (see Appendix A2). The breakfast was the last in a series of events

---

1 Significantly, the reviews of the *Travels* generally concur that Abu Talib's appraisal of national character is accurate. The *Critical Review* (June 1811), *British Critic* (Sept 1810) and *Monthly Review* (June 1813) all accept his catalogue of virtues and vices. It is only the *Eclectic Review* (Aug 1811) which questions both the authenticity of the text and its usefulness to the English reader (72-75). See Appendix B2.

celebrating the introduction of the Duchess's daughter Georgiana into society, and its guest list defined the upper echelon of social and political power in the nation. The very notion of publicly presenting a marriageable girl to the fashionable world would have been exceedingly strange to Abu Talib, and it is in this context that his account of the event needs to be read. Simply put, the celebration of Georgiana's marriageability operates as the exemplary and in some ways originary moment of women's exalted place in the public sphere. The key question is what distinguishes this social custom from the behavior of courtesans. Abu Talib lets that question fester and, after remarking on Georgiana's beauty, focuses instead on how he is cared for at the event. The Duchess assigns him to "Lady Elizabeth Foster, one of her intimate friends, to be [his] *Mehmandar* during the day" (2.74). [190] A *Mehmandar* is a guest-keeper and thus Lady Foster is the figural equivalent of the functionaries assigned to distinguished foreign visitors in the Persian courts. This not only elevates Abu Talib, but also places Lady Foster in a lower position. When she takes Abu Talib's arm, she both enacts public intimacy, but also sets up a key reversal of power:

> It so happened, that, as we were about to enter a door, we met the Prince of Wales. I immediately drew back, to make way for his Royal Highness, and consequently kept her ladyship back; but the Prince, with all that politeness which distinguishes his character, retreated, and made a sign to me to advance. I was quite lost in amazement; but Lady Elizabeth laughed and said, "His Royal Highness would not for the world take precedence of any lady: and as my arm was under yours, he would by no means allow that we should separate, to make way for him." From this circumstance, some idea of the gallantry of the, English towards ladies may be formed. (2.74-5) [190]

Abu Talib's amazement is important because it attests to his shock that in both real and symbolic ways even the most important men in the kingdom serve women. The fact that Lady Foster has already been established as *Mehmandar* suggests that the Prince's "gallantry" also constitutes an abasement in Abu Talib's eyes.

This staging of abasement is replayed after the breakfast, when, at the Duchess's insistence, Abu Talib goes to the Opera with the Duke of Gloucester (i.e., the King's brother) and others to attend Lady Georgiana, Lady Foster, and Lady Harvey. As

Mohamad Tavakoli-Targhi argues, "Mirza Abu Talib viewed the visit to playhouses as 'sensual enjoyment' (*mashghalah-'i nafs*)" and thus the entire assignation carries sexual implications perhaps not immediately apparent to English readers.[1] However, what is clear is that the men involved are abased by the women's lateness:

> I found the Duke was there before me, and waiting impatiently for the ladies. He sat with me for an hour; and as they did not make their appearance, he was irritated, and went away, but desired me to scold them, should they arrive. When the Opera was nearly finished the ladies came in. I taxed them, both on the Duke's and my own account, with their breach of promise. They made me one of those trifling and improbable excuses, which so become the fascinating mouth of an English beauty: "That the crowd of coaches was so great at the gates of Chiswick House, they could not get away sooner." I recollected some verses of a Persian Ode, which I thought applicable to the case, and spoke them, as if extemporary. (2.76-7) [191]

How are we to interpret the men's irritation? In the Duke's case, the issue seems to be one of respect. But in Abu Talib's eyes, this lack of respect is exacerbated by the Duke's seeming acceptance of his position vis-à-vis the ladies. Abu Talib argues that both the external insult and the self-abnegation of the Duke are symptomatic of a society "fascinated" or entranced by female beauty. The extemporary ode castigates the women for lying, but it also declares that the poet and by extension the Duke are slaves "and shall pay implicit / obedience to your wishes" (2.78). [191] Speaking for himself *and* the powerful men of fashionable society, Abu Talib seems to suggest that the sensual attractions of women hold the nation's most powerful personages in thrall. And such a reversal of "normative" power relations is explicitly linked at various moments in the text to the unstable future of the British empire.

The "Poem in Praise of Miss Julia Burrell" demonstrates the sophistication of Abu Talib's critique.[2] The poem is broken into

---

1 Tavakoli-Targhi, 59.
2 See Kate Teltscher's illuminating discussion of how this poem both adheres to the rhetorical conventions of the *masnavi* form and diverges from it through the specific address to Julia Burrell in "The Shampooing Surgeon and the Persian Prince: Two Indians in Early Nineteenth-century Britain," *interventions* 2.3 (2003): 420.

sections, one of which, "Praise of her Mole," makes links between sexual and political economy that are significant beyond the mere expression of specific desires:

Although her mole, by its charms, prove fatal to lovers;
Her beauty, like the Messiah, recalls them to life.
Say not, that it is a cypher to increase the beauty of her lip;
For it is a robber that lurks by a river's banks.
Not only have remained unshut the eyes of men, on account of that mole;
The pupil of her eye is also its constant attendant.
Although the European be ruler over a part of India;
Yet behold an Indian who is sovereign of all Europe.
What a mole! the essence of a hundred caskets of ottar makers;
What a face! the cure of a hundred diseased cities.
Her chin is not an apple of the garden;
It is a well full of the water of life.[1] [372]

The poem turns on the complex metaphor in line eight which takes the sovereign relationship of Britain over part of India to figure for the relationship between the white face and the dark mole. The comparability that allows the metaphor to operate relies as much on the implied darkness of India and the mole as it does on the historically tendentious suggestion that India is a part of Britain in the same way that the mole is a part of Julia Burrell's face. The suggestion is tendentious because, as Sudipta Sen has argued, the condition of sovereignty assumed here is historically only beginning to fully cohere and it may have more to do with the author or the translator's desire than with a functioning model of sovereignty.[2] Be that as it may, the metaphor is

---

1 Mirza Abu Talib Khan, *Poem in Praise of Miss Julia Burrell* trans. George Swinton (London, 1802), 9-11.
2 Sudipta Sen, in *Distant Sovereignty: National Imperialism and the Origins of British India* (New York: Routledge, 2002), argues not only that the institutional structures of sovereignty were not fully accommodated during the time of the composition and reception of Abu Talib's text, but also that sovereignty itself emerged from a complex negotiation between metropole and colony that exceeded conventional juridical understandings of the term. In that sense, Sen's argument resonates

interesting because it works in precisely the opposite direction. After establishing the "Indian" mole as an entrancing part of the "European face, Abu Talib argues that because of the desire elicited by the mole, it in fact "rules" over those who wish to "acquire" it. In sexual terms, this resonates with many of Abu Talib's remarks regarding British women's power over men in the sexual economy of Georgian life—that men's ostensible social superiority is continually undercut in the public performance of deference to the objects of their desire. This move is filled out in the opening and closing lines of the poem, which make the rather startling argument that the mole, like the apple in the garden of Eden, not only proves fatal to lovers, but also instantiates their revivification at the hands of Miss Burrell's messianic beauty. At one level, this performs a precise condensation of the fall and the subsequent resurrection, but it is important to recognise that this metaphorical assemblage is not simply about sexual desire, but has implications for understanding imperial desire as well.

Once the India/mole metaphor is set into gear in lines seven and eight, one can read back through the poem and argue that India's many "charms" prove fatal to those who wish to acquire them, but that the lover/imperialist is recalled to life not by the mole, but by the totality of the empire's beauty, here figured by the entirety of the face. Read in this way, the poem engages with widespread British fears that imperial activity will, like that of previous empires, end in corruption and ruin and argues that a proper understanding of the relationship between part and whole is as necessary for the "life" of the empire as it is for the resolution of sexual desire. In this context, the elaboration of the synecdoche in lines nine and ten suddenly takes on important political significance, for the beauty of the mole/India is metaphorically compared to that of a feminised commodity—ottar—whereas—the beauty of the sovereign face is figured as a cure for "a hundred diseased cities." The desire generated by the mole is strictly acquisitive, whereas that generated by the face is governmental in the sense that a proper negotiation of sovereignty will cure the corruption attending mere acquisition and accumulation both in London and in cities such as Calcutta and Bombay. In

---

with the work of Nancy F. Koehn in *The Power of Commerce* (1994) and with Ann Laura Stoler's Foucauldian arguments about the transcolonial emergence of social categories in the nineteenth century in *Race and the Education of Desire: Foucault's History of Sexuality and the Colonial Order of Things* (Durham: Duke UP, 1995).

this context, the openness of the phrase "a hundred diseased cities" allows the figure to traverse colony and metropole and figure forth a future desiring relationship between the various parts and the whole of the empire.

That said, it does not follow that the poem is arguing for a straightforward extension of British sovereignty over India, because the poem is explicit about the mole's agency. Lines three and four indicate that the mole is not simply a "cypher" that can add value to the sexual/imperial economy. Rather, it operates like a robber who will overcome those who come only in search of mere acquisition and leave them with nothing. The subtle threat here not only declares agency, but also suggests that only through a proper negotiation of the scene of desire will there be a possibility of averting the loss not only of the object of desire, but also of the very sense of subjectivity on which that desire is based. In short, such a reading of the poem suggests that a proper negotiation of imperial sovereignty (which was still very much up in the air), like a proper negotiation of sexual desire, will require the sovereign to subject itself to that which it rules to ensure the historical continuation of the relationship. Such a negotiation presents a possible future that supercedes the conventional notion of empire as much as it supercedes conventional notions of heterosexual desire. And yet it also lays out a very clear cautionary narrative if such a complex negotiation is not broached: the futurity of the metropole, like that of Adam and Eve after the fall, will be marked by death except that there will be no hope of messianic revivification. And this re-figuration of the trope of imperial decline needs to be read both as a significant elaboration of pre-existing fears in Britain itself and as a prophetic utterance on the part of Abu Talib. When he employs the language of sovereignty to talk about sexual desire, he is making more than an occasional metaphorical connection. He is linking the politics of empire to those of everyday life and in so doing is folding the dynamics of sociability in the metropole into a larger geopolitical critique whose implications impinge on the world-historical status of British imperialism.

If these sexual critiques of Britain's imperial designs seem extraordinarily indirect, then other aspects of the *Travels* are not. Abu Talib offers a scathing critique of the corruption of legal officials working on behalf of the East India Company in Calcutta (2.106-16). [202-05] And he engages in a direct attack on his former employer Nathaniel Middleton, the Company Resident at Oudh who was publicly humiliated during the impeachment of Warren Hastings (1.16) [63-64]. The same specificity extends to his implicit attack on Sir Elijah Impey, the former Chief Justice at Fort William who was also disgraced during the Hastings proceedings (2.255-6).[1] [251] That Abu Talib's specific criticisms are aimed at figures famously associated with Hastings is significant because ridiculing Middleton and Impey would not have been a problem for the East India Company in the post-Hastings era; in fact, it was part and parcel of the Company's own desire to distance itself from a past version of itself. As Nicholas Dirks has argued,

> Burke brought articles of impeachment against Hastings for what everyone knew was business as usual. In Burke's obsessional litany of Hastings's excess, what was embarrassing was neither Hastings's greed nor his methods so much as his manifest success in making the horrors and the pleasures of empire realizable. In the wake of Burke's attack, a colonial bureaucracy was established to monitor the greed with which all Britons went to India from the late eighteenth century on. Burke shifted the balance of power to the state rather than the mercantile elite, and it was under his scrutiny that the colonial state was born. Colonial rapacity could not be curtailed either by Hastings's recall or the India Act of 1784, however; it could only be bureaucratized through the high-minded rhetoric of the [Permanent Settlement]. British rule represented its interest in securing steady revenue through a language of improvement predicated on the rule of property and the benevolent intent of a new "postdespotic" state.[2]

In this context, Abu Talib's desire for legal reform dovetails nicely with the "civilizing mission" of British rule in India initiated during the tenure of Cornwallis as Governor General of Bengal (1786-93) and extending well through the nineteenth century. In other words, Abu Talib's explicit attacks on British governance in India serve the Company's interests quite well. This is why he can both critique legal corruption among government officials in India and promulgate plans for instruction in Persian as a way of improving bureaucratic governance. For

---

1 Abu Talib implies that Impey is complicit in the death of Nundcomar and thus ties him to one of the most famous and persistent examples of the despotism of Company rule.
2 Nicholas B. Dirks, *Castes of Mind: Colonialism and the Making of Modern India* (Princeton: Princeton UP, 2001), 123.

British readers committed to colonization and, most importantly, for the company officials publishing Abu Talib's narrative, many aspects of his discussion of British rule, including those that critique past excesses, have the virtue of placing the reformist objectives of colonial rulers in the mouth of a native informant.

That said, it is important to recognise that Abu Talib's enthusiasm for technological modernization, exemplified by his admiring descriptions of European achievements in technology and science, and his overall commitment to the economic objectives of British capitalists both in the metropole and the colonies, does not amount to a straightforward endorsement of Britain's imperial project.[1] The text stages a series of counter-narratives that not only predict the ultimate failure of that project but also puncture some of the most important ideological components of supposed British benevolence. The fantasy of benevolent British rule was grounded on the representation of Indian peoples, both Hindu and Muslim, as incapable of self-government. During the late eighteenth and early nineteenth centuries, the Hindu population was stereotypically figured as effeminate, passive, superstitious, and prone to slavery and thus easily dominated by the stereotypically despotic, hyper-masculinist, and violent Muslim minority.[2] These caricatures of entire populations and histories were widely disseminated and instrumentalised during Britain's extended wars with Tipu Sultan throughout the 1780s and 90s. After the temporary defeat of Tipu in 1792, two of his sons were transferred as hostages to Lord Cornwallis. As Kate Teltscher has argued, the event was staged as a moment of benevolent paternalism in which Cornwallis came to figure as the good father who would replace Tipu's deviant paternity.[3] It was a resonant moment whose familial dynamic would be extended to Britian's relation to Hindu and Muslim subjects alike following the defeat of Tipu in 1799 and of the Maratha Confederacy in 1803. After achieving military supremacy in India, the missionaries and bureaucrats set about "civilizing" India through the propagation of Christianity and the Anglicization of everyday life.

Abu Talib's text does not address these ideological formations directly. He has little to say about the Hindus, but his entire performance of civility in the *Travels* constitutes a rejoinder to Euro-

---

1 See *Travels*, 2.1-21 [165-71].
2 See Sen, 85-118 for a history of these ethnic profiles and the excerpt from Grant in Appendix D3 [451-56]
3 Teltscher, 248-51.

pean constructions of Muslim barbarism. However, his account of Ireland operates as a thinly veiled critique not only of the history of British greed, but also of how popular forms of representation further the self-justifying fantasies that ostensibly authorise British domination of subject peoples. This is most tangibly felt when Abu Talib argues that English representations of the Irish do not tally with his experiences of hospitality while in Ireland. This becomes quite pointed when he analyses a series of caricatures of Scottish, Irish, and English subjects (1.168-71). [113] His descriptions of the stereotypes of the upwardly mobile Scot and the violent Irishman are delivered flatly and by their flatness stand in contrast with his admiring portraits of various Irish and Scottish figures in the text (1.185-6). [118-19] The description of the caricature of the Englishman differs slightly in that he interprets the intention behind the image and thus identifies qualities that will be fleshed out later in the narrative:

The Englishman is represented as a fat bull (therefore named *John Bull*); and as that animal is remarkable for eating a great deal, and for excessive courage and obstinacy, so the English seem to consider eating and drinking as their chief happiness, are frequently blunt and uncouth in their manners, and often run blindly into danger and unnecessary expence. (1.170-1) [113]

This combination of greed, bellicosity, and "unnecessary expence" is a perfect summation of the qualities attributed to Hastings by his critics. When placed next to Abu Talib's detailed account of poverty in Ireland, it speaks truth to power in more than one colonial locale and suggests that, in order to meet the demands of metropolitan luxury, Indian people, like the Irish, will be impoverished and embattled under British rule. For observers of the various wars in the sub-continent and the famines in Bengal during this period, this observation would have needed little further support.

As we have already noted, entry points are extremely important in this text. Abu Talib enters Britain via Ireland, England's oldest and arguably most volatile colony. Thus Abu Talib's account of Ireland can operate as a space for imagining India's future. The first thing he does when he reaches Dublin is meet with Cornwallis. It is a curious encounter, for after declaring that he is on good terms with the former Governor-General of Bengal, he ridicules the European idolatry of statues—a remark that may be aimed at the recent erection of a statue to Cornwallis in Dublin (1.143-4). [105] It is important to remember Cornwallis's curious history as imperial icon: he was inextricably tied to the loss of Britain's Atlantic empire because of his catastrophic defeat at Yorktown; he figured simultaneously as military hero and benevolent paternal figure during his struggle with Tipu in the early 1790s; and he had recently achieved fame for brutally suppressing the Irish rebellion in 1798. Is Abu Talib alerting his readers to the political value of such iconicity? It is a question that persists throughout his account of Ireland and is most forcefully articulated in his account of going to the theatre in Dublin.

Just as Abu Talib is highly attuned to the theatricality of social life, he is extremely fascinated by the theatre. In many ways, the theatre at this historical juncture is the closest thing to contemporary mass culture, and thus its ideological function cannot be over-emphasised. But despite frequent visits to the theatre and the opera in London, Abu Talib chooses to discuss the theatre and other forms of spectacle in Dublin. Stewart's translation does not render Abu Talib's diagram of the playhouse, but nevertheless his recognition that this institution is marked by its technological display and by the class hybridity of its audience is manifest. However, it is the theatrical repertoire itself that engages his most telling remarks. He offers detailed accounts of two theatrical productions: an extremely racist pantomime featuring an Ethiopian magician and various "barbarous" Africans, and a production of Astley's *The Siege and Storming of Seringapatam*, which was performed repeatedly during Abu Talib's residence in Dublin (1.158-61). [109-11] The almost painful detailing of the plot of the pantomime reads in two directions, for he could be demonstrating the depths of meretricious racist display to critique the audience's self-justifying pleasure, or he could be claiming some kind of affiliation with the racist gaze that places civilised subjects like himself and his fellow audience members well above the "barbarous Ethiopians." Here we have the deployment of one form of racism to counteract the effects of another. And what are we to make of his assertion of amusement? Is the harlequinade amusing in and of itself, or is he laughing at the culture that revels in this type of entertainment, or both?

We can gain some purchase on these questions by looking more closely at his reaction to Astley's spectacular staging of the fall of Seringapatam and the death of Tipu because Abu Talib's description demonstrates the precarious state of imperial representation at this historical moment, when one opens the field of analysis beyond the immediate purview of the metropole. Astley's play was imported from London and generated a great deal of press:

A new and very splendid spectacle, the subject of which is founded on the death of this extraordinary character [Tippoo Saib or Tipu Sultan], was presented for the first time in this kingdom, yesterday evening, ... and as a performance of action and historical incident interspersed with a variety of new and beautiful scenery, dress, decoration and the costume of the East, we may say that this grand piece, bids likely to crowd the Amphitheatre to an overflow this night, and every evening this week.[1]

Astley's play was the last of a series of Tipu plays that re-enacted British victories in Mysore. During its London run, the play deployed horses, actors, and various explosive devices or "blow-ups" to demonstrate the technological superiority of British warfare against the disparate, animalised forces of the Sultan. The play ends violently not with a representation of the death of Tipu but with the immolation of the primary sites associated with Eastern despotism: the harem or zenana and the potentate's fortress. The following summary of the play gives some sense of the evening's entertainment:

In the course of this interesting Spectacle the following most striking Scenery will be displayed, viz. 1st, A view of an Indian Sea Port; 2d, A view near the River Cavery; 3d, The Banqueting Garden of Tippoo Sultaun; 4th, The Commander in Chief General Harris's Marquee; 5th, A correct view of the City of Seringapatam, the whole of Tippoo's Army, elephants, camels, &c. in motion, together with the Mysore Army, consisting of Peadars, Bungaries, Sirdars, &c. forming the Camp near Fort Periapatam; 6th, A British Battery opening brisk fire on Tippoo's Advanced Guard, particularly the blowing up of a Powder Mill; 7th, The Fortifications and City of Seringapatam, with the Springing of a Mine; 8th, External view of Tippoo's Palace, and his two Sons firing from the windows;

---

1 *Dublin Evening Post*, 17 December 1799. This is a puff for Astley's *The Siege and Storming of Seringapatam, or the Death of Tippoo Saib* which ran from 18-20 December 1799 at the Amphitheatre Royal in Dublin.

and 9th, The Zenana and City on Fire. With a variety of circumstances which attended this important conquest.[1]

By prominently enacting the strict regimen required for the
operation of the battery in the sixth and seventh scenes, the play
propagated a fantasy of extreme national consolidation in which
the audience was encouraged to identify with the British troops'
repudiation of individuality in favour of a highly amalgamated
form of national subjectivity. The effect shared a great deal with
Robert Ker Porter's concurrent panoramic representation of the
scene and constitutes a merging of pre-cinematic interpellation
with the dramaturgical techniques of the illegitimate theatre.[2]
Abu Talib's suggestion that the Irish are being "gratified" not only
with Astley's displays of horsemanship and the spectacle of the
fall of Tipu, but also with panoramas of British military
supremacy, is in itself resonant.[3] It is difficult not to read the
choice of entertainments discussed as symptomatic, for each performance seems to speak to key imperial anxieties and objectives.
Is Abu Talib registering the place of spectacular displays of
British military might in India and of ancillary racial fantasies in
the propagation of hegemonic British interests in Irish colonial
space? With Cornwallis's use of cavalry in the quashing of the
Irish Rebellion fresh in the minds of some audience members,
could Abu Talib be suggesting that the display of horsemanship,
which "far surpasses ... anything I ever saw in India," needs to be
read first and foremost as a prescient assertion of imperial
supremacy (1.160)?[4] [110] He describes the spectacle of the fall

---

1 *Morning Post/Gazetteer*, 5 May 1800. The London production of *The
Siege* was accompanied by the obligatory display of horsemanship,
feats of strength by "The Flemish Hercules," and concluded with "A
Serio-Comic Pantomime" entitled *The Daemon's Tribunal, or Harlequin's
Enterprizes*.

2 See Daniel O'Quinn, *Staging Governance: Theatrical Imperialism in
London, 1770-1800* (Baltimore: The Johns Hopkins UP, 2005).

3 The panorama of the siege of Gibraltar precedes the famous theatrical-
ization of the same event at Sadler's Wells in 1804. For a detailed discussion of Dibdin's *The Siege of Gibraltar* see Gillian Russell, *The Theatres of War: Performance, Politics, and Society, 1793-1815* (Oxford:
Clarendon, 1995), 71-74.

4 The East India Company forces were extraordinarily deficient in cavalry.
See Franklin and Mary Wickwire, *Cornwallis: The Imperial Years* (Chapel
Hill: U of North Carolina P, 1980), 101 for a discussion of the tactical
importance of that insufficiency.

of Tipu's fortress at Seringapatam as both "correct" and "affect-ing", but he does not specify the emotion generated by the play. His reticence here seems to partake of what Homi Bhabha has described as sly civility even if Tipu is understood as Abu Talib's enemy.[1] And finally, what exactly does he think about the panoramic representation of the seige of Gibraltar (1.161)? [110-11] On the one hand he seems to be astonished by its optical ingenuity, but on the other he recognises its status as mere pro-pagandistic illusion. Whichever way we read Abu Talib's text, it signals an important recognition. As the staging of war in Dublin and in London attempts to obviate the mediation of actors, far more complex mediations begin to emerge from the realm of the audience, especially when that audience is increasingly composed of subjects distanced geographically, ethnically, or politically from the fantasies of the metropole. The undecidability of Abu Talib's remarks perfectly captures the dialectical complexity of the history of representations of colonization and decolonization. Every gesture that seems to posit imperial supremacy also figures forth the fragility of that fantasy of governance. And every gesture that seems to register complicity also harbors the potential for figural reversals and future acts of resistance.

The complexity of Abu Talib's account of *The Siege and Storm-ing of Seringapatam* suggests a highly ambivalent relation to figures such as Tipu Sultan. That ambivalence is evidenced again in his description of British policy with regard to Tipu in Volume II. One of the most troubling things about Tipu for British observers was that he was actively building alliances with Napoleon during the late 1790s. Abu Talib's narrative offers an extremely astute account of the global war between France and Britain to that point, and interspersed throughout the text are brief discussions of his attendance at commemorative events and representations of British victory over French attempts to attack Britain through its colonial holdings. With some sense of Abu Talib's complex relation to British imperial policy and his incipi-ent critique of key aspects of metropolitan sociability, it is reveal-ing to examine in detail an incident where geopolitical and social/sexual desires are thoroughly intertwined. Abu-Talib's interest in the erotic dynamics of metropolitan life is intimately

---

1   See Homi Bhabha, "Sly Civility" and "Signs Taken for Wonders: Ques-tions of ambivalence and authority under a tree outside Delhi, May 1817" in *The Location of Culture* (New York: Routledge, 1994), 93-101 and 102-22.

related to his religious and political analysis of British imperial rule. The linkage between these domains is not simply proto-ethnographic, but rhetorical. As we will see, the point of contact between two different figural economies allows him to balance his desire for the technological and social modernization concomitant with British colonialism with his deep seated sense of ethnic and cultural autonomy. The remainder of this introduction argues that the text's erotic preoccupations are integrally related to its analysis of British imperial fantasy and implicitly predict the decline and fall of the British empire.

The Lord Mayor's Day of 10 November 1800 was an auspicious occasion because it was Lord Nelson's first public appearance in London after his epochal victory over the French Navy at Abu Qir. After being mobbed in the street, Nelson appeared at the dinner in full regalia wearing the mechanised diamond *chelengk* conferred upon him by the Ottoman Sultan Selim III, and he was awarded an extraordinary jewelled sword by the City.[1] But Abu Talib's description of the ensuing feast pays less attention to Nelson's costume than to the physical staging and performance of his own dubious celebrity and forces us to think about the performance of patriotic imperial nationalism in an intercultural context. Seated directly across from the Lord Mayor and Lord Nelson, Abu Talib starts his description of the party with an implicit comparison to the pleasures of the table promised in the Koran's representation of paradise and turns to a passage from Hafiz:

Come, fill the goblets with wine! And let us rend
     the vault of the Heavens with our shouts!
Let us overturn the present system of the Universe, and form
     a new Creation of our own! (2. 94-5) [198]

Hafiz is notoriously difficult to render in English, but the opening line corresponds quite closely to Ode 307 of *The Divan*. In Hafiz, the drinkers in the tavern shout the name of God

---

1 "As the Lord Mayor made his way from Westminster back to the City via Blackfriars, his party "was joined by the carriage of Lord Nelson, who was waiting to receive them. But as soon as the populace discovered the vehicle which was to convey the Hero of the Nile, they unharnessed the horses, and drew him in triumph to Guildhall...." *Oracle and Daily Advertiser*, 11 November 1800. All subsequent descriptions of the event are taken from this source. See Appendix A3 [381-84].

because they are intoxicated with love, but they do so in contrast to and in preparation for the silent tombs of death. By experiencing love/intoxication in this life they are frantically preparing for the end of the world and the entry into a new realm. What is interesting about this rendition is that the subsequent line not only diverges from Hafiz, but also attributes intense agency to the drinkers in the transition from one form of existence to another. The destruction of the Universe and the formation of "a new Creation of our own" curiously leaves God out of the process and emphasises the acquisition of a new world. There is also something unsettling about the temporality here. In Hafiz, the drinkers' actions are staged in relation to the futurity of the afterlife, but the lines here imply that the guests at the Lord Mayor's Feast believe themselves to be experiencing that futurity in the present apotheosis of British global supremacy. It is tempting to read this as a subtle indication of imperial hubris, and subsequent elements of the rout confirm this reading, but such a reading needs to be proposed cautiously at this point because both the translation and the question of intercultural reception have the potential to spiral into indeterminacy.[1] It is here that an act of willful misreading allows me to move forward, but with the explicit recognition that such a gesture marks my own historical complicity because it is based on a desire to strategically figure forth a version of these historical events that speaks to present forms of neo-imperialism by positing a different future.

In the face of these problems for reading, the newspaper reports of the event allow us to recognise not only how the text uses elision to downplay the performance of patriotism, but also how the text re-frames the performance to highlight its sexual dynamics. Immediately prior to the conferral of the commemorative sword, Chamberlain Clarke, in a long speech reported in the *Oracle and Daily Advertiser*, put Nelson's victory in global, historical, and theocratic context:

> The consequences of the action I am thus called on to applaud, are, perhaps, UNEQUALLED IN THE HISTORY OF MANKIND! A numerous army ... landed in *Egypt* under the command of him who now sways the Gallic Sceptre, with designs of the most ambitious and extensive nature. One of

---

1 For example, the largely apocalyptic connotations of the second line in the cited passage may be a function of Stewart's compromised understanding of the text.

their objects, as acknowledged by themselves, was to annihilate, by degrees, the English East India Trade, and finally, to get into their possession the whole commerce of *Africa* and *Asia*.

.... But, at this momentous period, the ALMIGHTY directed your Lordship, as his chosen instrument, to check their pride, and crush their force, as a maritime power, during the present contest.

These remarks emphasise the importance of the Battle of the Nile for the security of imperial holdings in India. But this geopolitical fact, of obvious import to Abu Talib, and for which Nelson was amply rewarded by the East India Company, is subsumed into a providential narrative that both figures Britons as God's elect, and activates key historical examples of the destruction and imperial subjugation of the inhabitants of the Middle East with whom Abu Talib would have felt some historical affiliation. Chamberlain Clarke implicitly compares the defeated French fleet not only to the decimated Persian navy at Salamis, but also to the subjugated peoples of Palestine.[1] This orientalization of the French, perhaps inadvertently, but no less suggestively, testifies to the other primary effect of Nelson's victory at Abu Qir. As Said and others have demonstrated, the stranding of Napoleon's forces in Egypt forced a transformative encounter between French Enlightenment and Egyptian Islamic culture. The French attempt to bring revolutionary principles to Egypt generated both the desire for modernization—something explicitly argued for in Abu Talib's text—and the emergence of differing forms of anti-imperial Islamic nationalism—something that haunts certain elements of his narrative, especially his account of Wahabism in Volume III. In short, the Chamberlain's speech rehearses both the geopolitical situation on which Abu Talib's desire for technological modernity is based and the set of metropolitan fantasies that not only derogate his religious and cultural traditions, but also consign him to antiquity.

It is in response to this double bind that Abu Talib chooses to elide the Chamberlain's speech altogether and counter it with the lines from Hafiz. This has the effect of not only eliminating the narration of imperial fantasy, but also of eliding the correlative decla-

---

1 See Appendix A3. See Herodotus *Histories* (8:70-94) for the account of the battle of Salamis. See Herodotus (2:110) for an account of Sesostris's conquest of Syria/Palestine.

ration of Christian election. The Chamberlain's speech concludes with the following utterance, which reprises a corresponding performance of the patriotic Psalm 115, "Non nobis, Domine":[1]

> you have enforced a most important truth, that the most independant CONQUEROR felt, in the most intoxicating point of time, the influence and protection of HIM, whom our enemies, to their shame and their ruin, had foolishly and impiously defied.

Is it reading too much into the Hafiz quotation to pull out the word "intoxicating" here, and see the interposition of a counter-discourse based on the rhetoric of intoxication that is so crucial to Hafiz and Abu Talib's figuration of divine and worldly love? Perhaps, but at the very least the substitution of Hafiz's lines for the Chamberlain's speech in the narration of the celebration turns attention away from declarations of Christian supremacy to moments of bodily performance whose enactment conflates the geopolitical with the erotic.

When Abu Talib represents the conferral of the sword, he is suddenly re-introduced as a significant performer in the scene:

> As many persons ... could not see who were at the upper table, a short time previous to the ladies quitting the company, a petition was sent to the Lord Mayor, to request they might be allowed to pass round the table, in small parties. His lordship, having asked my consent, directed that they might do so.... When they came opposite to Lord Nelson, or me, the men stooped their heads, and the women bent their knees, (such being the English manner of salutation). This mark of respect they thought due to Lord Nelson, for the victory of the Nile; and to me for my *supposed high rank*. This ceremony took up nearly an hour; after which the Lord Mayor presented Lord Nelson, in the name of the city, with an elegant scimitar, the hilt of which was studded with diamonds, as a testimony of their gratitude for his distinguished services. His lordship, having buckled on the sword, stood up, and made a speech

---

1 "DIGNUM, SALE, and other excellent Singers assisted in the festivity of the evening. The first air was *Non Nobis, &c*; the second, *God save the King!* And the third, after Lord NELSON'S brief but memorable speech, was *Rule Britannia!*" *Oracle and Daily Advertiser*, 11 November 1800.

...assuring them that, with the weapon he had now been invested, and the protection of the Almighty, he would chastise and subdue all their enemies. (2.95-7) [198]

In this narrative, Nelson's brandishing of the sword and the oratorical celebration of his victory are quickly dispensed with in favor of a lingering account of how the women in the room came by in procession to pay their respects to both Nelson and Abu Talib.[1] Abu Talib emphasises that the respect paid to him is an error due to the sanctioned ignorance of the English: because he is a foreigner, he is "supposed" to be of "high rank." But this error is merely the set-up for the insinuation of a related error, for he states that the guests also "thought" these marks of respect due to Lord Nelson and thus introduces the possibility that they may not be, or rather that they are a function of a delusion again based on ignorance.

If this move seems subtle, then it is important to remember that the political significance of this receiving line is traversed by a submerged erotics that Abu Talib mobilises for a further level of critique. By comparing the ladies at the Ball to the Houries (2.97-8), [199] he puts the final touches on a representation of the Lord Mayor's Feast as an analogue to the Koran's figuration of Paradise or Heaven that was started with his catalogue of the pleasures of the table at the beginning of the description.[2] In the Koran, the pleasures of wine, eating, and women enjoyed in Paradise are separated from any hint of excess and become figures for divine fulfillment.[3] Abu Talib suggests that the English are literalizing these passages of the Koran, and in so doing are misrecogizing the worldly pleasures of the present for the divine satisfaction of the heavenly future. Read in this way, the guests of the ball are enacting a blessing that only God has the authority to confer. This combination of atheism and pride resonates with Abu Talib's catalogue of the vices of the English in which these two defects are singled out not only as the greatest and most conspicuous defects in the English character (2.128-9), [208] but also as the harbinger of imperial decline.

---

1   This event happens at the height of the Emma Hamilton scandal. Abu Talib may be registering the imputation of vice which dogged Nelson's reception in Britain following his return from the Mediterranean.

2   The papers barely report on the Ball. The *Oracle* describes it as follows: "The LADIES were all dressed in the most elegant style; and the BALL, as usual, attracted the most expert at 'the light fantastic toe.'"

3   See *The Koran* 52:19-21.

The women and men at the Ball perform as if the British were already installed in Paradise and thus enact a level of imperial arrogance that is both politically unsound and arguably blasphemous. The suggestion that the British misrecognise their desire for luxury—as exemplified in the feast itself, in the sexual availability of the women at the Ball, in Nelson's ostentatious self-presentation, and in the imperial project itself—as divine election, amounts to little more than a careful analysis of the Chamberlain's mobilization of providential rhetoric. In other words, the Chamberlain's oratory is not presented directly by Abu Talib, but it is thoroughly critiqued by his presentation of the evening's pleasures.

Significantly, it is around the questions of luxury and enactment that he distinguishes himself from the other men at the event:

> This was one of the most delightful nights I ever passed in my life; as, independent of every luxury my heart could wish, I had an opportunity of gazing all the time on the angelic charms of Miss Combe, who sat in that assemblage of beauties like the bright moon surrounded with brilliant stars. (2.98-9) [199]

The careful disengagement from the scene of desire is intriguing because he retreats into figurality. In a gesture entirely in line with Hafiz's poetic tactics, Abu Talib turns Miss Combe into a figure of heavenly love so that he can relish her sexual desirability as an allegory of God's beneficence, and thus does not dance with her. His desire for her is "independent of every luxury" and thus stops short of enactment. When he does enter into social intercourse with her, all sense of her figural relation to the Houris dissolves and the encounter becomes radically demystified:

> One evening, I met her, by chance, at a masquerade, and, as the weather was warm, she wore only a short veil, which descended no lower than her upper-lip. As our meeting was quite unexpected, she thought she could converse with me without being known; but, in answer to her first question, I replied, "There is but one woman in London who possesses such teeth and lips; therefore Miss Combe may save herself the trouble of attempting to deceive her admirers." This speech was overheard, by some persons, and became the

subject of conversation in the polite circles next day. (2.99)
[199]

Earlier in the narrative, Abu Talib finds it amusing that the
British masqueraders frequently don ostensibly Eastern costumes
to play out erotic fantasies of the "Orient" and here he intervenes
in its most powerful phantasm. Contrary to prevailing doxa, Abu
Talib reads through the veil, through the figure, and recognises
Miss Combe's sexual desirability. This unmasking, placed immediately following the complex misrecognitions of the previous paragraphs, carries a double significance. It renders Abu Talib's gaze as
entirely of this world: his desire for Miss Combe has directly
acquisitive ends and is not misrecognised as anything else. Thus his
circulation in fashionable society allows him to unveil that which is
paradoxically not hidden. This presentation of the ideological
symptom stands in contrast not only to the figural sublation of
British imperial appropriation into fantasies of divine election, but
also to the re-codification of erotic satisfaction at the Ball as in
some way related to the paradisal state of British domination. In
other words, Abu Talib's frank adoption of sexual agency stands in
contrast to the mobilization of desire in the rhetoric of empire.

Abu Talib's intercultural deployment of erotic discourse
becomes the fulcrum on which he stages a geopolitical critique of
the orientalist fantasies that supplement British imperialism. This
is significant because he doesn't seem as concerned with the fact
of economic and military colonization. Perhaps because he has
always understood India as a colonised space, his attention is
directed less at largely European notions of economic and
"national" independence, than it is at the autonomy of social, cultural, and religious specificity. It is thus that his text can simultaneously endorse modernization under British rule and critique
the social practices and cultural fantasies that would eventually
delegitimise not only Islamic and Hindu culture in Asia, but also
the very knowledge practices that brought his narrative to the
British reading public.

With some sense of the complexity of Abu Talib's engagement
with geopolitical sociability circa 1800, it is difficult not to be left
with a sense of loss after reading this text. Abu Talib would be dead
only two years after the composition of the *Masir-i Talibi* and thus
one of the most learned commentators on the stakes of intercultur-
alism at this crucial historical juncture was lost. It is perhaps a blessing that he did not live to see the effects of the East India Charter
Act and of the momentous alteration of educational practice in

India, but it is important to recognise that his text has had notable after-lives. As Mohamad Tavakoli-Targhi has demonstrated, the *Masir-i Talibi* had a profound impact on the emergence of Iranian literary nationalism and on the construction of fantasies of the West, particularly those pertaining to the imagination of European femininity, in both Persian and Arabic texts. In a different sphere, Charles Stewart's translation of Abu Talib's narrative valiantly attempted to intervene in the debate surrounding Indian education, but failed to stem the tide of Anglicization. With this edition of *The Travels of Mirza Abu Taleb*, I am attempting to consolidate a further after-life for the text that perhaps can be best understood through a final comparison to a similarly complex intercultural text.

One of Lady Mary Wortley Montagu's most remarkable observations during her travels to Constantinople in the early eighteenth century was the degree to which a willful misreading of Ottoman culture could perform a historical intervention not accessible to her in the drawing rooms of London. The most famous instance comes during her account of a visit to the hammam in Adrianople (Sophia). Surrounded by naked bodies in what she styles the "women's coffee house," Montagu becomes the object of scopophiliac desire and overdetermined misreading:

> The lady that seemed the most considerable amongst them entreated me to sit by her and would fain have undressed me for the bath. I excused myself with some difficulty, they being however all so earnest in persuading me, I was at last forced to open my shirt, and show them my stays, which satisfied them very well, for I saw they believed I was so locked in that machine, that it was not in my own power to open it, which contrivance they attributed to my husband.[1]

At the very moment of partial divestiture, where one might expect revelations about Lady Mary, she offers instead a speculation regarding the "beliefs" of the Turkish women around her. It is a remarkable moment of transference because it allows her to say something about herself, that her liberty is in fact bound by a patriarchal contrivance whose ideological force is realised in the psychic and physical contours of fashion, by presenting precisely that which she has no access to: the thoughts of the women around her. Montagu presents her own reading of the limitations

---

1 Lady Mary Wortley Montagu, *The Turkish Embassy Letters* ed. Malcolm Jack (London: Virago, 1995), 59-60.

of the British sex/gender system as the misreading of foreigners and thereby makes a crucial proposition—namely, that the misreading inherent to intercultural interpretation, by nature of its ability to speak what intra-cultural tradition renders mute, has the capacity to open reading to that which has been previously foreclosed in the realm of sociability.[1]

Attributing misreadings to the women she desires enables Lady Mary to actively misread herself and those around her, and it is for this reason that the scene necessarily marks her entry into the "levant."[2] That her account so fully embraces error at the outset in turn enables fruitful interpolations of the kind presented so eloquently by Aravamudan, wherein the critic is able to narrativise certain political desires of cultural criticism itself. By actively embracing a tendentious reading practice, one dramatises the indeterminate condition of reading itself and foregrounds the question of a reader's historical responsibility. Such acts of misreading by their very nature involve levels of conscious and unconscious appropriation that both re-enact and resist the structures of privilege endemic to uneven geopolitical development.[3] This is most apparent in acts of translation where the violence of linguistic and cultural dislocation is required for intercultural communication. The *Travels* is one such translation whose provenance folds into the history of British domination in India, but whose hybridity continually offers traces of an anti-imperial imperative to the reader who accepts the responsibility of reading the text otherwise. However, that responsibility comes with little solace, for it only highlights the reader's complicity with the translator and his or her desire to re-constitute a level of resistance in the author that may only satisfy the reader's present desire for an effective counter-imperial politics. In short, the *Travels* has the sobering capacity to underline precisely the degree to which the history of orientalist scholarship haunts our own practice even at those moments when it is possible to imagine a pre-existing critique of such complicity.

---

1 For a useful discussion of the kind of foreclosure implied here see Mieke Bal's critical misreading of Gayatri Chakravorty Spivak's *Critique of Postcolonial Reason* in *Travelling Concepts in the Humanities: A Rough Guide* (Toronto: U of Toronto P, 2002), 291-307.

2 For bracing readings of Lady Mary's letters see Srinivas Aravamudan, *Tropicopolitans: Colonialism and Agency, 1688-1804* (Durham: Duke UP, 1999), 159-89 and Cynthia Lowenthal, *Lady Mary Wortley Montagu and the Eighteenth-Century Familiar Letter* (Athens: U of Georgia P, 1994), 80-113.

3 See David Harvey, *Justice, Nature and the Geography of Difference* (Cambridge, MA: Blackwell, 1996), 295-97.

Mirza Abu Talib and Charles Stewart: A Brief Chronology

1752   Abu Talib ibn Muhammad Isfahani born at Lucknow.
1763   The British are at war with Mir Kasim, Nawab of Bengal.
1764   British defeat the Wazir of Oudh (Awadh) and the Mughal Emperor at the Battle of Buxar. Charles Stewart born in Lisburn, Ireland.
1765   At the treaty of Allahabad, the Mughal Emperor grants *diwani* of Bengal to the East India Company. The East India Company suddenly finds itself governing millions of people and collecting revenues on a huge scale.
1766   Abu Talib leaves Lucknow with his family for Moorshedabad. His father dies shortly afterward.
1767-9 I-tisam al-Din, one of the earliest Mughal subjects to visit Britain, assists William Jones with orientalist studies at Oxford. His travelogue *Shigarg-nama-I wilayat* is composed and circulated in 1785. It is eventually abridged and translated into Urdu and English in 1827.
1772   Warren Hastings assumes the post of Governor General of Bengal. Sir William Jones publishes *Poems, consisting chiefly of translations from the Asiatick languages.*
1775   In the court of Asaf ud-Daula, the mesnud of Awadh, Abu Talib is appointed Aumildar of Etaya and adjacent regions. He works as a revenue collector in this position until 1777. Britain is at war with the Marathas in western India.
1775   Mir Muhammad Husain, like Abu Talib a court functionary at various Mughal courts who eventually served the British, travels to England and France. Upon his return he writes an important travelogue and is later recognised by Sir William Jones in the "Sixth Discourse on the Persians" as an important contributor to the Asiatick Society of Bengal.
1777   Asuf ud-Daula dies and is replaced by Hyder Beg Khan. As a result of this succession, Abu Talib loses his position at court and returns to Lucknow. Abu

	Talib spends the next three and half years working as an assistant to Colonel Alexander Hannay collecting revenues in and around Gorakhpur.
1780	Britain declares war on Haidar Ali of Mysore. Indian princes form a coalition against Britain. The East India Company forces sustain heavy losses.
1781	Charles Stewart becomes a cadet in the East India Company's Bengal Army.
1782	Abu Talib becomes entangled in the complex struggles over revenue collection in Awadh. Caught between the Resident Nathaniel Middleton and Hyder Beg Khan, Abu Talib will be eventually forced out of civil service when Middleton departs India.
1783	Sir William Jones assumes judgeship on the Bengal Supreme Court.
1784	The Asiatick Society of Bengal is founded by Sir William Jones.
1785	Hastings is recalled and leaves India.
1786	Marquess Charles Cornwallis becomes Governor General of Bengal.
1787	Abu Talib leaves Lucknow to find employment with the East India Company in Calcutta. In spite of support from Cornwallis and Sir John Shore, Abu Talib fails to find a position and instead commences a literary career.
1788	The impeachment proceedings against Warren Hastings commence in London. He will be acquitted seven years later.
1789	Abu Talib edits a collection of Hafiz's verse, prepares an edition of the *Riyaz al shu'ara* (Ali Quli Khan Walih's biographical dictionary), and a universal history.
1790	East India Company forces at war with Tipu Sultan of Mysore.
1792	Tipu is defeated, but not killed, by Cornwallis's forces at Seringapatam.
1793	Britain at war with France.
1794	The first book by an Indian in English, the *Travels of Dean Mahomet*, is published in London. William Carey, a Baptist minister, commences his missionary activities in Bengal.
1798	Wellesley becomes Governor General of Bengal. Cornwallis, as newly appointed Lord Lieutenant of Ireland,

puts down rebellion in Wexford. Napoleon leads an expeditionary force to Egypt. Nelson defeats the French Fleet at Abu Qir.

1799   Despite a successful literary career, Abu Talib decides to leave Calcutta with his friend Captain David Richardson on the journey that would become the subject of the *Masir-i Talibi*. Abu Talib arrives in Ireland. Tipu Sultan is killed in the Fourth Mysore War and, with the exception of ongoing conflict with the Marathas, Britain's rule in the Asian subcontinent is consolidated.

1800   On January 21, Abu Talib arrives in London and stays in the city for roughly two years and five months. In early November, Abu Talib is present at Lord Mayor's Day festivities celebrating Nelson's victory at Abu Qir. Governor General Wellesley establishes Fort William College in Calcutta for the education of British civil servants in Persian, Hindustani and other Indian languages. Charles Stewart is appointed assistant professor of Persian at Fort William College.

1801   The *Asiatic Annual Register* publishes Abu Talib's "Vindication of the Liberties of Asian Women." Later in 1802, the same periodical which followed his exploits with interest, reported that Abu Talib "has now acquired a significant knowledge of English to read it to his own satisfaction, and make himself understood in conversation." (Quoted in Khan, 98)

1802   The Peace of Amiens. During the temporary cessation of hostilities between Britain and France, Abu Talib decides to return to India. "Poem in Praise of Miss Julia Burrell," trans. George Swinton, is published in a limited edition in London shortly after Abu Talib's departure for France in early June. He visits Paris, Lyons, and Marseilles. By late July, he embarks for Genoa, travels the eastern Mediterranean and arrives in Constantinople in early November. In early December, he travels overland by caravan to Baghdad.

1803   For the first five months of this year, Abu Talib's journey takes on the character of a Shiite pilgrimage to important historical and religious sites in the vicinity of Baghdad. He sails from Basra in May and in June arrives in Bombay. After a short hiatus he returns by sea to Calcutta. Upon his arrival, he composes *Masir-i*

Talibi using diaries and letters written during his travels. Fully embroiled in the Napoleonic wars, Britain is also at war with the Marathas.

1805   Abu Talib dies in Calcutta.

1806   Charles Stewart returns to England.

1807-8 A translation of *Masir-I Talibi* is serialised from September 1807 to February 1808 in the *Supplement to the Calcutta Gazette*. Charles Stewart becomes Professor of Arabic, Persian, and Hindustani at the East India College at Haileybury. Stewart begins to publish an extensive array of biographical, bibliographical, historical, and philological works and becomes one of the foremost orientalists of his generation.

1809   Charles Stewart publishes *A descriptive catalogue of the oriental library of the late Tippoo Sultan of Mysore, to which are prefixed memoirs of Hyder Aly and his son, Tippoo Sultan.*

1810   *Travels of Mirza Abu Taleb Khan in Asia, Africa and Europe*, trans. Charles Stewart, is published in London by Longman.

1812   A Persian language abridgement of *Masir-i Talibi*, edited by Abu Talib's sons, is published by the Hindustani Press in Calcutta. This abridgement is re-issued in 1827 and 1836.

1813   East India Company Charter Act comes into effect. Trade restrictions are eased and missionaries are granted full access to India.

1814   A second edition of the *Travels* is published by Longman in London.

1827   Charles Stewart leaves his post at the East India College, Haileybury.

1835   Thomas Babington Macauley's "Minute on Indian Education" proves to be a decisive intervention in the cessation of education in Persian and other Asian languages in India. With Governor General William Bentinck's order, English education was officially introduced with wide ranging effects on Indian society and culture.

1837   Charles Stewart dies at Bath.

A Note on the Text

The source text for this edition is *Travels of Mirza Abu Taleb Khan in Asia, Africa, and Europe, during the years 1799, 1800, 1801, 1802, and 1803. Written by himself in the Persian Language. Translated by Charles Stewart.* 3 vols. (London: Longman, Hurst, Rees, Orme, and Browne, 1814). Stewart's translation was first published in 1810, but this text is based on the more readily available and slightly more extensive second edition of 1814. Stewart's translation includes four appendices, which are included in this edition. The sources for the editorial appendices are cited in the headnotes. All spelling and punctuation follows that of the source texts. In the critical apparatus—i.e., the Introduction, Chronology, and the footnotes—I have attempted to render names and titles according to accepted current usage. Most importantly I follow the contemporary practice of referring to the author of the *Masir-i Talibi* in the first instance as Mirza Abu Talib, but for reasons of brevity I have dropped the honorific "Mirza" throughout the Introduction and notes. I have chosen to diverge from Stewart's translation in order to follow the accepted practice of rendering the author's name as Mirza Abu Talib throughout the Introduction and notes.

TRAVELS

of

MIRZA ABU TALEB KHAN

IN

ASIA, AFRICA, AND EUROPE,

DURING THE YEARS

1799, 1800, 1801, 1802, AND 1803.

Written by Himself in the Persian Language.

............TRANSLATED BY

CHARLES STEWART, ESQ. M.A.S.

PROFESSOR OF ORIENTAL LANGUAGES IN THE HON.

EAST-INDIA COMPANY'S COLLEGE, HERTS.

VOL. I.

SECOND EDITION, WITH ADDITIONS.

Printed by R. Watts, Broxbourne, Herts.

AND SOLD BY

LONGMAN, HURST, REES, ORME, AND BROWN,

LONDON.

1814.

To the Most Noble the Marchioness of Hertford.[1]

Madam,

I fear I shall be accused of presumption in dedicating to your Ladyship a Work which may, at first sight, appear to be possessed of little literary value. It is to be considered, however, that the original is the production of a Native of the East, unacquainted with the sciences of Europe, whose only object was to inform and improve his countrymen, by a candid and simple narrative of what he saw, heard, and thought, during his Travels.

The remarks of such an observer, on the laws, manners, and customs of the different countries of Europe, particularly on those of our own, can never be without their interest and importance to an enlightened mind: and I am therefore encouraged to hope, that your Ladyship, after making due allowance for the disadvantages of a translation, may be induced to honour them with your countenance and protection.

I have the honour to be,
Your Ladyship's most obedient
and devoted Servant,
Charles Stewart.[2]
Hertford,
May 25th, 1810.

---

1 Isabella Anne Ingram Shepheard (1760-1834), was the second wife of Francis Ingram-Seymour Conway (1743-1822), second marquess of Hertford.
2 Charles Stewart (1764-1837), an orientalist scholar and a renowned professor of Persian, Arabic, and Hindustani. At the time of this dedication Stewart was professor of oriental languages at the East India Company College at Hertfordshire.

Translator's Preface

I will not trespass on the time of the Reader, by any apology for introducing to him the following Work. The free remarks of an intelligent Foreigner, and especially of an Asiatic, on our laws, customs, and manners, when they are ascertained to be genuine, must always be considered as an object of liberal curiosity.

The Author of these Travels was so well known in London, in the years 1800 and 1801, under the title of *The Persian Prince*, and has so clearly related the principal incidents of his life in the introduction and course of his narrative, that it is unnecessary to enter further into his personal history in this place; and it only remains for me to give some account of the Manuscript from which the Translation was made.

For several months after the Author's return to Bengal, he was without any employment; during which time he revised his Notes, and compiled his Narrative. He then employed several Katibs (writers) to transcribe a certain number of copies under his own inspection, which he distributed to his most intimate friends. One of these correct copies was presented by the Author to Captain Joseph Taylor, of the Bengal Artillery, who, in the year 1806, had a correct transcript taken of it at Allahabad, by Mirza Mohammed Sadik Moonshy; which copy he gave to Lieutenant-Colonel Lennon, who brought it to England in the following year, and from whom it came into my hands.

The Manuscript consists of three small octavo volumes, written in a neat hand; which, for the satisfaction of any persons who may have doubts of its authenticity, will be deposited with Messrs. Longman & Co. Booksellers, for three months.

With respect to the Translation, I shall only say, that I have endeavoured to render it as literal as the different idioms of the two languages would admit: and, except in a very few instances, for which I trust I shall be pardoned by the Reader, I have not ventured to curtail or omit any part of the narrative.

In some places, I have been under the necessity of transposing the Chapters, in order to preserve a connexion between the subjects; an object little attended to by Oriental writers in general.

We have several books of fictitious travels, ascribed to natives of the East; but I believe this is the first time the genuine opinions of an Asiatic, respecting the institutions of Europe, have appeared in the English language; and, as such, I trust they will be received with proportionate interest by the Public.

I take this opportunity of returning my public thanks to Mr. Northcote,[1] for the readiness with which he lent the Portrait whence the Engraving of the Author has been taken.

Hertford, May 1810.

Advertisement to this edition.

Some persons having entertained doubts of the authenticity of these Travels, the Translator has been induced to give in this Edition the names at full length, instead of the initials only; and has made such other additions as he trusts will completely satisfy the most incredulous reader.

He has also the satisfaction to state, that the Bengal Government, convinced of the policy of disseminating such a work among the Natives of the British Dominions in the East, ordered the Original in the Persian language to be printed. Forty Copies of the Book have arrived in England; and it may be seen either in the East-India Company's Library in London, or at their College in Hertfordshire.

The Translator still sensible of his inability to do justice to the Poetical part of the Work, has omitted it also in this Edition. The printed Copy has enabled him to rectify a few trifling mistakes of the Original Manuscript.

---

1 This is likely artist and author James Northcote (1746-1831), one of several men who painted a portrait of the author during his time in London.

In the Name of the Most-merciful God.
Introduction.

After Thanksgiving to God, and Praise of Mohammed, the Author details his reasons for publishing the account of his Travels.

Glory be to God, the Lord of all worlds, who has conferred innumerable blessings on mankind, and accomplished all the laudable desires of his creatures. Praise be also to the Chosen of Mankind, the traveller over the whole expanse of the heavens, (Mohammed), and benedictions without end on his descendants and companions.

The wanderer over the face of the earth, Abu Taleb the son of Mohammed of Ispahan, begs leave to inform the curious in biography, that, owing to several adverse circumstances, finding it inconvenient to remain at home, he was compelled to undertake many tedious journeys; during which, he associated with men of all nations, and beheld various wonders, both by sea and by land.

It therefore occurred to him, that if he were to write all the circumstances of his journey through Europe, to describe the curiosities and wonders which he saw, and to give some account of the manners and customs of the various nations he visited, all of which are little known to Asiatics, it would afford a gratifying banquet to his countrymen.

He was also of opinion, that many of the customs, inventions, sciences, and ordinances of Europe, the good effects of which are apparent in those countries, might with great advantage be imitated by Mohammedans.

Impressed with these ideas, he, on his first setting out on his Travels, commenced a journal, in which he daily inserted every event, and committed to writing such reflections as occurred to him at the moment: and on his return to Calcutta, in the year of the Hejira 1218 (A.D. 1803), having revised and abridged his notes, he arranged them in the present form.

I[1] have named this work *Musier Taleby fy Bulad Affrenjy*—"The Travels of Taleb in the Regions of Europe;" but when I reflect on the want of energy and the indolent dispositions of my countrymen, and the many erroneous customs which exist in all Mohammedan countries and among all ranks of Mussulmans, I

---

1 A transition from the third to the first person is not uncommon in Persian writers. This exordium was not inserted in the First Edition, as not being thought interesting to European readers in general. (Translator's note)

am fearful that my exertions will be thrown away. The great and the rich, intoxicated with pride and luxury, and puffed up with the vanity of their possessions, consider universal science as comprehended in the circle of their own scanty acquirements and limited knowledge; while the poor and common people, from the want of leisure, and overpowered by the difficulty of procuring a livelihood, have not time to attend to their personal concerns, much less to form desires for the acquirement of information on new discoveries and inventions; although such a passion has been implanted by nature in every human breast, as an honour and an ornament to the species. I therefore despair of their reaping any fruit from my labours; being convinced that they will consider this book of no greater value than the volumes of Tales and Romances which they peruse merely to pass away their time, or are attracted thereto by the easiness of the style. It may consequently be concluded, that as they will find no pleasure in reading a work which contains a number of foreign names, treats on uncommon subjects, and alludes to other matters which cannot be understood at the first glance, but require a little time for consideration, they will, under pretence of zeal for their religion, entirely abstain and refrain from perusing it.

I am however sensible, that my work is in many respects deficient, and that my inquiries have not had sufficient profundity, or that I have not been able satisfactorily to explain the result of them. I have also to regret that my poverty, and the want of rich patrons, have prevented my having drawings and plans made of the various machines lately invented, and of the edifices in which the Arts are cultivated in Europe: these would have elucidated my explanations, and rendered them easy to every comprehension; but, according to the Arabian Proverb, "We are not to abandon the whole, because we cannot obtain the whole." I am therefore hopeful that the enlightened reader, taking into consideration these difficulties, will not be deterred by the number of harsh and uncouth names which occur in this book from giving it a deliberate and unprejudiced perusal: and let him be assured, that by reading this account of the state of the Arts and Sciences in Europe, he will considerably add to the stock of his own knowledge.[1]

---

1   Besides this work, in which there are Odes on *every* subject, the Author wrote at the same time a *Poetical Description* of his Travels, which he named the *Mesnevy*, consisting of a thousand verses. This circumstance may account for the want of *climacterical warmth* complained of by some of his reviewers; and by others, that the descriptions are not sufficiently

CHAPTER I

The Author gives an account of his origin, and of his family. His father becomes a favourite of Abul Munsur Khan Sufder Jung, Nabob of Oude—is appointed Deputy to the Nabob's Nephew. The Nabob dies–is succeeded by his son Shujaa ad Dowleh, who becomes jealous of his cousin, and arrests and puts him to death—suspicious of the adherents of the deceased—he attempts to seize the author's father, who flies to Bengal. The author's journey to join his father at Moorshedabad. His father dies. The Nabob Shujaa ad Dowleh dies—is succeeded by his son, Assuf ad Dowleh, whose minister invites the author to return to Lucknow, and bestows on him the appointment of Aumildar, or collector of the revenues. The minister dies—his successor inimical to the author, who is superseded, and retires to Lucknow—appointed an assistant to Colonel Hannay, collector of Gorruckpore—is removed from his office, and returns to Lucknow—Insurrections in Oude. The author consulted by the English on the state of affairs—is employed to reduce Rajah Bulbudder Sing—surprises the Rajah's camp. Enmity of the minister, Hyder Beg Khan. The author proceeds to Calcutta—is well received by the Governor-general—settles in Calcutta. Lord Cornwallis recommends the author to the British Resident, and to the Nabob, at Lucknow. Lord Cornwallis leaves India. The Nabob quarrels with the Resident, and dismisses the author, who returns to Calcutta—Being unhappy, is invited to make a voyage to Europe—agrees—takes his passage—the ship is burnt—he engages another vessel.

In commencing the account of my Travels, I think it requisite that the Reader should be informed of some circumstances which occurred antecedent to my setting out, and be made acquainted with the general outline of my history.

My father was named Hajy Mohammed Beg Khan, by descent a Turk, but born at Abbassabad Ispahan. Whilst a young man,

---

replete with Oriental imagery, or flights of fancy. On this subject it may however be remarked, that the generality of Persian works which have hitherto been translated into the languages of Europe have been either Poems or Romances, in which such imagery is peculiarly appropriate; but that the Orientals can and do write in every kind of style, and on every subject, can only be doubted by those who are ignorant of their language. In proof of this, the reader is referred to the "Descriptive Catalogue of Tippoo Sultan's Library;" and particularly to the Appendix of that work. (Translator's note) dreading the tyranny of Nadir Shah,[1] he fled from Persia; and, on his arrival in India, was admitted into the friendship of the *Nabob* Abul Munsur Khan Sufder Jung. Upon the death of Nowil Ray, deputy governor of Oude, Mohammed Culy Khan, nephew of the Nabob, was appointed to that important office, and my father was nominated one of his assistants. From this circumstance, such an intimacy and friendship took place between them, that my father was considered as one of his faithful adherents.

The Nabob Sufder Jung died in the year of the Hejira 1167 (A.D. 1753), and was succeeded by his son, Shujaa ad Dowleh;[2] who becoming jealous of his cousin, Mohammed Culy Khan, arrested him, and put him to death. The Nabob being also suspicious of the adherents of the deceased, attempted to seize my father, who, previous to this event, had settled his wife and family in the city of Lucknow. My father received intimation of the Nabob's intentions, and fled, with a few of his faithful servants, to Bengal; but so sudden was his departure, that he only carried with him his gold and jewels. The rest of his property, being left, was plundered by the soldiers.

My honoured parent passed a number of years in Bengal, beloved and respected; and died at Moorshedabad, in the year of the Christian æra 1768.

My mother's father was named Abul Hussen Beg. He was a religious and devout person; and being a townsman of the Nabob Borhan Al Mulk Saadit Khan, great grandfather to the present sovereign of Oude, had such an affection for him, that, after the death of that nobleman, he abandoned all worldly affairs, and never more quitted his house.

I was born at Lucknow, in the year 1752: and although the Nabob Shujaa ad Dowleh was much displeased at my father's conduct, he nevertheless, recollecting the connexion between our families, supplied my mother with money for her expences, and gave her strict injunctions to let me have the very best education.

My father, having resolved to continue in Bengal, directed my mother to remove thither with all her family. We therefore left Lucknow in the year 1766, and proceeded by land as far as Patna, where we embarked on board a boat for Moorshedabad. This was

---

1 Nadir Shah, also spelled Nader (1688-1747), Shah of Iran from 1736 to 1747.

2 Shuja ud-Daula (d.1775), Nawab of Oudh (Awadh), lost to the British at Buxar in 1764, but was reinstated by the East India Company the following year.

my first journey; but being then only fourteen years of age, and accompanied by my mother, it was free from anxiety.

A year and a half after our arrival at Moorshedabad, my father died; and the whole charge of his affairs, both public and private, devolved upon me. Previous to this unfortunate event, my worthy parents had betrothed me to the daughter of a near relation of Muzuffer Jung,[1] Nabob of Bengal. In consequence of this connexion, I remained several years happy and contented in the service of that prince.

In the year 1775, Assuf ad Dowleh succeeded to the musnud of Oude. On this occasion, I received an invitation from his Prime-minister, Mokhtiar ad Dowleh, to return to Lucknow; and was appointed Aumildar[2] of Etaya, and several other districts situated between the rivers Jumnah and Ganges. In this situation I continued for two years; the greater part of which time I lived in tents, being obliged, in enforcing the collection of the revenues, to make frequent excursions through the districts.

After the death of my patron, and the appointment of Hyder Beg Khan to his office, I was superseded; and repaired to Lucknow, where I resided for nearly a year. At the expiration of that period, Colonel Alexander Hannay,[3] having been appointed collector of Gorruckpore, requested the Nabob's permission to take me with him as an assistant. In that situation I continued for three years, living the whole of the time either in tents, or temporary houses composed of mats and bamboos. When the Colonel was removed from his office, I accompanied him to Lucknow, and remained at home for one year unemployed.

During this period, great dissensions existed between the minister, Hyder Beg Khan, and the representatives of the East-India Company, Messieurs Nathaniel Middleton[4] and Richard Johnson;[5] in consequence of which, and the clandestine intrigues

---

1 Also spelled Muzaffer Jang (d.1796), Nawab of Furrukhabad during the trial of Warren Hastings.
2 This office, under the native governments, united the duties of our Lord-lieutenant and Receiver of the Taxes of the County: he had also a considerable military force under his command. (Original note)
3 Alexander Hannay (c.1742-82), Adjutant-general in India was supported and admired by Warren Hastings.
4 Nathaniel Middleton (1750-1807), East India Co. servant, was appointed by Warren Hasting as representative in the court of the Nawab of Oudh, Shuja ud-Daula.
5 Richard Johnson (1753-1807), East India Co. servant, collected oriental art and literary manuscripts.

of the former, the finances of the state were much deranged; and although the collectors extorted larger sums than usual from the Zemindars, the revenues annually decreased. The oppressions of the collectors were at length carried to such an excess, that many of the Zemindars rebelled, the principal of whom was Raja Bulbudder Sing. He was lineally descended from the ancient Hindoo monarchs of Oude; and having 100,000 Rajpoots (the military tribe of Hindoos) at his command, considered himself as equal to the Nabob Vizier, whose authority he therefore disclaimed.

To reduce this Raja to obedience, an army was sent, composed partly of the Nabob's troops, and partly of the Company's Sepoys; but, owing to the intrigues of Hyder Beg Khan and the collectors, this measure failed of success.

Such was the deranged state of the Nabob's affairs, that Mr. Hastings (Governor-general)[1] deemed it requisite to interfere. He, in consequence, ordered Mr. Middleton to send for and consult me on the best mode of reducing the Raja, and of restoring the country to order.

As I was convinced that Hyder Beg Khan was the person who had contrived to throw the Nabob's affairs into confusion; and that, while he continued in office, every endeavour on my part would only serve to irritate him, and be the probable cause of my own ruin; I declined any interference: but the Resident persisting in his entreaties, and swearing to support and protect me against all enemies, I at length consented to be employed.

During two years, I frequently defeated and pursued Bulbudder Sing; and at length, having surprised his camp, he was killed in endeavouring to make his escape. By this service, I rid the Nabob of an enemy of his family for the last sixty years, and restored order and good government in the country.

But from that period I may date the ruin of myself and family; for shortly after, Mr. Middleton having been removed from Lucknow, and Governor Hastings having proceeded to Europe, I

---

1 Warren Hastings (1732-1818) became Governor General of Bengal in 1772 and was impeached in 1787. He was a deeply cultivated man and fostered much orientalist research during his tenure. However, he also embroiled the East India Company in a series of intractable wars. This, and allegations of personal corruption, led to his impeachment for high crimes and misdemeanors largely through the efforts of Edmund Burke. The impeachment, which lasted seven years and ended with his acquittal, was arguably the most sustained attempt to scrutinize imperial governance in the eighteenth century.

was left without any protection against the machinations of my enemies.

Hyder Beg Khan, having by his cunning and hypocrisy gained the favour of the new Governor-general, behaved to me for some years ostensibly with attention and kindness, and even wished to ensnare me to accept of an employment under him; but failing in this attempt, he quarrelled with me, and stopt the allowance of 6,000 rupees per annum which I received from the Nabob for my support. I therefore found it impossible to remain at Lucknow, and resolved again to travel to Bengal.

In the year 1787, I embarked on the Ganges, and proceeded to Calcutta, where I stated my complaint to Lord Cornwallis.[1] His lordship received me very politely, and made many promises of assistance; but being just then about to embark for Madras, and to take the command of the army against Tippoo Sultan,[2] my business was delayed for four years. During this period, I sent for my family to Calcutta; and my friends, seeing no hope of my getting into office, dispersed themselves in various places.

The great expence which I had incurred by the removal of myself and family from such a distance, added to the building of a house in the vicinity of Calcutta for our residence, quite overwhelmed me with debt. My distress and misery were further increased by the death of my son, a beautiful boy of four years old, who fell a sacrifice to the unhealthy climate, and ignorance of the (native) physicians of Calcutta.

When Lord Cornwallis returned to Bengal, he recollected his promise to me; and Hyder Beg Khan being then dead, he sent me, in the year 1792, with letters of recommendation to Mr.

---

1 Charles Cornwallis (1738-1805), first Marquess and second Earl Cornwallis, was then Governor General of India. Cornwallis reformed the military and initiated the Permanent Settlement which sought to radically alter how property in land was taxed. He also played crucial roles in the British defeat at Yorktown and in the brutal curtailment of the Irish rebellion in 1798. At the time of Abu Talib's acquaintance with him, Cornwallis was seen as the great imperial hero who defeated Tipu Sultan of Mysore.

2 Also spelled Tipu Sultan, Tippoo Sahib, and Tipu Sahib (1749-99), sultan of Mysore; his alliance with the French in 1798 gave Marquess Richard Wellesley (1760-1842), Governor General of Bengal, justification to invade Mysore. Tipu and his father Hyder Ali offered the most sustained and effective resistance to British rule in India in the late eighteenth century. He was widely known as the Tiger of Mysore.

Cherry,[1] the Resident of Lucknow, and to the Nabob Assuf ad Dowleh,[2] with an assurance that they would speedily provide for me.

In consequence of these letters, I was most graciously received at Lucknow, both by the Nabob and his courtiers; and was in daily hopes of an appointment, when, unfortunately for me, Lord Cornwallis quitted India, and all my expectations were blasted; for, shortly after, the Nabob quarrelled with Mr. Cherry, and got him removed from Lucknow. He also sent me orders to quit that city; and although I remonstrated against such injustice, my complaints were not listened to. I therefore left a part of my family at Lucknow; and having sent the remainder to Allahabad, I proceeded, in the year 1795, a third time to Calcutta.

Sir John Shore (now Lord Teignmouth),[3] who was then Governor-general, received me kindly, and promised me assistance; but the Nabob Assuf ad Dowleh dying soon afterwards, the confusion created by Vizier Aly Khan,[4] and the multiplicity of business caused by that event, did not leave him leisure to think of my affairs before he embarked for Europe.

During the three years of expectation which I passed in Calcutta, all my dependants and adherents, seeing my distress, left me; and even some of my children, and the domestics brought up in my father's family, abandoned me. In this situation I was quite overcome with grief and despondency; when one day my friend Captain David Richardson, a Scotchman, came to visit me. As this gentleman perfectly understands both the Persian and Hindoostany languages, we conversed on various subjects: and at length he informed me, that, as he found his health on the decline, he meant shortly to embark for Europe, in hopes that his

---

1 This likely refers to George Frederick Cherry, a judge residing in Lucknow who was killed in Benares in 1799. The deposed Nawab of Oudh, Vizir Ali, was purportedly responsible for his murder.

2 Asaf ud-Daula (d.1797), Nawab of Oudh, died without heir. The short reign of his adopted son, Vizir Ali, was followed by that of his half-brother Saadat Ali (d.1814).

3 First Baron Teignmouth (1751-1834), Governor General of India 1793-98 and a member of the Board of Control following his return to England.

4 Vizir Ali (d.1817), Nawab of Oudh, remained in power from the end of 1797 to the beginning of 1798. He had been adopted by the previous Nawab, Asaf ud-Daula, but his anti-British stance led to his deposition by Sir John Shore.

native air might renovate his constitution; and that he should return to India in three years. He added, "As you are without employment, and appear depressed in mind, let me request you to accompany me. The change of scene, and the curiosities you will meet with in Europe, will disperse the gloom that now hangs over you. I will undertake to teach you English during the voyage, and provide for all your wants." After having considered his proposal for some time, I reflected, that, as the journey was long and replete with danger, some accident might cause my death, by which I should be delivered from the anxieties of this world, and the ingratitude of mankind. I therefore accepted his friendly offer, and resolved to undertake the journey.

That no time might be lost, I went on the following day and agreed for my passage in the Charlotte, one of the East-India Company's ships; but in a few days afterwards, this vessel was unfortunately burned. Notwithstanding this unpropitious event, as Captain Richardson and I were determined on the business, we went immediately and engaged a passage in the Christiana, Captain Nettleman, bound for Denmark.

CHAPTER II

The Author leaves Calcutta—arrives at Kedjeree—embarks on board a vessel bound to Denmark. Description of the ship—character of the captain and officers. The ship sails to the mouth of the river. Embargo—disagreeable state of suspense. An English vessel burned while at anchor—plundered by the Danish captain. The French frigate La Forte captured by an English frigate, both of which pass up the river. The embargo taken off. The author proceeds on his voyage.

On the 1st of Ramzan, A.H. 1213 (Feb. 7th, 1799), we took leave of our friends, and embarked at Calcutta, on board a *budgerow* (barge), in order to proceed to the ship.

On the third day we arrived at Kedjeree, where we found the vessel at anchor. We shortly after went on board; and each of us took possession of his cabin. We found the ship in the greatest disorder; the crew principally composed of indolent and inexperienced Bengal Lascars; and the cabins small, dark, and stinking, especially that allotted to me, the very recollection of which makes me melancholy. The fact was, that as Captain Richardson and myself were the last who took our passage, all the good apartments had been previously secured by our fellow passengers; but as we had paid our money in Calcutta, and it was impossible to get it returned, we were compelled to take what they chose to give us.

In the next cabin to mine, on one side was a Mr. Grand,[1] a very passionate and delicate gentleman; and on the other side were three children, one of whom, a girl three years old, was very bad tempered, and cried night and day: in short, the inconveniences and distresses which I suffered on board this ship were a great drawback from the pleasures I afterwards experienced in my travels.

Our agreement was, that the ship should be well supplied with water, liquors, and provisions; and that we were to be conveyed direct to Europe, without stopping any where on the way. On this account we looked forward to a speedy and pleasant voyage.

The first breach of promise we experienced from the captain, was his desiring us to go on board, stating that he would certainly follow us the next day; instead of which, he remained a fortnight longer in Calcutta, to finish his own business. It is unnecessary to say, how disagreeable such a delay was to us, who had nothing to amuse our minds, and were anxious to proceed on our voyage. At the end of fifteen days, he arrived, and gave orders to unmoor the ship.

This captain was a proud self-sufficient fellow. His first officer, who was by birth an American, resembled an ill-tempered growling mastiff, but understood his duty very well. The second officer, and the other mates, were low people, not worthy of being spoken to, and quite ignorant of navigation.

On the 16th of the month we left Kedjeree, and proceeded towards the mouth of the river. During our passage down, we had several narrow escapes. Our vessel drew thirteen feet and a half of water; and we passed over several sands on which there were not six inches more water than we drew. Had the ship touched the ground, as the tide was running out, we should have stuck there, and probably have been lost.

---

1 First husband of "'Madame Grand'" (née Werlee), George Grand brought Sir Philip Francis to trial for an affair with his sixteen-year-old wife. Francis was Warren Hastings's chief rival and a prominent player in his impeachment. Judges consisting of Sir Elijah Impey, Sir Edward Hyde, and Sir Robert Chambers found Francis guilty of "criminal conversation" and awarded damages. Catherine Grand later married French minister and ambassador, Charles Maurice Talleyrand (1754-1838). Abu Talib also knew Sir George Shee, who was deeply implicated in the Francis scandal. See p. 116, note 1.

The next morning, when we were about to weigh anchor, a pilot sloop came alongside, and informed us, that a French frigate, called La Forte, was cruising at the Sand Heads, and had taken several vessels; that an embargo had in consequence been ordered; and that we must not depart till it was rescinded.

As it would have been attended with delay and danger to return up the river, it was resolved we should remain at anchor where we were, till the embargo should be taken off. During our stay at Kedjeree, we had been regularly supplied with fresh bread, butter, eggs, fish, and vegetables, from the shore; but as the boats would not come down so far as where the ship now lay, we were reduced to eat biscuit and salt butter, and, in fact, to commence the consumption of our sea stores. We suffered another great inconvenience from flies, which, notwithstanding our distance from the shore, swarmed in such numbers on board, that we could not speak without holding our hands to our mouths, lest they should go down our throats.

We passed twenty days in this wretched state of suspense. One day we heard the sound of cannon at a distance, and concluded that some of the English ships of war stationed at Madras had been despatched to attack the Frenchman. Shortly after we saw three ships coming up with all sail crowded: this circumstance confirmed our conjectures; but when they arrived, we learnt that they were three out of four English ships which had fallen in with the enemy's frigate, and had engaged her; that *they* had escaped, but the fourth was taken.

A few nights after, an English ship which was anchored near us, loaded chiefly with Bengal cloths, caught fire, and dreadfully alarmed us. The crew abandoned her, and she burnt to the water's edge. Our captain, who was bound to his own country, and not fearing to be called to account by the English, sent his boat on board her for several days successively, and brought away a number of chests of half-consumed cloth. He had occasion, however, to repent this conduct in the sequel.

Another day we saw several ships coming up, one of which appeared to have French colours suspended under the English: we then concluded that the frigate had certainly been taken; but on their near approach, we discovered it was an Arab vessel, in which the Frenchman had sent up all his prisoners; and that those in company were only pilot schooners.

On the last day of the month, we received authentic intelligence that an English ship had arrived from Madras, and, after a severe contest, had captured the French frigate. Shortly after,

Captain Cook, commander of La Sibylle, who had been severely wounded in the action, and died some days after his arrival in Calcutta, passed by us.

On the 3d of the month Shual (4th or 5th of March), the two ships cast anchor near us. La Sibylle was severely injured; but La Forte, which was much the largest vessel, had not a mast standing, and was towed up the river by her conqueror. The English lost only twenty-five men during the engagement; whilst the French had their captain and 200 men killed or wounded. This circumstance was the cause of much astonishment to all of us. On the following day, fifteen sloops, each having on board a guard of soldiers, came down the river, for the conveyance of the prisoners to Calcutta.

Permission having been at length granted for the ships to proceed on their voyage, the pilot again came on board; and having, on the 8th of the month, carried us into the deep water, called, by the English, the Bay of Bengal, he took his leave.

CHAPTER III

Commencement of the voyage. The captain finds it requisite to go to the Nicobar Islands for water. Phænomena. Description of the Nicobar Islands—their produce, inhabitants, &c. Several of the Lascars, or Indian sailors, desert the ship, and conceal themselves in the woods— brought back by the natives—Infamous conduct of the captain on this occasion. The ship leaves the islands. Sun vertical. Calms. Polar star. Equinoctial line. Curious ceremony on passing the line. Shoal of flying-fish. Trade winds. The ship passes the longitudes of the islands of Mauritius and Madagascar. Gale of wind. Sufferings of the author. The coast of Africa in sight. Whales approach the vessel. We descry the Table Mountain of the Cape of Good Hope. The captain resolves to go into the port. The ship carried to the southward by the current. Dreadful storm. The author's reflections. The vessel loses her reckoning—is in great distress—again discovers the land—anchors in False Bay.

We proceeded for several days on our voyage with a favourable wind; when one morning we discovered that the captain had altered the ship's course, from south to south-east. This circumstance created in the passengers much astonishment; but the explanation only added to our mortification: the fact was, our stock of water had been so much expended during our detention at the mouth of the river, that it now became requisite to bear away for the Nicobar Islands, in order to replenish that indispensable article.

These islands, which are about seventeen in number, are more or less inhabited, and are frequently resorted to by ships in want of water or provisions. We attempted to reach the largest, which is called the *Carnicobar*, but were blown off. We were equally unsuccessful in attempting to gain the second; but with great efforts we anchored after midnight near the third.

In our approach to these islands, a circumstance occurred which was quite novel to me. When we came in sight of the land, I wished to behold it more distinctly, and for that purpose borrowed a telescope; but upon applying the instrument to my eye, I could not distinguish the land. Being astonished at this circumstance, I requested one of the most intelligent officers to explain to me the cause of it. He replied: "These islands are, in fact, still below the horizon, being concealed from our view by the spherical body of water between us and them; and what we now behold is caused by the power of refraction, which, in a dense atmosphere, apparently raises all bodies considerably above their real altitude." More plainly to elucidate this axiom, he threw a ring into a China bowl, and carried it to such a distance that I could no longer see the ring. He then filled the bowl with water, when, by the refractive power, the ring appeared to float on the top of the water. As this explanation, although interesting, does not solve the difficulty, it is probable the telescope was out of order, or that they played me some trick on this occasion.

After this digression, I return to my narrative. The island at which we anchored is named Tribiser, and is about forty-five miles in circumference: the two others in sight were called Rajoury and Bigou. Several of the inhabitants came off to us from all the three islands, and brought with them abundance of delicious cocoa-nuts, pine-apples, plantains, limes, and other fruits, also ducks and fowls, all of which they readily exchanged for cloth, tobacco, and any kind of cutlery; but they did not appear to set much value upon gold or silver, these precious metals not being yet current among them.

Cocoa-nuts are here in such abundance, that ten of them were given for a tobacco *cheroot* or *sagar*, which costs less than a farthing in Bengal.

These islands being situated near the Equinoctial line, have two Springs and two Autumns; and as the sun had lately passed to the north of the line, we had incessant showers of rain.

The inhabitants are well made, and very muscular. They are of a lively disposition, and resemble the Peguers and Chinese in features, but are of a wheat colour, with scarcely any beard. Their clothing consists merely of a narrow bandage round the waist. Being allowed to go on shore for the purpose of shooting, we had frequent opportunities of seeing their children, many of whom I thought very handsome. Their houses are built of wood and bamboos, with thatched roofs, and are always circular, resembling a stack of corn. Several of them, however, consist of three stories; the ground floor being kept for the goats, poultry, &c. The middle story is appropriated to the men, and the upper story to the women. They are of the Mohammedan religion, and keep their women concealed, not permitting then to have any communication with strangers. They build very neat boats, and have even constructed two or three ships in the European manner. I was so much captivated by the mildness of the climate, the beauty of the plains and rivulets, and with the kind of life and freedom which the men enjoyed, that I had nearly resolved to take up my abode among them.

Having replenished our stock of water, and received on board a considerable supply of provisions, our captain was about to depart, when a circumstance occurred which occasioned some delay, and much doubt whether we should have been able to proceed any further on our voyage. The fact was this: sixteen of our best Lascars (or Indian sailors), being much disgusted with the treatment they received on board this ship, deserted, and hid themselves in the woods; and it was discovered, that the remainder of the crew only waited the approach of night to follow the example of their comrades. In this dilemma, some of the principal people of the island fortunately came on board; and dreading the imputation of being in collusion with the deserters, they voluntarily offered to bring them back; and the captain, who at this period considered himself in a very critical situation, bound himself, by the most sacred promises, to give them for their trouble a number of pieces of the cloth which he had plundered from the ship burned in the Ganges. Stimulated by these promises, and being well acquainted with the woods and mountains, they in a short time caught the deserters, and during the night brought them on board. The ungrateful wretch of a captain, however, repaid their exertions and kindness by the grossest treachery; for, pretending that he could not open the hold while it was dark, to take out the cloth, he promised, that if they would then go away, and return in the morning, he would reward them liberally for their trouble; but as soon as the day broke, he weighed anchor, and, before the islanders were aware of his intention, the vessel had proceeded many miles to the southward.

We quitted these friendly islands on the 4th of April; and three days afterwards we had the sun vertical, in the seventh degree of northern latitude: the heat was consequently very great; and for a fortnight we had much rainy weather, attended with calms. Our progress was now very slow; and some days we had not above ten miles on our log-book. It is generally observed, that calms prevail in the vicinity of the Equinoctial line: this I suppose is caused by the influence of the sun.

On the night of the 16th, being then near the line, and the atmosphere perfectly clear, we observed the polar star with great attention. The constellations Ursa Major and Minor appeared to be elevated above the polar star, equal to the altitude which that star has in Calcutta; while the latter was sunk nearly to the margin of the horizon. I am therefore of opinion that the polar star is seldom seen nearer to the line than the fourth or fifth degree of northern latitude; and, in fact, we did not again see it till, after having doubled the Cape and re-crossed the line, we arrived a second time in the above latitudes.

On the 19th we crossed the Equinoctial line, in the 100th degree east longitude of London. For several days past we had seen a number of birds, some as large as a goose, and others about the size of a pigeon. They live entirely upon fish, and rest on the water during the night. When they wish to propagate their species, they gain the coast by degrees, and remain on shore during the time of incubation. One of the smaller kind alighted during the night upon a mast of our vessel, and was caught by the sailors: it was probably unwell, for when it was turned loose next morning, it could with difficulty fly away.

On this day the sailors exhibited a ridiculous farce. Three of the principal ones dressed themselves in a strange manner, and, having daubed their faces with red and yellow paint, came upon the deck, their clothes and artificial hair dripping with water. One of them carried a book, and another a trumpet: the third was more extravagantly dressed, and appeared the superior. Chairs having been offered, they seated themselves; when the trumpeter proclaimed, that *Neptune, god of the Sea*, had honoured the ship by a visit, on its approach to his residence. The mock deity then commanded, that all persons on board, who had not before crossed the Line, should be summoned to appear, and that they should be cleansed from all their former sins by immediate ablution. Many of the young men and boys, who had not before witnessed this ceremony, being alarmed, ran and hid themselves in different places, and some of them even climbed to the very top of the masts; but the secretary, opening his book, read over the name of every person who was liable to this discipline, and insisted upon his being brought to the presence. The culprit, having his eyes bound, was then forced to sit on a plank, which was laid across a tub, and several buckets of the sea water were poured over his head; and the plank being at the same time drawn from under him, he was immersed in the tub. When it came to my turn, by the mediation of one of the officers, and a present of some bottles of brandy, I was excused this disagreeable ceremony; and the farce having terminated, Neptune and his companions returned, apparently, to their submarine abode.

On the 25th we saw a numerous shoal of flying fish. Many of these rose three or four yards high, and flew nearly the distance of 500 paces. The motion of their wings was exactly like that of a bird; and although I had frequently heard them described by travellers, I could not credit the report, but supposed their motion was that of leaping; but I am now perfectly convinced they may be classed among the flying animals. Many of them fell upon the ship, and were served at table. I thought them good food, and fancied they had somewhat the flavour of a bird.

Having reached the fifth degree of south latitude, we perceived the weather get considerably cooler, although the sun was not yet twenty degrees from us. When we arrived in the twelfth degree, the atmosphere being remarkably clear, I sought in the heavens for some star which might point out the southern pole; but we could not even find any constellation corresponding either with the Ursa Major or Minor, much less a polar star.

On the 27th we entered the region of the trade winds. This being one of the phænomena of nature, it requires some explanation. The European navigators have, by experience, discovered, that between the 10th and 28th degrees of southern latitude the wind constantly blows from the south east, which is equally serviceable to ships coming to India or returning from it, and conveys them rapidly through eighty degrees of longitude. It is generally supposed, that if it was not for the intervening of the Cape of Good Hope and of South America, ships might circumnavigate the globe in these latitudes in a very short period. As these winds were first discovered by people employed in trade, and are very favourable to commerce, they have been named *Trade Winds*: but, except in the latitudes above mentioned, the course of the winds during the voyage is variable and uncertain.

During the first week of May, whilst we were sailing in the fifteenth degree of south latitude, the waves were so agitated by the winds, that they rose as high as the ship, and frequently entered by the quarter-galleries and stern-windows. It was impossible to sleep for the noise, and we could not walk on deck without great difficulty.

Although we were then only thirty-one degrees from the sun, yet the cold was so severe that we were obliged to put on our warm clothing, and spread blankets and quilts on our beds. It appeared to me very extraordinary, that the month of May, being the hottest part of the year in Bengal, should be so extremely cold here. We passed the island of Mauritius, and the south end of Madagascar, at the distance of sixty or seventy leagues. The latter, I understand, is governed by a Mohammedan king, and the Arabic language is spoken in some parts of it.

As from our first setting out on this voyage we had great apprehensions of being captured by the French, who were then at war with the English, our fears were increased ten-fold whilst in the vicinity of their islands; and if by chance a ship was discovered by our glasses, we concluded it was an enemy, and were almost reduced to despair: we were however fortunate enough not to be molested by any of them.

About this time we had a dreadful storm, which lasted four days, during which period the sea ran mountains high; and the force of the waves striking against the ship was such as to preclude the possibility of standing; and even when seated, our heads were knocked with violence against the sides of the ship. During this scene, Mr. Grand, who was of an enormous size, and whose cabin was separated from mine only by a canvas partition, fell with all his weight upon my breast, and hurt me excessively. What rendered this circumstance more provoking was, that if, by any accident, the smallest noise was made in my apartment, he would call out, with all that overbearing insolence which characterizes the vulgar part of the English in their conduct to Orientals, "What are you about? You don't let me get a wink of sleep!" and such other rude expressions.

During the storm, it was with much difficulty that we could get any provisions dressed; and these we were obliged to eat sitting in our beds. To add to our distress, the leaks of the ship, which at the commencement of the voyage were only trifling, now increased to such a degree, that the pumps were kept at work both day and night. This circumstance much alarmed many of the passengers; but, for my part, I was so tired of life, that I became perfectly indifferent about our fate.

Notwithstanding the raging of the elements, we saw several birds whose form did not appear calculated to contend with storms. Their body was not larger than a kite's, but their wings extended nearly four yards.

On the 24th of May we had a view of part of the continent of Africa, about 200 miles to the north of the Cape of Good Hope; and although we had not the most distant intention of going on shore here, yet the sight of land brought tears into my eyes. While sailing along this coast, we had frequent opportunities of seeing one of the wonders of the deep. Several fishes called *whales* approached so close to the ship, that we could view them distinctly. They were four times the size of the largest elephant, and had immense nostrils, whence they threw up the water to the height of fifteen yards. As these animals are obliged frequently to come to the top of the sea for the purpose of respiration, they are easily discovered, and are killed by the Europeans for the sake of their oil, spermaceti, and whalebone, all of which are articles of great value. The capture of them is however attended with much danger, and requires great dexterity.

During the remainder of the month, we had such dreadful weather, that for several days and nights we could not see either the sun or stars; and as the waves were constantly dashing over the ship, we were obliged to keep the hatches covered; thereby excluding all light, and compelling us either to sit in darkness, or constantly to burn candles, of which there was a great scarcity on board. In short, we passed our time like dead bodies shut up in dark and confined cells: and had it not been for the incessant noise and jarring of the elements, we might have supposed ourselves inhabitants of the nether world. Often did I think of the verse of Hafiz:[1]

"Dark is the night, and dreadful the noise of the waves and whirlpool.

---

1   Khwajeh Shams al-Din Mohammad Hafiz e-Shirazi (c.1319-89), commonly referred to as Hafiz or Hafez, was a Persian poet and proponent of Sufism; his writings are notoriously difficult to translate, but were the focus of intense interest among eighteenth-century orientalists. In general, "Hafiz" refers to one who has memorized the Qur'ān. His verse is characterized by elaborate celebrations of the sensual pleasures of wine and women which figure for the ecstasy of divine love. See Appendices C1, C2, and C3 [404-19].

Little do they know of our situation, who are travelling merrily on the shore."[1]

On the 4th of June we came in sight of the high land of the Cape, called Table Mountain; and shortly after had a view of Table Bay, at the bottom of which is situated the Cape Town. It was now made known, that our water and provisions being nearly expended, it was requisite we should go into the port for a fresh supply. Although this was contrary to our agreement with the captain, and the measure would probably be attended with much delay and expence to the passengers, yet, as there was no other remedy, we were obliged to consent. As but a few hours of the day remained, and it was thought dangerous, on account of the rocks, to enter the bay in the dark, it was determined that the ship should stand off and on during the night, and proceed in early next morning. It so happened, that throughout the night the wind was extremely favourable, and we might have been all landed without any trouble or expence at Cape Town; but, contrary to our hopes, the second officer, having gone to sleep during his watch, allowed the ship to run so far to the southward, that during the whole of the next day we could not regain the land. A second night was therefore passed in tacking backward and forward; and on the following morning, when we were about to enter the bay, a sudden storm, accompanied by thunder and lightning, came on, which carried us, before it ceased, five degrees to the southward. The ship was also struck by the lightning, three of the crew were killed, and two others severely burned.

For the benefit of my countrymen who may be inclined to travel, I shall here relate a few of the hardships and mortifications which I endured on board this ship, in hopes that they will take warning by my sufferings, and derive some advantage from my experience. In the first place, I must advise them never to embark in any but an *English vessel*; and if they are not possessed of sufficient wealth to provide themselves with a number of articles, not to undertake the voyage.

I shall comprise the miseries of this ship under four classes:

The first is that to which every ship is liable; viz. the want of good bread, butter, milk, fruit, and vegetables; to which are to be

---

1 This is a rendering of the fifth couplet of the first Ghazal in Hafiz's *Diwan*.

added, drinking stinking water, and washing the mouth with salt water; also the impurity of being shut up with dogs and hogs, and the difficulty of getting to and from the quarter-gallery, with the danger of being wet, or drowned, while there. To these I should add, the state of suspense and agitation to which a person is constantly exposed, the confinement in one place, and the sickness caused by the motion of the ship.

The second class arose from want of wealth; viz. a small and dark cabin, and the consequent deprivation of air and light; the neglect of servants; the want of a ship cot, on account of the deficiency of room; and the tyranny or rudeness of my neighbours, who ever studied their own convenience at my expence.

The third class is confined to foreigners, by which, I mean persons who are not Europeans; viz. the difficulty of shaving oneself; the cutting of one's own beard and nails; not having any private place for ablution; the necessity of eating with a knife and fork; and the impossibility of purification. From the latter I suffered much inconvenience; for as it was only customary on board to draw up water in buckets early in the morning, at which time all the crew washed themselves and whatever else they required, I was frequently under the necessity of drawing it up when I wanted it, in one of my own copper vessels; but during the rough weather many of these were lost in the attempt, and I was at last reduced to one ewer. I therefore relinquished the practice of purification, and was consequently incapacitated from the other duties of our religion.

The fourth class is confined to ships *not* belonging to the *English*; viz. noise and tumult when any business is done; the abusive language made use of while heaving the anchor; the quantity of bilgewater allowed to remain in the ship; and the unnecessary destruction of every thing on board. To these may be added, the quantity of stinking salt fish and putrid eggs of which the sea store is composed, and the absurd custom of the crew lying on the wet decks; with a total want of discipline in the sailors, and science in the officers.

It was from a thorough knowledge of all these circumstances, that my good friend Mr. Augustus Brooke of Calcutta strongly advised me not to embark in any but an English ship; but finding I was determined to go in the Dane, he repeatedly desired I would carry on board a number of dried fruits, preserves, biscuits, &c. and also take with me a plentiful supply of warm clothing. Not content with this advice alone, he sent me a present of all these things: and fortunate it was for me that I had such a friend, as without these articles I should either have died of hunger, or perished with the cold.

The gale abated on the 13th of the month, but our condition was not much improved thereby; as, in consequence of our not seeing the sun for several days, and not having a correct Ephemeris on board, together with the want of skill in the officers, we had completely lost our reckoning; and not a person in the ship could tell where we were, or how we ought to steer. To add to our distresses, it was now discovered that we had only water for a few days remaining. Thus we were nearly reduced to despair; and had it not been for the mercy of God, we must have perished. During this dreadful state of suspense, and at a time when all the officers supposed we were far to the west of the Cape, and nearly half way to St. Helena, it happened that the steward of the ship, who possessed a keen sight, and who had made several voyages to India, came on the poop to ascertain the quantity of poultry remaining. Having cast his eyes astern of the ship, he exclaimed, "There is the land! You are leaving it behind you." On hearing this joyful news, some of the officers went to the mast head, and with their spy-glasses clearly discerned the land, but even then could not say what place it was: they however put the ship about and stood towards it, and in the course of a few hours ascertained it to be the Table Mountain and Sugar-loaf Hill of the Cape.[1] This intelligence roused the drooping spirits of the crew, and every exertion was made to gain the wished-for port.

On the 21st we we were opposite the entrance of Table Bay; but the monsoon having changed, it became requisite that we should now go to False Bay; no vessel being permitted to enter the former after a certain period, when the wind, coming to the south west, renders it, for four months in the year, a very unsafe anchorage. On this account the Governor has positive orders not to allow any ship to enter the port, and even to fire cannon at them if they refuse to obey the signal.

On the evening of the 23d of July we with some difficulty entered False Bay; but as it soon became dark, we were obliged to cast anchor, lest the ship should run on the rocks. On the following morning we again got under weigh, and at noon anchored opposite the town.

This town is situated at the bottom of a verdant mountain, clothed with a variety of flowers and odoriferous herbs. It consists

---

1 Two mountains so called from their resembling those articles. (Original note)

of about thirty houses only: these are, however, very regular and well built, and each of them contains a pipe of running water: it is therefore peculiarly well adapted as a place of refreshment for ships during the south-west monsoon. We accordingly found sixteen vessels lying here, two of which were men of war, stationed to protect the harbour against the French. As a long time had elapsed since I had seen the habitations of men, I was much struck with the appearance of this town, and the beauties of its port; nor did I ever before experience such pleasing sensations as when I landed there.

On the 24th, all the passengers, except myself, went on shore; for as I had very little money with me, I dreaded the expence, and remained on board. My situation was however rendered more comfortable by the supplies of fresh provisions, fruit, &c. which were daily received from the shore.

CHAPTER IV

The author disembarks, and hires lodgings at False Bay—description of his landlord and family—is hospitably received by the Commandant of the British troops—marked attention of the officers of the Royal navy—improper conduct of his landlord—he determines on proceeding to Cape Town—account of his journey. Description of the town, and remarks occasioned thereby. Character of the Dutch inhabitants, and their conduct to slaves. Description of the climate, and of the country in the vicinity of the Cape; also of the fruits, vegetables, animals, and other productions. People of various nations settled at the Cape. The author meets with several Mohammedans. Panegyric on General Dundas and the British officers. The author sells his slave and some other property, in order to support his expences. The Danish ship brought from False Bay to Table Bay—her captain prosecuted for plundering the vessel in the river Ganges, and his ship thereby prevented from proceeding on her voyage. The other passengers prosecute the captain, and recover half the sum they had paid. The author takes his passage for England.

After some days, I learned that all the passengers, being disgusted with the bad conduct of the captain, had resolved not to return on board again, but to proceed to the Cape Town, and wait there the arrival of some English vessel, in which they might embark for Europe. I was therefore under the necessity either of abandoning my companions, or of incurring a heavy expence by quitting this disgusting ship: and having resolved upon the latter, I went on shore, and took up my residence at the house where the other passengers were staying.

Our landlord, who was called Barnet, was a very smooth speaker, and appeared very polite. He said he was by descent a Scotchman, though born and bred amongst the Dutch. With this person I agreed for my board and lodging, at the rate of five rupees a day. His family consisted of his wife, two children, and five slaves; and notwithstanding there were fifteen of us, including servants, who lodged in the house, they attended minutely to all our wants, and even anticipated our wishes, without any noise, bustle, or confusion.

Some time previous to our arrival at the Cape, it had been taken possession of by the English, and was garrisoned by about 5000 European soldiers, under the command of General Dundas[1] (a nephew of the celebrated Mr. Dundas, one of the principal Ministers of the British Empire), who also acted as Governor during the absence of Lord Macartney.[2] The troops at False Bay were commanded by Captain Collins, on whom I waited, and was received with great attention and politeness. He returned my visit on the following day, and invited me to dine with him. We found a large company assembled, and were entertained in a very sumptuous manner. Although I then understood English but imperfectly, yet the marked attention of Captain and Mrs. Collins and their friends was so flattering, that I never spent a more agreeable day in my life. On taking leave, they requested me to drink tea with them every evening I was disengaged, during my stay at False Bay. From the commanders of the ships of war, Captains Lee and Gouch, I also received the greatest attention. They invited me twice to entertainments on board, and sent their own barges to convey me. Upon entering and leaving the ship, I was saluted by the discharge of a number of pieces of cannon, and was treated in every respect as a person of consequence.

---

1 Francis Dundas (c.1759-1824), first Viscount Melville, was the nephew of Henry Dundas. See p. 122, note 2.

2 George Macartney (1737-1806), first Earl Macartney, started his diplomatic career as British envoy to Russia and was Governor of Madras from 1781 to 1785. His tenure in Madras was controversial and he was often in conflict with Warren Hastings during the Second Mysore War. After resigning his post at Madras, he was sent as British envoy to Peking (Beijing) and was eventually appointed governor of Cape Town in 1796. He returned to England in 1798.

After a short residence with Mr. Barnet, I experienced a very great change in his behaviour. Our table became daily worse supplied, and his conduct was sometimes rude. He one day came and desired I would change my apartment for a smaller one, as he expected more guests, and could put up two or three beds in *my* room. After I had removed my luggage to another, he then told me *that* room was pre-engaged, and that I must remove to a third, in which I found a gentleman's trunks, who was gone to Cape Town, and might possibly return during the night. I was much irritated at such conduct, and asked him what he meant. He replied, that he had let me have my lodgings too cheap; and that if I wished to remain there, I must pay him ten rupees (£.1. 5s.) a day. I observed that his behaviour was that of a *blackguard Dutchman*, and that I should quit his house the next day. I accordingly made my preparations for proceeding to Cape Town; and although I left his house before sun-rise, he insisted on my paying him for the whole of that day. He also charged very extravagantly for my washing, and other matters wherein I had employed him. But I was still more provoked at the behaviour of his wife, to whom, on the day of my arrival, I had presented a bag of fine Bengal rice, worth at the Cape forty or fifty rupees: she was in consequence very polite for three or four days, but afterwards totally changed her conduct.

On the 2d of July I set out for Cape Town, in a coach drawn by eight horses, all of which were driven by one man, and with such dexterity as I have never witnessed. Part of the road was through water up to the horses' bellies; in another place the wheels sank nearly up to the axle-trees in sand; and although we climbed and descended very steep mountains, we were seldom out of a gallop. When we approached within four or five miles of the town, we found the road broad and even, lined on each side with hedges; the country was also well cultivated, and adorned by groves and gardens, with here and there windmills and farmhouses, which much ornamented the scenery. On this road the English and the genteel Dutch families take the air, either on horseback or in carriages, every day from noon till four o'clock.

At the distance of three miles, the town appears very beautiful and superb, and much delights the beholder. The distance from False Bay to Cape Town is a day's journey; but as there are houses for the entertainment of travellers on the road, we had a comfortable breakfast and dinner at the proper hours.

It was nearly dark when we entered the town; and lodgings having been secured for me by one of my ship-mates, I drove directly to Mr. Clark's, the best house of that description in the place.

Two sides of the town are surrounded by mountains; and some of the houses are so near the Table Land, that a stranger is in dread of its falling on them. These mountains are covered with a variety of flowers and sweet herbs, and afford an excellent pasture for cattle; they also abound with springs of delicious water, which not only supply the inhabitants with that indispensable element, but also serve to turn mills, and to irrigate the lands when requisite.

The inhabitants of the Cape frequently form parties of pleasure on the top of the Table Land; and although several places in the road are so steep that they cannot be ascended without the aid of ropes, the Dutch ladies are so accustomed to climb precipices, that they always accompany the men on these excursions.

On another side of the town is Table Bay; on the shore of which are erected very formidable batteries, sufficient to prevent any enemy from entering it. Some batteries have also been constructed on the land side. In short, the fortifications of this place were so strong, that when the English came to attack the Cape, they found it expedient to proceed to False Bay, and effect their debarkation at that point: they thence proceeded by land, and having with great difficulty clambered over the mountains, made their attack on that side, and thus compelled the Hollanders to capitulate.

The town is about six miles in circumference. A few of the houses are built of stone, but the generality of them are only brick and mortar. The streets are very broad and straight, and paved on each side with large bricks or flag stones. Each street is also provided with one or two channels for carrying off the water, so that even in winter there is scarcely any mud or dirt to be seen. Each side of the street is also planted with a row of trees, which afford an agreeable shade; and along the front of every house is erected a seat of masonry, about a yard high, for the inhabitants to sit on and smoke their pipes in the summer evenings. This custom, which is, I believe, peculiar to the Hollanders, appeared to me excellent.

The furniture of some of the houses is very elegant, consisting of mirrors, pictures, girandoles, lustres, and a great quantity of plate. The walls of the rooms were covered with variegated paper, and hung with handsome window curtains, some of chintz, others of velvet; in short, the splendour of this town quite obliterated from my mind all the magnificence of Calcutta, which I had previously considered as superior to any thing to be found between India and Europe. In the sequel I changed my opinion respecting the Cape; and indeed I may say, that from my first setting out on this journey, till my arrival in England, I ascended the pinnacle of magnificence and luxury; the several degrees or stages of which were, Calcutta, the Cape, Cork, Dublin, and London; the beauty and grandeur of each city effacing that of the former. On my return towards India every thing was reversed, the last place being always inferior to that I had quitted. Thus, after a long residence in London, Paris appeared to me much inferior; for although the latter contains more superb buildings, it is neither so regular, kept so clean, nor so well lighted at night as the former, nor does it possess so many squares or gardens in its vicinity; in short, I thought I had fallen from Paradise into Hell. But when I arrived in Italy, I was made sensible of the beauty of Paris. The cities of Italy rose in my estimation when I arrived at Constantinople; and the latter is a perfect Paradise, compared to Bagdad, Mousul, and other towns in the territory of the *Faithful*. All these places I shall describe more particularly in the course of my Travels.

Nearly in the centre of Cape Town is a large handsome square, two miles in circumference, in which the troops are exercised. Two sides of the square are inclosed with streets of lofty houses, a third is bounded by the Fort, and the fourth faces the sea. The Fort is regular, and much resembles that of Calcutta, but smaller. The *bazars* are well built, and well supplied with every requisite.

Having said so much of the place, I will now take the liberty of describing the inhabitants. All the *European* Dutch women whom I saw, were very fat, gross, and insipid; but the girls born at the Cape are well made, handsome, and sprightly; they are also good natured, but require costly presents. Even the married women are suspected; and each of the Englishmen of rank had his particular lady, whom he visited without any interruption from the husband, who generally walked out when the admirer entered the house. The consequence was, that the English spent all the money they got; while the Hollanders became rich, and more affluent than when under their own government.

The generality of the Dutchmen are low-minded and inhospitable, neither do they fear the imputation of a bad name, and are more oppressive to their slaves than any other people in the world. If a slave understands any trade, they permit him to work for other people, but oblige him to pay from one to four dollars a day, according to his abilities, for such indulgence. The daughters of these slaves who are handsome they keep for their own use, but the ugly ones are either sold, or obliged to work with their fathers. Should a slave perchance save money sufficient to purchase his freedom, they cause him to pay a great price for it, and throw many other obstacles in his way.

I saw a tailor, who was married, and had four children; he was then forty years of age, and had, by great industry and œconomy, purchased the freedom of himself and wife; but the children still continued as slaves. One of them, a fine youth, was sold to another master, and carried away to some distant land: the eldest girl was in the service of her master; and the two youngest were suffered to remain with their parents till they should gain sufficient strength to be employed.

As the female slaves are employed in making the beds, and looking after the rooms of the lodgers, they frequently have opportunities of getting money; great part of which they are, however, obliged to pay to their avaricious owners.

During my stay at the Cape, I suffered great inconvenience from the filthiness and stench of their privies, which they take no pains to keep clean. Neither have they any baths, either hot or cold, in the town; and ablution is quite unknown to the inhabitants.

Although I was ignorant of the Dutch language, and could not converse with the young women, yet in dancing they made use of so many wanton airs, and threw such significant looks towards me, that I was often put to the blush, and obliged to retire to the other side of the room. A party of these girls once attacked me: one of them, who was the handsomest and most forward, snatched away my handkerchief, and offered it to another girl of her own age; upon which they all began to laugh aloud: but as the young lady did not seem inclined to accept the handkerchief, I withdrew it, and said I would only part with it to the *handsomest*. As this circumstance was an allusion to a practice among the rich Turks of Constantinople, who throw their handkerchief to the lady with whom they wish to pass the night, the laugh was turned against my fair antagonist, who blushed, and retreated to some distance.

I continued to reside with Mr. Clark till the 15th of July, during which time I formed several acquaintances, and found that a number of Mohammedans dwelt at the Cape. My landlord in a short time proving himself to be a true Dutchman, by the exorbitance of his charges, and various impositions, I quarrelled with him; upon which he was very abusive, and threatened to summon me before the court of justice. I thereon complained to my ship-mate, Captain Williamson; but he, having formed an attachment to one of the females in the house, took my adversary's part, and insisted upon my paying all his demands. He had occasion, in the sequel, to repent his conduct; for the girl having been detected, was severely punished, and compelled to pay to her oppressive master all the money the captain had given her, who thereupon quitted the house, and apologized to me for his conduct.

In consequence of my dispute with Mr. Clark, I hired lodgings in the house of a worthy Mussulman, who behaved to me with the greatest attention and kindness; and as I had constant invitations from the English officers, I passed my time very pleasantly, and lived at a small expence.

Although it was now winter at the Cape, the trees were all in full verdure, and the gardens were replete with flowers of every kind: the fruits were also delicious, and in such variety, that we found here the produce of both the torrid and frigid zones. At a short distance from the town is situated a celebrated garden, called Constantia, the grapes of which are superior to any I have ever tasted, and from which they make an excellent sweet wine, that is much admired, and carried to all parts of the world.

The markets are well supplied with good beef, mutton, and goat. The sheep are of the large-tailed species, and afford a great quantity of grease and tallow. The vegetables here are also very good, and in great variety; but their wheat and rice are indifferent. Fresh butter is with difficulty procured: and notwithstanding there appeared a great abundance of every thing else, the prices were high. Meat was seven-pence halfpenny a pound; bread three-pence a pound; and eggs three-pence each. Washing is also very dear.

The horses of the Cape are very strong and active, and under excellent command: they have probably some of the Arab blood in them. Here are also very good mules, which are principally used for carriages: the waggons are drawn by oxen. Ostriches are found in this part of Africa; and they shewed me a particular species of dogs and cats, both of which run wild in the woods.

Besides the Dutch, there are to be found at the Cape people of many other nations; and at least seven or eight languages are spoken here. The common people are principally Malays and Negroes. Most of these were originally slaves, who have either purchased their freedom, or have been manumitted by their masters. Among them I met with many pious good Mussulmans, several of whom possessed considerable property. I had the pleasure of forming an acquaintance with Shaikh Abdulla, the son of

Abd al Aziz, a native of Mecca, who having come to the Cape on some commercial adventure, married the daughter of one of the Malays, and settled there. He was very civil, introduced me to all his friends, and anticipated all my wishes.

From Mr. Bomgard, a Dutch gentleman, who had resided twenty years in Bengal, and had been for some time governor of Chinsura, I experienced much kindness. His wife was a very agreeable and clever woman, and spoke seven languages.

Were I to relate all the civilities I received from General Dundas and the other British officers, they would fill a volume. I cannot however refrain mentioning the many delightful evenings I passed at the house of Lady Anne Barnet,[1] who was generally called the Princess of the Cape, and every week gave an entertainment to all her acquaintances, and constantly did me the honour to number me among her guests. Lady Anne is the daughter of an English nobleman, and has all the dignified manners of a person of quality. At her house I frequently met with a Mrs. Crawford,[2] a young Irishwoman, who was exceedingly beautiful, but spoke little, and was rather reserved: in short, she had quite the elegant behaviour of our Indian princesses, and completely won my heart. These were the only two English women of rank whose husbands were at the Cape. The rest of the officers were obliged to amuse themselves with the Dutch ladies, several of whom, in consequence, got well married.

Although I lived with the greatest possible œconomy during our long stay at this place, I could not have borne the expence, but for the sale of some articles. Of these, the most valuable was a Negro slave, whose manners and disposition had been so much corrupted on board ship, that I found it requisite to part with him, and disposed of him for 500 dollars. I also sold a talisman and some pieces of muslin for 200 dollars more. By these means I was enabled to live without incurring any debts, till an opportunity offered of proceeding on our voyage.

During our stay at the Cape, the monsoon having changed, Captain Nettleman was enabled to bring his ship, the Christiana, from False Bay to Table Bay: but immediately on his arrival, he was accused by Mr. Pringle, the East-India Company's agent,

---

1 Lady Anne Barnard (1750-1825; née Lindsay), writer and hostess whose journals written at the Cape recount colonial politics and society. She corresponded frequently with Henry Dundas. See the editor's "Introduction" for her account of Mirza Abu Talib's visit (9-10).
2 Lady Barnard's daughter, who married Col. James Crawford.

with having plundered the burnt ship in the river Ganges; and a prosecution was filed against him in the court of justice. The fact was easily proved, and he was sentenced to pay £.2000 damages. During the prosecution, the ship was laid under sequestration; and the crew having dispersed themselves in various situations, Captain Nettleman found it impossible to proceed on his voyage. He was however, I believe, not sorry for the event; for he shortly after married a Dutch lady, and settled at the Cape. His passengers thereon prosecuted him for the amount of their passage money, and compelled him to repay them half the sum they had given him. I very imprudently declined joining in the prosecution, for two reasons; in the first place, I was afraid of the chicanery of Dutch lawyers; and, secondly, Captain Nettleman assured me, that if the cause was decided against him, he would repay me in proportion to the others. This agreement he afterwards denied, and I lost my money. Glad, however, to get rid of such a wretch, and an opportunity offering at this time of proceeding to England, I engaged a passage, for forty guineas, on board the Britannia, a South-Sea whaler, bound to London.

CHAPTER V

The Author quits the Cape, and embarks on board the Britannia. Description of the ship, and character of the captain. Discover St. Helena—anchor in the port—description of the island, town, and fortifications—hospitable and friendly conduct of the Governor. Leave St. Helena. Pass the island of Ascension—some account thereof. Recross the equinoctial line. Anecdote related by the captain. Fall in with an American and an Hamburgh vessel. Again see the polar star—pass a fleet of outward-bound Indiamen— pass the Canaries and the entrance to the Mediterranean Sea. Arrive at the mouth of the English Channel—contrary wind—obliged to bear away for the Irish or St. George's Channel. Fall in with an overset vessel. Cold and disagreeable weather. The captain determines to enter the Cove of Cork.

On the 29th of September, my friend Captain Richardson and I embarked on board the Britannia, and were soon under weigh. This was one of the vessels employed in catching whales, and was loaded with the oil of that fish. She had also a *Letter of Marque*, and was therefore well equipped for war; and had been fortunate enough to capture a Spanish prize on her way out, which sold for a large sum of money. The crew consisted of between thirty and forty men; but as they were all able seamen, and kept under the same discipline as on board a ship of war, the duty was performed with great alacrity, and without any noise or confusion. Although our accommodations were rather confined, every thing was so well arranged, and the guns, arms, &c. so well secured, that we felt none of the inconveniences which we had suffered in the Dane.

The Britannia sailed very fast; and during the voyage we pursued several ships, but did not succeed in making any captures. The captain was named Clark: he was an excellent navigator; and whenever we approached any land, he predicted to an hour when we should arrive at it. Soon after leaving the Cape, we were again favoured by the trade winds, and in two days ran 400 miles.

On the morning of the 13th of October we discovered the Island of St. Helena, and at noon cast anchor in the port. I soon after landed, and was honoured by Governor Brooke[1] with an invitation to dinner. This gentleman, having served thirteen years as an officer in India, some part of which period he resided at the court of the Emperor Shāh Aalum,[2] spoke Hindoostany with great fluency, and conversed with me a long time on Indian politics.

St. Helena is an island in the midst of the Great Western Ocean, situated many hundred miles from any other land, in the sixteenth degree of south latitude, and is about twenty-eight miles in circumference. The cliffs from the sea appear black and. burnt up; but, in the interior, some of the valleys are clothed with delightful verdure: the hills are also adorned with a variety of beautiful shrubs, and every spot fit for culture is laid out in picturesque gardens. The inhabitants have with great labour formed zigzag roads up the hills, fit for two horses to ride abreast; but on account of the steepness of the ascent, carriages are seldom made use of. The most elevated of the mountains is said to be about a mile high; from some of the crevices in which a smoke and strong smell of sulphur are often emitted. There are only two considerable streams of water in the island; and as the vegetation is therefore entirely dependent on the rain, it often happens, that, from

---

1 Robert Brooke (1744-1811), officer of East India Co. and colonial administrator, was governor of St. Helena from 1787 to 1801.
2 Shah Alam (1728-1806), Mughal emperor of India, was defeated by the British in 1764 and received a stipend from the East India Co.; he returned to regain power in 1772 but was blinded and deposed by the Rohillas. He was restored to the throne in 1803 by the British.

a want of moisture, the grass for the cattle and the produce of the gardens are destroyed, which causes much distress to the inhabitants. In favourable seasons, the quantity of apples and other fruits produced in some of the gardens is astonishing. A garden belonging to an officer yielded in *one* year a clear profit of £.1250. As this island does not produce any grain, it is principally supplied with flour and other articles of food from Europe. Beef, mutton, and poultry, are procurable, but at very high prices. Milk is not in plenty, but so rich, that it produces cream twice. Here you meet with the trees and fruits both of Europe and Asia, and perhaps some of the most romantic spots in the world. Whilst walking in Colonel Robertson's garden with his beautiful daughters, the contrast between my then situation, and the confined cabin of a ship, made me fancy, for some moments, that I had suddenly been transported into Paradise.[1] But the most surprising thing about this island is, that thunder and lightning are never heard nor seen.

The only town on the island is situated in a narrow valley, which seems to have been formed by torrents from the mountains: this valley is about two miles in length, and from twenty to a hundred yards in breadth. The town was founded by the English, about forty years after they had obtained settlements in India. It contains some good buildings formed of stone, but the roofs of the houses are thatched or tiled. Here are several good shops, in which both Indian and European commodities are sold; and also a tavern and coffee-house. In the broadest part of the valley there is a small square, used as a parade for the troops: towards the sea there are several very heavy batteries erected; and on the tops of two of the hills are two strong forts, which could with ease sink any enemy's ship that should venture to anchor in the Roads. Some little way in the interior there is a remarkable strong tower, built entirely of stone, the walls of which are fifteen feet thick. The engineer told me it was impregnable; that it was as solid as the rock on which it is built; and that he hoped it would be as durable.

The only place at which ships can anchor is opposite the town: and the water is here so deep, that they lie within a hundred yards of the shore.

I was told, that when the English first settled here, the island was overrun by wild goats; and that these animals, in bounding

---

1 Mohammed's Paradise is of course meant. (Translator's note)

from rock to rock, frequently threw down large stones, which falling on the roofs of the houses built under the precipice, occasioned much damage; that a reward was in consequence set upon their heads; and every person who brought the skin of one of them to a particular office, received a sum of money for it; by which means the goats were gradually extirpated.

The lower class of people here are of a tawny colour, being a mixture of European, Indian, and Negro extraction. Of the two latter denominations there are still a number of slaves on the island.

Governor Brooke, whose hospitality and liberality were extended to every person who visited the island, having requested me to live with him during my stay, supplied me with a horse, and directed his son to attend me into the country; by which means I visited the Governor's and Deputy Governor's gardens, and every other place worth seeing. When we were about to embark, he sent on board a large stock of fruit and vegetables for my use.

On the evening of the 15th, after having dined with the worthy Governor, we repaired on board. The anchor was immediately weighed, and in a short time we quitted this romantic scene.

On the 20th we passed by the Island of Ascension, at the distance of only two miles. This island, like St. Helena, is also a rock, situated in the great Western Ocean, in the eighth degree of south latitude; but as it does not possess any springs of fresh water, it is not a place of rendezvous for ships; they however often stop here to catch turtle, for the number and goodness of which this place is celebrated. These animals come on shore during the night to deposit their eggs, and the people employed to catch them then turn them on their backs, and carry them off at their leisure during the day. A few goats are also to be seen here, which probably find rain water deposited in the cavities of the rocks, or in some stagnant pools, which enables them to subsist. On this day we again had the sun vertical; and although we were only eight degrees from the equinoctial line, we found the necessity of putting on our warm clothing.

On the 25th we re-crossed the line, the weather still continuing uncommonly cold. In this latitude we caught great numbers of fish: we were also followed by a number of birds resembling swallows. It is said that these birds never go to the land, but form nests of weeds and the scum of the sea, which constantly float on the water, in which they lay their eggs and bring forth their young; but this story appears very improbable.

I was however told a circumstance which is more extraordinary than the above. Captain Clark, who was not addicted to fiction, related to me, that once he went on shore on the coast of Africa, with two boats, to procure water for the ship; that while he was there, nearly 300 animals, of a size between a horse and an ass, which they call sea-horses (probably seals) came out of the sea, and went above a mile on land, leaving very deep impressions of their feet in the sand. When they were returning, he (the captain) fired his musket at, and killed one of them; that the others, in order to revenge the slaughter of their companion, instantly pursued him; and that he and some of his companions only escaped by hiding themselves among the rocks. Some of the party got on board one of the boats, and pushed off to the ship; but the other boat was broken to pieces by the enraged animals.

On the 26th, at noon, we saw a ship at a distance, which the captain believing to be a French vessel, cleared his own for action. As we were then in the track between Europe and America, and most of the kings of Europe were at war with each other, these latitudes are considered to be more replete with danger than any other part of the ocean; it being the practice of Europe, that whenever the ships of two enemies meet at sea, the most powerful carries his adversary with him into one of his own ports, and there sells both ship and cargo for his own advantage.

After a run of some hours, we discovered that it was an American ship; and although the English were not at war with that nation, Captain Clark ordered the master to bring to, and to come on board with his papers. The poor fellow, being much frightened, came on board, and brought with him his Journal and certificates. During the whole of the day he was kept as a prisoner, but in the evening obtained liberty to proceed on his voyage.

On the following day we fell in with another vessel, from Hamburgh, laden with salt provisions for the Island of Mauritius. This was a fine large three-masted ship; but the captain, upon being ordered to stop, immediately complied, and came on board with his papers: he also brought us a present of some fresh cheeses, which were very acceptable; and he was permitted shortly to depart.

On the night of the 27th, being then in the fifth degree of north latitude, we had again the pleasure of beholding the constellations Ursa Major and Minor, and the polar star. About this time we had a great deal of rain; and the captain assured me that he had constantly experienced wet weather in these latitudes.

On the 7th of November we a third time entered the region of the trade winds, for these also prevail between the tenth and twenty-seventh degrees of north latitude; which carried us on with such rapidity, that sometimes the ship went ten miles in the hour; the waves were in consequence much agitated, and the sea ran nearly as high as off the Cape; but, as the ship was well secured and well managed, we did not suffer those inconveniences which had been experienced on board the Dane.

On the 11th we passed within a mile of six English Indiamen, under convoy of a ship of war. We shewed our colours to each other, and passed on. During this part of the voyage we also passed by the islands, called, by the English, *The West Indies*; but did not see any of them, as they lie far west of the track we pursued.

On the 14th we were opposite the Canaries, or Fortunate Isles, whence the Mohammedans commence their longitude. These islands are in the thirty-third degree of north latitude: we however passed far to the westward of them. We shortly after passed the entrance of the Mediterranean Sea, which runs east as far as Aleppo.

From the 19th to the 27th we had contrary winds, and the sea ran very high; but we suffered no other inconvenience than the want of food and sleep. On the 29th we were opposite the entrance of the channel which runs between England and France, but which takes its name from the former; and expected to have cast anchor in two days at Portsmouth, one of the most celebrated ports of England; but a strong easterly wind continuing to blow right against us, we were unable to enter it, and were obliged to bear away for the coast of Ireland.

It becomes in this place requisite to explain (to my countrymen) the signification of several English terms, in order that they may more fully comprehend my meaning.

A *Channel* means a narrow part of the sea, confined between two lands, but open at both ends.

A *Bay* extends far into the land, is of a circular form, and open only on one side.

A *Sea* (sometimes called a *Gulf*) is a large extent of the ocean, but nearly surrounded by land; as the Mediterranean Sea, the Gulf of Persia, the Red Sea, &c.

As the English Channel runs nearly east and west, it is impossible to enter it if the wind blows from the former quarter: when therefore a ship arrives at this place, if the wind be easterly, she is obliged to beat about till it changes. This was precisely our situation; and for two days we continued to tack from one side to the other, without gaining any advantage.

Thus situated, and our captain seeing no prospect of a change of wind, and being also apprehensive of falling in with some of the French cruizers, resolved to go into the channel which runs between Ireland and England, called St. George's Channel, as being a much more safe place, and out of the track of the enemy.

In consequence of this determination, we changed our course, and during the day fell in with a two-masted vessel, which had overset in the late gale, and been abandoned by her crew; but which, being laden with buoyant articles, floated on the water like *a half-drowned animal.* Captain Clark ordered out his boat, and went on board her; and with the assistance of his men, who were good divers, he got out several chests of excellent wine, and a quantity of delicious fruits and sweetmeats. As we were now near the land, and the weather was excessively cold, we were permitted to have a fire in the cabin, over which we enjoyed these good things; and were thus in some measure compensated for the want of a favourable wind, though at the expence of our fellow-creatures, who had lost or rather abandoned their property.

After cruizing for several days in the Irish Channel, and the wind still continuing adverse, the captain resolved, instead of wasting his time in contending with the elements, to go into the *Cove of Cork,* and pass some days there.

CHAPTER VI

The ship enters the Cove, and casts anchor. Description of the bay. The author lands at the town, and is hospitably treated—visits the city of Cork, which he describes—returns to the ship, and determines on visiting Lord Cornwallis at Dublin—quits the ship, and sets out for Cork, where he visits Captain Baker. Description of that gentleman's house and family. The author sets out for Dublin—account of his journey.

On the 6th of December we had a view of the land in the vicinity of the Cove of Cork: it consisted of a range of hills, approaching the sea with a gentle slope, and divided by inclosures into numerous fields. We soon after entered the mouth of the Cove, between two forts, which have been erected to prevent the ships of an enemy from entering the harbour. After proceeding some distance, we came to another fort, built with stone, upon a rock in the middle of the bay, which is thereby divided into two channels. Having passed the fort, we in a short time came opposite the town of Cove, and cast anchor.

We found here not less than forty or fifty vessels of different sizes, three of which were ships of war. The bay resembles a round basin, sixteen miles in circumference. On its eastern shore is situated the town, which is built in the form of a crescent, and defended at each end by small forts. On one side of the bay, a large river, resembling the Ganges, disembogues itself: this river extends a great way inland, and passes by the city of Cork. The circular form of this extensive sheet of water, the verdure of the hills, the comfortable appearance of the town on one side, and the number of elegant houses and romantic cottages on the other, with the formidable aspect of the forts, and so many large ships lying securely in the harbour, conveyed to my mind such sensations as I had never before experienced: and although, in the course of my travels, I had an opportunity of seeing the Bay of Genoa, and the Straits of Constantinople, I do not think either of them is to be compared with this.

In the afternoon we landed at the town, but found that its interior did not correspond with its exterior appearance. It does not contain any handsome buildings, and is, in fact, merely the anchoring place for ships engaged in the commerce of the city of Cork. It consists only of one street, little more than half a mile long: in the shops, however, were abundance of apples, pears, and grapes; also a variety of dried fruits. Having satisfied our curiosity, we went to the post-office, to despatch our letters. The mistress of the house being of a hospitable disposition, insisted upon our staying to dinner, and, assisted by her sons and daughters, waited upon us at table. Our meal consisted of fish, beef, butter, potatoes and other vegetables, all of so excellent a quality, that in my whole life I never tasted any equal to them. Cork is celebrated for all these articles; and ships are sent here, *all the way* from London, to procure them for that market. When we were about to return to our ship, we wished to pay for our dinner, as is the custom in Europe; but our hostess would not accept a farthing, and strongly advised us to come on shore in the morning, and proceed to the city, which she assured us was well worth seeing. We agreed, and early next day went to her house. She furnished us with horses; and ordered her son, a fine youth of fifteen years of age, to accompany us. The conduct and appearance of this amiable woman astonished me: she had been the mother of twenty-one children, eighteen of whom were then living, and most of them present in the house; notwithstanding which she had not the appearance of old age, and I should not have supposed her more than thirty.

After travelling about three miles, we came to the bank of the river (Lee), in which we found a number of small ships at anchor. At this place there is a good ferry; and our horses being very quiet, we easily got them into the boat, and in a short time crossed over. From hence to the city was nine miles, the whole of which extent is highly cultivated, and adorned with country-houses, groves, gardens, &c.

We arrived at the city about noon, and put up at an excellent hotel, the apartments of which we found elegant, and the servants attentive. After a short time we walked out to see the town; but it being the winter season, and the streets very dirty, we did not derive so much satisfaction as we otherwise should. The part of the town we visited consists of houses built of brick and mortar, very regular, and four stories high, with handsome doors and glazed windows, and fitted up in the interior with great elegance. The shops were handsome, and filled with every requisite, either for use or luxury; but as this city has been erected for the purposes of commerce, more pains have been taken to facilitate the importation and exportation of goods, than to preserve uniformity and regularity: it has therefore no extensive squares, and is intersected by canals lined with stone, by which vessels can either approach the warehouses of the merchants, or may be hauled into dock, to be repaired. Over these canals are thrown draw-bridges, which can be opened and shut at pleasure; but, owing to the stagnant water, and the filth which is thrown into them, disagreeable smells frequently arise, which are not only nauseous, but must be unwholesome. The situation of the city is also so low, that you scarcely discover it till you come close to it.

Having made a hearty dinner at the hotel, and the captain being in expectation of a change of wind, we deemed it imprudent to remain any longer: we therefore mounted our horses, and returned by the same road we came, to the Cove, and slept on board our ship.

During my visit to Cork, I learned that Lord Cornwallis (late Governor of India),[1] who was the representative of the King in this island, having quelled the rebellion which had disturbed this country for several years, was settled in Dublin. As this city was only three days' journey from Cork, and it had always been my intention, after seeing England, to pay my respects to his lordship, it now occurred to me, that it would be better, as chance had thrown me in his vicinity, to anticipate my intentions, and to

---

1 See p. 65, note 1.

take this opportunity of waiting on him. I was further induced to this determination by the beauty of the country, and from having learnt that two ships had lately been lost in the English Channel. I therefore resolved to quit the ship at this place, and, after first visiting Dublin, proceed thence to London. Having communicated my intentions to my friend, Captain Richardson, he resolved to accompany me: we therefore left our heavy luggage and servants on board the ship, and, having landed with a small trunk of clothes, again set out for Cork. This time we proceeded by water, in an open boat, and took up our lodgings at the hotel where we had formerly dined.

On the day after our arrival, we were agreeably surprised by a visit from Captain Baker, an old friend of Captain Richardson, and a gentleman with whom I had formed an acquaintance in Rohilcund during the war with Ghoolam Mohammed Khan.[1] He had heard of our arrival, and came to see us. After the usual inquiries respecting our health, &c. he insisted that we should accompany him to his house, which was situated a few miles in the country; to which we agreed, and were most hospitably entertained. I was delighted with the beauty of his park and gardens, and the regularity and good arrangement of all his apartments and offices. I was particularly pleased with his cook-room, it being the first regular kitchen I had seen: the dressers for holding china, the racks for depositing the dishes after they were washed, the pipes of cold and boilers of hot water, which, merely by turning a cock, were supplied in any quantity that could be required, with the machinery for roasting meat, which was turned by smoke, all excited my admiration. At Cove I saw a spit for roasting meat turned by a dog. The poor animal was put into a hollow wheel, and, being impatient at his confinement, endeavoured to clamber up the wheel: by this exertion he gave the machine a rotatory motion, which

---

1 Ghulam Mohammad Khan (1762/3-1828), ruler of the Rohilla state of Rampur (later known as Rohilkhand) for a brief period in 1794. The British had defeated the Pashtun Rohillas in 1774 and the region was ruled by Nawab Faizullah Khan for twenty years. His son Muhammad Ali Khan was killed by the Rohilla Leaders shortly after becoming Nawab and Ghulam Muhammad Khan, the brother of the deceased, was proclaimed Nawab. The East India Company intervened, and after a reign of less than four months Ghulam Muhammad Khan was defeated by its forces, and the Governor General made Ahmad Ali Khan, son of the late Muhammad Ali Khan, the new Nawab.

was communicated by a chain to the spit, and thus regularly turned every part of the meat towards the fire. I was told that the dog had been thus employed, for two or three hours every day, for fifteen years.

Captain Baker informed me that he had purchased this estate, which was situated on the bank of the river, and only four miles from Cork, for 20,000 rupees (£2,500). Part of it was arable land, some of it meadow, and the rest, except the garden, was laid out in pasture for sheep and cows. He told me that it supplied him with more corn, straw, and hay, than he could use, also with abundance of milk, fruit, potatoes, and other vegetables; that he reared his own sheep and poultry; and was only obliged to go to market for beef, groceries, and wine: in short, he lived on this little estate with more comfort and plenty than an English gentleman could in India upon an annual income of a lac of rupees (£. 12,500).

This gentleman's family consisted, in all, of twelve persons, two of whom were his nieces. One of these ladies was witty and agreeable; the other handsome, but reserved. Several of the young men of Cork had made them offers of marriage; but they were so impressed with their own powerful attractions, that they were difficult to please, and would not yield their liberty to any of their admirers. These ladies, during dinner, honoured me with the most marked attention; and as I had never before experienced so much courtesy from beauties, I was lost in admiration. After dinner these angels made tea for us; and one of them having asked me if it was sweet enough, I replied, that, having been made by such hands, it could not but be sweet. On hearing this, all the company laughed, and my fair one blushed like a rose of Damascus.

Another remarkable person in this family was named Deen Mohammed.[1] He was a native of Moorshedabad in Bengal, and had been brought up from his childhood by an elder brother of Captain Baker's, who, on his return to Europe, brought this lad with him, and sent him to school in Cork, to learn to read and write English. At the school he became acquainted with a pretty girl, the daughter of respectable parents, and persuaded her to elope with him. They went to another town, where they were married, and then returned to Cork. They had several fine chil-

---

1 This person lately kept the Hookah Club-House in George Street, Manchester Square. (Translator's note)

dren; and he has published a book, giving some account of himself, and of the customs of India.[1]

On the 8th of December, having previously engaged places for Dublin, at the rate of three guineas each, we set out in the mail coach. As this carriage has the privilege of conveying the letters from the post-office, and the roads were not yet quite secure, we were escorted by three dragoons, who were regularly relieved whenever we stopped to change horses. For the above reason we also stopped during the night. On this road we found ample supplies of every thing requisite. We breakfasted the first day at a small newly-built town, called Fermoy, and dined and slept at Clonmell. The people of the inns, on hearing the sound of the coachman's horn, had every thing prepared, so that there was never the smallest delay. We however could not either eat or sleep comfortably for the hurry of the coachman, who threatened, if we were not ready on the blowing of his horn, that he would leave us behind; in which case we should not only have lost our passage, but probably our luggage, and at all events have been separated from our companions. The second day we breakfasted at Kilkenny: this city is celebrated throughout Ireland for the purity of its air, the fineness of its water, the healthiness of its situation, and the beauty and urbanity of its inhabitants. I was so delighted with the transient view I had of it, that I would not sit down to breakfast, but, having taken a piece of bread in my hand, walked to the river: this I found came rolling down a verdant hill at some distance, but was in its progress interrupted by a fall, which added much to the beauty of the scenery. On the opposite side of the river, the ground was laid out in gardens and orchards, resembling a terrestrial paradise; in short, I am at a loss for words to express the delight I felt on beholding this charming place. During the night, we slept at the town of Carlow, and on the following evening entered Dublin.

---

1 Formerly Dean Mahomet (1759-1851), he served in one of the Bengal army's European regiments before emigrating to Ireland in 1784. He converted to Anglicanism and eloped with an Anglo-Irish woman in 1786. He attempted several business ventures, but is most known for his bath houses and shampooing (Indian therapeutic massage) and his Indian restaurant, the Hindostanee Coffee House, in Portman Square. In 1793-94 he wrote *The Travels of Dean Mahomet* and published a treatise entitled *Shampooing, or; Benefits resulting from the use of Indian medicated vapour bath* (1822) and thus became the first Indian to publish in Britain.

This three days' journey was through a hilly country, so that we were constantly ascending and descending; we did not however meet with any very steep mountains. The villages in this country much resemble those of India. The roofs of the houses are thatched with straw, and bound down with osiers; but in some instances they are covered with sods, which have the grass growing out of them a span high. Few villages contain more than a dozen houses. The poverty of the peasants, or common people, in this country, is such, that the peasants of India are rich when compared to them. This poverty arises from two causes; first, the high price of provisions; and, secondly, the quantity of clothes and fuel requisite to keep them warm in so cold a climate. Notwithstanding the sharp stones over which they are obliged to travel, and the excessive cold of the climate, they never wear a shoe, but during the whole year go about with bare legs and bare arms; in consequence of which, these parts of them are as red as the feet of a Hindoo woman who has been embellishing herself with *Mendee* (the leaves of the *Sphæranthus Indicus*).

I was informed, that many of these people never taste meat during their lives, but subsist entirely upon potatoes; and that, in the farm-houses, the goats, pigs, dogs, men, women, and children, lie all together. Whilst on our journey, the boys frequently ran for miles with the coach, in hopes of obtaining a piece of bread.

Notwithstanding the poverty of the peasants, the country is well cultivated, and very fertile; it produces great quantities of wheat, barley, peas, turnips, and, above all, potatoes. Rice, both of Bengal and America, is procurable every where, though at a high price. Wherever I dined, a plate of this grain was always boiled, and brought to table for my exclusive use; my host and his other guests contenting themselves with bread and vegetables. The horses and cows are fed during winter, while the ground is covered with snow, on dry grass and grain, and the sheep on turnips.

Here is found a kind of earth, called *Turf*, which is unfit for tillage, but makes tolerable fuel: it is however not equal to the other kind of fuel used in these countries, called *Coal*, which is a species of black stone, dug out of mines, and affords a great heat.[1] Turf is nevertheless better than the composition of cow dung, used by the poor in India.

---

1 In a Persian work entitled "The Wonders of Creation," a long description is given of *Coal*; but it is not generally known in India, although it is to be found in the Ramghur Hills. (Original note)

CHAPTER VII

The Author arrives at Dublin, and hires lodgings. Description of the city, and of the interior of the houses. Lighting of the streets at night. Squares. Infatuation of Europeans respecting Statues. Account of Phoenix Park— the Light-house and Pier—the river, and canals. Description of the College—Parliament House—Custom House, and Exchange—Churches— Barracks, and Hospitals. The Author visits the Theatre—his account of an Harlequin entertainment, and other public exhibitions.

Upon our arrival in Dublin, we found the inn, at which the coach stopped, quite full: we were therefore obliged to go to an hotel frequented only by lords and dukes, and where, of course, the charges were very high. But, by the advice of a gentleman who came in the coach with us from Cork, I went next day and hired a lodging in English Street, near the College, at the house of a Mrs. Ball, a widow lady of an amiable disposition, who had several very fine children. In this country it is not customary to take lodgings by the month, but only by the week: I therefore engaged two rooms, at a guinea a week. I always breakfasted at home, the servants of the house purchasing for me excellent tea, sugar, bread, and butter.

During the first week of my residence in Dublin, I daily accompanied Captain Richardson to some of the coffee-houses, where we dined at about five shillings expence; but in a short time I had so many invitations, that I was seldom disengaged. Every gentleman who wished to invite me to his house, first called, and then sent a note, to request I would dine with him on such a day. Sometimes they brought the note with them, and, if I happened to be absent from home, left their names written on a card, together with the invitation.

Captain Richardson, having paid his respects to the Lord Lieutenant, and seen every thing he deemed worthy of observation in Dublin, determined to proceed immediately to London: but, as I had no particular object in view, and was highly gratified by the attention and hospitality of the Irish, I resolved to continue some time longer in this country, even at the risk of parting with my friend, and trusting myself entirely among strangers. Of this, however, I had no cause to repent; for my acquaintances, finding that after the departure of Captain Richardson I was left without a companion, redoubled their attentions to me: and I found, that by not having any person to interpret for me, I made much more progress in acquiring the English language.

As my principal object in undertaking the journey to Dublin was to pay my respects to Marquis Cornwallis, the second day after my arrival I sent my compliments to his lordship, and, if agreeable, I would wait upon him: in reply to which, I received a polite message from his lordship, expressive of his happiness at my safe arrival, and desiring to see me at a certain hour on the following day. I accordingly waited upon his lordship, by whom I was most graciously received. He directed his secretary to provide me with whatever I required, and depute some person to shew me all the curiosities of the place. He further requested that I would favour him frequently with my company at the Castle. During my stay in Dublin, I paid my respects to his lordship every week, and was each time honoured with fresh proofs of his kindness and friendship.

I shall here endeavour to give my Readers some description of this city, certainly the most magnificent I had hitherto seen.

Dublin is the capital of Ireland: it is situated within a few miles of the sea, and is about twelve miles in circumference. Many of the houses are built of stone, and do not appear as if any mortar was used in their construction, the stones fitting so exactly into each other. The generality of the houses are, however, built of brick and mortar, neatly laid together: the bricks are of a large size, and the mortar appears as a white border round their edges. All the houses in a street are of the same height, which gives an uniformity of appearance that is very pleasing: in the inside they are generally painted white, or of different colours, and have all glazed windows. Most of them consist of four stories, one of which is under ground; in this they have apartments fitted up for cooking, washing, and keeping coals, wine, &c. The ground floor is appropriated to shops or offices, and eating rooms. The next story is the most elegantly ornamented, and is used for the reception of company: the one above that is divided into bed rooms, for the master and mistress, or their visitors: and the upper story of all, the windows of which rise above the roof of the house, and where the ceilings are low, is allotted as sleeping apartments for the servants. The roofs of the houses are covered with thin blue stones, which are closely fitted, and nailed on narrow slips of board, and are much handsomer and more durable than tiles.

The apartments are in general fitted up with great elegance. The window curtains are either of beautiful chintz, silk, or velvet. The rest of the furniture consists of mirrors, girandoles, pictures, mahogany tables, chairs, couches, &c. In every apartment there is a place for a fire, the machine for holding which is composed of steel and brass, very highly polished, and ornamented. The front of the fire-place is adorned by marble slabs, one of which is laid horizontally, upon which, in the summer, they place bouquets of flowers, and, in the winter, various ornaments of china, spars, &c. Nothing in their houses attracted my admiration so much as what I have just described, utility and ornament being therein happily blended. The walls of the rooms are covered with variegated paper, with which the pattern of the carpets in general correspond. The entrance to the house is by a door on the eating floor, on which the number of the house and the name of the master are either painted, or engraved on a brass plate. On every door there is fixed a knocker, by striking of which you give notice to the servants, when you wish to enter; but in some houses they have bells fixed for this purpose. In the room below stairs, where the servants assemble, there are several bells fixed, which communicate by wires with the different apartments; and being all numbered, upon the ringing of any bell the servants immediately know where their presence is required.

The streets of this city are in general wide, and are divided into three portions: the two sides, which are flagged, are appropriated to foot passengers; and the middle part, which is paved with stones, is used for horses and carriages. In front of the houses of noblemen and gentlemen there is an iron railing which projects some yards into the street, by which light and air are admitted into the lower floor, and heavy or dirty articles can be taken out or in through a door in the railing, without defiling the house.

Many of the best streets are entirely occupied by shops: these have all large glazed windows, in which the articles are exhibited to attract purchasers. They have also over the doors a plank painted black, on which is inscribed, in gold letters, the name and profession of the owner. These shops are at night brilliantly lighted up, and have a handsome effect. In them is to be found whatever is curious or valuable in the world. My attention was particularly attracted by the jewellers' and milliners' repositories; nor were the fruiterers' or pastrycooks' shops without their attractions. I generally spent an hour between breakfast and dinner in some one of these places.

At night, both sides of the street are lighted up, by lamps suspended in glass vases at the height of ten or twelve feet from the ground; which, with the addition of the numerous candles in the shop windows, render it as light as day. One of the streets thus lighted up, in which were several chemists' shops containing glass vases filled with different coloured liquids, put me in mind of the

Imam Bâreh (Mausoleum) at Lucknow, when illuminated, during the reign of the late Nabob Assuf ad Dowleh.[1] This being the first town I had seen well lighted at night, it impressed me with a great idea of its grandeur, nor did it afterwards suffer in my estimation with a comparison with London.

The crowd of people who are constantly walking the streets is astonishing; and they have acquired such dexterity by habit, that they never run against each other. I could not help admiring some girls, who, either from the coldness of the weather or their natural high flow of spirits, disdained to walk deliberately, but bounded through the crowd, without touching any one, as if they had been going down a dance.

In this, and all the other cities of Europe, there are so many carriages of different kinds, that I may safely aver, from the day I arrived in Dublin, till I quitted Paris, the sound of coach wheels was never out of my ears. There are seven hundred registered coaches here, which never go out of the town, but merely carry passengers from one street to another. Besides these, every nobleman and gentleman of fortune keeps his own carriage, some of which are drawn by two horses, others by four or six. The horses are of a large breed peculiar to these kingdoms; and they are used for all kinds of work, even for ploughing the ground. The only use made of bullocks in this country is to *eat* them. The sheep here have not large tails, but are very delicious food. The fowls are also very fine, of the size of geese, and give very large eggs.

In this city there are several extensive and beautiful squares: in the centre of each is generally a fountain, over which a cupola is erected, to shelter it from the sun: the water issues from the heads of lions, or some other animal, carved in stone; but, to prevent the water being wasted, every pipe has a screw to it, which, when the person has filled his buckets, he turns, and the water ceases to flow. In some of the squares there is a stone platform erected, on which is placed the equestrian statue of one of their kings; and when seen from a distance, it appears as if the horse was curvetting in the air. These fountains and statues have an iron railing round them; and at night, lamps are affixed thereto, to prevent people from hurting themselves by running against them.

---

1 An Imambara is the residence of the Imam or religious leader of an Islamic community and of particular importance to Shiites who celebrate Muharram or the Islamic new year on the site. Bara Imambara was a large imambara complex built by Asaf ud-Daula in 1784, which featured a bhulbhulayah (or lovers' maze) and the Asfi mosque.

In this country, and all through Europe, but especially in France and in Italy, statues of stone and marble are held in high estimation, approaching to idolatry. Once in my presence, in London, a figure which had lost its head, arms, and legs, and of which, in short, nothing but the trunk remained, was sold for 40,000 rupees (£. 5000). It is really astonishing that people possessing so much knowledge and good sense, and who reproach the nobility of Hindoostan with wearing gold and silver ornaments like women, should be thus tempted by Satan to throw away their money upon useless blocks. There is a great variety of these figures, and they seem to have appropriate statues for every situation: thus, at the doors or gates, they have huge janitors; in the interior they have figures of women dancing with tambourines and other musical instruments; over the chimney-pieces they place some of the heathen deities of Greece; in the burying grounds they have the statues of the deceased; and in the gardens they put up devils, tigers, or wolves in pursuit of a fox, in hopes that animals, on beholding these figures, will be frightened, and not come into the garden.

The centre part of some of the squares is laid out in handsome gardens, where the genteel inhabitants walk every morning and evening, and from which the common people are excluded. Bands of wandering musicians also come here, and play for a small reward.[1]

Besides the squares, they have in Europe other places of recreation for the inhabitants, called *Parks*: these are an extent of ground inclosed with a wall, containing rows of shady trees, verdant pastures, and brooks of water, over which are thrown ornamental arches, either of stone or marble. Cattle and sheep are permitted to graze in these parks; and deer are frequently allowed to run wild in them, and increase their numbers. The flesh of the last-mentioned animals is highly prized; and when one of them is required for the table, a good marksman is employed to kill him with a musket. In some of the parks there are handsome buildings and delightful gardens, to which the inhabitants of the city resort in great numbers on Sundays.

The country all round Dublin is very picturesque, and in that respect it far surpasses London. At the distance of few miles from the city, there is a great variety of hamlets and country-houses, where the people of opulence reside during the summer.

---

1 In the original, the plan of the square is delineated. (Translator's note)

The most charming place I have ever beheld is Phoenix Park. Besides the beauties which I have described as belonging to parks in general, it contains several buildings of hewn stone; and the Dublin river runs through the middle of it, the banks of which are sloped, and formed into verdant lawns; and over the stream are erected two elegant stone bridges: it also contains several rising grounds or hills, on the shaded sides of which, during the winter, snow is sometimes to be seen, while the other parts retain their verdure: this forms an agreeable contrast, and renders the whole of the scenery peculiarly interesting. On viewing this delightful spot, I was made sensible of the just sentiments of the English gentlemen in India, who, notwithstanding their high rank and great incomes, consider that country as merely a place of temporary sojourn, and have their thoughts always bent upon returning to their native land.

Another captivating scene near Dublin is the sea-side, the prospect from which is beautiful, and enlivened by the view of many hundred ships at anchor. All along the shore, for several miles, they have wooden houses placed upon wheels, for the convenience of private bathing. These machines are drawn by horses into the proper depth of water: a door then opens towards the sea, and a person may perform his ablutions with the greatest privacy, and benefit to his health.

The greatest curiosity of this city is a tower which is built in the sea, at the distance of two miles, and is united to the shore by a wall or pier forty yards in breadth. On this tower they every night light up an immense lantern with a great number of lamps; by seeing which, the people on board ships bound for this harbour, steer their course, and avoid the shoals and rocks which obstruct the free navigation of this port. Besides the advantage of a safe communication with the Light-house, the Pier is useful, to prevent the sea from encroaching on the city.

The river which runs through Dublin is called the Liffy, and is as large as the Goompty (of Lucknow), when full: both banks of it are lined with stone; and there are six handsome bridges over it. The sides of these bridges are defended by iron railings, to which are affixed a number of the glass vases I have before described, for holding lamps; and at night, when these are lighted up, they have quite the appearance of illuminations made by the nobility of Hindoostan, on a marriage, or some other rejoicing. In this country there are numerous canals, for the conveyance of coals and other heavy goods from one part of the kingdom to another. There is one which runs from Dublin to Limerick, upon which are several covered boats resembling our budgerows: but some of these are much larger, and will carry a great number of passengers. These boats are drawn by horses, which proceed along a level road formed on the bank of the canal, which is generally shaded by rows of trees. By the contrivance of gates or locks,[1] a sufficient quantity of water is always retained in the canals; and in case of its overflowing, it can be let off into other channels. In the vicinity of this city are also several docks for building ships, the construction of which is very curious.

Of the public buildings, the College is the most celebrated. The entrance to this is through a lofty arched gateway; opposite to which is a building five stories high, containing the apartments of the students, of whom there have been, some years, as many as twelve hundred at the same time. The Library is a very elegant room, one hundred yards in length, and twenty in breadth: the walls are all fitted up with shelves, which contain above 40,000 volumes, in various languages, and every branch of science. I was much pleased to find here several Persian books; among which were two very elegant manuscript copies of the *Shahnameh* (an heroic poem on the ancient history of Persia), and the Five Poems of Nizamy.[2] The Museum is also a fine room: it contains a great number of curiosities, principally collected from foreign countries: one of these was a human body wrapt up in cloths and gum, which had been brought from the pyramids of Egypt. At the back of the College is an extensive meadow, divided into walks, and shaded by trees, which serves as a place of recreation for the students.

At the time of my visit to the College, the chief or head of the University was Provost Guerney.[3] He first honoured me with an invitation to inspect the College, and afterwards requested I

---

1 In the original a drawing of the lock is given. (Translator's note)
2 The *Shahnameh* or The Epic of Kings was composed around 1000 by Ferdowsi. It is the most important text in Persian literature, for it recounts the mythical and historical past of Iran from the creation of the world until the emergence of Islam. Nezami was one of the great Persian poets of the twelfth century and the undisputed master of the *masnavi* style of double rhymed verses. The Five Poems referred to here are collectively known as the *Quinary* which is composed of five books: "The Storehouse of Mysteries," "Khosrow and Shirin," "Layla and Majnun," "The Book of Alexander," and "The Seven Beauties."
3 This is likely John Kearney (1744-1813), who was appointed provost of Trinity College in 1799.

would favour him with my company to dinner. He, and his lady, a very sensible and intelligent woman, behaved to me with the most marked attention and politeness. At his table I had the pleasure of meeting with Dr. Brown, a member of Parliament, and a great favourite of the people of Ireland; also a Dr. Hall; both of whom afterwards honoured me with their friendship. I was so much pleased with the wit and agreeable conversation of Mrs. Brown, that I wrote a poem in her praise, and sent it to her from London.

Next in rank among the public buildings, is the Parliament House.[1] This is divided into two large apartments, and several offices. In one of the apartments the Lords meet; and in the other, the Commons, or representatives of the people, assemble. These rooms are hung round with *tapestry*, on which are depicted the representations of battles,[2] and other events that occur in their history. At first I thought they were paintings, but, upon examination, discovered, to my great astonishment, that the figures were all worked on the cloth.

I next visited the Custom House, and the Exchange: these are both noble buildings. In the former, the duties upon all goods exported or imported are received; and in the latter the merchants assemble to negotiate their concerns. One of the greatest curiosities I observed here was a *wind clock*: it had a dial resembling a common clock, with two hands, which indicated the exact point whence the wind blew. I afterwards proceeded to the Courts of Law, and then to a superb dome called the *Rotunda*. This latter place was built for a public music-room, and will hold 4000 persons, but is now used by Government as a barrack for soldiers.

The five buildings I have mentioned are constructed of beautiful hewn stone; and the four latter have, in the centre of each, a lofty dome, whence, through large glazed windows, the light is communicated to the interior: they are also adorned in front by arcades of lofty pillars.

In this city there are a great number of places of public worship, several of which I visited. The most celebrated of them

---

1 Abu Talib visits the Houses of Parliament just prior to the abolition of the Irish parliament by the Act of Union. The last session was held in August of 1800.

2 The tapestries represent the "Battle of the Boyne" and the "Defence of Londonderry." They were designed by Dutch landscape painter William Van der Hagen and woven by John Van Beaver and date from 1733.

is called Christ Church: it is very large, and above 600 years old. In it, they never permit the men and women to sit together, which appears to me an excellent regulation. The barracks of Dublin are very extensive; and there are two handsome parades, well paved and flagged, for the exercise of troops in rainy weather.

The public hospitals of this city are numerous, and are admirable institutions. One of these is for the delivery of poor pregnant women; another for the reception and education of orphans; and a third for the maintenance of wounded or worn-out soldiers.

In these countries it is common for persons, when dying, to bequeath estates, or large sums of money, to endow hospitals, or for other charitable purposes. This custom is truly praise-worthy, and should be accepted as an excuse for those who, during their existence in this world, hoard up their riches, and often deny themselves the enjoyments of life.

In this city there are but two hot baths, the roofs of which resemble large ovens. They are not properly fitted up; and are so small, that with difficulty they hold one person; and even then the water does not rise above his middle. Being a case of necessity, I bathed in one of them; but there were not any attendants to assist me; and instead of a rubber, I was obliged to use a brush, made (*I hope*) of horse's hair,[1] such as they clean shoes with. The fact is, that in winter the people of Dublin never bathe, and in summer they go into the sea or river: these baths are therefore entirely designed for invalids or convalescents.

Dublin can boast but of two public Theatres or Play-houses, each of which will contain about 1500 persons.[2] The half of the building which is appropriated to the audience is divided into three parts, denomininated, the Boxes, Pit, and Gallery:[3] the first of these is intended for the nobility and gentry, the second for the tradesmen, and the third for the lower classes of people. The prices of admittance are, five shillings, three shillings, and one shilling. The other half of the building is occupied by the stage, on which the actors exhibit: this is subdivided by a number of curtains and scenes, upon which are painted cities, castles, gardens, forests, &c. The whole of the house is well lighted, by candles placed in chandeliers, lustres, &c.

---

1 Hog's bristles are an abomination to Mohammedans. (Translator's note)
2 The Theatre Royal in Crow Street and the Amphitheatre Royal in Peter Street.
3 In the original, the plan of the Playhouse is given. (Translator's note)

In the exhibition which afforded me the greatest amusement, the actors spoke in some barbarous language. One of them represented an Ethiopian magician, called *Harlequin*, with whom the daughter of a nobleman falls desperately in love: the magician in consequence conveys her, while asleep in her bed, to his own country. Here she is visited by the Queen of the Fairies, and several of her attendants, all of whom descend on the stage in flying thrones: they reproach her for her partiality to such a wretch, and advise her to discard him: she, after showing evident proofs of her attachment to the magician, yields to their advice, and requests they will assist her to return home. The queen orders one of the attendants to accompany the young lady, and to remain with her as a protection against the power of the magician, and to assist her father and her intended husband. Harlequin, however, contrives to visit his mistress; and the lovers being soon reconciled, they attempt at one time to escape in a coach, at another in a ship, but are always brought back. At length, in one of the affrays, the father is wounded, and confined to his bed: here he is visited by the Angel of Death, represented by the skeleton of a man with a dart in his hand, who tells him he must either marry his daughter to Harlequin, or accompany him. The father consents to the marriage, which is celebrated with great rejoicings; and thus ends the farce. Another of their exhibitions was named *The Taking of Seringapatam*: all the scenes in this, were taken from a book recently published, containing an account of the late war in Mysore, and the fall of Tippoo Sultan. The representation was so correct, that every thing appeared natural; and the conclusion was very affecting.

I was much entertained by an exhibition of *Horsemanship*, by Mr. Astley[1] and his company. They have an established house in London, but come over to Dublin for four or five months in every year, to gratify the Irish, by displaying their skill in this science, which far surpasses any thing I ever saw in India.

I was also much astonished on seeing a new invention of the Europeans, called a *Panorama*. The scene was Gibraltar, a celebrated fort belonging to the English, at the entrance of the

---

1 Philip Astley (1742-1814), an equestrian performer, opened Astley's Royal Amphitheatre in London in 1798 and also brought his traveling shows to Dublin and Paris. Astley's *The Siege and Storming of Seringapatam* was based on Alexander Beatson's *A View of the Origin and Conduct of the War with Tippoo Sultan* (London: 1800), and was staged in Dublin from 18 to 20 December 1799.

Mediterranean Sea, on the coast of Spain. I was led by a dark entrance into the middle of a large room, round which a picture of this famed fortress was hung; but, by some contrivance, the light was so directed, that every object appeared as natural as life. They also exhibited an engagement between an English and a French fleet, in which not only the noise of cannon was distinctly heard, but also the balls flew about, and carried away the masts and sails of the adversaries' ships.

CHAPTER VIII

Character of the Irish. Caricatures. Troublesome curiosity of the common people. Heavy fall of snow. Severe cold. Climate of Ireland—advantages thereof. Skaiting. Account of the author's particular friends or patrons. Mode of living of the Irish. The author leaves Dublin—his passage to England—he lands at Holyhead. Description of Wales, and of the city of Chester. The author arrives in London.

I shall here endeavour to sketch the character of the Irish. The greater number of them are Roman-Catholics, or followers of the religion of the Pope; only a small proportion of them being of the religion of the English, whom the former call Dissenters or Philosophers (i.e. Deists or Atheists).

They are not so intolerant as the English, neither have they the austerity and bigotry of the Scotch. In bravery and determination, hospitality, and prodigality, freedom of speech and open-heartedness, they surpass the English and Scotch, but are deficient in prudence and sound judgment: they are nevertheless witty, and quick of comprehension. Thus my landlady and her children soon comprehended my broken English; and what I could not explain by language, they understood by signs: nay, before I had been a fortnight in their house, they could even understand my disfigured translations of Persian poetry. When I was about to leave them, and proceed on my journey, many of my friends appeared much affected, and said: "With your little knowledge of the language, you will suffer much distress in England; for the people there will not give themselves any trouble to comprehend your meaning, or to make themselves useful to you." In fact, after I had resided for a whole year in England, and could speak the language a hundred times better than on my first arrival, I found much more difficulty in obtaining what I wanted, than I did in Ireland.

In Dublin, if I happened to lose my way, and inquired it of any person, he would, immediately on perceiving I was a foreigner, quit his work, and accompany me to the place where I wished to go. One night, as I was going to pay a visit at a considerable distance, I asked a man, which was the road. He instantly accompanied me; and when we arrived at a particular spot, I knew where we were, and, having thanked him for the trouble he had taken, said I was now perfectly acquainted with the remainder of the road, and begged he would return home. He would not consent; but, after we had gone some distance further, I insisted upon his leaving me, otherwise I should relinquish my visit. He apparently complied; but I could perceive, that, from his great care of me, he still followed. Being arrived at the door of my friend's house, I waited for some time, that I might again have an opportunity of thanking him; but as soon as he saw that I had reached a place of security, he turned round, and went towards home.

The Irish, by reason of their liberality and prodigality, seldom have it in their power to assist their friends in pecuniary matters: they are generally in straitened circumstances themselves, and therefore cannot, or do not aim at the comforts and elegance of the English: neither do they take pains to acquire riches and honours like the Scotch, by limiting their expences when in the receipt of good incomes, and paying attention to the Great. In consequence of this want of prudence, they seldom attain to high dignities, and but few of them, comparatively, make much progress in science.

Their great national defect, however, is excess in drinking. The rich expend a vast deal in wine; and the common people consume immense quantities of a fiery spirit, called *whiskey*, which is the peculiar manufacture of this country and part of Scotland.

One evening that I dined in a large company we sat down to table at six o'clock: the master of the house immediately commenced asking us to drink wine, and, under various pretences, replenished our glasses; but perceiving that I was backward in emptying mine, he called for two water glasses, and, having filled them with claret, insisted upon my taking one of them. After the table-cloth was removed, he first drank the health of the King, then of the Queen; after which he toasted a number of beautiful young ladies with whom I was acquainted, none of which I dared to refuse. Thus the time passed till two o'clock in the morning; and we had been sitting for eight hours: he then called to his servants to bring a fresh supply of wine. Although I was so much intoxicated that I could scarcely walk, yet on hearing this order, I was so frightened, that I arose, and requested permission to retire. He said he was sorry I should think of going away *so soon*; that he wished I would stay till the wine was finished, after which he would call for tea and coffee. I had heard from Englishmen, that the Irish, after they get drunk at table, quarrel, and kill each other in duels; but I must declare, that I never saw them guilty of any rudeness, or of the smallest impropriety.

The painters of these countries sometimes draw ridiculous figures, called *Caricatures*, which it is impossible to behold without laughing. They, in general, are intended to exhibit the defects or follies of the Ministers or other great men, and sometimes to turn into ridicule the prevailing passion or vice of the people at large. These pictures are sold in sets, and consist of several pieces. One of them which was shewn to me contained a caricature of each of these nations. The first exhibited a Scotchman, quitting his country to seek his fortune: and the itch being a very common complaint in Scotland, this poor fellow is drawn, rubbing his back against a mile-stone, on the road to London. In the next page he is shewn in the habit of a postman, carrying a bag of letters from one village to another. In the third page, he becomes a gentleman's steward: in this situation, by his industry, and attention to the wishes of his master, he acquires some money, which he lends out at interest to his master, and thus becomes rich. In the fourth page, he gets acquainted with an opulent English widow, whom he marries, and thereby acquires some degree of importance. In the fifth page, he is represented as an attendant on the minister, with whom, by his assiduity and flattery, he becomes a favourite, and obtains a post under Government. In the last page, he is seated in the chair of the Vizier, having, by industry and perseverance, thus raised himself, from the most abject state of poverty, to the highest situation which can be held by a subject.

The Irishman's career is not so long, nor so varied. He enlists as a soldier, and, having distinguished himself by his bravery, is promoted by degrees to the rank of General. He then quarrels at table with another officer; they fight, and he is killed in the duel.

The Englishman is represented as a fat bull (therefore named *John Bull*); and as that animal is remarkable for eating a great deal, and for excessive courage and obstinacy, so the English seem to consider eating and drinking as their chief happiness, are frequently blunt and uncouth in their manners, and often run blindly into danger and unnecessary expence.

The Irish *women* have not such elegance of manners, nor the handsome eyes and hair of the English; neither are they as tall nor so good figures as the Scotch; but they have much finer complexions, are warm in their affections, lively, and agreeable.

For some time after my arrival in Dublin, I was greatly incommoded by the common people crowding round me, whenever I went out. They were all very curious to see me, but had no intention of offending me. Some said I must be the Russian General, who had been for some time expected; others affirmed I was either a German or Spanish nobleman; but the greater part agreed that I was a Persian *Prince*. One day, a great crowd having assembled about me, a shopkeeper advised me to walk into his house, and to sit down till they should disperse. I accepted his kind invitation, and went into the shop, where I amused myself by looking at some penknives, scissars, &c. The people however thronged so about his windows, that several of the panes were broken; and the crowd being very great, it was in vain to ask who had done it.

About a fortnight after my arrival, there fell a very heavy shower of snow. As I had never before seen any thing of the kind, I was much delighted by it. The roofs of the houses and tops of the walls were soon covered with it, and in two or three days the fields and mountains, as far as the eye could reach, became a white surface. During the time it continued to snow, the cold was not very great; but when it ceased, notwithstanding I had all my doors and windows shut, and had three blankets on my bed, I felt the frost pierce through me like an arrow. The fire had scarcely any effect on me; for while I warmed one side, I was frozen on the other; and I frequently burned my fingers before I was aware of the heat. At length I discovered, that the best remedy was walking; and during the continuation of the frost, I walked every day seven or eight miles. I was apprehensive that my health would have suffered from the severity of the climate; but, on the contrary, I had a keen appetite, and found myself every day get stronger and more active.

I recollect that in India, when I only wore a single vest of Dacca muslin, if I walked a mile I was completely tired; but here, when my clothes would have been a heavy load for an ass, I could have run for miles without feeling the smallest fatigue. In India, I slept daily seven or eight hours, at different times, without feeling refreshed; but during the two months I remained in Ireland, I never slept more than four hours any night, and yet I never felt an inclination to lie down in the day time.

The coldness of the climate in these islands is, I am convinced, very beneficial, and attended with many advantages to the inhabitants. In the first place, it renders the men vigorous both in mind and body, and the women fair and handsome. Secondly, it obliges them to take exercise, which hardens and invigorates the constitution, and inspires them with that valour, by which they are enabled to encounter the greatest hardships, and to acquire *immortal fame*. During my residence in Ireland and England, I have frequently received contusions without being sensible of them at the time, the tenth part of which would in India have laid me upon the bed of sickness. Thirdly, it renders them open-hearted and sincere, steady in the pursuit of knowledge, and not led away by the flights of fancy or sallies of imagination. I have frequently seen both men and women of *twenty* years of age, who possessed not an idea that could interfere with their acquirement of science or the useful arts. The excessive cold prevents their sitting idle; and the mind being therefore engaged, is prevented from wandering to, or dwelling on things that are improper. Boys and girls of fifteen years of age are, here, as innocent as the children of India of five or six, and have no wish beyond the amusement of playthings, or the produce of a pastry-cook's shop. I have even seen grown-up persons, who had acquired reputation in their own line of business, and many of them had accumulated fortunes, but who were as ignorant of the world as boys in the East. Another great advantage of the coldness of the atmosphere, is their being accustomed to wear a number of tight-made clothes, which are troublesome to take off, and are very inconvenient for lying down: thus they are prevented from indulging in indolent habits during the day; and their nights are passed in harmless sleep, contrary to the custom of India, where the day is frequently devoted to sensuality and repose, and the night to business or conviviality.

What I am now about to relate will, I fear, not be credited (by my countrymen), but is, nevertheless, an absolute fact. In these countries it frequently happens that the ponds and rivers are frozen over; and the ice, being of sufficient strength to bear a great weight, numbers of people assemble thereon, and amuse themselves in *skating*. For this purpose it is requisite to be provided with a kind of wooden shoes, having pieces of iron fixed to the soles. At first this appears a very difficult operation, and many get severe falls; but, after some months' practice, they can slide along the ice with the rapidity of a horse on a fine road, and turn, in all directions, quicker than the best-trained charger. I have even seen them engrave the name of a lady on the ice with the. heel of their skate. In England and Ireland this art is only practised for amusement; but in Holland, I have been informed, the women will carry a basket of eggs or butter, in this manner, twenty miles to market, and return home to dinner.

I remained forty-four days in Dublin; and, in the course of my whole life, never spent my time so agreeably. Were I to mention the name of every person from whom I experienced hospitality and civility, I should tire my readers. I shall therefore only enumerate a few of my particular friends. The principal of these were Sir George and Lady Shee.[1] He had resided for many years in India, and was for some time paymaster at Ferrokhabad. He was at this time employed by the Government of Ireland, was a great favourite with Lord Cornwallis, and did me the honour of being my interpreter with his Lordship. Lady Shee was remarkable for mildness of disposition, elegance of manners, skill in music, and sweetness of voice.

From Lord and Lady Carleton[2] I experienced much attention and politeness: their house was a repository of every thing that was grand or curious. Many of the articles attracted my wonder and astonishment; but they were so numerous and extraordinary as to exceed the powers of description. His lordship held the honourable office of Chief Justice of Ireland.

The Duke of Leinster,[3] the first of the nobles of this kingdom, honoured me with an invitation: his house is the most superb of any in Dublin, and contains a very numerous and valuable col-

---

1 Sir George Shee (1754-1825) of the East India Co. married Lady Elizabeth Maria Shee (1764?-1838; née Crisp) at Hugli near Calcutta in 1783. Shee was a protegé of Edmund Burke's and a close associate of Warren Hastings's arch-rival Philip Francis while posted in Bengal. His reputation was sullied during the sexual and political scandal that enveloped Francis in 1778, yet Francis retained enough power to have Shee appointed Resident and Collector of Revenues at Farrukhabad, where he remained until 1782. Upon his return to Calcutta he gathered damaging evidence against Hastings, which would eventually be used by Burke during Hastings's impeachment. Shee returned to Ireland in 1788, secured a baronetcy in 1794, and supported the Act of Union in 1800. See p. 68, note 1.

2 Hugh Carleton (1739-1826), Viscount Carleton, was an Irish judge and politician who married his second wife, Mary Carleton, (d.1810; née Buckley) in 1795.

3 William Robert Fitzgerald (1749-1804), second Duke of Leinster. See p. 189, note 1.

lection of statues and paintings. His grace is distinguished for the dignity of his manners, and the urbanity of his disposition. He is blessed with several angelic daughters.

I here had the good fortune to meet with Colonel Wombell,[1] a gentleman I had long known in India, from whom I experienced many acts of friendship, and with whom I daily spent some happy hours. This gentleman was much attached to the natives of India, and spoke their language fluently. He was, at this period, Colonel of the Norfolk Volunteer Militia, and asked me several times to dine at the regimental mess, where he introduced me to some of the finest-looking young men I ever saw in my life. Norfolk is celebrated above all the countries in England for fine poultry, abundance of game, and handsome women.

I here had the pleasure of forming an acquaintance with General Vallancy,[2] an officer of artillery, who, although of a remarkable short stature, had a most expanded heart: he was a great adept in acquiring languages, and was much delighted with the Hebrew, Arabic, and Persian dialects: he informed me, that there was a considerable analogy between the Hindoostany and Irish languages. To Lords Shannon and Newcomen,[3] Mr. White, Mr. Irving, and Mrs. Humphries, I feel grateful for their attention and hospitality.

The various acts of kindness and hospitality I received from Mrs. Fleming are innumerable. This lady having been informed that I had become acquainted with her husband at the house of our mutual friend, Mr. W. A. Brooke, in Calcutta, immediately sent a gentleman to request I would call on her. She afterwards gave me many invitations to her house, and introduced me to a numerous circle of her acquaintance. This lady one day asked me, if her husband spent his time pleasantly in Calcutta. I replied, "How is it possible he can be happy while separated from so charming a companion as you." She smiled, and said she

---

1   Sir George Wombell (1769-1846), second baronet of Wombell, was known primarily for his race horses. His father was an extensive East India proprietor and was a Director of the East India Co. from 1766 to 1768 and from 1775 to 1778.
2   Charles Vallancey (c.1726-1812), antiquary and general, developed an improbable argument suggesting that Irish civilization was ultimately descended from Eastern origins.
3   Richard Boyle (1728-1807), second Earl of Shannon, was then First Lord of the Treasury in Ireland. Sir Thomas-Gleadowe Newcomen (1776-1825), Viscount Newcomen, was a wealthy banker in Dublin.

believed I only flattered her. Two of her daughters had accompanied their father to India, but there still remained at home three girls, beautiful as the *Houries* of Paradise.

Having hitherto omitted giving any description of the mode of living of the Irish, I shall here state, that the breakfast is generally confined to the family. At dinner, they meet at each other's houses, in large parties: this meal is divided into three parts, at the end of each of which, a table-cloth is removed. After dinner the gentlemen continue to drink wine for one or two hours: they then join the ladies, and drink tea or coffee: and at night they again sit down to what is called *supper*. This last meal I enjoyed more than any other, as there is less ceremony observed at it than at dinner: the servants are soon dismissed, and the guests help themselves.

The mode of paying *complimentary* visits here is very easy; they merely knock at each other's doors, and give their names, written on a square piece of pasteboard, called a *card*, to the *servant*; but if they wish to see the master of the house, they go in, and sit with him half an hour.[1]

Nothing pleased me more in Europe than the attendance of servants being dispensed with. In India, they remain constantly in the room; but here they retire as soon as dinner is over, and remain till summoned by the bell.

I was also much pleased to observe, that in European society, when a person is speaking, the others never interrupt him, and the conversation is carried on in a gentle tone of voice. One evening, while I was engaged in conversation with the lady of the house, the servant entered with a large tray of costly china; and his foot catching the edge of the carpet, he fell, and broke the whole to pieces: the lady, however, never noticed the circumstance, but continued her conversation with me in the most undisturbed manner.

It affords me much satisfaction thus to record the amiable qualities of the Irish; as, previous to my landing, I had conceived strong prejudices against them, in consequence of the misrepresentation of some of the passengers on board our ship, who had described them as rude, irascible, and savage.

Captain Williamson, one of the passengers on board the Christiana, (who was of a sarcastic disposition) used constantly to frighten me, with accounts of the uncivil treatment I should

---

1 The natives of India always send a message before, to ask whether the visit will be convenient. (Translator's note)

meet with in England: thus one day at dinner, when, for want of employment, I had laid a piece of bread on the table-cloth, and was cutting it with great caution, he called out to me, "If in England you cut your bread in that manner, the ladies, alarmed for their table-cloths, will never invite you to their houses a second time; nor will you ever find any person there who will assist you to carve your meat as we do here." If ever I chanced to spill the gravy or soup on the cloth, or my own garments, he used to look at me with aversion, and say, "If you do so in London, nobody will sit at table with you." Notwithstanding this, both in Dublin and in London, wherever I was invited, the master and mistress of the house not only excused my awkwardness, but pressed me to eat in my own country manner; and when I refused, always cut the meat for me. Another time he told me, that in London no person would assist another with sixpence; and that without a bribe they would not even let me pass along the street, much less point out the road. In contradiction to this, often under pretence of inviting me to take a walk, my acquaintances have carried me to see various places, which cost them at least four or five shillings. Numberless also were the presents forced upon me, of books, pen-knives, spectacles, watches, and other English curiosities; and I was even frequently solicited to accept the loan of 1000 or 2000 guineas. I have been induced to relate these anecdotes, that the difference between the dispositions of the English in India, and the genuine unsophisticated English, may be known.

On the 16th of January, 1800, having taken leave of all my friends, I embarked on board one of the vessels called *Packets*, which convey the letters and passengers from one island to another. About the middle of the night we quitted the Irish shore; and the wind being very favourable, we cast anchor early next morning at Holyhead. We were soon after landed, and went to the best inn in the town, kept by a person named Jackson. This man, seeing that I was a foreigner, thought that he could reap some advantage by detaining me at his house: he therefore endeavoured to persuade me to remain a short time at Holyhead: but two Irish gentlemen, who, accompanied by a beautiful young woman, were then at the inn, perceiving his intention, abused him for it, invited me to dine with them, and in the evening put me into the mail coach, which was setting out for Chester.

Holyhead is a small and dirty town, and only known as being the port opposite Dublin: it is situated in a small island, separated from Wales by an arm of the sea almost as broad as the river

Ganges at Calcutta. Wales is one of the three divisions which, with England and Scotland, constitute Great Britain. The Heir Apparent, or eldest son of the King, takes his title from this province, and is called *Prince of Wales*.

After travelling twenty-five miles, we arrived at the arm of the sea above mentioned, and in a short time were ferried to the opposite side, where there is a town called Bangor Ferry. Here we were refreshed by an excellent breakfast, and immediately after proceeded on our journey. Our next stage was to Aber-Conway, a very ancient city, situated between lofty mountains, on the banks of a fine river, which joins the sea a little below the town.[1] This place was formerly fortified, and several of the walls are still standing, which much resemble those of *Allahabad*.[2] After dinner we again entered the coach, and at midnight arrived, without any accident, at Chester. Our route during this journey was over lofty hills, so that we were frequently obliged to alight from the coach, and walk up the steepest of them. Although Wales is a very mountainous country, it nevertheless contains a great quantity of arable land and excellent pastures for cattle.

Chester, being the principal town of the county, where all the public business is transacted, is large and populous, and is said to be more ancient than London. In several particulars it differs from any other place I have seen. Some of the streets have colonnades, running from one end to the other of them, under which the foot passengers can walk perfectly dry, at all seasons of the year. The middle of the streets is paved, and contains ample space for the carriages and horsemen. Many of the houses have handsome porticoes in front, supported by stone pillars, which give them a magnificent appearance. These islands produce great abundance of fine stone, and even the common walls of the gardens and yards are built of this material.

As several of my Irish friends had recommended me to gentlemen in Chester, the latter had been for some time in expectation of my arrival. I was in consequence, early next morning, waited upon by a Mr. Fleming, and three or four other persons, who loaded me with invitations, and accompanied me to look at

---

1 Conwy Castle in northern Wales, built by Edward I between 1283 and 1289.

2 One of the most famous fortresses in India, built by the Mughal emperor Akbar in the 1570s. The implicit comparison between Akbar and Edward I is part of a larger strategy to align Mughal rule with the legacy of British kings.

the city. At the hour for dinner, a large party, consisting of some of the principal inhabitants of the town, assembled; and in the evening we were most agreeably entertained with music and dancing. When we broke up, many of these hospitable people requested that I would stop for some time at Chester, and favour them with my company: but, as I was very anxious to get to London, I declined their polite invitations.

By the advice of my friends, I agreed with the owner of the stage coach, that, instead of continuing the journey to London without intermission, I should sleep one night on the road. It was between one and two in the morning when we quitted Chester; and after a journey of forty-nine miles we breakfasted at Stafford. It was midnight before we reached Northampton, where I stopped for the remainder of the night, and felt truly grateful to my friends for their good advice, as I thereby enjoyed a comfortable supper, and a refreshing sleep, after the fatigue of a long day's journey. On the following morning I again set out in the coach; and on the 25th of Shaban, corresponding to the 21st of January 1800, arrived safe in London, being five days short of a Lunar year from the period of my leaving Calcutta.

CHAPTER IX

The Author hires lodgings in London. Interview with the President of the Board of Controul. Is introduced at Court—Attention of the Princes, and of the Nobility. Public amusements. The Author's original view in coming to England—disappointment—compensated by the kindness of his friends. He visits Windsor—arrives at Oxford—account of the University—proceeds to Blenheim—description of the park and house—visits Colonel Cox. Mode of sporting in England. The Author proceeds to the house of Mr. Hastings—Returns to London. Ode to London.

Previous to my departure from Dublin, I had taken the precaution of writing to my friend and shipmate, Captain Richardson, to hire apartments for me in the same house where he resided; and immediately on my arrival, I proceeded to Margaret Street, where I had the pleasure of finding him: but as the lodgings he had provided for me were up two pairs of stairs, I thought them inconvenient, and, after remaining there a week, removed to others in the same street. Being dissatisfied with these, I went to Ibbetson's Hotel, in Vere Street: this situation was very agreeable, but the expences were beyond my means: I therefore again removed to a house in that neighbourhood, where there were both hot and cold baths, and where I enjoyed the luxury of daily ablution. I continued in this residence for seven months; at the end of which time, having a dispute with the master of the house, I hired apartments in Upper Berkeley Street. The mistress of this house was an Irish woman, and was employed........................[1] Although I was much gratified by seeing a number of beautiful women, who frequently visited at the house, I could not agree with the temper of my landlady, and once more changed my residence, removing to Rathbone Place.

A few days after I was settled in my new lodgings, some of my friends called, to remonstrate with me on having taken up my abode in a street, one half of the houses of which were inhabited by courtezans. They assured me that no ladies, or even gentlemen of character, would visit me in such a place: however, as I found my house very comfortable, and the situation was in many respects convenient, I determined to remain where I was; and as my reputation in the minds of the English was as deeply impressed as the carving on a stone, my friends had the condescension and goodness to overlook this indiscretion; and not only was I visited there by the first characters in London, but even ladies of rank, who had never in their lives before passed through this street, used to call in their carriages at my door, and either send up their compliments, or leave their names written on cards. After a residence of fourteen months, I removed thence to Wardour Street, and afterwards to Berwick Street.

Shortly after my arrival in London, I sent a note to Mr. Dundas,[2] then one of the principal Ministers of the Empire, to solicit an interview: he immediately appointed a day, and, when I waited on him, received me with the greatest attention and kindness. He afterwards invited me to his country-house at Wimbledon, where I was entertained in the most agreeable and courte-

---

1 Abu Talib is using these ellipses to indicate that the Irish woman in question is running a brothel.

2 Henry Dundas (1742-1811) was Home Secretary at this time. His knowledge of Indian affairs was formidable and he had long taken a critical view of the actions of the East India Company. During the Hastings impeachment he was the principal Tory analyst of India policy. Prior to and following Abu Talib's visit, Dundas was a key strategist in the war against France.

ous manner, by Lady Jane Dundas, one of the most charming and sensible women in England.

A few weeks subsequent to my visit to Mr. Dundas, I had the honour of being introduced to the King; and on the following day was presented to her most gracious Majesty Queen Charlotte.[1] Both of these illustrious personages received me in the most condescending manner, and, after having honoured me with some conversation, commanded me to come frequently to court. After this introduction, I received invitations from all the Princes; and the Nobility vied with each other in their attention to me. Hospitality is one of the most esteemed virtues of the English; and I experienced it to such a degree, that I was seldom disengaged. In these parties I enjoyed every luxury my heart could desire. Their viands were delicious, and wines exquisite. The beauty of the women, and their grace in dancing, delighted my imagination; while the variety and melody of their music charmed all my senses.

I may perhaps be accused of personal vanity by saying, that my society was courted, and that my wit and repartees, with some *impromptu* applications of Oriental poetry, were the subject of conversation in the politest circles. I freely confess, that, during my residence in England, I was so exhilarated by the coolness of the climate, and so devoid of all care, that I followed the advice of our immortal poet Hafiz, and gave myself up to love and gaiety.

I often visited all the public places of amusement in London; and frequently had so many Opera tickets sent me by ladies of quality, that I had an opportunity of obliging many young Englishmen, by transferring the tickets to them. My amusements were not however confined to the metropolis; I had many invitations to the distance of forty, fifty, or eighty miles from it; on which occasions my friends were so obliging as to take me down in their own carriages, so that I thereby did not incur any expence.

When I first arrived in London, it had been my determination to have opened a Public Academy to be patronized by Government, for instructing such of the English as were destined to fill important situations in the East, in the Hindoostany, Persian, and Arabic languages. The plan I proposed was, that I should commence with a limited number of pupils, selected for the purpose, who were not to go abroad; but, each of these to instruct a

---

1 Charlotte of Mecklenburg-Strelitz (1744-1818), married George III in 1761.

number of others: thus as one candle may light a thousand, so I hoped to have spread the cultivation of the Persian language all over the kingdom. By these means I expected to have passed my time in England in a rational and advantageous manner; beneficial both to myself, and to the nation I came to visit. I therefore took an early opportunity of mentioning the subject to the Ministers of the Empire: but whether it was owing to their having too many other affairs to attend to, or that they did not give my plan that consideration which, from its obvious utility, it deserved, I met with no encouragement. What rendered their indifference on this subject very provoking, was: many individuals were so desirous of learning the Oriental languages, that they attended *self-taught masters*, ignorant of every principle of the science, and paid them half-a-guinea a lesson.

A short time before I left England, the Ministers, having become sensible of the advantages likely to arise from such an institution, made me an offer of 6000 rupees (£.750) annually, with liberty to reside either in Oxford or London, to superintend it; but as I had then resolved to return to India, and was disgusted with their former apathy on the subject, I politely excused myself. I, however, promised that if I should return to England, I would then accept it, and give my aid in establishing so laudable and requisite an institution.

I have already stated, that the marks of attention, and proofs of friendship, which I received in London, from various persons in all ranks, were innumerable: in justice, however, to my most particular friends, I shall take the liberty of reciting a few of their names. Among the foremost of these, was Mr. Charles Cockerell.[1] Had I been his brother, he could not have behaved with more kindness. He liberally supplied me with money for my drafts on Calcutta, and offered to advance any other sums I required: he also escorted me to all the places of public amusement, and invited me once every week to dine at his table, where I had an opportunity of meeting some of the handsomest women and the most agreeable company in England. I was present at one entertainment he gave, where seven hundred persons of rank and consequence sat down to a supper, at which were served up all

---

1 Sir Charles Cockerell (1755-1837), first baronet, was banker and agent for the East India Co. and bought Sezincote (as it is more commonly known) from the estate of his brother, John Cockerell. With the help of a third brother, architect Samuel Pepys Cockerell, he converted the house to exemplify Indian architecture and culture.

the choicest fruits and rarities procurable in London: many of these were produced by artificial heat; for the English, not content with the fruits of their own climate, contrive, by the assistance of glass and fire, to cultivate those of the torrid zone; and, as a contrast to these, they form *ice* into the shape of peaches, &c. which frequently deceive the beholder. This gentleman resided many years in India, and there acquired a large fortune in the most honourable manner.

It is customary for gentlemen of fortune to quit London during the summer months, and to amuse themselves by travelling about the country. In one of these tours, Mr. Cockerell did me the favour to take me with him. We travelled in a *barouche* or open carriage, drawn by four beautiful horses. Our first day's journey was to Windsor, the country residence of the King. The Palace, or Fort, is situated in an extensive and beautiful park, and contains a number of elegant apartments. These are ornamented with a great variety of pictures, principally of the ancient Kings, Queens, and Princesses of England. One of these rooms contained the portraits of twenty-four celebrated Beauties, who gave brilliancy to the court of one of their Sovereigns. They were painted from life, by command of the monarch, and are the most charming countenances I ever saw. The chapel belonging to the palace is an ancient building, and fitted up in a very peculiar style. In it are deposited the crown, the throne, and complete armour of each of the former Kings, all of which may be considered as very great curiosities.

The following day we proceeded to the house of Mr. Addington,[1] the prime minister, who possesses very extensive gardens, and where I had an opportunity of seeing a large collection of exotics. During the summer, these trees are exposed in the open air; but in winter they are shut up in rooms covered with glass. Our next stage was to the house of Mr. Goolding, where we were most hospitably entertained; and in the evening, were amused by music, and the singing of the young ladies. On the fourth day, soon after noon, we entered Oxford, and took up our residence at the Star Inn.

Oxford is a very ancient city, and the most celebrated *Seat of Learning* of the Empire. All the public buildings are constructed of hewn stone, and much resemble in form some of the Hindoo

---

1 Henry Addington (1757-1844), first Viscount Sidmouth, was Prime Minister from 1801 to 1804.

temples. The streets are very wide and regular, and several of them are planted on each side with trees. In this place are assembled the most learned men of the nation, and students come here from all parts.

There are twenty-three different colleges, each containing an extensive library. In *one* of these libraries I saw nearly 10,000 Arabic and Persian manuscripts. The collective name of these twenty-three colleges is *The University*, meaning an assemblage of all the sciences. For the use of the University, a very magnificent *Observatory* has been erected, with much philosophical and astronomical skill. It contains a great variety of instruments, and some very large telescopes.

There is here, also, a large building for the sole use of anatomy. One of the Professors did me the favour to shew me every part of this edifice, and to explain many of the mysteries of this useful science, which afforded me very great satisfaction. In the hall, were suspended the skeletons not only of men, women, and children, but also of all species of animals. In another apartment was an exact representation of all the veins, arteries, and muscles of the human body, filled with red and yellow wax, minutely imitating Nature. The Professor particularly pointed out to me the great nerve, which, commencing at the head, runs down the back-bone, where it divides it into four great branches, one of which extends down each arm, and leg, to the ends of the fingers and toes. In another room were, preserved in spirits, several bodies of children, who had something peculiar in their conformation. One of these *lusus Naturæ* had two heads and four feet, but only one body. The mother having died in the act of parturition, the womb, with the children, was cut out, and preserved entire.

In one of the lower apartments appropriated to dissection, I saw some students at work on a dead body. They also shewed me some candles which they said were made of human tallow, and a great number of other curiosities.

As Europeans are much more experienced than we are in the science of anatomy, I shall here explain some of their opinions, which are in opposition to ours.

★ ★ ★ ★

[N.B. Although this dissertation evinces that the Author lost no opportunity to acquire knowledge, yet, as the subject is not a pleasing one, and can be interesting only to few, the Translator has thought it better to omit it.]

★ ★ ★ ★

Having seen every thing that was curious in Oxford, we proceeded to Blenheim, the seat of the Duke of Marlborough. This place is, without comparison, superior to any thing I ever beheld. The beauties of Windsor Park faded before it; and every other place I had visited was effaced from my recollection, on viewing its magnificence. The park is fourteen miles in circumference, planted with large and shady trees. The house, or rather palace, is lofty and superb, and, with its various offices, covers half a mile of ground. Many rivulets of clear water run through the park; and over the largest of these are erected several handsome bridges. In the middle of the park stands a stone pillar, seventy yards high, on the top of which is sculptured, in marble, a statue of the great Duke, as large as life. This illustrious person was the Generalissimo of Anne,[1] one of the most celebrated Queens of England; and, in return for his eminent services, was rewarded with this mansion, and a pension of 50,000 rupees annually. The trees in the park are said to have been planted to resemble an army drawn up in battle array; and on the tapestry of the large rooms, the plans of his most celebrated battles are faithfully delineated in needle-work.

After looking at the house and gardens, we drove round the park, and thence proceeded to the house of Mr. Molony, a friend of Mr. Cockerell's. Here we found a party invited to meet us; and I had the pleasure of being introduced to Mrs. Cox, the sister of Mrs. Pringle of Lucknow, under the care of whose worthy husband I left my fortune and family when I quitted that city. I was much rejoiced by this unexpected pleasure; and Colonel Cox having invited us to visit them at Sandford Park, we went there the following day, and were most hospitably entertained by that gentleman and his charming wife, with whose conversation and affability I was quite delighted.

Our next visit was to Mr. Stratton, a very engaging young man, who possesses an estate of 4000 acres in that neighbourhood. This gentleman is a great sportsman, and keeps a number of horses, dogs, &c. As I was anxious to see the mode of sporting in England, he kindly offered me the use of one of his horses, and a gun. We set out early in the morning, accompanied by two servants, to lead our horses and carry the game. We were out for nearly ten hours, sometimes walking, and at others riding, and returned with twenty partridges and five hares.

---

1 Anne (1665-1714), was Queen of Great Britain and Ireland from 1702 until her death.

No country in the world produces a greater variety of sporting dogs than England. They have them trained for every species of game. They have greyhounds for coursing, and other hounds for killing deer, foxes, &c.: these hunt together, in packs of fifty or sixty. They have also two distinct species of dogs for the gun. Those which accompanied us, were of the kind that, as soon as they smell the game, stop until the sportsman comes close up, when, at his command, they move gently forward and rouse the game. I was much delighted at the sagacity of these animals; for, although there were several beating about us on all sides, whenever one of them stopped, the others followed his example, and became immoveable. I was told an anecdote of one of these pointers, which is very surprising. While in the act of jumping over a wall, he perceived a hare on the opposite side; when, by a great effort, he stopped himself on the wall, and waited there till his master came up and shot the hare.

In England, game is considered as private property; and if any person kill it on the land of another, he is liable to a severe penalty. There is, however, an exception to this rule: when deer, foxes, or hares, are hunted by *hounds,* in that case the hunters pursue them over the country, sometimes to the distance of forty or fifty miles: and should the game even swim across a river, both dogs and horsemen follow. If the fox runs into a hole, they send in a small kind of dog, called a *terrier,* who drives him out. The horses that are trained to this sport will leap over walls two yards high, and rivulets or ditches six yards wide, without moving an experienced rider from his seat.

After having changed our clothes, and refreshed ourselves from the fatigues of the field, we sat down to dinner. Here our society was again enlivened by the presence of Mrs. Cox and some other ladies: and our host entertained us with some of his own-fed mutton, which was superior to any I had ever eaten, and a great variety of game, fruits, wines, &c.

Early next morning we pursued our journey: we breakfasted at Chipping Norton, and dined at Stowe; after which we proceeded to Seisincot, the house of Mr. Cockerell. This estate had been purchased by the late Colonel Cockerell, who built thereon a new house, and, at his death, bequeathed the whole to his brother. We spent two days in this delightful spot, and then proceeded to the residence of Mr. Hastings, the late worthy Governor-general of India.

As I had promised Mr. Hastings, while in London, that, if ever I visited Oxfordshire, I should pass a week with him, he therefore now claimed the fulfilment of my promise. I was much rejoiced to find this great man released from all the toils and anxieties of a public life, amusing himself in rural occupations, and enjoying that happiness in his domestic society which is unattainable by the monarchs of the world.

I was much pleased with viewing his grounds and gardens, which were laid out with great taste and judgment; but I was particularly struck with the arrangement and economy of his farm-yard and dairy. As the latter surpasses any thing of the kind I have seen, and is an office unknown in a gentleman's family in the East, I shall attempt a description of it.

A *dairy* is a large room for preserving milk, butter, and cheese. The one I now speak of, was well shaded from the sun, and had large glass windows on the four sides, which were opened or shut at pleasure. Within each window stood a frame of netted wire, which admitted the air, but obstructed the entrance of flies, or other insects. Around the room were placed a number of vessels, made of white marble, for holding the milk. There were also several marble slabs for pressing and shaping the cheese on; and even the floors and seats were composed of the same delicate and costly material.

As Mr. Hastings prefers living in the country to London, he has spared no expence in fitting up this residence; in which elegance and utility are so happily blended, that it resembles more the work of a *Genii*, than of human art.

During my stay at this delightful abode, Mr. Hastings treated me with the utmost attention and kindness and when I was about to depart, he offered to supply me with money as long as I should remain in England. I returned him my acknowledgments for his kindness; but not being in want of assistance, I declined his friendly offer.

Mr. Cockerell having some business which would require his staying a fortnight at Seisincot, wished me much to return thither, and pass that time with him: but as, previous to my leaving London, Cupid had planted one of his arrows in my bosom, I found it impossible to resist the desire of returning to the presence of my fair one; and therefore, on leaving Mr. Hastings's, we separated.

On my way to town, I had an opportunity of seeing Henley. It is advantageously situated on the river Thames, and said to be one of the handsomest towns in England. I did not think it superior, however, either to Richmond or Kilkenny.

A few days after my arrival in London, I composed the following Ode, in imitation of Hafiz.

ODE TO LONDON,

Henceforward we will devote our lives to London, and its heart-
alluring Damsels:
Our hearts are satiated with viewing fields, gardens, rivers, and
palaces.

We have no longing for the Toba, Sudreh, or other trees of
Paradise:
We are content to rest under the shade of these terrestrial
Cypresses.

If the Shaikh of Mecca is displeased at our conversion, who
cares?
May the Temple which has conferred such blessings on us, and
its Priests, flourish!

Fill the goblet with wine! If by this I am prevented from
returning
To my old religion, I care not; nay, I am the better pleased.

If the prime of my life has been spent in the service of an
Indian Cupid,
It matters not: I am now rewarded by the smiles of the British
Fair.

Adorable creatures! whose flowing tresses, whether of flaxen or
of jetty hue,
Or auburn gay, delight my soul, and ravish all my senses!

Whose ruby lips would animate the torpid clay, or marble
statue!
Had I a renewal of life, I would, with rapture, devote it to your
service!

These wounds of Cupid, on your heart, Taleba, are not
accidental:
They were engendered by Nature, like the streaks on the leaf
of a tulip.

See Appendix (I).

CHAPTER X

Character of the Author's friends in London. His mode of passing the time. He visits Greenwich, and other places in the vicinity of the metropolis. Account of the Freemasons. British Museum. The Irish Giant. Chimney-Sweepers. King's Library. Pictures. Hindoostany Ladies. Panegyric on Mr. Swinton, one of his pupils.

After I was again settled in the metropolis, I paid my respects to my friends, and was again introduced into the best societies. I generally spent one evening every week at the house of Mr. Plowden.[1] This gentleman resided many years in India, at the court of Lucknow; where his services were so much approved, that he has since been chosen one of the Directors of the Company. Mrs. Plowden is a most charming lively woman, and the delight of all her acquaintance: she is blessed with a numerous family of beautiful children, several of whom are grown up, and possess the amiable qualities of their parents. As the whole family are admirers of music, their parties were always enlivened by dancing or singing; and I had frequent opportunities of meeting the first connoisseurs in that delightful science, at their house. I also there had the pleasure of becoming acquainted with some of the most beautiful and charming ladies I have ever met with in my travels. Two of these were Miss Hyde and Mrs. Anstruther: their singing and playing were, in my opinion, superior to either Mrs. Billington or Madame Banti,[2] although the first of these actresses was esteemed the best singer at the Theatre, and the latter the most admired at the Opera house; notwithstanding the performers of the last-mentioned institution are all natives of Italy, a country which is considered by Europeans as the *Treasury of the Science of Music*; and in fact the melody of Italy approaches nearer to the soft tones of Hindoostan than any other I have ever heard.

To Sir T. and Lady Metcalfe[3] I was much obliged for the many

---

1 Richard Chicheley Plowden (1743-1830), was Director of the East India Co. for a series of three-year terms from 1803-29.
2 Brigita Banti (c1756-1806; née Giorgi), was principal soprano in the King's Theatre Italian Opera Company and retired in 1802. Elizabeth Billington (1765-1818; née Weichsel) was offered Banti's position in the Company towards the end of her own successful operatic career.
3 Theophilus John Metcalfe (1783-1823), East India Co. servant and older brother of Charles Theophilus Metcalfe, a noted colonial governor.

agreeable parties I met at their house. One summer evening that I spent with them at their country residence near Windsor, the company drank tea under the shade of a large tree: among the female visitors were two young beautiful ladies, a Miss Taylor, and a Miss Hosea: the latter was the daughter of Dr. Hosea, who was lost when returning from India in the ship Grosvenor, on the coast of Africa;[1] and she being an orphan, Sir Theophilus had afforded her an asylum in his house. During an interval in the conversation, Lady Metcalfe observed, that trees of the species under which we were seated generally extended their branches to a great distance, but were seldom high; that this was an exception to the general rule, being not only of a great circumference, but also very tall. I immediately replied, it was by no means astonishing; as had I the honour of being so often the companion of Miss Hosea as it had, my head would proudly exalt itself still higher than the tree. They all laughed heartily at this speech, and applauded my warmth in the cause of beauty.

At the house of Sir T. Metcalfe I often had the pleasure of meeting Miss—. As it is impossible for simple prose to do justice to her angelic qualities, I have attempted to describe them in the following Ode.

[The Translator acknowledges himself unable here to follow the Author.]

Sometime before I quitted England, this Miss— married an old man on account of his wealth: on which event a number of the young ladies who were envious of my attachment to her, whenever they had an opportunity, ran to condole with me on my misfortune, saying, "Do you know that your Miss— is married?" and then attempted to make some sarcastic remark on the object of her choice. This I would not permit them to do: but answered them in such a manner as made them laugh, by saying, "It is a long time since my attachment to her ceased; she therefore, being in despair, has prudently taken to herself a husband."

To my friend Mrs. Rickets I shall ever be grateful for her civil-

---

1 William Hosea was Resident at the Durbar of the Nawab of Bengal in Murshidabad through much of the 1770s. He died in the famous shipwreck of the *Grosvenor* off the coast of South Africa on 4 August 1782. His daughter Mary was one of three women who was ostensibly abducted by a group of Caffre tribesmen after the wreck.

ities. She is the granddaughter of *Begum* Johnson,[1] well known in Calcutta.

I had the good fortune to form an intimacy with Mr. Ferary,[2] an Italian gentleman, so well skilled in music, that many of his compositions were introduced at the Opera. He was also well versed in chess, which gave me an opportunity of improving myself in that game. He one evening took me to visit a countryman of his, who played three games of chess at the same time, without looking at any of the boards, and beat all his adversaries.

At the house of Sir J. Macpherson,[3] late Governor of Bengal, I had frequent opportunities of meeting the Princes; who all behaved to me with the greatest condescension and kindness.

Among the literary characters with whom I had the honour of being acquainted, were Sir Frederic Eden, Sir John Sinclair, and Sir Joseph Banks.[4] The first of these has written several treatises on different subjects. The second is well skilled in husbandry and agriculture, and has therefore been placed by the King at the head of a Society for the encouragement of these useful arts. This gentleman paid me much attention, and frequently took me with him ten or twenty miles into the country to look at various objects of curiosity. One evening, when we were returning from visiting his son, who was at the school of Sunbury, (with the inspection of which I was much delighted,) and were arrived at his door, he ordered the coachman to drive on to my house, and first put me down. I represented to him, that although my house

---

1   Begum Johnson (1728-1812; née Frances Croke), was a hostess renowned for her long residency in India and her influential sphere of friends and acquaintances. Her daughter, Sophia Watts (1753-1830) married George Poyntz Ricketts and thus the Mrs. Rickets referred to above is likely one of her daughters or the wife of one of her sons.

2   Probably Italian composer Giacomo Ferrari (1763-1842).

3   Sir John Macpherson (c.1745-1821), first baronet, succeeded Warren Hastings as Governor General, but his term in office lasted only nineteen months.

4   Sir Frederick Eden Morton (1766-1809), writer on England's social and economic conditions; Sir John Sinclair (1754-1835), first baronet, noted agriculturalist and politician; and Sir Joseph Banks (1743-1820), renowned explorer, collector, and naturalist. Banks was famous for his role in Captain Cook's first voyage and for his role in the foundation not only of the British Museum, but also of the Royal Botanical Gardens at Kew. Abu Talib's discussion of Banks would no doubt have reminded British readers of Banks's patronage of Mai, commonly referred to as Omai, of Raitea during his widely discussed visit to London in 1774-76.

was still two miles further off, as I was in the constant habit of walking the streets, I should prefer going home on foot, and would not either trouble his servants to carry me so far, or encroach upon his time by carrying him so much out of his way. He however refused either to put me down or get out himself: and when I pressed him to explain the motives of his conduct, he replied: "In this world we are all liable to accidents; and if it should by chance happen, that you this night met with any misfortune, I should never forgive myself." At the house of Sir John I frequently had the pleasure of meeting some of the most respectable characters in England. He did me the honour of introducing me to Lord Sheffield,[1] by whom I was most sumptuously entertained.

The third is one of those persons who sailed round the world with Captain Cook; is esteemed the greatest Philosopher of the age; and is President of the Royal Society. From each of these gentlemen I received the most pointed marks of regard and esteem.

At the house of the latter gentleman, I became acquainted with some of the most celebrated painters in England, several of whom requested me to sit for my portrait. Thus, during my residence in London, no less than six pictures were taken of me, the greater number of which were said to be very good likenesses. The following are the names of the persons who did me this honour: Mr. Edridge, also celebrated as an engraver, Mr. Devis, Mr. Jesit, Mr. Drummond, Mr. Ridley, and Mr. Northcote.[2] I thought Mr. Edridge's was the best likeness; but Mr. Northcote's was esteemed the finest picture. The merits and celebrity of all these gentlemen are far beyond my feeble panegyric; but some of the portraits of the last appeared as if starting from the canvas. His picture of my lovely friend Miss Burrell afforded me the highest gratification; and, with the recollection of the original, will ever remain deeply impressed on my memory.

At Sir J. Banks's weekly meetings, to which I was first introduced by Colonel Symes,[3] I had frequent opportunities of con-

---

1 John Baker Holroyd (1741-1821), first Earl of Sheffield, was a politician and writer.
2 Henry Edridge (1769-1821), painter; Arthur William Devis (1763-1822), portrait artist and historical painter; Samuel Drummond (1765-1844), historical painter; likely William Ridley (1764-1838), portrait artist; for Mr. Northcote, see note 3 in preface.
3 Michael Symes (1761-1809), East India Co. officer, published an account of his time spent at the Burmese Court.

versing with Mr. Wilkins.[1] This gentleman resided many years in India; and, besides acquiring a knowledge of the Persian language, has the merit of being one of the first Englishmen who made any progress in Sanscrit lore. He has even translated a poem, called the *Bhagvunt Geeta*, from that abstruse language.

In the same manner I became acquainted with Sir W. Ouseley.[2] This gentleman, being possessed of a great taste for Oriental literature, has by uncommon perseverance acquired such a knowledge of Persian, as to be able to translate freely from that language; and has published one or two books to facilitate the study of it. He did me the honour of frequently calling on me; and I received much pleasure from his acquaintance.

From General Wilkinson, Dr. Neal, and Sir John Talbot,[3] I received the most marked attention, and many proofs of hospitality.

Another of my most particular friends was Lady Elford;[4] to do justice to whose merit far exceeds the powers of my feeble pen. She is distinguished by a dignified deportment, ease and elegance of manners, affability and politeness of conversation. She is also imbued with so much piety, and endued with so great a share of sensibility, that she never heard of any instance of God's mercy, the loss of any friend, or any act of cruelty, but the tears flowed from her compassionate eyes: notwithstanding this softness of temper, she possesses a ready wit, great soundness of judgment, and an excellent taste for poetry. She made a large collection of my Odes:[5] and although the idiom of our languages is so very different, she readily understood my meaning, and was much pleased with my

---

1 Sir Charles Wilkins (c.1749-1836), orientalist who played an integral role in establishing printing presses for oriental languages.

2 Sir William Ouseley (1767-1842), orientalist scholar and author, was knighted for his works in 1800 and later journeyed to Persia to continue his investigations. His *Persian Miscellanies: an essay to facilitate the reading of Persian manuscripts* (1795) and the three volume *Oriental Collections* (1797-99) were standard works of British orientalism. He is also notable for his relationship with Mirza Abul Hasan, the Persian envoy to Britain who was the focus of widespread interest, in the early nineteenth century.

3 Admiral John Talbot (1769-1851) resided in England during the period between his Irish and Canadian stations.

4 Mary Elford (1753-1817; née Davies) married artist and politician Sir William Elford (1749-1837) in 1776. They had three children and it is presumably their daughters Grace Chard (1781-1856) and Elizabeth (1782-1837) to which the author refers below.

5 See Appendix (II). (Translator's note)

performances. One day she took me to see a new invention, which was exposed for view in her neighbourhood; it was the representation of things in coloured *cork*, and in fidelity of representation far exceeded many pictures I had seen, whether delineated by the pencil or worked with the needle. While we were viewing the different articles, the owner of the exhibition came up, and presented Lady Elford with a free-admission ticket: which surprising me much, I asked her to explain the reason of his conduct: she informed me, that it was customary at these exhibitions, if any persons had been there frequently, to present them with a ticket of that kind, in order to induce them to continue their visits, and to bring their friends. Her Ladyship also did me the favour to take me with her to Ranelagh; a particular description of which place I have given in my *Poetical Tour*; also to see the barracks of the worn-out soldiers at Chelsea; and to Sir Ashton Lever's Museum,[1] and various other places of amusement. Her husband, Sir William Elford, is a colonel in the army and a member of Parliament, and celebrated for his wisdom and integrity. He also possesses an ample knowledge of the Arts and Sciences. May God Almighty preserve Lady Elford, and her two angelic daughters, Betsy and Jessy! whose transcendant qualities I have attempted to describe in the following Ode.

[Here the Translator has again to lament his want of poetical talents.]

In short, the delight I experienced in the society of Lady Elford and her amiable daughters will never be obliterated from my memory. When I was about to quit England, and went to take my leave, each of them gave me some curiosity, as a token of remembrance; and made me promise to write to them frequently. Her Ladyship was so overpowered by her feelings, that she could not bid me adieu.

In London I had the happiness of again meeting my friend Mr. R. Johnson. We had been many years acquainted in India; and it was at his suggestion that I printed in Calcutta an edition of the poet Hafiz. He was my banker during my residence in England; and I had a general invitation to his table, where I often had the honour of meeting some of the most respectable characters in London. It was rather a curious circumstance, that, in the persons of my London bankers, Mr. N. Middleton, and Mr. R. Johnson,[2] I should meet the two gentlemen who were the repre-

---

1   Sir Ashton Lever's (1729-88) collection of natural curiosities and artefacts (many from Cook's expedition) were housed at the Holophusikon in Leicester Square.
2   See p. 63, note 4 and note 5.

sentatives of the East-India Company at the Court of Lucknow during a very eventful period; and who originally marred my fortune, by forcing me to accept of an employment under that government.

Mrs. Johnson is an amiable and accomplished woman, and frequently had musical parties in the evening. It was at her house that I first had the pleasure of hearing Lady Hamilton[1] sing. Her ladyship has, without doubt, one of the finest voices in Europe, and possesses great skill in music.

To Lady Burrell, and her amiable daughter,[2] I shall ever feel grateful for their hospitality and kindness; and to the latest hour of my life I shall recollect with pleasure the many happy days I passed in their society. In my poetical work, entitled *The Mesnevy*,[3] I have dedicated three Odes to Miss Burrell: these, however, but faintly express my admiration of her wonderful perfections; in her person are united the beauty and accomplishments of Europe, with the grace and modesty of India. The eyes of the heavens never beheld more loveliness, nor did the inhabitants of Paradise ever hear more delightful melody than issues from the harp when touched by her angelic fingers.

But, above all my friends, I shall ever regret my separation from Colonel Symes.[4] He was a man of the strictest honour and integrity, and had passed several years in India. During the government of Sir John Shore (now Lord Teignmouth) he was sent ambassador to Ava, and conducted himself in that situation much to his own credit, and to the advantage of the British nation. On his return from thence, he wrote a book, describing all the curiosities of that country, and the peculiar customs of its

---

1   Emma Hamilton (bap.1765-1815; née Lyon) was the wife of the diplomat and art collector Sir William Hamilton (1731-1803) and the mistress of Horatio Nelson at the time she met Abu Talib. The relationship between these three personages at the turn of the century was an open scandal. She was well known for her famous "attitudes," but while in Italy with her husband she received vocal training.

2   Lady Sophia Burrell (1753-1802; née Raymond) was a playwright and poet. She and her first husband, the antiquarian William Burrell (1732-96), had two daughters among their seven children. The author is likely referring to their eldest daughter, Julia Ann (Juliana) Burrell (1780-1856), though he may also be referring to her younger sister, Emily Elizabeth Burrell (c.1789-1838). See Appendix A1 for Abu Talib's "Poem in Praise of Miss Julia Burrell."

3   See Note to the Introduction. (Translator's note)

4   See p. 359, note 1.

inhabitants; which was universally read and admired. From this gentleman I received many proofs of friendship; and, in fact, he behaved to me as if I had been his brother. When I had the honour of being introduced to his Majesty, he acted as my interpreter; and he took me to see all the places in London where any information or knowledge could be acquired. He also introduced me to a number of his acquaintances, and frequently pressed me to accept of money for my expences. He agreed with me, that we should return to India together, and share in each other's fortunes. He literally performed his promise; but just as I was about to take my passage on board the ship he had engaged, Lord Pelham, one of his Majesty's Ministers, prevailed upon me to forego my intention, and we took leave of each other with tears in our eyes.[1]

The principal person to whom I was introduced by Colonel Symes was Lord Carhampton.[2] He is a nobleman of high dignity, and was the deputy of Lord Cornwallis during the period he was Lord-lieutenant of Ireland: he did me the honour of inviting me twice to his house, and entertained me in a very superb style.

To the introduction of Colonel Symes I was also indebted for my acquaintance with Sir James Earle.[3] He is one of the King's Physicians, and of a most amiable and liberal disposition. He frequently took me with him ten or twelve miles from London, to see various gardens, and other places of curiosity. He often asked me to dine with him: and I had numerous invitations from Lady Earle to her routs and evening parties; where I met a number of beautiful young ladies, and heard exquisite music and singing. The most accomplished of these *Houries of Paradise* was Miss Marian. Her beauty transcends all praise; and from the first moment I saw her, her image has never been effaced from my mind.

At Sir James Earle's I had the pleasure of forming an acquaintance with Lady Charlotte, the sister of Lord Carbury; who frequently invited me to her routs, where I met some of the first company in England.

By the means before mentioned, I was introduced to Mr.

---

1 See Appendix (III). (Translator's note)
2 Henry Lawes Luttrell (1737–1821), second earl of Carhampton, was Lieutenant General of the Ordnance of Ireland 1789–97. He led the British suppression of the Irish Rebellion of 1798.
3 Sir James Earle (1755-1817) was appointed surgeon-extraordinary to George III in 1786 and eventually head of the Royal College of Surgeons.

Nepean,[1] Secretary to the Admiralty: he is a sensible well-informed man; and during the summer gave me several invitations to his country-house, in the village of Fulham; and in the winter I attended Lady Nepean's routs in London.

From Sir John and Colonel Murray, both of whom had held high official situations in Bengal, I experienced much kindness; but as their place of residence was Scotland, and they only came occasionally to London, I did not see so much of them as I wished.

It would be the height of ingratitude to omit the name of Mr. Debrett[2] from the list of my friends; for although a bookseller, he is a person of elevated sentiments and noble mind: his house used to be the rendezvous of all the members of Parliament who opposed Mr. Pitt.[3] His wife is also a person of a very good family, and of a very hospitable disposition. From my first arrival in London till the day I left it, I experienced from this worthy couple much attention, and many acts of friendship.

I had also the pleasure of being acquainted with Mr. Sewell, another bookseller, who has a very large shop in the city. He was very anxious to promote the study of Persian in England; and invited me frequently to his house. He took me into the country, to see Colonel Alexander Robert's Observatory and Greenhouses; both of which are well worth visiting, and proved that the proprietor's philosophy and knowledge comprehended the objects of the heavens and the productions of the earth.

From Mr. Rousseau,[4] a celebrated printer, I received numberless marks of attention; and in the preface to many of his books he inserted my name by way of remembrance.

Lady Winifred Constable, a venerable Scotch lady, but whose mind still retained all the vigour of youth, and who every week,

---

1 Sir Evan Nepean (1751-1822) was an extremely influential figure socially and politically. His friends included William Pitt and Henry Dundas, and George III often relied upon him as an advisor. He was Governor of Bombay from 1812 to 1819.

2 John Debrett (d.1822) was a bookseller whose shop provided a gathering place for Whig politicians and supporters.

3 William Pitt (1759-1806) was prime minister from 1783 to 1801 and then again from 1804 to 1806.

4 Samuel Kent Rousseau (1763-1820) was an orientalist scholar and printer. Aside from his various linguistic treatises, *The Flowers of Persian Literature* (1801), which presented Persian and English texts in parallel, was an important introduction to Persian literature for British readers.

during the winter, invited all her acquaintance twice to her house, did me the honour, without any introduction, of sending me a card for her rout; and I was so much taken with her affability and elegance of manners, that I became her constant visitor: I also received much delight from the agreeable society that frequented her house. This good lady's principal residence was in Edinburgh, the chief city of Scotland; and when she was about to depart for that place, she told me it would be a great pity if I should return to India without having seen Scotland: she therefore urged me to accompany and spend some time with her; but being then in the same predicament as when I visited Oxford, I wished to decline her kind invitation: she however would accept of no excuse; and on the day she was setting off, stopped her coach at my door, and pressed me to go along with her. I was quite overcome by this uncommon act of kindness and attention, and promised, nay swore, that I would certainly follow her in two months, and put up at her house. With this declaration she was at length satisfied, and bade me farewell. At the end of the prescribed period, I made preparations for my journey, and was about setting out, when I received the melancholy tidings of her death. I was sincerely affected by this intelligence, as she was an excellent woman, and the most benevolent and obliging person of her nation that I ever met with: for be it known, that of my European friends, many more of them were Scotch than English; more particularly Mr. G. Johnstone, who had resided long at Lucknow, and with whom I had been intimate for twelve years; and Dr. Blane,[1] who was formerly at Gorruckpore with Colonel Hannay, and whom I had known for thirty years: from both of these gentlemen I naturally expected much civility, and an invitation to pass some time with them in *Scotland*; but they totally neglected the right of friendship and hospitality, while this amiable lady, to whom I was a perfect stranger, offered me the means of visiting a very interesting and distant part of the kingdom.

To Colonel Brathwaite,[2] and his charming wife, I was under many obligations, for their hospitality, and shewing me many of the public places in London, particularly the Tower and the

---

1 Sir Gilbert Blane (1749-1834), a renowned physician, did much to improve medical conditions for naval officers; he also worked on the implementation of the Quarantine Act.
2 Colonel John Brathwaite suffered a crushing defeat to Tipu Sultan in 1784 during the Second Mysore War, but went on to have an extensive career in India.

British Museum. The Colonel had served long in India, and was much pleased with the society of Natives of that country. I consider the Colonel as one of the most fortunate men in this world; for although a single glance from his wife is worth £. 100,000, he received a marriage portion with her of ten lacks of rupees, upon the easy condition of taking her name, she having been the daughter of General Brathwaite, commander in chief of Madras. Such was her affection for her husband, that she always wore his picture suspended round her neck.

In the house of Mrs. Gordon, and the society of her charming family, which consisted of her amiable daughter, her grandson who studied Persian under me, and her nephew Captain Losack, an officer in the Royal Navy who had highly distinguished himself during the war by attacking and bringing away a French ship which was under the protection of a heavy battery, I spent many delightful evenings: the amusements of which were sometimes varied by the pleasure of playing at chess with General Money;[1] and of seeing and hearing the beautiful Miss Latour, whose praises far exceed my powers of description, and is one of those *belles* who has left a scar on my heart.

Mrs. Gordon did me the favour to introduce me to Mr. Hankey, Colonel Peach, and Mr. Macpherson; from each of whom I experienced much attention.

At the table of Earl Spenser[2] I had the honour of being introduced to Lord Macartney.[3] This celebrated nobleman has been employed by the King on the most difficult missions. He was for some years Ambassador in Russia; where he is said, by his manly figure and accomplishments, to have gained the affections of the Empress. He was sent many years afterwards to China, where he acquitted himself much to the satisfaction of his Court. During the war with Hyder Aly, he was Governor of Madras; and had the offer of succeeding to the government of Bengal, but declined it. Although seventy years of age, he had the appearance of a handsome man of forty-five. His lordship frequently did me the favour of calling on me; and entertained me several times in a very superb manner.

---

1 This may be John Money (1752-1817), one of England's first aeronauts. He made two hot air balloon ascents in 1785.
2 George John Spencer (1758-1834), second Earl Spencer, politician and literary collector; his wife, Lady Lavinia Bingham (1762-1831), was a renowned social hostess and is mentioned further in Volume II.
3 See p. 81, note 2.

I had also the honour of forming an acquaintance with Lord Hardwicke,[1] a nobleman of very ancient family, and who succeeded Lord Cornwallis as Governor of Ireland. As his Lordship was married to the sister of Lady Ann Barnet, whom I had the pleasure of knowing at the Cape of Good Hope, and by whom I was recommended to his lordship, he in consequence called on me, and invited me to spend some time with him at his country-house, forty miles distant from London. As this event occurred a short time before he went to Ireland, he urged me to return thither, to pass a month or two with him; but I had so many engagements on my hands, that I was obliged to decline the honour.

At the house of Lord Hardwicke I had the pleasure of meeting Mrs. Montague, the daughter-in-law of the lady whose superb mansion adjoins Portman Square;[2] and of whom I shall hereafter relate an extraordinary anecdote. His Lordship also did me the honour of introducing me to Mr. Hope,[3] one of the most celebrated commercial men in Europe. Notwithstanding he is said to have lost half his property by the French Revolution, he is still considered as the wealthiest merchant in London. The variety of wines, and the richness of the plate, at his banquets, exceeded any entertainment I have ever seen.

I was much indebted to Sir Charles Rouse Boughton[4] for many acts of kindness and friendship. This gentleman had resided many years in India, and perfectly understood the Persian language. The first time I met him was at Court; where, by command of his Majesty, he officiated as interpreter, and stood between me and the King.

I have also to acknowledge my obligations to the Marquis of Townshend,[5] to Colonel Neville, and to Dr. Carshore, for their numberless civilities.

The Honourable Mr. Bruce,[6] brother of Lord Elgin, did me

---

1 Philip Yorke (1757-1834), third Earl of Hardwicke, married Lady Elizabeth Lindsay (1763-1858).
2 See p. 148, note 2.
3 This is likely Thomas Hope (1769-1831), a wealthy collector and connoisseur.
4 Sir Charles William Rouse Boughton (1747-1821), writer for the East India Co.
5 George Townshend (1724-1807), first Marquess Townshend, politician and caricaturist.
6 Charles Andrew Bruce (1768-1810), son of Charles Bruce, fifth Earl of

the favour to introduce me to his mother, who held the high and honourable office of Governess to the Princess Charlotte of Wales (who, after her father, is likely to succeed to the throne of England, in preference to her uncles, such being the law of this country).[1] When Mr. Bruce was returning to India, he resolved to proceed thither by the route of Constantinople, in order to visit his brother, who was then Ambassador at the Turkish Court; and was very solicitous that I should accompany him: but, as I was not then satiated with London, I declined his kind offer.

I often visited at the house of General Charles Morgan, in Portland Place. This officer commanded the East-India Company's army in the field at the period that Zeman Shah, the Abdally, threatened to invade their northern provinces; and had acquired a large fortune in India in the most honourable manner. I was quite enraptured with his daughter, who has since married Mr. Lushington; and have therefore dedicated one of my Odes to her.[2]

To Mr. Biddulph I was extremely obliged for his attention. He is one of the most extensive merchants in London; is a person of excellent manners, and sound sense: he frequently executes commissions for the Prince of Wales:[3] and it was by his introduction that I viewed Carlton House, the apartments of the Princess Charlotte, and many other places in London.

From Dr. Macdonald, the son of my old friend Colonel Macdonald of Bengal, I received the most marked civility and friendship, and had a general invitation to dine with him whenever I was disengaged.

Colonel Mackenzie, who had long resided in India, and who spoke Persian with great fluency, often called upon me; frequently entertained me at his house; and kept up a constant intercourse with me till I quitted England.

Mr. Christie[4] the Auctioneer also paid me much attention,

Elgin and Martha Whyte (d.1810), governess to Princess Charlotte. His brother, Thomas Bruce (1766-1841), was the seventh Earl of Elgin and British ambassador to Constantinople during Abu Talib's visit. See p. 278, note 1.

1 Charlotte Augusta Matilda (1766-1828), the princess royal.

2 This man is likely Stephen Lushington (1744-1807), East India Company director intermittently from 1782 to 1805.

3 George IV (1762-1830).

4 James Christie the elder (1730-1803) was a prominent antiquary and auctioneer. It is possible that the author is here referring to his son, also James Christie (1773-1831), though not likely since he assumed responsibility for the business only at the time of his father's death.

and gratified me highly, by shewing me the articles he had for sale. He once exhibited to me a number of pictures which he valued at £60,000; and when I called there a few days afterwards, they were all disposed of.

At the house of Counsellor Dowse I had the pleasure of seeing a large collection of Persian and Hindoostany pictures, and other rarities of the East: some of which I thought superior to the paintings of Europe.

I had the pleasure of being acquainted with Mr. Hartman, who lived in a very magnificent style in Portman Square. At his parties I met a number of Frenchmen: among these was the gentleman at whose house Napoleon Buonaparté was educated; but the Emperor, so far from being grateful to him for the favours conferred, compelled him to flee, and take refuge in England from his tyranny. At the same place I was also introduced to the father-in-law of General De Boigne,[1] who acquired so large a fortune in the service of the Mahratta chief Mahdajee Scindia: this gentleman had been one of the courtiers of the murdered King of France, and was of course obliged to abandon his country.

Mr. Strachey,[2] who had held an important situation at Madras, used frequently to call on me, and invite me to his house. He spoke Persian fluently, with the modern pronunciation of Irān (Persia), the style of which is *well known*; (i.e. grammatically erroneous).

Sir Robert Chambers,[3] who had been for many years Chief Justice in Bengal, frequently invited me to his house; but as he was then preparing for his journey to eternity, our intimacy was never matured.

To Mr. Ducarrol,[4] Colonel Osborne, and Mr. Huddleston, all of whom had resided in India, I was under many obligations.

---

1   See p. 149, note 2.
2   Sir Henry Strachey (1736-1810), first baronet, was appointed private secretary to Robert Clive in 1764.
3   Sir Robert Chambers (1737-1803) was appointed to the supreme court of Bengal following the East India Regulating Act, along with Warren Hastings and Elijah Impey. He returned to England in 1799 but was plagued by ill health until his death.
4   This is likely Gerard Gustavus Ducarel (1745-1800), an East India Co. employee who likely married Elizabeth (Bibi) Mirza during the 1780s. Their relationship began a decade earlier in India. She returned to England with him in 1784.

Mr. Wedgewood,[1] whose compositions and inventions in the manufacture of Chinaware are celebrated throughout the world, paid me much attention, and at one period was very anxious to accompany me by the route of Persia to India; but afterwards meeting with a traveller who had returned from India that way, and who described the journey as very perilous, he was alarmed, and abandoned his design.

Mr. Hagar a celebrated painter, Mr. Poole, and Mr. Hamilton, two famous musicians, and Mr. Rotton,[2] a proprietor of one of the Theatres, shewed me much civility in the line of their different professions.

Lord Teignmouth, Mr. Ives a long time the East-India Company's representative at Lucknow, Colonel Mark Wood,[3] and Major Marsac, were all very polite, but did not manifest any warmth of friendship; which, as they had been all many years in India, I was rather disappointed at.

Many other noblemen and gentlemen paid me much attention: but as a recital of their names would be the cause of prolixity, I shall here close the account.

Notwithstanding the constant round of my engagements in London, I passed a considerable portion of my time in writing *poetry*, and in seeing every thing or place that was curious, either in the metropolis or its vicinity. I went one day, with a party of friends, to see Greenwich, once the residence of the Sovereign, but now an Hospital for Invalid Seamen, of whom there were 1500 present, when I inspected it. It is a noble institution, and worthy of imitation. Here is also a very celebrated Observatory, furnished with the largest and finest instruments procurable; and it is from this spot that the English calculate their longitude.

By the kindness of Mr. Sewell, I was invited to spend the day at the house of Dr.—, situated eight miles from London. This gentleman was celebrated for his knowledge of chymistry, and his invention of several curious and useful machines. He exhibited

---

1 This is likely Josiah Wedgwood (1769-1843), namesake of his father. Following the death of the elder Josiah Wedgwood in 1795, the younger assumed responsibility for the family's renowned china and pottery business.

2 Richard Wroughton (1748-1822; née Rotten), actor and theatre manager, began using 'Wroughton' c.1769; he acted and managed at Drury Lane during the author's visit.

3 Sir Mark Wood (1747-1829), was first baronet, colonel, and employee for Bengal Engineers.

before me many specimens of his art, which *appeared* to be the effect of magic. He dissolved gold and silver, and even a ruby, by a few drops of aqua-fortis. He made fire to pass through water. He changed water into air, and air into water. He separated the bodies of several substances, and again united them; with many other things too tedious to relate, but which afforded me the greatest amusement.

At the distance of — miles from London there is a beautiful garden solely appropriated to the use of the *Freemasons*. Many wonderful stories are told of this sect. They have several regulations peculiar to themselves, and are able to know each other, at first sight, by some sign, which cannot be perceived by any other person. Even the fear of death will not make them betray the secrets of their order. It is reported that the King, having some suspicions of them, ordered the Heir Apparent to become a Freemason, and to inform him if there was any thing in their tenets prejudicial to good government, or dangerous to the State. The Prince, in obedience to the Royal orders, was initiated into all the mysteries of the sect; and declared to his father that their principles were favourable to his government, and that they were among the most loyal of his subjects. Thus far the Prince disclosed; but nothing respecting their mysteries ever issued from his lips.

The only information I could obtain on this subject was, that when King Solomon made his preparations for building the Temple of Jerusalem, he collected masons and workmen from all parts of the world, especially from Europe; and that these people, when assembled together, being desirous of commemorating the circumstance, and proud of their profession, invented certain mysteries, which should only be communicated to persons of their own craft.

Many of their customs are very praiseworthy. They do not interfere with any man's religion, nor attempt to alter his faith. They are liberal to the poor; and always relieve each other when in distress. Variance and strife are banished from among them; and they consider each other as *Brothers.*

I visited Spa Garden one evening when the Prince of Wales attended the Lodge. The garden was elegantly illuminated; and there was a great concourse of people of both sexes. Supper was served upon tables placed under the trees; each of which held about twenty persons, and was superintended by one of the superior Freemasons. Many of the guests were of the lower order of the people; whose spirits, being exhilarated, either by the gay scene before them, or by the wine they had drunk, talked in the most familiar but affectionate style of their *Brother George*.

My appearance in the garden having attracted much attention, I received invitations from many of the tables to favour them with my company; and as they would not take any refusal, I was compelled to pay my respects to them in turn. I was therefore obliged to take a bumper of wine at each table; and having been frequently challenged by some beautiful women to replenish my glass, I drank more wine that night than I had ever done at one time in the course of my life.

During supper, there was a grand display of fire-works, and the Prince's band of music played several delightful airs: in short, this entertainment realized the scenes described in the *Fairy Tales*, or the Arabian Nights' Entertainments.

I was frequently urged by several of the Freemasons to become one of their brethren; but as I was not perfectly convinced that their principles were conformable to my mode of thinking, I begged leave to decline the honour. They however prevailed upon Effendi Ismael, the Turkish ambassador, and Effendi Yusuf, his secretary, to embrace their tenets; and both these Mohammedans were initiated into all the mysteries of Freemasonry.

In a former part of this work I have said that the English are fond of making large collections of every thing that is rare or curious. The place where these articles are deposited is called a *Museum*. The most celebrated of these, in London, is the *British Museum*; it being a National institution, that is, the whole expence is paid by Government.[1] This building contains nearly 100 apartments, each of which is named from the articles it contains. It would be a vain attempt to enumerate the curiosities which are here preserved. All Nature has been ransacked to procure them. I was however particularly attracted by the sight of two horns, as long as those of a deer of two years old, which were extirpated from the forehead of a woman after her death. A picture of the woman is also preserved with the horns.

This Museum is situated nearly on the limits of the city: and from its windows are to be seen, at the distance of four miles, the beautiful villages of Hampstead and Highgate, both of which stand upon lofty hills, bounding the horizon. The intermediate

---

1 The British Museum was established in 1753. Founded primarily on the collections of Sir Hans Sloane, by the time of the author's visit the Museum at Montagu House contained vast collections of natural and cultural artefacts and also housed the King's Library.

space is filled by rich meadows and verdant fields. However attracting the objects in the inside, I could not refrain from turning my eyes to this delightful prospect.

One of the objects which I saw in London, that most astonished me, was a man called a *Giant*.[1] He was born in Ireland. His height was seven cubits, the length of his foot one cubit, the breadth of his hand two thirds of a cubit, and all his other limbs in proportion. My head scarcely reached to his waist; and when he stood, he was obliged to stoop, lest he should strike his head against the ceiling. This poor fellow led a miserable life, as he was never permitted to walk out, for fear he should frighten the women and children; and was compelled to shew himself to every person who would pay a shilling for admittance.

My attention was one day attracted, as I passed through Portman Square, by seeing a great assemblage of boys clothed in sooty rags, who were singing and rejoicing. I asked the reason of their apparent happiness, and was informed, that Mrs. Montague[2] had for several years lost one of her sons; that at length he was brought back to her by some chimney-sweepers; and, in gratitude for his restoration, she every year gave all the children of that description in London a grand entertainment, and they were then celebrating the anniversary of the joyful event.

I was much gratified by an inspection of the King's private Library. It contains a vast number of books in all the European languages, bound in a very elegant manner. It also contains some choice Persian and Arabic Manuscripts. I saw there a copy of the *Shāh Jehān Nāmeh*, or History of the Emperor Shah Jehan of Hindoostan; in which were inserted the Emperor's portrait, and those of his most celebrated courtiers.[3] After the plunder of

---

1   This is likely Charles O'Brien (1761-83), whose remains were on display in the Hunterian Museum in Lincoln's Inn Field.

2   Elizabeth Montagu (1718-1800; née Robinson) author and hostess, owned Montagu House on the north-west corner of Portman Square. The daughter-in-law referred to by the author above is most likely Elizabeth Montagu (née Charleton) who married Montagu's nephew, Matthew Robinson Montagu (1762-1831) in 1785. Elizabeth Montagu's only natural son died in 1744 but she adopted her nephew in 1776, at which time he assumed her surname. Records show that Elizabeth Montagu did invite young chimney sweepers to her home on an annual basis, but her motives are generally given as purely philanthropic.

3   Shah Jehan (1592-1666) was the Mughal Emperor from 1628 to 1658. During his rule Mughal art and architecture were at its pinnacle. He built the Taj Mahal at Agra and the Red Fort at Delhi.

Dehly, this book had been purchased by the Nabob Asuf ad Dowleh, and was highly prized by him. He gave it, as a mark of his special favour, to Sir J. Shore, late Governor of Bengal, who presented it to his Majesty.

In the house of Mr. Daniel,[1] I saw the portraits of many of my Indian acquaintance, and some beautiful paintings of the *Taje Mahal* (Tomb of Momtazī Zemān, the Empress of Shāh Jehān, King of the World) at Agra, and of several other places in Hindoostan, most accurately delineated. As many of the English had an opinion that there were not any buildings worth looking at in India, I was much rejoiced that Mr. Daniel had, by his skill, enabled me to convince them of the contrary; and I insisted upon several of my friends accompanying me to his house, to look at these pictures, which they could not behold without admiration.

During my residence in London, I had the good fortune to form an acquaintance with two or three Hindoostany ladies, who, from the affection they bore to their children, had accompanied them to Europe. The most distinguished of these was Mrs. Ducarrol. It is generally reported that she was a young *Hindoo* widow of rank, whom Mr. Ducarrol rescued from the funeral pile of her former husband, and, having converted her to Christianity, married her. She is very fair, and so accomplished in all the English manners and language, that I was some time in her company before I could be convinced she was a native of India. This lady introduced me to two or three of her children, from sixteen to nineteen years of age, who had every appearance of Europeans.

I visited Noor *Begum*,[2] who accompanied General De Boigne from India. She was dressed in the English fashion, and looked remarkably well. She was much pleased by my visit, and requested me to take charge of a letter for her mother, who resides at Lucknow.

---

1 This is likely Thomas Daniell (1749-1840), an artist and printmaker who traveled throughout India painting its landscape and geography. His works were widely collected and played a significant role in representing the Indian landscape to Europe.

2 Nur Begam (1770-1853; née Halime Banu), wife (by Islamic rite) of General Benoît de Boigne (1751-1830), French general in India from 1784-96. The couple came to England with their two children in 1797. She remained in London after the general's marriage to Adèle d'Osmond (1781-1866), a French writer and daughter of the Marquis d'Osmond, a French diplomat.

When General De Boigne thought proper to marry a young French woman, he made a settlement on the *Begum*, and gave her the house in which she resides. She has two children, a boy and a girl, of fifteen and sixteen years of age, who, at the time of my visit, were at school, but always spend their holidays with her.

I have before mentioned, that one of the objects I had in view, in coming to Europe, was to instruct young Englishmen in the Persian language. I however met with so little encouragement from the persons in authority, and had so many other engagements to amuse me, that I entirely relinquished the plan. I could not, however, refuse the recommendations that were brought to me by an amiable young man, Mr. Swinton;[1] and I agreed, that, if he would attend me at *eight* o'clock in the morning, I would instruct him. As he was full of ardour, and delighted with the subject, he frequently forsook his breakfast, to come to my house in time. Thanks be to God, that my efforts were crowned with success! and that he, having escaped the instructions of *self-taught* masters, has acquired such a knowledge of the principles of that language, and so correct an idea of its idiom and pronunciation, that I have no doubt, after a few years' residence in India, he will attain to such a degree of excellence as has not yet been acquired by any other Englishman!

CHAPTER XI

General description of England. Soil. Animals. Division of Land—state of cultivation. Roads. Description of London—Squares—Coffeehouses and Taverns—Clubs—Literary and other Societies—Opera, and Play-houses—Orrery—Masquerades—Routs—Public Buildings—Charities—Bank of England—Royal Exchange—Bridges—Canals.

Having, I fear, tired my Readers, by being so long the hero of my own tale, I will for some time drop this subject, and endeavour to give a description of London, and some remarks on England in general; together with a short account of the customs and manners of the people, the nature of its government, and its naval and military systems.

England, according to the ideas of a native of Hindoostan, may be said to be a mountainous country. Its soil is composed of two kinds of clay mixed with stones, and is equally adapted for

---

1 See Appendix A1 for Swinton's translation of Mirza Abu Talib's verse.

the rearing of animals or for the cultivation of grain. The rainy season not being here of any continued duration, the earth is never too much saturated. The roots of the vegetable kingdom having, in consequence, a firm hold, extend themselves to a considerable distance, and are thereby enabled to support the lofty stems and spreading branches of the numerous trees which adorn this happy land, or to yield an abundance of delicious fruits to its inhabitants. I have seen a single vine, which grew in a small courtyard paved with flat stones, cover the whole side of a house, and produce sufficient grapes for all the family during the season; some of its bunches weighing six pounds. Here also is to be found every species of flower that grows either in Persia or India. There must certainly be something very peculiar in the climate and soil of England, which causes it not only to yield such a variety of the productions of the earth, but also such a difference in the tempers and manners of its inhabitants, that no two of them appear to think or act alike.

The domestic animals of England are all excellent in their kind, especially the horses, dogs, and cattle. The latter are much larger than those of India; and the cows give a much greater abundance of milk, which yields delicious butter and cheese: their flesh also is admirable.

The English have particular horses for every kind of work. Those for draught are so very large and powerful, as to be considered a curiosity in other countries. They are used only for heavy carriages, or for ploughing the land; it not being customary to use bullocks for that purpose, as with us. One of these horses will carry as great a load as a camel, and will work day and night. The saddle-horses are not handsome, but very useful; and so quiet, that one man may lead ten of them at once with a halter, and they will follow him over wall or ditch without any trouble or difficulty. All the land in England is divided into fields and parks, which are inclosed either with hedges or walls. Many of the parks contain *country-houses*: these are the rural habitations of the nobility or people of fortune, and comprehend, besides the house and offices, gardens, orchards, fish-ponds, and pasture-grounds for both sheep and deer. Many of these estates have also rivers running through them, and extensive woods of valuable timber. Some of the proprietors of these houses reside in them the whole year; or, when they have business in London, hire a ready-furnished habitation for the time: but the people of wealth seldom remain in them above five or six months. Like the Arab tribes, they forsake the cities during the summer season, and seek, in the fresh and wholesome air of the country, a supply of health and vigour for the ensuing winter.

Every part of this country appears highly cultivated: though, to judge from the few people whom I saw in the fields, or met on the road, I should think the population very scanty; and I was frequently astonished how the agriculture was carried on.

The roads throughout England are very good; they are wide, and formed of stone or gravel; and wherever they are intersected by ravines or rivers, good and substantial bridges are erected; by which means travelling in this country is not attended with any difficulty; and, at the distance of every six or seven miles, there are inns, which afford all things requisite either for rest or recreation. The villages resemble those of India, as, although the houses are generally built of brick or stone, and have chimneys, the roofs are low and thatched.

London is the capital of the Empire, and is the largest city I have ever seen: it consists of three towns joined together, and is twenty-four miles in circumference: but its hamlets, which to a foreigner appear a continuation of the city, extend several miles in every direction; and new streets are each year added to the town, the houses of which are frequently bought or rented before they are finished, and in the course of twelve months are completely inhabited. Thus during my residence there, ten new streets were added to the town. The houses in London are generally built of brick, though a few of them are of hewn stone: they are commonly four stories high, and have regular rows of glazed windows in front. A few of the noblemen's houses have courts or porticoes before the door, which add to their grandeur. The roofs are sloped like a tent, and are covered either with tiles, or thin stones called *slates*. The interior is divided and furnished like those already described in Dublin; and the streets and shops are also lighted at night, in the same manner. The shops are in regular rows; and are very rich, extensive, and beautiful, beyond any thing I can describe. The greatest ornament London can boast, is its numerous squares; many of which are very extensive, and only inhabited by people of large fortune. Each square contains a kind of garden in its center, surrounded with iron rails, to which every proprietor of a house in the square has a key, and where the women and children can walk, at all hours, without being liable to molestation or insult.

In this city the coffee-houses are not so numerous as in Paris: here is scarcely a street, however, in which there is not either an inn, hotel, or coffee-house, to be found: many of these have a magnificent appearance, and are on so extensive a scale, that in the London Tavern they can prepare a dinner for five hundred persons of rank, at a few hours' notice. I frequently dined at this tavern, with the Indian Club, by invitation; and although several other large parties were assembled there at the same time, we were not sensible, either from a want of attendance, or from any noise or confusion, that any other persons were in the house.

Of the many admirable institutions of the English, there was none that pleased me more than their *Clubs*. These, generally speaking, are composed of a society of persons of the same rank, profession, or mode of thinking, who meet at a tavern at stated times every month, where they either dine or sup together, and confer with each other on the topics most interesting to them, or discuss such matters of business as, for want of room, could not be easily done in a private house.

These societies frequently consist of one or two hundred members; but, as seldom above thirty or forty assemble at one time, they are easily accommodated. The absent members pay a small fine, which is carried to the account of the expences of the dinner, and the remainder is paid by those present.

There are a great variety of these clubs. Some are appropriated to gambling, or chess; others are entirely composed of painters, artists, authors, &c. &c. The Indian Club consists of a number of gentlemen who have resided for some years in the East. At these clubs, no person but a member is admitted, without a particular invitation; and, in order to become a *member*, every person must be ballotted for; that is, his name and general character are submitted to the society; and if any gentleman present objects to him, he is immediately rejected.

They have also societies of nearly a similar nature, which meet at the house of the president, where they are entertained with tea, coffee, sherbet, &c. Of this kind is the Royal Society, who meet every Sunday evening at the house of Sir J. Banks, where all new inventions are first examined; and if any of them are found deficient, they are rectified, by the joint consultation of the members. All the great literary characters assemble here, and submit their works to the inspection of the society. Through the kindness of the President, I was frequently present at these meetings, and derived much mental satisfaction from them.

I also frequently attended the meetings of the Musical Society, at the house of Lady Charlotte— , where I was always much delighted by the harmonious voices and skill of the performers.

In London there is an Opera, and several Play-houses, open to every person who can pay for admission. As these differ but little from the Play-houses described in my account of Dublin, it is unnecessary to say more respecting them. There are also so many other places of public amusement, that a stranger need never be at a loss to pass his time agreeably.

A philosopher named Walker[1] lately hired one of the old Play-houses, in which he exhibited, every night during the summer, an astronomical machine, called an *Orrery*, by which all the revolutions of the planets and heavenly bodies were perfectly described. From the centre of a dome twenty yards in height was suspended a glass globe, in which a bright lamp was burning that represented the Sun, and turned round, like the wheel of a mill, on its axis. Next to the Sun was suspended a small globe that represented Mercury; a third representing Venus; a fourth, the Earth; and a fifth, the Moon: the sixth was Mars; the seventh, Jupiter, attended by four satellites; the eighth, Saturn, with five attending satellites; and the ninth, Georgium Sidus, a lately-discovered planet, with six attending satellites. All these globes were put in motion by the turning of a wheel; and exhibited, at one view, all the revolutions of the Solar system, with such perspicuity as must convince the most prejudiced person of the superiority, nay, infallibility, of the Copernican System. I was so much delighted by the novelty of this exhibition, and the information I received from it, that I went to see it several times.

The English have an extraordinary kind of amusement, which they call a *Masquerade*. In these assemblies, which consist of several hundred persons of both sexes, every one wears a short veil or mask, made of pasteboard, over the face; and each person dresses according to his or her fancy. Many represent Turks, Persians, Indians, and foreigners of all nations; but the greater number disguise themselves as mechanics or artists, and imitate all their customs or peculiarities with great exactness. Being thus unknown to each other, they speak with great freedom, and exercise their wit and genius.

At one of these entertainments, where I was present, a gentleman entered the room dressed in a handsome bed-gown, night-

---

1   Adam Walker (c.1730-1821), lecturer and writer, issued publications on astronomy, mathematics, and philosophy. Walker's eidouraion, a transparent orrery which demonstrated planetary movements, was widely exhibited, but Abu Talib is likely referring to its exhibition in the Theatre Royal, Haymarket, where it was accompanied by a mechanical harpsichord of Walker's invention.

cap, and slippers, and, addressing the company, said he paid several guineas a week for his lodgings above stairs; that they had kept him awake all night by their noise; and that, notwithstanding it was near morning, they did not appear inclined to disperse; they were, therefore, a parcel of rude, impudent people, and he should send for constables to seize them. I thought the man was serious, but my companions laughed, and applauded his ingenuity.

Several of the ladies of quality permit their acquaintances to come to their houses in masquerade dresses, previous to their going to the public room, where they exhibit their wit and skill at repartee.

They have other public amusements, called *Balls*, which are confined to dancing and supper; but there are so many private entertainments of this kind given, that the public ones are not well attended in London.

I one day received an *invitation card* from a lady, on which was written, only, "Mrs.— at home on — evening." At first, I thought it meant an assignation; but, on consulting one of my friends, I was informed that the lady gave a *Rout* that night; and that a rout meant an assemblage of people without any particular object; that the mistress of the house had seldom time to say more to any of her guests than to inquire after their health; but that the servants supplied them with tea, coffee, ice, &c.; after which they had liberty to depart, and make room for others. I frequently afterwards attended these routs, to some of which three or four hundred persons came during the course of the night.

The public buildings in London are innumerable, and a description of them alone would fill a volume. They are generally built of stone, and many are very massy and grand. The principal of them are, Westminster Abbey, which contains the tombs of all the Kings; the Cathedral of St. Paul's; the Foundling and Lying-in Hospitals; and those of Greenwich and Chelsea, for naval and military pensioners. There are also a number of Colleges, such as I have described at Oxford; and several Schools, which contain four or five hundred boys each, supported entirely by subscription, or by charitable donations. These schools may be considered as a little world, in which the English are taught every thing useful, honourable, and virtuous.

English charity does not consist in giving a small sum of money to a beggar, or a poor poet, or a starving musician. These persons they have a great aversion to; and should one of them follow a coach for miles, he would lose his labour, and not be able to soften the hearts of those seated therein. But their charities are of a public nature; for in every parish there is a house built for the poor, where they may reside, and receive a daily allowance of food. If a family be reduced to poverty by any accident, they have only to make known their condition to the parish officers, who are obliged immediately to admit them to the established allowance.

These poor-houses are supported by a tax paid by every housekeeper in the parish; and the amount of their revenues has been estimated at *three crores of rupees*, or £.3,000,000, annually. Notwithstanding this immense expenditure, I saw a number of beggars in London, but was told they were idle, worthless people, who preferred this mode of a life to a regular stipend. Sometimes the receipts of the Play-houses or Opera, &c. are dedicated to charitable purposes; and such is the attention of Government to the welfare of the poor, that if any individual can devise a scheme by which they will be benefited, the Ministers lay it before Parliament, and obtain permission to appropriate *lacs* of rupees for its support.

In this city there are several hundred bankers, who have very extensive concerns all over the world. There is, however, one house vastly preeminent over all the others, which is called the *Bank of England*: it is a very massy building, and contains nearly two hundred apartments, each of which is appropriated to a particular office. The partners of this bank are numerous, and constitute a *Company*, similar to the *East-India Company*, the business of which is managed by a certain number of Directors. In this bank is lodged all public money, and all the treasure of the nation. It is said to contain not less than £.100,000,000, in specie and bullion. The profits of this Company must be immense, as they seldom pay any demand in money; and their notes, which do not bear any interest, pass current, as cash, all over the empire.

Opposite the Bank is situated another public building, called the *Exchange*, where all the merchants of the city assemble every day, to make their bargains; and where intelligence is daily brought from every part of the world, whether of a commercial or political nature.

It has been before mentioned, that the present capital is composed of three towns; called, Westminster, the City, and the Borough. The latter is situated on the south bank of the river, and is united to the others by three handsome stone bridges, each of which is from a quarter to half a mile long. Lower down the river, at a place called Gravesend, they are constructing a very extraordinary bridge, if such it can be called. It is an iron tunnel, which is to extend from one side of the Thames[1] to the other, all the way under ground. It will, consequently, be quite dark; but, by the aid of lamps, horses and carriages are to pass at all hours, while ships of the greatest burthen are sailing over their heads. This appears to me one of the boldest undertakings, and will be the most surprising work of art in England, if it succeed.

All the foreign trade enters London by the Thames; but there are various canals, communicating with this river, to every part of the country, by which the internal commerce is carried on. By means of these canals, all heavy articles are conveyed from one part of the kingdom to another, at one third of the expence they could be conveyed by land; and, consequently, the proprietors are enabled to sell them at a lower price.

CHAPTER XII

Of the state of the Arts and Sciences in England. Utility of the Art of Printing. Newspapers. Facility of travelling. Price of Provisions. Hothouses. Excellence of the British Navy. The Author gives an account of the War with Denmark. He visits Woolwich—Description of the Docks and Iron-Foundry. Account of the British Army. Grand Review at Windsor. Tower of London.

Of the inventions of Europe, the utility of which may not appear at first sight to an Asiatic, the art of printing is the most admirable. By its aid, thousands of copies, of any scientific, moral, or religious book, may be circulated among the people in a very short time; and by it, the works of celebrated authors are handed down to posterity, free from the errors and imperfections of a manuscript. To this art the English are indebted for the humble but useful publication of *Newspapers*, without which life would be irksome to them. These are read by all ranks of people, from the prince to the beggar. They are printed daily, and sent every morning to the houses of the rich; but those who cannot afford to subscribe for one, go and read them at the coffee-rooms or public-houses. These papers give an account of every thing that is transacting, either at home or abroad: they contain a minute description of all the battles that are fought, either by sea or by land; the debates in the Houses of Parliament; the state of

---

1   The Thames at this part is as wide as the Ganges. (Original note)

the crops in the country; the price of grain and all other articles; the death or birth of any great personage; and even give information, that, on such a night, such a play will be performed, or such an actor will make his appearance.

Soon after my arrival in London, an entertainment was given at Vauxhall for the benefit of some public charity.[1] Previous to its taking place, the managers sent me a polite message, requesting I would favour them with my company; but that, as my appearance would be attended with great benefit to the undertaking, they hoped I would excuse their not accepting any thing for my admission. As I was ever ready to assist any public charity, I agreed to go; and it was immediately inserted in the newspapers, that the *Prince Abu Taleb* would honour the gardens with his presence on the appointed night. As Vauxhall is situated on the opposite side of the river, and I had never been seen in that part of the town, the crowd of people who assembled in the evening was greater than ever before known, and it was with much difficulty I could pass through them. Whenever I went to Court, or paid my respects to one of the Princes or ministers of state, the circumstance was always reported by the newspapers of the following day. In all these advertisements, they did me the honour of naming me *The Persian Prince*. I declare I never assumed the title; but I was so much better known by it than by my own name, that I found it in vain to contend with my godfathers.[2]

I am convinced no country in the world affords so much facility of travelling as England. People of fortune, who travel in their own carriages, need never feel fatigue; but if a person is in a hurry, he has only to take a place in the *Mail Coach*, and may be conveyed a thousand miles in seven or eight days, well secured from all the inclemencies of the weather, and sure of a good breakfast and dinner. These carriages pay a tax to Government, and are used by people of all ranks. Although these vehicles are in use in France, and all over Europe, there is no country where

---

1 By the late eighteenth century, Vauxhall Gardens, one of London's premier venues for public entertainment, featured illuminated walkways, various architectural caprices (including structures in ostensible oriental styles), and regular musical performances.

2 *Mirza* means a Prince, but it should follow the name: prefixed, it shews the person to be a descendant of Mohammed. Some people have supposed, because the author was not a *Prince,* he was unworthy of the attention paid him: this however is a mistake; he was a Gentleman by birth, education, and employment, and a Khān (Lord) by creation. (Translator's note)

the same attention is paid to the comfort and ease of the passengers as in England. I complained of the inconvenience I suffered in Ireland by the jolting of the carriage, and what I then thought the rudeness of the coachman; but after experiencing the mode of travelling in France, I was convinced my former complaints were all groundless. This will be further explained in the sequel.

Living is very expensive in England; and a good appetite is a serious evil to a poor man. Some idea of the rate of the expence may be formed by the prices of the common articles of food. Meat of all kinds sells, upon an average, for seven-pence half-penny a pound; bread, four pounds for fifteen-pence; and porter, five-pence a quart. Vegetables and fruit vary in their prices, according to the season of the year.

One of the greatest luxuries the English enjoy is the produce of their hot-houses. In these buildings they raise vegetables and fruit in the coldest season of the year; and the tables of the rich are covered with pine-apples, melons, and other fruits of the torrid zone. In this instance they excel us; for none of the Emperors of Hindoostan, in all the plenitude of their power, could ever have forced a gooseberry or a cherry, two of the most common fruits in Europe, to grow in their dominions.

[Here follows a minute description of a hot-house, which is omitted.]

★ ★ ★

The great perfection to which the English have brought their navy is, doubtless, the chief cause of their prosperity, and the principal source of all their wealth. By means of their navy, they can at all times send an army to invade their enemy's country. If they succeed, it is well; if not, they can return with little loss. Their neighbours, the French, on the contrary, although they possess an innumerable army of brave troops, cannot injure the English, who are constantly well protected by their floating batteries, which suffer not a Frenchman to pass the sea.

The wisdom and skill manifested by the English, in the construction and navigation of their vessels, with the excellent regulations for preserving the health and discipline of the crew, are beyond my powers to describe. The following instance of their coolness and dexterity may give some faint idea of their character. Lord Teignmouth[1] informed me, that when returning from

---

1 See p. 66, note 3.

India, and during a gale of wind off the Cape of Good Hope, the mainmast of the ship was struck by lightning, which instantly set fire to the sails and rigging; and before they could extinguish the flames, the mast was burned down nearly level with the deck: but, by the activity and dexterity of the crew, the fire was prevented from communicating with the other sails, or any other part of the ship. All this was done with so little noise and confusion, that neither he, nor any of his family, who were below deck, in the great cabin, (although it happened in the day-time) knew any thing of the matter till several hours after, when, the gale having abated, they went on deck, and observed the mast gone.

During the late war, four of the kings of Europe, viz. the sovereigns of Russia, Prussia, Denmark, and Sweden, being irritated against the English for searching their ships, from a suspicion of their having French goods on board, entered into a confederacy to punish the English navy, if they persevered in this system. They also ordered all the merchant vessels of that nation in their ports to be seized, and prohibited the exportation of any naval stores from their countries. When this intelligence was brought to Great Britain, the generality of the people were much alarmed; but the Government shewed no apprehensions, and sent Lord Nelson,[1] with fifty ships of war, large and small, to cruize in the North Sea, on the coasts of these four kings; and gave him orders to seize, burn, or sink, all the ships he should meet with belonging to those nations, and thus revenge the affront offered to the British flag.

Lord Nelson having proceeded with his fleet up the North Sea, arrived at the narrow entrance of the Baltic Sea. Here his passage was warmly opposed by two forts, one on the Denmark, the other on the Norway shore, assisted by several large ships moored close to the land. The English however forced the passage, and cast anchor opposite Copenhagen, the capital of Denmark, when they commenced a dreadful fire, both on the

---

1 Horatio Nelson (1758-1805), Viscount Nelson, had recently returned after defeating the French at Abu Qir Bay. Britain's foremost naval hero, at the time of Abu Talib's visit his victories in the Mediterranean were the cause of much celebration in London. However, it is important to recognize that his victory at Abu Qir had lasting effects on the Islamic world, because it stranded French forces in Egypt. During their occupation, the French initiated the process of modernization which catalyzed both reform and resistance among communities ostensibly under the rule of the Ottoman emperor.

town and on the ships in the harbour. The Danes were not deficient either in skill or bravery, and the contest was long doubtful. Many of the English ships were severely injured, and 6000 of their men killed; when, at length, the Danes sued for peace, and acknowledged Great Britain to be sovereign of the ocean. All the English merchant ships were immediately restored; and the Emperor of Russia dying very soon after, the other kings were glad to make peace, and comply with the terms of the conqueror.

VERSE.

> Better is a living body, and laughing enemies,
> Than a dead body, and crying friends!

In short, the British seamen look with much contempt upon the navy of all other nations, and consider them to be only fit for tenders, or carriers of provision, for their own fleet.

In the year 1801, the number of ships of war belonging to the Royal navy was eight hundred and three, carrying from sixteen to a hundred guns each; and there was a sufficient supply of timber and marine stores in the kingdom to build as many more. Of the number of their merchant ships, He only knows, who knows all things, whether in heaven or on earth!

The service of the navy is esteemed not only very honourable, but often very lucrative; for whatever ships of the enemy are taken, whether by the fleet or by a single ship, they become the property of the captors. The only restriction is, that if the ship so taken, or its guns, are thought worthy of his Majesty's service, the king can take them for that purpose, at a reasonable price. Thus the *Victorieux*, in which I made the voyage from Leghorn to Constantinople, was a French vessel, taken by the fleet under the command of Lord Duncan,[1] and was purchased from the captors for a large sum of money for his Majesty's service.

In England, there are several Royal dockyards, for fitting out and repairing these ships; but the two principal ones are Portsmouth and Woolwich. The former is also a celebrated seaport, or rendezvous of the fleets, previous to their sailing on any expedition. As it is at a considerable distance from London, I did not visit it; but, by the kindness of my friend Colonel Peach, I had an opportunity of inspecting every part of Woolwich. I there saw

---

1 Adam Duncan (1731-1804), Viscount Duncan, was then an admiral in the British navy.

several large ships on the stocks; and such stores of timber, iron, canvas, &c. that had the war continued for ten years longer, they would not have required a fresh supply. I was particularly attracted by the mode of casting the cannon-balls and shells; also by the manner of boring and shaping the exterior surface of the guns at the same time, all done by the motion of a wheel turned by a steam-engine, which so facilitated the work, that an old woman or a child might have performed the rest of the operation.

In conclusion of this subject, I think I may venture to assert, that one half of the people of England are either sailors, or in some way connected with the navy.

The British army consists of cavalry, infantry, and artillery, and is very numerous and well disciplined; but, as it is dispersed in different parts of the empire, it is seldom that more than twenty or twenty-five thousand can be seen at one time; and this only happens when they are assembled to be reviewed either by the King or by the Commander-in-chief.

I had the good fortune to be present at one of these reviews, but found considerable difficulty in effecting it. All the troops in the vicinity of London, amounting to 25,000, having been ordered to assemble near Windsor, to be reviewed by his Majesty, Mr. Clive and I set out from London the day previous to the time appointed, and arrived at Windsor early the same evening; but so many people had come on the same errand, that we could not get any accommodation at the inns; and although we offered six guineas for the use of two beds at any private house for the night, we could not obtain them. We wandered, for some time, up and down the town, in the greatest distress; but at length my friend recollecting that he had an acquaintance who kept a large school in the neighbourhood, we proceeded thither, and fortunately reached the house just as the family were going to supper. The worthy schoolmaster received us most hospitably; and having directed four of his boys to sleep in two beds, he gave us their vacant ones.

Next morning, after breakfast, we proceeded on horseback to the parade, where we found an immense multitude of spectators assembled. I can safely aver there were five thousand carriages, filled, both in the inside and on the tops, with handsome women, dressed in their best attire. During the whole of my residence in Europe, I never saw so much beauty assembled as on that day.

The troops were drawn up in a circle, into the middle of which the King, attended by the Princes and general officers, rode. His Majesty was first welcomed by a discharge of cannon from each brigade, after which he was saluted by all the troops with their muskets. They then broke into columns, and marched past the Duke of York[1] in grand divisions. I was lucky enough to obtain a station near his Royal Highness, opposite to whom a select band of music, belonging to the third regiment of Guards, was drawn up, and played some of the most charming tunes and melodious pieces of music I ever heard. It was nearly four o'clock before all the troops had passed the Commander-in-chief: we therefore hurried back to London as soon as the review was over, not wishing either to sleep on the road, or again to annoy our friends at the school.

The *Horse Races* at Newmarket annually occasion a vast assemblage of people; but as that diversion may be seen in Calcutta, I pass it over.

The object most worthy of visiting, in or near London, is, I think, the fort commonly called the Tower. By the introduction of my friend Colonel Brathwaite, I was permitted to see every part of this fortress. Immediately on my entrance, I was conducted to the Royal Menagery, where I was shewn lions, tigers, panthers, and some other savage animals which had been chiefly brought from Africa, but of whose names I had never before heard. We then proceeded to the Jewel Office, where they exhibited to us the crown, the mace, and all the coronation jewels, both of the King and Queen: amongst these were a ruby and an emerald, each of which cost ten lacs of rupees (£.125,000), and a number of valuable diamonds and other precious stones. During this exhibition we were locked up in the room, although all the articles were well secured by glass-cases and iron gratings. We afterwards went to the Armoury, in the yard of which were lying an innumerable quantity of cannon of all sizes: two of these were each twenty-five feet long. The room under the armoury was a quarter of a mile in length, and said to contain bridles, saddles, harness, and other equipments for 60,000 cavalry and artillery horses. The armoury is seven hundred paces long: in it are disposed, in a very curious and beautiful manner, muskets, bayonets, halberds, swords, and pistols, sufficient for an army of 120,000 men. At one end of the room is an apartment containing the statues of eighteen of the Kings of England, on horse-back, with all the armour which they were accustomed to wear in their life-time; and, in fact, they

---

1 Prince Frederick (1763-1827), Duke of York and Albany, second son of George III.

looked as if still prepared for battle: each horse has also his groom attending him.

The armour which is here preserved is of a very ancient date, and is not composed of chains, like that of Hindoostan, but each limb has a complete piece of iron to cover it, and the whole fits the body as exactly as a suit of clothes: there is also a mask for the face, and iron gloves with joints at the knuckles, so that a person may even write in them. They assert that, formerly, the kings wore this armour the whole day, and never took it off but when they wished to sleep.

End of Vol. I.

CHAPTER XIII

The science of Mechanics much esteemed in England—various uses to which it is applied—Mills—Founderies—Steam Engines—Waterworks, &c. Account of the modes of Engraving. Manufactories. Staple commodities of England. Public Illuminations on the Proclamation of Peace. Character of the London Tradesmen.

In England, labour is much facilitated by the aid of mechanism; and by its assistance the price of commodities is much reduced: for if, in their great manufactories, they made use of horses, bullocks, or men, as in other countries, the prices of their goods would be enormous. It is impossible, without the aid of drawings or plates, to describe the mode and the various uses to which it is applied: I shall however mention a few of the instances, that some general idea may be formed of the subject. I shall only add, that the English are so prejudiced in favour of this science, that they often expend immense sums, and frequently fail two or three times, before they succeed in getting the machinery of any extensive work in order. The French, on the contrary, although good mathematicians, are content with manual labour, if any difficulty occurs in erecting the machinery.

The first and most simple of all these works are the mills for grinding corn: these are of two kinds, water-mills and wind-mills, and are both known in *some parts* of India. The only hand-mills ever used in London are small iron things, for the purpose of grinding coffee or pepper. I however think *our hand-mills* might prove very useful with an army, where it will often happen that the hungry troops make a seizure of wheat or barley without having the means of grinding it: they should also be provided with iron plates, for baking cakes on.

Another kind of these works are iron-founderies, the great wheels of which are worked by *steam*, in a very surprising manner. In these they cast cannon, beat out anchors, and do all other large work, which could not be effected by manual labour, the sledge itself being more than any man could lift.

By similar machinery they can beat out sheets of copper and lead to any extent: and, as they have not the art of making a cement of lime in this country which will keep out water, they cover all their flat-roofed houses with lead. I have seen some buildings, twenty yards square, covered with this metal.

The manufacture of needles astonished me. A bundle of steel wires was thrown into a wheel, which, at *one turn*, threw them out on the opposite side, cut into a number of pieces of the proper length: these were caught in a basket by a boy, who handed them to a person whose business it was to form the eyes and sharpen the points, both of which he effected by machinery in the shortest time imaginable.

If my astonishment was excited at the needle manufactory, it was much more so when I saw a *spinning engine*. By the turning of one large wheel, a hundred others were put in motion, which spun at the same time some thousand threads, of sufficient fineness to make very good muslin. A few women or boys are sufficient to attend the machine, for the purpose of joining the threads when they break, or of giving a fresh supply of cotton. It must however be acknowledged, that the cloth made of this thread is not equal to that sent from India: it neither wears nor washes so well, which is perhaps owing to the thread being over twisted. The wire and the rope manufactories are also very curious. It is asserted, that they can draw or spin out either of these articles to the length of twenty miles, if requisite, without any junction being perceptible.

I accompanied my friend Mr. Kelby to his Porter Brewery, which was of an immense extent, and contained many thousand barrels. His steam-engine for raising water was of the largest size; and he assured me, that if he had not that machine, he should be under the necessity of constantly employing fifty horses; the expence of which, and of their grooms, if added to the price of the porter, the favourite beverage of the populace of London, would render it so dear, that an insurrection might be apprehended.

The English are celebrated for their manufacture of *paper* of all kinds. I was told they could make a sheet of it twenty yards square; and during my residence amongst them, they discovered that excellent paper might be made of common straw.

The hydraulic machine for supplying London with water is a stupendous work. By its means, an ample supply of water is raised from the river Thames, so as constantly to keep full a lofty reservoir, whence, by means of conduits and leaden pipes, it is conveyed all over the town, and even to the upper rooms of houses four stories high, to the great comfort and ease of the inhabitants. Besides this supply, there is generally in every square or large yard a machine called a *pump*, whence, by the slightest exertion of the arm, the water is easily forced: it is a very simple contrivance, and much preferable to our wells.

They have engines for expressing oil from seed, and others for thrashing and winnowing corn. In short, the English carry their passion for mechanics to such an extent, that machinery is introduced into their kitchens, and a very complete engine is used even to roast a *chicken*. I was also told, that an instrument had lately been invented for mincing meat and chopping onions. The English are naturally impatient, and do not like these trifling and tedious employments; besides which, the expence of a common servant in England is eight times more than in India.

The art of printing being well understood in Calcutta, I have said but little on that subject. There is, however, another science, nearly similar, called *engraving*, much in use in Europe; of which I shall endeavour to give some description. This art is subservient to painting; and by its aid, the copies of a picture may be multiplied at pleasure, though generally on a smaller scale. For this purpose, a sheet of copper must be procured first of the size required, on which is spread a coat of thin white wax or similar substance; on this the outlines of the picture are drawn with black lead; and the engraver, with various sharp instruments, then cuts through the wax into the copper: or it may be done by aquafortis, (as the lines drawn by a pen dipped in that liquid soon eat their way into the copper,) and afterwards finished by the engraver, who must also possess a considerable knowledge of painting. The plate being ready, the prints are struck off nearly in the same manner as books are. If it be wished to have them coloured, so as to resemble the pictures more nearly, this can be done by boys or women, at a very cheap rate. By these means, the copy of a picture may be procured for a guinea, the original of which would have cost a hundred.

On entering one of the extensive manufactories in England, the mind is at first bewildered by the number and variety of articles displayed therein: but, after recovering from this first impression, and having coolly surveyed all the objects around, every thing appears conducted with so much regularity and precision, that a person is induced to suppose one of the meanest capacity might superintend and direct the whole process. Whatever requires strength or numbers is effected by engines; if clearness of sight is wanted, magnifying-glasses are at hand; and if deep reflection is necessary to combine all the parts, whereby to insure a unity of action, so many aids are derived from the numerous artists employed in the different parts of the work, that the union of the whole seems not to require any great exertion of genius. Thus, in all kinds of clock-work, the wheels, chains, springs, &c. are made by different artists, and only require a person who is conversant in the business to select and put the pieces together.

The manufactories in which the English excel the other nations of Europe, are, cutlery, and all kinds of iron work; furniture made of the most valuable species of wood; leather of every denomination; clocks and watches; broad-cloth; satins and silks of various sorts; glass ware of every description; guns, pistols, and pictures. These articles are carried to all parts of the world, and sold to great advantage.

The sword-cutlers' and gun-smiths' shops in London are particularly well worth seeing, as they generally contain many curiosities. They shewed me a new-invented lock that, if the gun should be immersed for a week in water, the powder in the pan would suffer no injury; and they assured me, that it was even possible to discharge the gun *under water.*

It is customary in London to illuminate the town, either on the King or Queen's birth-day, on the intelligence of any great victory, or on the proclamation of peace. Although I had seen a number of illuminations in Hindoostan, and was present at Lucknow during the marriage of Vizier Aly the adopted son of the late Nabob, when a fort five miles in circumference, with regular bastions, towers, and gateways, was formed with bamboos, and covered at night with lamps which required 20,000 men to attend them, yet there was so much sameness and want of variety in this display, that, in my opinion, it fell far short of the illuminations of London.

In England, on account of the uncertainty of the weather, all the lamps are composed of glass; many are cut with a diamond, and others are coloured; these are suspended either on nails driven into the walls of the houses, or on frames of wood, formed into various figures and devices. When the lamps are lighted, and properly disposed, being of different colours, they can be so arranged as to represent any figure or inscription that is required. Thus I have seen a good representation of the King, and of the Queen, seated on their thrones, with crowns over their heads. But, as this is a voluntary act, and every person illuminates his house at his own expence, he is allowed to indulge his fancy, either in displaying the fertility of his imagination, or the extent of his loyalty, by the device he exhibits; and this circumstance produces a great variety of matter. On the proclamation of the late peace, previous to which the price of all the necessaries of life had risen to an enormous height, one of the tradesmen had the figures of a loaf of bread and a butt of porter very well imitated, in a falling position, with the following inscription under them: "WE ARE ABOUT TO FALL." This device was the subject of much mirth and laughter among the common people.

These illuminations, beheld from the middle of a square, whence the four grand streets leading in different directions can be viewed, surpass any thing of the kind I have ever seen. The concourse of people, both in carriages and on foot, on these occasions, is so great, that I have been sometimes for an hour in one of the widest streets, viz. Oxford or St. James's Street, without being able to advance the flight of an arrow. In this situation I have been much alarmed, as the people are constantly discharging muskets and letting off fire-works on all sides; so that if a weak person was to fall in the crowd, it is probable he would never rise again.

On the third day of the rejoicings for peace, having heard that M. Otto,[1] the French Envoy, had expended £2000 in preparations for a grand illumination which was to be exhibited on that night, I resolved, in order to avoid the crowd, to go and examine the devices during the day; supposing, that however better they would look when lighted up, I should still be able to form a just idea of the plan, and should avoid all risk of being trodden to death. I therefore proceeded towards Portman Square, where the Envoy resided; but, on approaching the square, I found a great crowd assembled, and the mob abusing the Envoy. Upon inquiring the cause, I learned that the Frenchman had chosen for his motto, "PEACE AND CONCORD." Some of the soldiers who had barracks in that neighbourhood, having more courage than wisdom, and more skill in the use of their swords than their pens, thinking he meant a reflection on the English, and that they were glad to make *Peace* because they were *Conquered*, began to break his lamps. M. Otto, surprised and alarmed at this circumstance, came out, and endeavoured to explain, that *Concord* bore no allusion to the events of the war, but was synonymous with Unanimity and Friendship. They would not however be convinced, until he agreed to change the motto to "PEACE AND AMITY."

---

1 Louis-Guillaume Otto (1753-1817) was the French Commissioner who negotiated and signed the Treaty of London in October 1801 which set the stage for the Peace of Amiens. The author's description of the celebrations tallies with overwhelming public enthusiasm for the Treaty.

Having been disappointed in my morning excursion, I determined to run all risks, and to see the grand display at night. Between eleven and twelve o'clock I left my own house, and attempted to go up Oxford Street, but was soon interrupted by the assemblage of coaches and crowd of foot people. I therefore turned off into one of the cross streets, and, knowing that part of the town well, succeeded in reaching one of the streets that led into the square. Here I was obliged to lay fast hold of the iron railing, and, as opportunity offered, pushed on a step or two at a time. At length I reached the square; but the press was so excessive, that my clothes were torn, and I lost my cane. The women were at the same time crying out, for God's sake, to be liberated, or that they should be squeezed to death; but no one listened to their complaints, and most of them lost their hats, ear-rings, and necklaces. In this situation I endeavoured to return home; but this I found more difficult than to advance. However, after much perseverance, I got into a corner of the square, where, being more at my ease, I resolved to remain till morning should thin the spectators. In this plan I succeeded, and was completely satiated with M. Otto's exhibition, which fell far short of my expectations, and by no means equalled Mr. Hope's in Cavendish Square.

The shopkeepers and tradesmen in London are in general people of education; in their dress and manners they are not distinguishable from noblemen or gentlemen; and are so courteous and polite, that, should the purchaser be ever so troublesome or litigious, they never give a rude or angry answer.

One day, a gentleman, either by way of a joke, or wishing to try the temper of a tradesman, went to his shop, and desired to see some broad-cloth. The man took down several webs of cloth, all of which were rejected: these were taken away, and another set displayed; but some were thought too coarse, others too dear, and none of their colours approved. At length, having kept the shopkeeper employed for a whole hour, the gentleman appeared satisfied with a piece of uncommon elegance at twenty-five shillings a yard, and the tradesman expected to have received an order for at least five or six yards; but was much surprised by his eccentric customer's taking out of his pocket a shilling, and desiring to have the worth of that coin cut off the cloth. The tradesman, however, preserved his temper; and taking the shilling, laid it on the corner of the web, from which he cut a piece exactly the same size, and presented it to the gentleman. They then parted, bowing respectfully to each other.

My watch having met with an accident, I determined to buy

another, but of a low price. I therefore went into a silversmith's shop, and looked at several. Having at length fixed on a silver one, the price of which was seven guineas, I told the man where I lived, and informed him I should keep the watch till next day, when, if it was approved of, I would pay him; otherwise, I would return his property. Notwithstanding I was a perfect stranger, he consented; and I carried away the watch, for one or two of my friends to examine; but they all found fault with it, and strongly advised me to return it. I was however so overcome by the watch-maker's courtesy, that I was ashamed to follow their advice, and therefore paid him his money.

These shopkeepers will send home the most trifling parcel that is purchased of them, even from one end of the town to the other; and often give one or two months' credit to people they know nothing about: they are, in consequence, frequently liable to be taken in by swindlers.

One of the ladies of light reputation, who lived in the same street with me, contracted a number of these debts, and went off without paying them. Although she was afterwards discovered, and carried before a magistrate, as she had no property remaining, her creditors thought it more advisable to let her go, than to put her in jail, where they would have been obliged to support her.

CHAPTER XIV

Mode in which the English spend their time. Of the length of the days and nights in England. Mode of living of the English. Division of employment between the Sexes. Regulations respecting Women. Liberty of the Common People. Anecdotes of the Prince of Wales and Governor Hastings. English Servants. Liberty of the higher classes. Duels. Education of Children.

I shall here endeavour to give some account of the mode in which the English pass their time. The middling class, in London, divide their time in the following manner: they rise from eight to nine o'clock in the morning: their dressing employs them an hour; after which they sit down to the breakfast-table, where they spend another hour: from that time till five in the evening, they employ themselves either in business or in walking and riding: at six they sit down to dinner; and if there is company invited, the men seldom rise from table before nine o'clock: they then join the ladies, to drink tea and coffee; after which they play cards, or listen to music, till eleven, when the party breaks up, and they retire to their beds.

It is thus evident, that for sixteen hours they do not indulge themselves in repose; and being constantly employed, the time does not appear tedious: the remaining eight hours is therefore passed in innocent sleep.[1]

Those who are unmarried frequently go, after dinner, to the Play, or other places of public amusement, and remain there till a late hour: others go to the gambling-houses, where they often stay till near morning. The common people rise earlier, and go to bed sooner than those above mentioned; but the nobility and higher classes have seldom done breakfast before one or two o'clock, and are never in bed before the same hours after midnight.

What I have said respecting the division of time may be considered as a general rule; but the length of the days and nights in England is so very unequal, that considerable variations will often occur. Thus, in the middle of winter, the sun does not rise till past eight, and sets a little after three o'clock; which, allowing two hours for the morning and evening twilight, makes the day, at the utmost, nine hours long: there consequently remain fifteen hours of night. On the contrary, in the middle of summer, the sun rises at four, and sets at nine; which, with three hours of twilight, curtails the night to about four hours. But in the northern part of the island, I understand there is scarcely any night at midsummer, as, during the few hours the sun remains under the horizon, there is a twilight by which a person may read: and in the winter, their nights are full eighteen hours long.

The shortest day in England is on or about the 21st of December. From that time, till the 21st of March, it gradually increases; at which period the day and night are of an equal length. The length of the day continues to increase till the 2lst of June; after which it decreases till the 2lst of September, when the day and night are again equal; and continues to decrease till the return of the 21st of December.

The English, in general, are not fond of high-seasoned cookery; and their dinners mostly consist of plain roast or boiled meats. But the rich, or higher classes, have a great variety on their tables, which is divided into three courses; the first consisting of soups and fish; the second, of roast and boiled meats, fricasees,

---

1   This is meant as a contrast to the custom of the East, where several hours of the day are devoted to repose. (Translator's note)

&c.; and the third, of puddings, pies, and game; after which there is a great display of fruit of all kinds, called the *dessert*.

The regular meals of the English are, breakfast, dinner, and supper; but in London they frequently stop at the pastry-cooks' shops, which are generally kept or attended by handsome women, and eat something between breakfast and dinner. They also eat bread and butter, or cake, with their tea or coffee in the evening; so that they may be said to eat five times a day; yet, as they eat but little at any one time, they cannot be called *gluttons*.

The English legislators and philosophers have wisely determined, that the best mode of keeping women out of the way of temptation, and their minds from wandering after improper desires, is by giving them sufficient employment; therefore, whatever business can be effected without any great exertion of mental abilities or corporeal strength, is assigned to the women. Thus they have all the internal management and care of the house, and washing the clothes. They are also employed to take care of shops, and, by their beauty and eloquence, often attract customers. This I can speak from my own experience; for I scarcely ever passed the pastry-cook's shop at the corner of Newman-street in Oxford-road, that I did not go in and spend money for the pleasure of talking to a beautiful young woman who kept it. To the men is assigned the business of waiting at table, taking care of the horses and cattle, and management of the garden, farm, &c. This division of labour is attended with much convenience, and prevents confusion.

Besides the above important regulation, the English lawgivers have placed the women under many salutary restraints, which prevent their making an improper use of the liberty they have, of mixing in company, and conversing with men. In the first place, strangers, or persons whose characters are not well known, are seldom introduced to them; secondly, the women never visit any bachelor, except he be a near relation; thirdly, no woman of respectability ever walks out (in London), unless attended by her husband, a relation, or a confidential servant. They are upon no account allowed to walk out after dark; and they never think of sleeping abroad, even at the house of their father or mother, unless the husband is with them. They therefore have seldom an opportunity of acting improperly. The father, mother, and whole family, also consider themselves disgraced by the bad conduct of a daughter or a sister. And as, by the laws of England, a man may beat his wife with a stick which will not endanger the breaking of a limb, or may confine her in a room, the women dare not even give their tongues too much liberty.

If, notwithstanding all these restraints, a woman should be so far lost to all sense of shame as to commit a disgraceful action, she is for ever after shunned by all her relations, acquaintances, and every lady of respectability. Her husband is also authorized by law to take away all her property and ornaments, to debar her from the sight of her children, and even to turn her out of the house; and if proof can be produced of her misconduct, he may obtain a divorce, by which she is entirely separated from him, and loses all her dower, and even her marriage portion. From what has been stated, it is evident that the English women, notwithstanding their apparent liberty, and the politeness and flattery with which they are addressed, are, by the wisdom of their lawgivers, confined in strict bondage: and that, on the contrary, the Mohammedan women, who are prohibited from mixing in society, and are kept concealed behind curtains, but are allowed to walk out in veils, and to go to the baths (in Turkey), and to visit their fathers and mothers and even female acquaintances, and to sleep abroad for several nights together, are much more mistresses of their own conduct, and much more liable to fall into the paths of error.

DISTICH.
Let him who reads take warning!

[N. B. This subject will be further discussed in the Appendix; the Author having, while in England, written a tract "On the Liberty of Asiatic Women."]

★ ★ ★

Liberty may be considered as the idol, or tutelary deity, of the English; and I think the common people here enjoy more freedom and equality than in any other well-regulated government in the world. No Englishman, unless guilty of a breach of the laws, can be seized, or punished, at the caprice or from the gust of passion of the magistrate: he may sometimes be confined on suspicion, but his life cannot be affected, except on positive proof.

I was informed, that the Heir Apparent of the throne, while one day walking, was jostled by an impudent fellow; that the Prince struck him with his cane, and chastised him for his insolence. The man, however, sued his Royal Highness in one of the courts of justice, and compelled him to pay a considerable sum of money.

Governor Hastings came one day to visit me, immediately after the hall door had been newly painted, and even while the man who had done it was collecting his pots and brushes on the steps. The Governor, not perceiving the circumstance, lifted the knocker of the door, and spoiled a new pair of gloves; on which he turned round angrily to the man, and asked why he did not inform him the door had been just painted: the fellow, in a surly manner, replied, "Where were your eyes, that you could not see it?" Mr. Hastings smiled; and when he came in, informed me of the circumstance. From these anecdotes, some idea may be formed of the liberty and freedom of the common people in England: in many instances, they carry it too great a length, and I have even felt the inconvenience of it. Their lawgivers are however of opinion, that this freedom tends to make them brave.

In England, no gentleman can punish his servant for any crime (except by turning him away), but must make his complaint before a magistrate. The servants in England receive very high wages, are as well fed, sleep as comfortably in raised beds (not on the floor, as in India), and are as well clothed, as their masters, who, in general, prefer plain clothes for themselves, while their servants are covered with lace; nor are they obliged to run after their masters while they are riding (as our grooms do): if the master is on horseback, the servant has also a horse to ride; and if the former is in a carriage, the latter has also a seat either before or behind.

In their newspapers and daily publications, the common people often take the liberty of abusing their superiors: also, in all public meetings, and even at the playhouses, they frequently hiss and reproach any nobleman or gentleman they dislike. Another mode they have of expressing their displeasure is by *caricatures*: in these, they frequently pourtray the Ministers, or any other public characters, in ridiculous situations, either talking to each other, or conversing with *John Bull*, who, by his blunt but shrewd observations, is always made to have the best of the argument, and to tell his opponent some disagreeable truths. In these pictures the Minister is always placed in so ludicrous a point of view, that even when he sees it himself he cannot refrain from laughing.

After all, this equality is more in appearance than in reality; for the difference between the comforts of the rich and of the poor is, in England, much greater than in India. The servants are not at liberty to quit their masters without giving proper warning; and, in general, they are as respectful in their behaviour as the slaves of Hindoostan.

The rich, or higher classes, also enjoy some privileges from this equality. They can walk out at all times, and go wherever they please, without being watched by a retinue of spies, under the denomination of servants, as in the East: and if *they* are abused by the common people, they can also indulge their spleen, by abusing the Ministers, Princes, and even Royalty itself.

I can scarcely describe the pleasure I felt, upon my first arrival in Europe, in being able to walk out unattended, to make my own bargains in the shops, and to talk to whom I pleased; so different from our customs. It is not to be inferred however, from what I have said, that every man is at liberty to follow the bent of his own inclinations. There are certain rules established in society, and a degree of decorum to be observed, the transgression or omission of which would be attended with bad consequences. Thus, were a gentleman seen to enter a public-house, and to drink with low companions, or to walk about the streets with a common prostitute, he would be shunned by all his acquaintances: and were he in any point to offend against the laws, he would immediately be seized, and sent to prison; or, were he to be guilty of sedition, treason, sacrilege, or blasphemy, he would be severely punished. Even the Ministers of the empire, when they find any ancient law or custom inapplicable to the present times, or even contrary to common sense, dare not boldly and openly propose its being cancelled in Parliament; but they endeavour by degrees to effect a change in the system, by proposing special modifications, uncertain whether the law may not have been framed for some good reasons not understood by them, but which may be discovered by their opponents.

Amongst the customs which are, I believe, peculiar to the British, may be reckoned their duels and boxing-matches. The first are confined to the higher classes, and are effected by the use of pistols or swords: they are now always fought in the presence of seconds or witnesses, who take care that no treachery or foul play is practised. The other mode is used by the common people, either to obtain satisfaction for an injury, or as a trial of skill. In these combats, it is not fair to lay hold of or grapple with the adversary, in which strength might get the better; but the whole contest must be decided, as fencing is in India, by skill and dexterity. If either of the combatants fall, the other must not strike him while down; but if it be discovered that one of them falls purposely, he is hooted and abused by the spectators. These combats are carried on with such violence as frequently to occasion the death of one of the parties. The loss of an eye, breaking of the nose or jaw, or having the cheek laid open, is a common consequence. The lower classes are so fond of, or are so convinced of the utility of this science, that there are few of them who do not learn pugilism; and even many of the nobility and gentlemen encourage these matches, and argue, that it serves to preserve their courage and inures them to hardship. During my residence in England, I was present at least at one hundred of these matches: two of these were drawn battles, that is, both combatants were carried off the field with cut lips, broken teeth, and covered with blood, without either having gained the victory.

The mode of education prescribed for boys in England is admirably adapted to render them honourable, courageous, and capable of enduring hardships. They are, at an early age, sent from their parents' house to a public school, where they are frequently obliged to contend with boys of a more advanced age than themselves, not only in a competition for prizes in learning, but often in defending themselves against superior strength. In this situation they remain for five or six years; during which period they must preserve a character, untainted by dishonour, and unblemished by cowardice.

The education of girls tends to render them accomplished, rather than to endue them with philosophy: they are instructed to sing, to dance, to play on musical instruments, and to be witty and agreeable in company. The children of both sexes are taught to reverence their parents, and to esteem their brothers, sisters, and other near relations. Perhaps nothing conduces more to the success in this respect, than the *single marriages* of the Christians, where, the progeny being all of the same stock, no room is left for the contentions and litigations which too often disturb the felicity of a Mohammedan family, perhaps the offspring of a dozen mothers. The parents also endeavour, by an impartiality of conduct, to preserve harmony amongst the children; and if they have a preference for any one of them, they strive to conceal it as much as possible. If the children are guilty of a fault, they do not severely beat or abuse them, but either send them to bed, or confine them to their rooms; they also frequently reason with them, and excite them to good behaviour more by hope than by fear. Owing to this mode of treatment, I have often seen an English child of five years old possess more wisdom than an Asiatic of fifteen. Even the play-things of children in Europe are made to convey lessons of instruction; and the alphabet is learned by infants, who suppose they are only playing with cards.

As far as I was able to judge, there are not so many dissensions or quarrels among relations in England as with us; the cause of which is probably owing to a certain degree of distance and respect that is always observed between the nearest connections: so that if the head of a family has it in his power to confer any favour on the other branches of it, they receive it with gratitude. Not so in Hindoostan, where the whole family depend upon their chief, and consider it *his duty* to provide for them, or to share his fortune with them; and if he does not, they are discontented and abusive.

CHAPTER XV

Analysis of the British Government. Authority of the Sovereign— Eulogium on his present Majesty—Condescending and liberal conduct of his Majesty to the Author. Description of the Queen's Drawing-room. Political situation of the Heir Apparent—Character of the Prince. Description of Carleton House. Duties of the Ministers of State—of the Chancellor of the Exchequer—of the Secretary for the Foreign Department—of the Secretaries for the Home and War Depart-ments—of the First Lord of the Admiralty—Author introduced to Lord Spencer. Of the Master General of the Ordnance—of the President of the Board of Controul—of the Lord Chancellor—of the Archbishop of Canterbury.

I shall now endeavour to give some account of the nature of the British Government, and of the rank, situation, and character of the principal persons composing it.

The British Constitution is of the mixed form, that is, an union of the monarchical, aristocratical, and democratical governments, represented by the King, Lords, and Commons; in which the powers of each are so happily blended, that it is impossible for human wisdom to produce any other system containing so many excellences, and so free from imperfection.

The King is, of course, the head of the Government, and the source of all honour and promotion. It would be tedious and difficult to define all his powers; but it may be sufficient to say, that no law can be valid without his consent; that he has the entire command of the army; and that he can pardon criminals condemned by the law and the judges.

As a proof of the power of the Sovereign, and of the excellence of the government, I shall relate an event that occurred during my residence in England. For seventeen years, the reins of government had been guided by the able hands of the celebrated minister, Mr. Pitt, for whom his Majesty had the warmest esteem, and the highest opinion of his abilities; but that minister, trusting too much to his influence over the King, and his general popularity, endeavoured to abrogate a law, in opposition to the Royal will, and to the opinion of some other members of the Council.[1]

Thus circumstanced, his Majesty suspended Mr. Pitt from his office; and although that minister was firmly supported by five other *Viziers*, who declared they would resign if their chief was not restored to power, the King dismissed them *all, the same day.*

This circumstance happened during the height of the war with France, and at a time when, unfortunately, the King was so unwell that no arrangement could be made for forming a new Ministry. For two months, affairs remained in this situation, and much business was suspended; but owing to the well-established laws and regulations of the kingdom, no confusion or disturbance of any kind took place.

It has formerly happened that the Kings have carried their authority to a great excess, and have attempted to govern the realm without consulting their Parliament, and even in opposition to it: in this attempt, however, they have always failed. But nothing of this kind has ever been apprehended during the reign of his present Majesty, George the Third, (may God preserve him!) whose mind is an assemblage of every virtue, and whose sole wish is, to instruct, and render his people happy, rich, and good: for this purpose he encourages the Arts and Sciences, by frequently visiting the colleges and other public institutions, and inquiring into the progress and conduct of the students: he also sets his subjects a laudable example of industry, by devoting his spare time to agriculture and husbandry, without a due attention to which no country can flourish, but must ever be dependent for food on its neighbours.

It would be an endless task to recite all the praise-worthy and disinterested acts of his Majesty; but how shall we sufficiently

---

1   Abu Talib is referring to the political conflict between Prime Minister William Pitt (1749-1823) and George III over the question of Catholic emancipation which resulted in Pitt's resignation on 3 February 1801. A new administration was formed by Henry Addington. See p. 181, note 2.

appreciate the merits of a monarch who could divest himself of all authority over the Judges, by conferring upon them *their offices for life*; thus relinquishing all those powers which stimulate and bias the actions of mankind, whether of hope or of fear?

It is for the reasons above stated, that for forty-two years which his Majesty has been seated on the British throne, he has been the idol of his people, and that his subjects are ever sincerely affected by every event which gives him pain or pleasure.

During my residence in England, I frequently attended the drawing-room both of the King and of the Queen; and in every instance, both these illustrious personages did me the honour of addressing me: and although I constantly had a gentleman with me to interpret, they condescendingly commanded that I should answer them; and they were even pleased to say, they perfectly comprehended my broken English. When I had the honour of taking leave of his Majesty, he kindly inquired into my wants, ordered his private treasurer to pay me a sum of money, and his Ministers to furnish me with letters of recommendation to his envoys and ambassadors at those Courts which I was likely to visit on my route to India.

The King dislikes pomp and finery; therefore, on his Court days, there is not any grand display: but when the Queen holds a Court, the spectators are lost in amazement at the value and brilliancy of the diamonds, pearls, and every other costly ornament worn by the ladies, who on this occasion wear *hoops,* which extend the dress, and display the embroidery, lace, &c. to the greatest advantage. These hoops are of a very ancient date, and are now never worn but at Court: some of them are so large, that a lady cannot enter a door without much difficulty. The men also, on these occasions, wear old-fashioned and costly dresses, either embroidered, or covered with lace.

Next in rank and dignity to the King and Queen, is the Heir Apparent, or *Prince of Wales.* During the life of his father, he seldom interferes in the government; and should he die before the King, he is succeeded by his eldest son. If he has no son, the right to the crown devolves to his daughter; but, in default of issue, it goes to the King's second son, who is, *in general,* the chief of the nobles, and commander of the army. By this well-regulated and systematic code of inheritance, all disputes between the brothers are prevented, and the blood of the subject is spared; no one daring to assert a right to the throne, unless duly qualified by law.

On this subject I once had a disagreeable altercation with a gentleman in London, who affirmed that the natives of Hindoostan were hard-hearted, treacherous, and cruel: and, in support of his argument, adduced the instances of the Emperor Aurungzebe confining his father, and destroying his three brothers; and of the wars between Behadur Shah and his brethren. I replied, that princes were not to be judged of by the same rules as other men; that if, in England, the only alternative left them was a throne or a coffin, such scenes would often have occurred in their history.

The present Prince of Wales is esteemed a gentleman of the most polished manners, and of the utmost liberality and benignity of heart. His Royal Highness's principal residence is in the street called Pall Mall: it is a superb building, and contains many fine rooms.[1] I went several times to view it, and was particularly attracted by the apartment called the *China Hall*: this contains a number of curiosities brought from Pekin: it is also elegantly furnished with the largest mirrors, and the most brilliant lustres, I have ever seen. Not the least remarkable of its curiosities is a *clock* resembling an Ethiopian woman, who by the motion of her eyes points out the hour.

The first time I visited Carleton House, the Prince, having received information of my intention, was pleased to order a cold collation to be prepared for my refreshment; and in every instance where I had the honour of meeting his Royal Highness, he always behaved to me with the greatest kindness and condescension.

The persons of importance next to the Princes are the *Ministers of State*: they are nine in number, and by them all the affairs of the kingdom are managed. The *chief* of these is the Chancellor of the Exchequer, the office lately held by Mr. Pitt, and now by Mr. Addington.[2] He has charge of the revenues of the State, arranges the taxes, and superintends the principal disbursements. He is considered as the King's deputy in the House of Commons; and the most difficult part of his office is, to preserve a majority of the members in his interest: to effect this, he frequently gives to some of them appointments, and to others titles. By these means, and the assistance of those persons who are attached to him either from principle or connexion, he is able to withstand the attacks of his adversaries, that is, the *Ex-Ministers,* or those

---

1 Carlton House was the palatial residence of the Prince of Wales from 1783 to 1826. The building was remodeled by Henry Holland and featured a Chinoiserie drawing room.

2 Henry Addington (1757-1844), Viscount Sidmouth, was Speaker of the House from 1789 to 1801 and Prime Minister from 1801 to 1804.

that *would be Ministers*; at the head of whom, during my residence in England, were the Duke of Norfolk and Mr. Fox.[1] Every subject that is proposed in Parliament is openly discussed, and determined by a majority of votes: if therefore the Minister cannot ensure the greater number of voices in his favour, it is impossible for him to carry on the business, and he had better resign.

Mr. Pitt was enabled, by his great abilities and wonderful powers of persuasion, to obtain always a large majority in his favour; and might be said to have governed, for seventeen years, with despotic sway.

By the introduction of my friends, Sir W. Elford, Sir C. Talbot, Sir J. Macpherson, and Mr. G. Johnston, I had frequent opportunities of being present during the proceedings of the House of Commons. The first time I saw this assembly, they reminded me of two flocks of Indian paroquets, sitting upon opposite mango-trees, scolding at each other; the most noisy of whom were Mr. Pitt and Mr. Fox. In short, during the administration of Mr. Pitt, all Parliamentary proceedings were perfectly nugatory, as, by his decided majorities, he could carry any measure he proposed. It is not however to be inferred, from this circumstance, that Parliaments are of no utility; on the contrary, they are of the greatest service. In the first place, they regulate the taxes for the year; they are a check upon all contractors and public agents; and restrain the Ministers within proper bounds, upon every occasion. Thus, during the indisposition of his Majesty, when many sensible persons thought it was requisite that the Heir Apparent should be immediately appointed Regent with extensive powers; and others were of opinion that a Regency should be nominated, composed of men of the first abilities of the country, one of whom should be the Heir Apparent; the Parliament, having taken into consideration the many virtues of the King, and the possibility of his recovery, resolved that the Ministers and public officers should continue to exert themselves to the utmost in the execution of their several duties, until the physicians should be able to determine on the probability of his Majesty's recovery; after which they would decide on the measures that might be requisite to be

---

1 Charles James Fox (1749-1806), prominent Whig politician and noted bon vivant, was Prime Minister for a brief period in 1783 as part of a coalition with Lord North. The coalition fell over his attempts to reform the relationship between the East India Company and Parliament, which were stymied by the political interference of George III.

taken. This wise determination had the happy effect of calming the minds of the people; and the business of the empire was conducted as usual. Much to the honour of the Princes, none of them interfered during the discussion of this delicate question, but submitted their private opinions entirely to the wisdom of Parliament.

The Minister next in importance to the Chancellor of the Exchequer is the Secretary of State for the Foreign Department: it is he who conducts the correspondence with Foreign States, and transacts business with all the ambassadors. During my residence in England, this office was most ably filled by Lord Pelham.[1] From his lordship I received the most unbounded proofs of kindness and friendship; nor have I language to express in dull prose my gratitude to her Ladyship, for the many favours conferred upon me. The third Minister in rank is the Secretary of State for the Home Department: this office was held by Lord Hawkesbury,[2] with whom I had not the honour of being acquainted. The fourth Minister, and who has charge of the War Department, was lately Mr. Dundas, but now Lord Hobart:[3] from both of these great persons I received many favours. These four Ministers are superior to all the others, and may be said to have the entire direction, or, at least, controul, over all the affairs of Government.

The fifth Minister is at the head of the Naval Department, and is called First Lord of the Admiralty: his powers are much greater than those of the Commander-in-chief of the land forces. This office is at present held by Lord St. Vincent,[4] to whom I have not

---

1 Thomas Pelham (1756-1826), second Earl of Chichester, was part of a group of Whigs who supported Pitt's administration in the late 1790s. Abu Talib's text is inaccurate here: under Addington he was in charge of the Home Office from 1801 to 1803.

2 Robert Banks Jenkinson (1770-1828), second Earl of Liverpool and Lord Hawkesbury, was the Foreign Secretary in the Addington cabinet from 1801 to 1804, the Home Secretary from 1804 to 1806 and became Prime Minister in 1812. As Foreign Secretary he negotiated the Treaty of London with his French counter-part Louis-Guillaume Otto.

3 Robert Hobart (1760-1816), Baron Hobart, fourth Earl of Buckinghamshire, was made Secretary of War by Addington in 1801, but he lost his office when William Pitt returned to office in 1804. During his service in India from 1784 to 1798 he advocated harsh military intervention and played a key role in precipitating the final war against Tipu Sultan.

4 John Jervis (1735-1823), Earl of St. Vincent, was First Lord of the Admiralty from 1801 to 1804 during the Addington administration.

the pleasure of being known. But to his predecessor, Lord Spenser, I am under infinite obligations. I first had the honour of meeting his lordship at the house of Sir J. Banks, and, in consequence of this introduction, received frequent invitations to dine with his lordship. Lady Spenser is esteemed one of the most sensible and learned women in England. She often did me the honour of conversing with me, and listened with apparent earnestness and approbation to my wretched translations of Persian poetry. Her ladyship particularly requested, and made me promise to publish an account of my Travels, and to state my opinion, candidly, of all the customs and manners of the English; and, without either fear or flattery, freely to censure whatever I thought reprehensible amongst them.

The sixth Minister is the Master General of the Ordnance, who has charge of all the fortifications in the kingdom. This office was held by Lord Cornwallis, whose kindness to me, both in India and in Ireland, I have before related.

The seventh Minister is the President of the Board of Controul: he it is who directs the affairs and guides the reins of the East-India Company. On my first arrival in England, this office was held by Mr. Dundas, but latterly was entrusted to Lord Dartmouth.[1] His lordship is descended from a very ancient and noble family, and possesses a highly-cultivated understanding. I became acquainted with his lordship through the introduction of my friend Lord Pelham, and received many solid proofs of his lordship's esteem. At his house I frequently met with several of the Directors of the East-India Company, who, although *the Masters of the Governors of India*, were invariably seated below me at table.

His lordship wished to have deputed me as Ambassador to the King of Persia,[2] and to Zeman Shah. The route he proposed to send me, was by Constantinople and the Black Sea, to Khuarizm; whence I was to travel to Taheran; and having settled the business at that Court, to proceed to Cabul, and thence, through the Punjab, &c. to Calcutta. I must confess I was alarmed at the length and dangers of the journey, and requested his lordship would permit me first to return to India; whence, after having

---

1 George Legge (1755-1810), third Earl of Dartmouth, was president of the India Board from 1801 to 1802.
2 Fath (also Feth) Ali Shah (1771-1834) ruled Persia from 1797 to 1834. A great patron of the arts, he was at war with Russia for much of the early nineteenth century.

seen and properly settled my family, I could without difficulty proceed to Cabul, and thence, if requisite, to Persia. To this plan his lordship acceded; and when I was leaving England, he gave me letters of recommendation to the Governor-general of India;[1] desiring him, in the first instance, to recover for me the amount of my pension, which, through the intrigues of my enemies at Lucknow, had been stopt for so many years; and then to send me to Cabul, with powers to remain (if agreeable to the Shah) as the East-India Company's representative at that Court.

The eighth Minister is the Lord High Chancellor:[2] he is supreme over the Law Department, and possesses extensive powers.

These eight Ministers attend the King every day, and lay before him the state of affairs in their respective departments, and obtain his Majesty's signature to such papers as require it. They then deliberate, collectively, with the King, on any subject that is to be laid before Parliament; and having arranged the plan, give it to the Chancellor of the Exchequer, who carries it to the House of Commons, for their discussion.

The ninth Minister is the Archbishop of Canterbury.[3] He is next in rank to the Princes: it is he who takes cognizance of every thing belonging to religion, and is the King's counsellor in all *spiritual affairs*. Immediately in subjection to the archbishop, are the bishops, or prelates of the Church, each of whom possesses ecclesiastical authority over a certain district, and superintends the conduct of the clergymen, or persons ordained for performing the public functions and ceremonies of their religion. It is

---

1 Richard Wellesley (1760-1842), Marquess Wellesley, was Governor General of Bengal from 1797 to 1806. He oversaw the defeat of Tipu Sultan of Mysore in 1799 and won a decisive victory against the Maratha leader Delaut Rao Sindhia at Assaye in 1803 which effectively curtailed the Maratha threat to British interests in India. Further conquests ended the last vestiges of French influence in north India. The remaining years of his tenure focused on governmental issues and he founded, amidst much controversy, Fort William College, an institution aimed at training civil servants in both classical and Asiatic languages. The College played a vital part in orientalist learning and in the publication of Abu Talib's text. See editor's Introduction.

2 During the author's visit, this was most likely John Scott (1751-1838), first Earl Eldon. He replaced Alexander Wedderburn (1733-1805), first Baron Loughborough and first earl of Rosslyn, when Pitt resigned, and continued in the post until 1827.

3 John Moore (1730-1805) held this office from 1783 to 1805.

requisite to explain to Mohammedans, that, in England, Law and Religion are distinct branches; and that the duty of a clergyman is limited to watching over the moral and spiritual conduct of his flock, to burying the dead, visiting the dying, uniting persons in marriage, and christening children; for, according to their tenets, children are born without any religion, and, until they have been christened, are not admitted into the pale of the Church. In recompence for their trouble, the clergy are entitled to a tenth of the produce of the land, whether of the vegetable or animal kind. For this purpose, England is divided into an immense number of parishes, in each of which there is a church, built at the public expence; and to each of these churches are attached a priest and deputy, who, on every Sunday, and other holidays, read prayers, preach to their congregation, and perform the other ceremonies before mentioned. A certain number of these parishes constitute a diocese, to each of which one of the bishops is attached, who, in addition to the duties before stated, has the power of ordaining and dismissing clergymen. The bishops are addressed as Lords, and have seats in the House of Peers, but seldom interfere, unless spiritual affairs are discussed. When a bishop dies, the King, by the advice of his Minister, selects one of the most worthy clergymen to supply his place.

I had the good fortune to be intimately acquainted with the Bishop of London:[1] he was a sensible and philosophic man, and took much pleasure in disputing with me on points of religion. I one day had a controversy with him respecting our Prophet Mohammed, and insisted that his coming had been foretold by the holy Messiah, in the *original* New Testament. He positively denied the premises, but agreed to examine the book, and give me further information in a week. On the day appointed I waited on him, and he produced a very ancient Greek version of the Testament, in which he candidly acknowledged that he had discovered the verse I alluded to, but said he supposed it might have been interpolated by some of the renegadoes of Constantinople, long after the preaching of Mohammed. I replied, that as copies of the New Testament were in the hands of every person at that time, it was impossible any interpolation could have taken place without having been noticed by some of the contemporary historians or writers. But, independently of that circumstance, it is a well-authenticated fact, that Mohammed himself had declared to the Christians, he was the Ahmed (*Paraclete*) promised by Jesus

---

1 Beilby Porteus (1731-1809) was Bishop of London from 1787 to 1808.

Christ, and quoted to them the passage in the Evangelists; that the Christians did not then object to the verse, but merely denied that he was the Comforter so promised, and that they should look for another. This was sufficient evidence to prove that the above passage was in the original, and not an interpolation. The bishop laughed, and said he supposed I was come to England to convert the people to Mohammedanism, and to make them forsake the religion of their forefathers.

I also had the honour of being known to the Lord Bishop of Durham,[1] who was a man of great liberality and extensive charity. He frequently invited me to his house; and marked his attention, by always asking some of the gentlemen who understood Persian to meet me. During the year of great scarcity in England, he daily fed a thousand poor people at his private expence. Hence may be formed some idea of the incomes and charity of English bishops.

In my account of the duties of his Majesty's Ministers, having mentioned *the Parliament*, it becomes requisite to explain the meaning of the term. Parliament properly means an assemblage of the three estates; viz. the King, Lords, and Commons; but it is generally applied to the two latter. The Lords have a particular apartment, where they assemble, and deliberate on the business which has passed the House of Commons; and which, if they disapprove, becomes nugatory. It is in the House of Lords that the Parliament assembles on the first and last days of the session. On these occasions, the King goes to the house in great state, attended by all the public officers in their robes and insignia of office. I once had an opportunity of being present at this interesting scene. I was introduced into the house by my friend Mr. Debrett; but had it not been for the kind attention of the Duke of Gloucester,[2] the King's brother, I should have seen little of the ceremony. His Royal Highness observed me soon after I entered the house, and sent one of the attendants to procure me a seat near the throne. In this situation I not only saw the King enter and go out, but also heard distinctly every word that he addressed to the Bishops, the Lords, and the Commons. In the course of my life, I have never witnessed so grand or so impressive a scene. The King was seated upon a superb and elevated throne, over which

---

1 Shute Barrington (1734-1826) was Lord Bishop of Durham from 1791 until his death.
2 William Henry (1743-1805) was first Duke of Gloucester of the fifth creation.

was erected a stately canopy. On his Majesty's right hand sat the Heir Apparent, and on his left the other Princes according to seniority, upon chairs of yellow velvet embroidered with gold. Near to these were placed a number of forms, covered with broadcloth, for the King's favourites or more distant relatives, and for the wives of the noblemen. On the right of the throne, but below the Heir Apparent, stood the Foreign Princes and Ambassadors. The sword of state was borne by Lord Spenser, and the *cap of Liberty* by Lord Winchelsea:[1] these two noblemen were close in front of his Majesty. Sir P. Burrell, now Lord Gwydir,[2] presided, as Lord High Chamberlain, over all the ceremonies. The Lords were seated to the right and left, in a line with the Princes; and the Commons were arranged, in due order, opposite the throne. His Majesty's speech was listened to with the utmost silence and respect; immediately after which the King withdrew. As I was engaged to dine with a person of rank, I endeavoured to make my escape from the house as soon as possible, but in vain; for the crowd was so great, that the hour of dinner was past before I could get free; and I was obliged to make many apologies to my host for my seeming inattention.

Among the hereditary nobility of England, there are several degrees of rank, as Duke, Marquis, Earl, Baron, and Viscount; although, when assembled in the House of Lords, their prerogatives and duties appear exactly the same.

The title next in rank to Prince is Duke. Several of these Dukes are the King's sons; and his present Majesty has made it a rule not to raise any person but his own relations to that dignity. The families and titles of many of these Dukes, and of some of the Earls, are of very ancient date. They originally took their titles from their estates, or from towns dependent on them. Their possessions are very great; and several of them have incomes equal to the allowance of the King. Their property, contrary to the general custom of England, is not divided among the children, but goes to the eldest son. By this means, the wealth and influence of the family remain stationary; and, as they are always generous and liberal to their tenants, they acquire such a host of dependants, that the government has had frequent occasions to

---

1 George Finch-Hatton (1752-1826), ninth Earl of Winchilsea, was a politician.

2 Peter Burrell (1754-1820), first Baron Gwydir, was a politician and legendary cricketer. Abu Talib knew both his sister Frances Julia Burrell and his cousin Julia Ann Burrell. See p. 192, note 2, and p. 137, note 2.

be jealous or distrustful of them. Thus, some years ago, a brother of the Duke of — rebelled in Ireland against the King, and, having been joined by a great number of the Irish, very nearly effected a revolution in that kingdom. At length, however, by the great wisdom and military abilities of Lord Cornwallis, the rebels were vanquished, and Lord— was taken prisoner.[1]

I had the honour of being acquainted with several of these Dukes. From the late Duke of Bedford[2] I experienced much civility: he was an amiable man, and of a most prepossessing appearance. He was succeeded by his brother, who, I understand, inherits many of his virtues. The Duke of Devonshire,[3] who married a sister of Lord Spenser, invited me several times to his house; and his Duchess, who is one of the most delightful women in England, paid me the greatest attention.[4] Their daughter, Lady Georgiana, surpasses in beauty and elegance the boasted nymphs of China or Tartary, and her voice thrills to the soul, like the elixir of life.

---

1 Lord Edward Fitzgerald (1763-98), brother of the second Duke of Leinster, William Robert Fitzgerald (1749-1804). Edward Fitzgerald was a central figurehead and leader of the United Irishmen's rebellion that occurred in Dublin in 1798. He was betrayed and arrested on 19 May 1798. He died on 4 June 1798 in Newgate gaol in Dublin from bullet wounds sustained during his arrest.

2 Francis Russell (1765-1802), fifth Duke of Bedford, agriculturalist and politician, was the subject of Edmund Burke's *A Letter to a Noble Lord* (1796).

3 William Cavendish (1748-1811), fifth Duke of Devonshire, married Georgiana Cavendish (1757-1806; née Spencer). Their daughter, Georgiana Cavendish (1783-1858) was one of two children born before the death of the Duchess and the Duke's remarriage to his longtime mistress, Lady Elizabeth Foster (1757-1824; née Hervey).

4 The Duchess of Devonshire was arguably the most famous woman in Britain in the late eighteenth century. She was a leader of fashion as well as an extremely influential political hostess. A long-time friend and associate of the Prince of Wales, Charles James Fox, and other prominent Whigs, she was extremely active in the contentious election of 1784 and in the Regency crisis of 1788-89. She went into exile for the 1790s, gave birth to an illegitimate daughter in France, but returned to England following the resignation of William Pitt in 1801. She was instrumental in bringing together a coalition to remove Prime Minister Henry Addington from power in 1804. Abu Talib's contact with the Duchess comes at this time of triumphant return to public life. See Introduction for a discussion of this passage.

VERSE.

> Since the Sphere commenced its revolutions, it has not
>   beheld such a Star:
> And since the Earth began to produce, it has not yielded
>   so fair a Flower
> As Georgiana, lovely daughter of the Duke and Duchess
>   of Devonshire.

His Grace has for many years past been in the habit of giving, annually, an entertainment to all his acquaintances, at Chiswick House.[1] I had the honour of being present at one of these entertainments; when the Duchess, taking into consideration my forlorn situation, among such a crowd of great people, to most of whom I was a stranger, kindly appointed Lady Elizabeth Foster, one of her intimate friends, to be my *Mehmandar* during the day. Her ladyship, according to the English custom, immediately put her arm under mine, and led me, through bowers of roses and walks of jessamine, over all gardens. She then conducted me to the concert and ball rooms. It so happened, that, as we were about to enter a door, we met the Prince of Wales. I immediately drew back, to make way for his Royal Highness, and consequently kept her ladyship back; but the Prince, with all that politeness which distinguishes his character, retreated, and made a sign to me to advance. I was quite lost in amazement; but Lady Elizabeth laughed, and said, "His Royal Highness would not for the world take precedence of any lady: and as my arm was under yours, he would by no means allow that we should separate, to make way for him." From this circumstance, some idea of the gallantry of the English towards ladies may be formed. When the company sat down to breakfast, I had the honour of being placed at the same table with the Prince.

Previous to breaking up, the Duchess presented me her ticket for the Opera of that evening. I at first declined accepting it, saying, it would be so late before I got home, that I should not have time to dress before the Opera commenced. The Duke of Gloucester, brother of the King, who was at the same table, overheard me, and said my excuse was not a sufficient one; that he meant to be there, and hoped to have the pleasure of seeing me. Lady Elizabeth Foster, Lady Harvey,[2] and Lady Georgiana, also

---

1 See Appendix A2.
2 Depending on the date of this encounter, the author could be referring to Lady Foster's mother, Lady Elizabeth Hervey (c.1732-1800; née Davers).

said that they should be at the Opera at eight o'clock, and if I did not meet them, they would severely fine me. I therefore promised to attend; and, after having arrived at home, I quickly changed my dress, and proceeded to the Opera House. I found the Duke was there before me, and waiting impatiently for the ladies. He sat with me for an hour; and as they did not make their appearance, he was irritated, and went away, but desired me to scold them, should they arrive. When the Opera was nearly finished, the ladies came in. I taxed them, both on the Duke's and my own account, with their breach of promise. They made me one of those trifling and improbable excuses, which so become the fascinating mouth of an English beauty: "That the crowd of coaches was so great at the gates of Chiswick House, they could not get away sooner." I recollected some verses of a Persian Ode, which I thought applicable to the case, and spoke them, as if extemporary. They insisted upon my giving them a translation, which I complied with; and the verses were handed about to all their acquaintances. They were nearly as follow.

EXTEMPORARY ODE.

> Although no person ever experienced the truth of your
>   promises,
> Yet are we ever deceived by those eloquent and ruby lips.

> Sin against me as much as you please: you need not ask
>   forgiveness;
> For I am your slave, and shall pay implicit obedience to
>   your wishes.

> Fear not to enter the ranks at the day of judgment
>   unveiled;
> For, should some of your murdered lovers demand
>   retribution,

> The Angels, ordered to drive you from Paradise,
>   captivated by your looks,
> Will offer themselves, as an atonement for your errors.

> That carriages round the gates of Chiswick House pre-
>   vented your coming, is not probable;
> Say rather, the crowd of those smitten by your charms
>   detained you.

Such was my desire of your presence, that I noticed not
the passing scene:
Now you are come, the sound of your voice banishes all
my anxiety.

As long as Abu Taleb can behold your charming
countenance,
He will not sigh for the bowers of the garden of Eden.

The Duke of Northumberland[1] is said to possess the greatest
riches, and most extensive property in the kingdom. At the
request of my friend Miss Burrell, and by desire of the Duchess
of Northumberland, who is a cousin of Miss Burrell's, I received
an invitation to visit Sion House: but as his Grace did not con-
descend to pay me that attention I had received from other
noblemen, I gratified my curiosity at the expence of my finer
feelings.[2]

The Dukes of Marlborough, Portland, Norfolk, Richmond,
Gordon,[3] &c. are all descended from ancient and noble families,
who have long possessed this title; for since the commencement
of the present reign, but one person, except the Royal Family, has
been promoted to that dignity.

The King's sons, during their infancy, are all called Princes;
but, as they arrive at the age of manhood, are created Dukes.
There are seven of them, all pleasing, unaffected men. They associate with the nobility, and do not assume any superiority in
company, but enter, without fastidiousness, into all the amusements that are going forward. Thus, the Duke of Gloucester, who
possessed a lively disposition and much ready wit, frequently
jested the young ladies, in my presence, on their attachment to
me, and their jealousy of each other on that account. This had

---

1 Sir Hugh Percy (1742-1817), second Duke of Northumberland, was a
   harsh critic of both Pitt and Addington at this period.
2 Frances Julia Burrell (1752–1820). Her father was William Burrell's
   brother Peter, therefore she is Miss Julia Burrell's cousin. See p. 137,
   note 2.
3 George Spencer (1739-1817), fourth Duke of Marlborough; William
   Henry Cavendish Cavendish Bentinck (1738-1809), third Duke of Portland (he assumed the second Cavendish in 1755); Charles Howard
   (1746-1815), eleventh Duke of Norfolk; Charles Lennox (1735-1806),
   third Duke of Richmond and Lennox; Alexander Gordon (1743-1827),
   fourth Duke of Gordon.

always the effect of making the company laugh, and of exciting good humour.

The next persons in rank to the Lords are the Members of the House of Commons. Their number is above three hundred and fifty. Two of them are elected by the inhabitants of every town in the kingdom, to be their agents or representatives in Parliament. They are, in general, men of very superior abilities and considerable property. For seven months in the year they remain in London, and attend five days in the week at the Parliament House. Some of their duties have been before described; but when their attention is not taken up with great political subjects, they employ themselves in considering the internal regulations, and plans for improving the state of the country, and in fact, take cognizance of every thing that is going forward. Even the laws respecting culprits are abrogated or altered by Parliament; for the Christians, contrary to the systems of the Jews and Mohammedans, do not acknowledge to have received any laws respecting *temporal* matters from Heaven, but take upon themselves to make such regulations as the exigencies of the times require.

CHAPTER XVI

Description of the East-India Company. Of the Board of Controul. Of the Lord Mayor of London—the nature and extent of his jurisdiction—Procession to Westminster and Guild-Hall. The Author is invited to the Lord Mayor's Feast—account thereof. Anecdote of Miss Combe.

In political importance, the East-India Company ranks next to the House of Commons. It is well understood, by every person possessing common information, that '*Company*' means an association of merchants, or other persons, who subscribe a certain sum of money, for the purpose of carrying on trade, or any other extensive concern, which exceeds the capital of an individual. Such was the origin of the East-India Company.

It is little more than a hundred years since the Company obtained their regular Charter, granting to them the entire monopoly of the trade with India and China. Their capital at that time was about three crores of rupees (£3,000,000), divided into shares of £1000 each, but has since been increased to double that amount; and, in consequence of their extensive conquests in India, the value of each share is now worth nearly twice the original subscription.

The Affairs of the Company are managed by twenty-four

Directors; six of whom go out of office every year, in rotation, and six others are appointed in their room. They are elected by those proprietors who possess a full share of £1000 stock. The Directors annually elect two of the most intelligent of their own body to be their President and Vice-President, who are called Chairman and Deputy Chairman; and these two gentlemen may be said to represent the Company; as, although they occasionally call on the other Directors to assist them with their advice, they have in general determined on the measure before they propose it to the court. It is evident, that to fill such a situation with propriety, requires a person of very superior understanding and well conversant in all kinds of business, and that therefore only a few of the Directors can aspire to this honour: some of them never attain to the dignity, and others are sometimes elected several years successively. The Directors most esteemed for their abilities, during my residence in England, and to whom the office of Chairman had generally fallen, were, Mr. H. Inglis, D. Scott, S. Lushington, Mr. Devaynes, and C. Grant.[1] I had the honour of being known to all these gentlemen; but had little acquaintance with any of the other Directors, except Sir T. Metcalfe, and Mr. Plowden, who has lately been elected.

The proprietors of East-India stock are of all ranks and professions; and some of them are such low people, that they do not presume to sit in the presence of their own *deputies*. They attend twice a year at the India House, to receive their dividends, or to give their votes, when called on, for the election of a new Director. They have nothing further to do with the business of the Company.

The India House is a very extensive and superb building, and contains an immense number of apartments for all the public offices. It is situated in the city, and, including the warehouses, is not less than a mile in circumference. Here all the business of the Company is transacted. The Chairman and his Deputy attend every day in the week, except Sunday; and the other Directors assemble once, twice, or three times in the week, according to the quantity and nature of the business that is transacting.

In consequence of the supposed misconduct or neglect of the Company, or their Governors abroad, his Majesty's Ministers some years ago deemed it advisable to create a *Board of Controul*,

---

1 Sir Hugh Inglis (1744-1820); David Scott (1746-1805); for Sir Stephen Lushington see p. 143, note 2; Charles Grant (1746-1823). See Appendix D3.

to superintend and direct the affairs of the Company. This Board is invested with great powers, and frequently opposes the measures of the Directors: it examines all their accounts, and controuls all their correspondence. The Company cannot now send out any order or letter to their Governors, unless sanctioned by this Board; and, as the President is always one of his Majesty's Ministers, no step of importance can be taken, or any new measure adopted, without being known to Government.

It nevertheless sometimes happens, that measures sanctioned both by the Court of Directors and the Board of Controul are brought under the cognizance of Parliament. Thus Lord Clive's[1] depriving the heir of the Nabob of the Carnatic of his powers, and the assumption of part of the territory of Oude by Lord Wellesley,[2] have been severely animadverted on, both in the House of Lords and of Commons; nor is it yet known how the business will be decided. Mr. Meheux, the Secretary to this Board, was a sensible pleasant man, and frequently asked me to dine with him at his house in Sloane-street.

When I first arrived in England, several of the Directors imagined that I had been sent as an agent by some of the Princes of India, to complain against their servants. They were therefore, for some time, very distrustful, and reserved in their conduct; but after they were convinced of their error, they received me kindly, and paid me much attention.

I have before mentioned, that London is composed of three towns; viz. the City, Westminster, and the Borough. The former was, many years ago, a walled or fortified town; is the residence of the principal merchants in England; and is still governed by a particular jurisdiction of its own. The ruler or governor of the city

---

1   Robert Clive (1725-74), Baron Clive, statesman and former governor of Bengal. As military commander in Bengal in the 1750s, he defeated Suja ud-Dowlah at Plassey and Buxar. In the wake of these victories, Clive was awarded the *diwani* on behalf of the East India Company and henceforth the Company collected revenues and assumed governmental responsibility for the residents of Bengal

2   Richard Wellesley (1760-1842; né Wesley), Marquess Wellesley, was Governor General of Bengal from 1797-1805. Under his command, the military forces working for the East India Company defeated Tipu Sultan of Mysore at Seringapatam in 1799 and seriously weakened the Maratha Confederacy. The elimination of these resistant forces paved the way for unrestrained British domination in the Asian subcontinent for the rest of the nineteenth century.

is called the Lord Mayor: he is endowed with great authority, and governs his own dominions as a sovereign. If I have been rightly informed, the constitution of the city is nearly as follows. Every person who has served his regular apprenticeship, or possesses certain property within the walls, is a freeman of the city. At stated periods, the housekeepers of each ward elect a number of persons to be the organ or channel of their opinions, who are called Common-councilmen: twenty-six of these are selected to be Aldermen, who hold their situation for life, and each of whom is magistrate of a particular ward or district of the city: he is answerable for its police, and has the power of calling any number of the Livery or freemen of his ward to his assistance, either to consult them, or to quell any disturbance. At his tribunal all the petty disputes of the district are adjusted. The mode of electing the Lord Mayor is this: On a particular day in the year, all the Livery-men assemble in a large building, called the *Common Hall*, where, having canvassed the merits of all the Aldermen, they select the names of two, and send them up to the Court of Aldermen, which is then sitting, who are obliged to elect one of the persons named by the Livery, as the Lord Mayor for the ensuing year.

The Lord Mayor is the chief magistrate of the city, and presides daily in a court of justice. He has two assistants, called Sheriffs, and a great number of officers under him. He is allowed a superb palace to reside in, and has a number of horses, servants, &c. kept for him at the public expence. One of his prerogatives is, that no body of soldiers or armed men shall pass through the city without his permission: and although his boundaries are divided from Westminster, or the *King's Town,* only by an old gateway, his Majesty never enters the city without giving information to the Lord Mayor, who, on all occasions of state or ceremony, meets the King at the gate, and makes an offer of the keys of the city: he then joins his Majesty's retinue, and accompanies him wherever he is going.

The annual election of the Lord Mayor is celebrated, by the inhabitants of the city, with as much pomp and rejoicing as is observed in Westminster on the anniversary of the King's birthday.[1] At noon, the Lord Mayor, dressed in his robes of state, and attended by all the city officers, embarks in a number of splendid boats prepared for the purpose, and proceeds up the river, to the

---

1 See Appendix A3.

great hall of justice at Westminster; where having taken the oaths of office, he returns in the same state to the city; and after having landed, he enters his state coach, drawn by six horses, and is conveyed to Guildhall, where a dinner is prepared for four thousand of the most respectable inhabitants of London, of both sexes.

Some months after my arrival in England, Alderman Combe[1] was elected Lord Mayor, and did me the honour of inviting me to his dinner. As soon as I alighted at the door, fifty of his lordship's attendants, with spears and maces in their hands, came to meet me, and a band of music at the same time commenced playing. I was then conducted, with great ceremony, to the room where his lordship was sitting with several of the King's Ministers and other noblemen.

On my entering the apartment, the Lord Mayor took me by the hand, and, having inquired respecting my health, introduced me to the Lady Mayoress, who was dressed as fine as a *Queen*, and seated with great pomp on a superb sofa. Although it is not customary, on these occasions, for the Lady Mayoress to return the salutation of any person, yet, in compliment to me as a foreigner, her ladyship rose from her seat.

The dinner having been announced, the Lord Mayor again took my hand, and led me to a table which was raised a step or two above the others. He then placed me opposite himself, that he might have an opportunity of attending to me. His lordship sat on the right of the Lady Mayoress; and on his right hand were seated Lord Cholmondeley,[2] Lord Spenser, Lord Nelson, and several other noblemen. On the left of her ladyship were placed the late Mayor[3] and his family. The remainder of the company at this table consisted of the Judges, Aldermen, &c.

The table was covered with a profusion of delicious viands, fruits, wines, &c. All the dishes and plates were of embossed silver; and the greater number of the goblets and cups, and the

---

1 Harvey Christian Combe (1752-1818), a brewer with radical Whig politics, was Lord Mayor during 1799-1800. Affluent and public minded he was also known as a prominent socialite and a gambler. His wife, the Lady Mayoress, was Alice Combe (d. 1828; née Christian).

2 George James Cholmondeley (1749-1827), fourth Earl of Cholmondeley and first Marquis of Cholmondeley, was a notorious womanizer who reportedly cavorted with Elizabeth Bridget Armistead, Fox's mistress, and Gertrude Mahon.

3 Sir Richard Carr Glyn (1755-1838), first baronet, was a banker who served as Lord Mayor in 1798.

candlesticks, were of burnished gold. In the course of my life, I have never seen such a display of wealth and grandeur. The other tables also appeared to be plentifully and elegantly served; and, if I could judge them from the apparent happiness of the people at them, they were equally pleased with their entertainment as myself.

After dinner, the health of the Lord and Lady Mayoress were drank, with great acclamations; then the health of the King, and of the Queen; after which, "The prosperity of Lord Nelson; and may the victory of the Nile be ever remembered!" was drank with loud applause.

When the whole of this company, consisting of several thousand persons, stood up, and, having filled their glasses, proclaimed the *toast* with loud huzzas, it immediately recalled to my mind the verse of our Poet Hafiz;

> Come, fill the goblets with wine! and let us rend the vault
> of the Heavens with our shouts!
> Let us overturn the present system of the Universe, and
> form a new Creation of our own!

As many of the persons who were seated at the lower end of the room could not see who were at the upper table, a short time previous to the ladies quitting the company, a petition was sent to the Lord Mayor, to request they might be allowed to pass round the table, in small parties. His lordship, having asked my consent, directed that they might do so. In consequence of this permission, they divided themselves into small parties, and walked round the table. When they came opposite to Lord Nelson, or me, the men stooped their heads, and the women bent their knees, (such being the English manner of salutation). This mark of respect they thought due to Lord Nelson, for the victory of the Nile; and to me, for my *supposed high rank*. This ceremony took up nearly an hour; after which the Lord Mayor presented Lord Nelson, in the name of the city, with an elegant scimitar, the hilt of which was studded with diamonds, as a testimony of their gratitude for his distinguished services. His lordship, having buckled on the sword, stood up, and made a speech to the Lord Mayor and to the company, assuring them that, with the weapon he had now been invested, and the protection of the Almighty, he would chastise and subdue all their enemies.

This interesting scene being finished, I thought it was time to retire, and went up to the Lord Mayor to take leave. His lordship, however, seized me by the hand, and led me up stairs to a superb apartment, where we found the Lady Mayoress, and nearly five hundred other ladies, richly dressed, some of whom were as beautiful as the *Houries of Paradise*, waiting our appearance, before they commenced dancing. As few rooms in the world would have held such an assemblage of people, if furnished in the usual manner, this apartment was fitted up with long ranges of seats rising above each other, (resembling the stone steps of a large tank or reservoir in India,) which were continued all round the room, for the use of the spectators, leaving but a moderate space in the middle for the dancers.

When we had been seated a short time, twelve or fifteen of the principal young men present were permitted to enter the circle, and to choose their partners. After they had gone down the dance, they were relieved by an equal number of others; and in this manner the ball was kept up till daylight; and the sun had risen ere I reached home.

This was one of the most delightful nights I ever passed in my life; as, independent of every luxury my heart could wish, I had an opportunity of gazing all the time on the angelic charms of Miss Combe, who sat in that assemblage of beauties like the bright moon surrounded with brilliant stars.

After what I have said, it may be unnecessary to repeat, that this young lady is one of the greatest beauties in London. One evening, I met her, by chance, at a masquerade, and, as the weather was warm, she wore only a short veil, which descended no lower than her upper lip. As our meeting was quite unexpected, she thought she could converse with me without being known; but, in answer to her *first* question, I replied, "There is but one woman in London who possesses such teeth and lips; therefore Miss Combe may save herself the trouble of attempting to deceive her admirers." This speech was overheard by some persons, and became the subject of conversation in the polite circles next day.

CHAPTER XVII

Description of the Courts of Law in London—of English Juries—of the Judges and Lawyers. The Author prosecuted by a tailor—his reflections

In London, there are several public courts of justice, each of which has its particular department, and separate judges. The court in which criminals are tried is called the *Old Bailey*. As I had the happiness to be acquainted with several of the judges of this court, and was anxious to obtain some insight into English jurisprudence, I frequently attended their sittings.

The first circumstance that attracted my attention, and consequent applause of the English law, was the right which every British subject possesses, of being tried by a jury. These juries are composed of twelve respectable inhabitants of the city, who, being summoned to attend without having any previous information on the subject to be tried, or any opportunity of conversing with the parties, come into court perfectly disinterested and unbiassed: they then take an oath to act impartially, and to decide according to the evidence. It is the duty of the jury to attend scrupulously to the whole of the proceedings, and particularly to the examination of the witnesses both by the counsellors and the judge: they are then to determine, whether the person accused is guilty, or not, of the crime laid to his charge. If they are unanimous in their opinions, the affair is immediately determined, and the judge pronounces the sentence of the law; but if they are of contrary opinions, they are locked up in an adjoining apartment until they come to a decision on the case. Notwithstanding this is the boasted palladium of English liberty, it does not appear to me free from imperfections. The judge, being a person of great consequence and superior abilities, often impresses the jury with such awe, that, if he is inclined to pass an unjust sentence, he can, in his interpretation of the law, and his address to them, dictate what they are to do. I have frequently seen the judge reprehend the jury for their decisions, and send them back, once or twice, to reconsider their verdict. If, by the above means, the judge can bring a few of the jury over to his opinion, he can frighten the rest, by threatening to lock them up without food; while he and the lawyers retire from the court, and refresh themselves, for three or four hours. From the above circumstance, it appears to me that the decision in all cases depends more on the judge than on the jury.

The English judges are doubtless men of the strictest honour and probity, and, being independent both in their fortunes and situation, are above all temptation to act unjustly; but the laws being excessively voluminous, and in many instances either con-tradictory or obscure, the lawyers, whose only income arises from their practice (that is, the fees they receive from the plaintiff and defendant), endeavour to delay the decision of the business as much as possible, and frequently prevail on the judge to postpone the trial to another year: in this manner, civil causes are often carried on for twenty years, to the ruin of both parties. In other instances, the judges allow the lawyers to puzzle and intimidate the witnesses, in such a manner, that it is impossible for a person unaccustomed to their proceedings to give his evidence correctly; and it sometimes happens, that the judge yields his own better judgment to the interested arguments of a bribed counsellor, who, to serve his client, will undertake to prove that black is white.

I was disgusted to observe, that, in these courts, law very often overruled equity, and that a well-meaning honest man was frequently made the dupe of an artful knave; nor could the most righteous judge alter the decision, without transgressing the law.

I myself had the misfortune to acquire a little experience in this way. Having purchased some cloth, I agreed with a tailor to make me a coat for ten shillings. Although there were two witnesses present, and I even had the agreement in his own handwriting, he denied it, and sent me a bill for twenty shillings. I gave him the ten, but refused to pay him any more: he said it was well, he should complain to the court of justice, and make me pay the remainder. He went immediately, and procured a summons for me to appear, but this he never delivered; and, after a certain time, produced a decree from one of the courts, ordering me immediately to pay the ten shillings, and a further fine of six shillings, for not having obeyed the summons. This I thought extreme injustice, and consulted one of my friends, who was an attorney, what I should do. He replied, "Although the case is very hard, you must *immediately* pay the money: you may then sue him for having withheld the summons, and for having, by that means, obtained an unjust decision against you." I was however perfectly satisfied with the experience I had already gained, and quietly paid the money. After that transaction, whenever any *unjust claim* was made on me, I endeavoured to compromise the matter, by offering to pay a third, or a half of the amount; and, as my adversaries found it troublesome to go backward and forward in attendance on the court, they were, in general, reasonable enough to comply with my wishes. This is the plan adopted by many sensible Englishmen, who find it easier to settle with their opponents in this manner, than to contest the point in a court of law.

I cannot pass over this opportunity of freely expressing my sentiments with respect to the establishment of British courts of law in India; which, I contend, are converted to the very worst of purposes, and, unless an alteration take place in the system, will some time or other produce the most sinister consequences.

In Calcutta, few months elapse that some respectable and wealthy man is not attacked by the harpies who swarm round the courts of judicature. Various are their modes of extorting money; and many of them have acquired such fortunes by these nefarious means, as to live in great splendour, and quite eclipse the ancient families.

Their general mode of proceeding is this: having by some means connected themselves with one of the attorneys of the court, they then, under a fictitious name, purchase a large quantity of goods on credit from some country trader; and when the time of payment arrives, they bring forward false witnesses, to prove that the merchandise was bought for half the price actually agreed on.

Another mode of acquiring money, is by frightening people with the terrors of the English law. They first make a demand on a person for a large sum of money, which they say is owing to them, either by himself or his father; to prove which they frequently forge bonds. If he is alarmed, and compromises the matter with them, it is well; but if he disputes their claim, they proceed to the court, and in the most hardened and villanous manner, make oath, or twenty oaths if requisite, that such a person owes them 50,000 rupees (£6250), and is about to abscond to one of the foreign settlements within twenty miles of Calcutta. A summons is *instantly* issued: and the person accused, being seized and brought to the court, is told he must either give immediate security for a lac of rupees (£12,500), or go to jail: if he is fortunate enough to have opulent friends, who will immediately come to his assistance and give their security, he may escape the disgrace of being carried to prison, on condition of agreeing to attend on the day of trial: if, on that day, he should arrive in the court an hour too late, he is fined perhaps a hundred or two hundred pounds: but if he should, by any accident, neglect to attend, his securities are obliged to pay the whole of the lac of rupees. These circumstances are all very distressing to a native of India, unacquainted with the English laws and customs; and many of them, rather than have the trouble and run the risk, willingly pay a sum of money: but if the person accused is a resolute man, who determines to go through the whole process, he is obliged to employ an attorney, who understands not a word of his language, and to intrust an important concern in the hands of a counsellor, whom he cannot understand but through the medium of an interpreter; and the attorney, not being paid by the year, month, or day, as is the custom of India, makes what charges he pleases, and postpones the trial till it suits his convenience. After a lapse of many months, or perhaps years, the cause comes on, and if the defendant is fortunate enough to prove that the plaintiff and his witnesses have perjured themselves, he obtains a verdict in his favour, and the plaintiff is ordered to pay the *costs of suit*. It frequently happens, that the plaintiff, aware of the event, absconds on the day of trial: if he does not, he may be arrested for the amount of the costs, and carried to jail: he there pleads poverty, and the defendant, after such injuries, is obliged to pay him a weekly allowance; in failure of which the scoundrel is liberated, and again let loose on the world, to recommence his villanies.

Hitherto we have taken the favourable side of the question. But suppose the defendant unable to give security for so large a sum of money: He is detained, the first day, in the court-house, under charge of the constables; where, if he is a Hindoo, he cannot eat; and if a Mohammedan, he is precluded from performing the duties of his religion. The following day he is carried to the same prison in which the felons are confined, to the great disgrace of himself and family: there he is every night shut up in a dark and hot cell, where he lingers for months. Many are the respectable persons who die under such misfortunes, before the trial comes on. If the supposed debtor survive till the day of trial arrives, he is then conveyed, under a guard, to the court, where, probably, the plaintiff plays the same tricks as before described; and the only consolation the poor man receives, is, that the court are very sorry he should have suffered so much trouble.

The hardships and inconvenience which witnesses also suffer, when summoned to Calcutta, are so great, that no man in India will now give voluntary evidence in any cause. The witnesses are sometimes brought down the country a month's journey; they are then detained five or six months in Calcutta: when brought into court, they are kept standing for two or three hours; and if puzzled by the various questions and cross-questioning of the lawyers and judges, they are then accused of being liars; and obliged to return home, at their own expence, without any remuneration for their loss of time and trouble.

An anecdote is related of a clever woman, who, having been summoned to give evidence before the court of judicature in Calcutta, deposed that such a circumstance occurred in her presence. The judge asked where it happened: she replied, In the verandah of such a house. "Pray my good woman," said the judge, "how many pillars are there in that verandah?" The woman, not perceiving the trap that was laid for her, said, without much consideration, that the verandah was supported by four pillars. The counsel for the opposite party immediately offered to prove that the verandah contained five pillars, and that, consequently, no credit could be given to her evidence. The woman perceiving her error, addressed the judge, and said, "My lord, your lordship has for many years presided in this court, and every day that you come here ascend a flight of stairs: may I beg to know how many steps these stairs consist of?" The judge confessed he did not know: "Then," replied she, "if your lordship cannot tell the number of steps you ascend daily to the *seat of Justice*, it cannot be astonishing that I should forget the number of pillars in a balcony which I never entered above once or twice in my life." The judge was much pleased with the woman's wit, and decided in favour of her party.

In short, the ambiguity of the English law is such, and the stratagems of the lawyers so numerous, as to prove a source of misery to those who are unfortunate enough to have any concern with it or them.

As it may not appear fair or candid to censure any system so freely without an endeavour to point out some remedy to correct its defects, I shall here take the liberty of suggesting a few hints, which, I think, might be usefully applied.

For many years after the establishment of the Mohammedan religion, every person pleaded his own cause; and the cazies, being then men of great learning and sanctity, gave their decisions gratuitously.

As the English judges are at present paid from the public funds, and therefore cannot benefit themselves by prolonging suits, I recommend, that the counsellors, attornies, &c. shall be placed on a similar footing, and that they shall not receive any fee or bribe from the litigating parties under a severe penalty. In order to defray the expence of this establishment, either let a small additional tax be laid on the nation at large, or a duty of so much per cent. be levied on all litigated property. By this plan, I am convinced that the number and length of suits would be much curtailed, the time of the witnesses would be saved, the law would be purified from those imperfections which are now a reproach to it, and the courts purged of those pettifogging lawyers, who are a disgrace to their profession.

CHAPTER XVIII

Of the Finances of England. Mode of assessing the Taxes. Government Loans. National Debt. Effects of the Heavy Taxes, on the Poor, the Rich, and the Middling Classes of the People. Plan proposed by the Author for the liquidation of the National Debt.

In a work of this kind, it may be expected I should say something of the Finances of England; but, as the system is tedious and complex, I shall confine myself to the principal points of it only.

The public revenue of England is not, as in India, merely raised from the land, or by duties levied on a few kinds of merchandise, but almost every article of consumption pays its portion. The taxes are levied by the authority and decrees of Parliament. They are, in general, so framed, as to bear lightly on the poor, and that every person should pay in proportion to his income. For this reason, bread, meat, and coals, being articles of indispensable use, are exempt from duties; but spirits, wines, &c. are taxed very high. The proprietors of land pay one fifth of their rents, besides the tenth of its produce to the clergy. The rich are taxed for every dog, horse, and man-servant, they keep: they are also obliged to pay for the liberty of throwing *flour* on their heads, and for having their *arms* (insignia of the antiquity and rank of their family) painted on their carriages, &c. Since the commencement of the present war, a new law has been framed, compelling every person to pay, annually, a *tenth* of his whole income. Most of these taxes are permanent, but some of them are changed at the pleasure of Parliament.

When the Chancellor of the Exchequer discovers that the revenue is not equal to the estimate of the expences for the following year, he does not increase the taxes to supply the deficiency, but, by a refinement in finance, he borrows the amount, on Government security, and increases the duty upon some particular article of consumption, an eighth, or a tenth part, which suffices to pay the *interest* of the sum so borrowed. At first sight, it appears, that an additional duty, levied upon any particular article, would be an injury to the vender of it: the fact is, however, quite the contrary; for the vender, under pretence of realizing the duty, enhances the price of the commodity in a greater proportion than is requisite, and thus becomes a gainer by the circumstance, while the whole burthen of the tax falls upon the consumers.

This system of Government loans commenced about a hundred years ago: and as the surplus revenue, during peace, has never been equal to the discharge of the debt contracted during a war, the national debt has been gradually increasing, and now amounts to the enormous sum of some hundreds of millions. As it seldom happens that any part of this debt is paid off, it appears extraordinary that people are willing to lend their money on such terms, particularly when the annual interest is not more than five or six per cent. But the state of the case, I conceive, is this. The moneyed capital in England far exceeds the amount required for carrying on the commerce of the nation: and as the legal interest of money is limited to five per cent by law, the bankers prefer lending it to Government on these terms, rather than to individuals upon indifferent security: and although they have no hopes of ever being repaid by the borrowers, yet has this ideal property received such sanction by time, and the regular payment of the interest every six months, that a number of persons are always ready to purchase the Government bonds from them, even at an advanced price. The amount of the debt is however become so enormous, that the payment of the interest, in addition to the current expences of the empire, is severely felt by every person in the nation. It is therefore impossible that this system can continue much longer. The poor, being exempt from most of the taxes, do not feel the severity of them, except in the price of provisions and clothes; and the rich have it in their power to avoid many of the taxes, by dispensing with the use of some of the articles of luxury: but the middling classes of people, who have been accustomed to live in a certain degree of comfort and respectability, feel more severely than others the pressure of the times. They have already greatly curtailed their expences; and they cannot further reduce their establishments, without descending into a lower rank of life than they and their ancestors have been accustomed to move in.

This subject is well understood by some of their most intelligent politicians, who have calculated, that if the whole surface of both islands was covered with gold, it would not suffice to pay off the national debt. But as these gentlemen have not yet pointed out any remedy for this evil, I shall take the liberty of giving a few hints on the subject, the adoption of which may perhaps avert a calamity, that, I foresee, will one day overwhelm Great Britain, and lay her glories in oblivion.

Let the creditors of Government be assembled, in the presence of the Parliament; and let the Minister, clearly and dispassionately, explain to them, that the state of affairs is arrived at such a crisis, that is impossible the nation can continue longer to pay the amount of the enormous taxes which oppress them; that a revolution is to be apprehended; that the first act of the leaders of the revolution certainly will be *to cancel the national debt*, and that the rich may consider themselves fortunate if left in possession of their real wealth; that the national debt, being thus cancelled, they, the creditors, will lose *the whole* of their property invested in the funds; that therefore it will be much wiser to enter into an immediate compromise, and relinquish a part. For instance; those who have been receiving *interest* from the nation for a great number of years, shall give up half their claim; those who have received interest for a moderate number of years, shall yield a third of their demand; and those whose bonds are of a late date, shall relinquish a quarter of the amount. Now, as the creditors of Government are all rich persons, and, besides their property in the funds, possess great wealth, in gold, silver, merchandise, houses, and lands, there can be no doubt, if they were convinced of the danger of a revolution, by which they would risk much more fatal consequences, they would immediately comply with this requisition. By this plan the national debt would, in one day, be decreased at least one half. The Parliament should then curtail every unnecessary expence, and apply, each year, the surplus revenue to the payment of the remainder of the debt. By such means, in twenty or thirty years, the whole of the debt would be liquidated; some of the most oppressive taxes might be immediately abolished, and others gradually relinquished; provisions would, in consequence, become cheaper; and the people be rendered happy, and grateful to their Government.

CHAPTER XIX

The Author apologizes for the censure he is obliged to pass on the English character. He accuses the Common People of want of religion and honesty, and the Nation at large of a blind confidence in their good fortune, also of cupidity. A desire of ease, one of their prevailing defects. Picture of a London Gentleman. The English irritable, bad economists of their time, and luxurious. The advantages of simplicity, exemplified in the histories of the Arabs and Tartars. The English vain of their acquire-ments in learned or foreign languages—Governed by self-interest, licen-tious, extravagant. An instance of meanness and extravagance united—Bad consequences of these vices. The English too strongly prejudiced in favour of their own customs. The Author's mode of defending the Mohammedan customs. The English blind to their own imperfections.

It now becomes an unpleasant, and perhaps ungrateful, part of my duty, by complying with the positive desire of Lady Spenser[1] and several other of my friends, to mention those defects and vices which appeared to me to pervade the English character, but which, perhaps, only existed in my own imagination. If the hints I shall give are not applicable, I hope they will be attributed to want of judgment, rather than to malice or ingratitude: but if my suggestions are acknowledged to be correct, I trust they (the English) will thank me for my candour, and endeavour to amend their errors.

VERSE.

> He is your friend, who, like a mirror, exhibits all your
>   defects:
> Not he, who, like a comb, covers them over with the
>   hairs of flattery.

As my experience and knowledge of the common people were chiefly acquired in London, it may, and with great probability, be objected, that there are more vicious people to be found in the capital than in all the rest of the empire.

The first and greatest defect I observed in the English, is their want of faith in religion, and their great inclination to philosophy (atheism). The effects of these principles, or rather want of prin-ciple, is very conspicuous in the lower orders of people, who are totally devoid of honesty. They are, indeed, cautious how they transgress against the laws, from fear of punishment; but when-ever an opportunity offers of purloining any thing without the risk of detection, they never pass it by. They are also ever on the watch to appropriate to themselves the property of the rich, who, on this account, are obliged constantly to keep their doors shut, and never to permit an unknown person to enter them. At

---

1 See p. 189, note 4. That the Duchess of Devonshire was such an impor-tant public and political figure is important to what follows.

present, owing to the vigilance of the magistrates, the severity of the laws, and the honour of the superior classes of people, no very bad consequences are to be apprehended; but if ever such nefarious practices should become prevalent, and should creep in among the higher classes, inevitable ruin must ensue.

The second defect, most conspicuous in the English character, is pride, or insolence. Puffed up with their power and good fortune for the last fifty years, they are not apprehensive of adversity, and take no pains to avert it. Thus, when the people of London, some time ago, assembled in mobs on account of the great increase of taxes and high price of provisions, and were nearly in a state of insurrection,—although the magistrates, by their vigilance in watching them, and by causing parties of soldiers to patrole the streets day and night, to disperse all persons whom they saw assembling together, succeeded in quieting the disturbance,—yet no pains were afterwards taken to eradicate the evil. Some of the men in power said, it had been merely a plan of the artificers to obtain higher wages (an attempt frequently made by the English tradesmen); others were of opinion that no remedy could be applied; therefore no further notice was taken of the affair. All this, I say, betrays a blind confidence, which, instead of meeting the danger, and endeavouring to prevent it, waits till the misfortune arrives, and then attempts to remedy it. Such was the case with the late King of France,[1] who took no step to oppose the Revolution, till it was too late. This self-confidence is to be found, more or less, in every Englishman: it however differs much from the pride of the Indians and Persians.

Their third defect is a passion for acquiring money, and their attachment to worldly affairs. Although these bad qualities are not so reprehensible in them as in countries more subject to the vicissitudes of fortune, (because, in England, property is so well protected by the laws, that every person reaps the fruits of his industry, and, in his old age, enjoys the earnings or economy of his youth,) yet sordid and illiberal habits are generally found to accompany avarice and parsimony, and, consequently, render the possessor of them contemptible: on the contrary, generosity, if it does not launch into prodigality, but is guided by the hand of prudence, will render a man respected and esteemed.

The fourth of their frailties is a desire of ease, and a dislike to exertion: this, however, prevails only in a moderate degree, and

---

1 Louis XVI (1754-93), King of France, was guillotined during the French Revolution.

bears no proportion to the apathy and indolence of the smokers of opium of Hindoostan and Constantinople; it only prevents them from perfecting themselves in science, and exerting themselves in the service of their friends, upon what they *choose* to call trivial occasions. I must, however, remark, that friendship is much oftener cemented by acts of courtesy and good-nature, than by conferring permanent obligations; the opportunities of doing which can seldom occur, whereas the former happen daily. In London, I had sometimes occasion to trouble my friends to interpret for me, in the adjustment of my accounts with my landlord and others; but, in every instance, I found that, rather than be at the trouble of stopping for five minutes longer, and saying a few words in my defence, they would yield to an unjust demand, and offer to pay the items I objected to at their own expence: at the same time, an aversion to the employment of interpreter or mediator was so conspicuous in their countenance, that, latterly, I desisted from troubling them. In this respect I found the French much more courteous; for if, in Paris, the master of an hotel attempted to impose on me, the gentlemen present always interfered, and compelled him to do me justice.

Upon a cursory observation of the conduct of gentlemen in London, you would suppose they had a vast deal of business to attend to; whereas nine out of ten, of those I was acquainted with at the west end of the town, had scarcely any thing to do. An hour or two immediately after breakfast may be allotted to business, but the rest of the day is devoted to visiting and pleasure. If a person calls on any of these gentlemen, it is more than probable he is told by the servant, his master is *not at home*; but this is merely an idle excuse, to avoid the visits of people, whose business they are either ignorant of, or do not wish to be troubled with. If the suppliant calls in the morning, and is by chance admitted to the master of the house, before he can tell half his story, he is informed, that it is now the hour of business, and a particular engagement in the city requires the gentleman's immediate attendance. If he calls later in the day, the gentleman is just going out to pay a visit of consequence, and therefore cannot be detained: but if the petitioner, unabashed by such checks, continues to relate his narrative, he is set down as a brute, and never again permitted to enter the doors. In this instance, I again say that the French are greatly superior to the English; they are always courteous, and never betray those symptoms of impatience so conspicuous and reprehensible in the English character.

Their fifth defect is nearly allied to the former, and is termed irritability of temper. This passion often leads them to quarrel with their friends and acquaintances, without any substantial cause. Of the bad effects of this quality, strangers seldom have much reason to complain; but as society can only be supported by mutual forbearance, and sometimes shutting our eyes on the frailties or ignorance of our friends, it often causes animosities and disunion between the nearest relatives, and hurries the possessor into dilemmas whence he frequently finds it difficult to extricate himself.

The sixth defect of the English is their throwing away their time, in sleeping, eating, and dressing; for, besides the necessary ablutions, they every morning shave, and dress their hair; then, to accommodate themselves to the fashion, they put on twenty-five different articles of dress: all this, except shaving, is repeated before dinner, and the whole of these clothes are again to be taken off at night: so that not less than two complete hours can be allowed on this account. One hour is expended at breakfast; three hours at dinner; and the three following hours are devoted to tea, and the company of the ladies. Nine hours are given up to sleep: so that there remain just six hours, out of the twenty-four, for visiting and business. If they are reproached with this waste of time, they reply, "How is it to be avoided?" I answer them thus: "Curtail the number of your garments; render your dress simple; wear your beards; and give up less of your time to eating, drinking, and sleeping."

Their seventh defect is a luxurious manner of living, by which their wants are increased a hundred-fold. Observe their kitchens, filled with various utensils; their rooms, fitted up with costly furniture; their side-boards, covered with plate; their tables, loaded with expensive glass and china; their cellars, stocked with wines from every quarter of the world; their parks, abounding in game of various sorts; and their ponds, stored with fish. All these expences are incurred to pamper their appetites, which, from long indulgence, have gained such absolute sway over them, that a diminution of these luxuries would be considered, by many, as a serious misfortune. How unintelligible to them is the verse of one of their own Poets:

"Man wants but little here below,
Nor wants that little long."[1]

---

1   Edward Young, *Night Thoughts* iv. 1. 118.

It is certain, that luxurious living generates many disorders, and is productive of various other bad consequences.

If the persons above alluded to will take the trouble of reading the history of the Arabians and Tartars, they will discover that both these nations acquired their extensive conquests, not by their numbers, nor by the superiority of their arms, which were merely bows and arrows, and swords: no, it was from the paucity of their wants: they were always prepared for action, and could subsist on the coarsest food. Their chiefs were content with the fare of their soldiers; and their personal expences were a mere trifle. Thus, when they took possession of an enemy's country, they ever found the current revenue of it more than requisite for their simple but effective form of government; and, instead of raising the taxes on their new subjects, they frequently alleviated one half their burthen. The approach of their armies, therefore, instead of being dreaded, was wished for by the neighbouring people, and every facility given to their conquests. To this alone must be ascribed the rapidity with which they overran great part of the globe, in so short a period.

An anecdote is related of the Commander of the Faithful, Aly,[1] (on whom be the grace of God!) which will corroborate what I have stated. The son-in-law of the Prophet, previous to setting out on an expedition, ordered a quantity of barley-bread to be baked at once, sufficient to last him for twenty days. This he carried on his own camel, and every day ate one of the cakes, moistened with water, which was his only food. His friends remonstrated with him on his abstemiousness, and requested he would order some other victuals to be dressed. He replied: "My time is fully taken up with two things: first, my duty towards God; and, secondly, my care of the army. I have therefore no time to throw away on the indulgence of appetite."

The following anecdote of the Emperor Timour (Tamerlane)[2] will also, I hope, be considered as applicable to the subject under discussion. When that great conqueror was returning to Samarcand after the conquest of Persia, he left a considerable army, under the command of some of his most experienced generals, in Azerbijan; but, previous to quitting that province, he summoned the generals to his presence, and, having given them much good advice respecting their conduct, and the government and security

---

1   See p. 437, note 1.
1   See p. 299, note 1.

of the territories entrusted to their charge, concluded thus: "By the blessing of God, and the prowess of our victorious arms, all our enemies have been extirpated from this part of the world, save Sultan Ahmed Jellair, and Kara Yusuf the Turkoman, both of whom have taken refuge in the territories of the Ottomans of Constantinople. The former of these is a king, and the son of a king; but as he has been bred up in Persian luxury, and habituated to ease and comfort, I have no apprehensions of him. But beware of Kara Yusuf; he is an experienced soldier, hardened in adversity, accustomed to privations, and capable of undergoing toil and labour: let all your views be directed towards him." The penetration of the Emperor, and the justness of his remarks, were, in the sequel, fully proved; for, shortly after his death, both these princes invaded the province of Azerbijan. Sultan Ahmed was quickly defeated, and put to death; but Kara Yusuf, supported by the qualities ascribed to him by the Emperor, took advantage of the want of energy and the tyranny of the Tartars, and not only recovered his own province, but expelled them from great part of Persia.

The eighth defect of the English is vanity, and arrogance, respecting their acquirements in science, and a knowledge of foreign languages; for, as soon as one of them acquires the smallest insight into the principles of any science, or the rudiments of any foreign language, he immediately sits down and composes a work on the subject, and, by means of the Press, circulates books which have no more intrinsic worth than the toys bestowed on children, which serve to amuse the ignorant, but are of no use to the learned. This is not merely my own opinion, but was confirmed to me both by Greeks and Frenchmen, whose languages are cultivated in England with more ardour than any others. Such, however, is the infatuation of the English, that they give the author implicit credit for his profound knowledge, and purchase his books. Even those who are judges of the subject do not discountenance this measure, but contend, that a little knowledge is better than entire ignorance, and that perfection can only be acquired by degrees. This axiom I deny; for the portion of science and truth contained in many of their books is so small, that much time is thrown away in reading them: besides, erroneous opinions and bad habits are often contracted by the perusal of such works, which are more difficult to eradicate, than it is to implant correct ideas in a mind totally uncultivated.

Far be it from me to depreciate the transcendant abilities and angelic character of Sir William Jones;[1] but his Persian Grammar, having been written when he was a young man, and previous to his having acquired any experience in Hindoostan, is, in many places, very defective; and it is much to be regretted that his public avocations, and other studies, did not permit him to revise it, after he had been some years in India. Whenever I was applied to by any person for instruction in the Persian language, who had previously studied this grammar, I found it much more difficult to correct the bad pronunciation he had acquired, and the errors he had adopted, than it was to instruct a person who had never before seen the Persian alphabet. Such books are now so numerous in London, that, in a short time, it will be difficult to discriminate or separate them from works of real value.

A ninth failing prevalent among the English is selfishness. They frequently endeavour to benefit themselves, without attending to the injury it may do to others: and when they seek their own advantage, they are more humble and submissive than appears to me proper; for after they have obtained their object, they are either ashamed of their former conduct, or dislike the continuance of it so much, that they frequently break off the connection. Others, restrained by a sense of propriety, still keep up the intercourse, and endeavour to make the person they have injured, or whom they have deceived by promises, forget the circumstance, by their flattering and courteous behaviour. I had few opportunities of experiencing this myself in England; but the conduct in India of Colonel Hannay, Mr. Middleton, Mr. Johnson, and Dr. Blane, gave me convincing proofs of it;[2] for, whenever they had any point to carry, they would accept of no excuse from me; and having, by persuasion and promises, prevailed upon me to undertake their business, as soon as they had obtained their wishes they forgot their promises, and abandoned

---

1 Orientalist scholar and judge (1746-94) whose translations, essays, and poetry had a lasting impact on how the East was represented. He founded the Asiatick Society of Bengal and argued that the classical languages of India, the Near East, and Europe all emerged from a common source. Despite his extraordinary achievements, Abu Talib questioned his linguistic abilities.

2 See p. 63, notes 3, 4 and 5. Sir Gilbert Blane (1749-1834) did not serve in India but during his career as a physician he implemented a number of hygienic measures which radically improved the health of British seamen. His measures were particularly instrumental in combating the plague during the British engagements in the Mediterranean in 1799.

me to the malice of my enemies. It might have been unnecessary to quote these instances; for this defect in the character of the English is so evident, that no doubts remain on the subject.

It is well known, that when Lord Hobart was Governor of Madras he wanted to interfere in the internal management of the revenues of the Carnatic, and for this purpose solicited the sanction of his superior, Sir J. Shore.[1] In this, however, he was disappointed, for the Governor-general would not acquiesce in the measure; saying, "Although it might be politic, it would be unjust, and an infraction of the treaty between the Nabob and the East-India Company." To this observation his lordship replied; that, "If ever, in any former instance, the English had manifested this spirit of forbearance in aggrandizing themselves, he should not have proposed the measure to his Excellency; but as it was evident to all the world that the contrary system had ever been pursued, he thought, to let the present opportunity pass by would be little less than an act of folly."

The tenth vice of this nation is want of chastity; for under this head I not only include the reprehensible conduct of young women running away with their lovers, and others cohabiting with a man before marriage, but the great degree of licentiousness practised by numbers of both sexes in London; evinced by the multiplicity of public-houses and bagnios in every part of the town. I was credibly informed, that in the single parish of Maryla-bonne, which is only a sixth part of London, there reside sixty thousand courtezans;[2] besides which, there is scarcely a street in the metropolis where they are not to be found. The conduct of these women is rendered still more blameable, by their hiring lodgings in or frequenting streets which from their names ought only to be the abode of virtue and religion; for instance, 'Paradise Street,' 'Modest Court,' 'St. James's Street,' 'St. Martin's Lane,' and 'St. Paul's Churchyard.' The first of these is to be the residence of the righteous; the second implies virtue; and the others

---

1 Sir Robert Hobart (1760-1816), fourth earl of Buckinghamshire, was stationed at Fort St. George (Madras) from 1794-1798 during Sir John Shore's tenure as Governor General. He was responsible for governing the Carnatic, the region of southern India between the Coromandel Coast and the Eastern Ghats. After the death of Mohammad Ali (1749-95), Nawab of Arcot, Hobart's attempts at fiscal reform were met with resistance from both Shore and the new Nawab Umdat Ul-Umra (1795-1801). For his efforts he was recalled in 1798.
2 It is unclear how Abu Talib arrives at this estimate.

are named after the holy Apostles of the Blessed Messiah. Then there is 'Queen Anne Street,' and 'Charlotte Street'; the one named after the greatest, the other after the best, of Queens. I however think, that persons who let the lodgings are much more reprehensible than the unfortunate women themselves.

The eleventh vice of the English is extravagance, that is, living beyond their incomes by incurring useless expences, and keeping up unnecessary establishments. Some of these I have before alluded to, under the head of luxuries; but to those are now to be added the establishments of carriages, horses, and servants, two sets of which are frequently kept, one for the husband, the other for his wife. Much money is also lavished in London, on balls, masquerades, routs, &c. Sometimes the sum of £.1000 is thus expended in one night's entertainment. I have known gentlemen in the receipt of six or seven thousand pounds a year, who were so straitened by such inconsiderate expences, that if asked by a friend for the loan of *ten* pounds, could not comply with this trifling request. This spirit of extravagance appears daily to increase; and being imitated by merchants and tradesmen, must have the worst of consequences: for if these people find the profits of their trade not sufficient to support their expences, they will attempt to supply the deficiency by dishonest means, and at length take to highway robbery. It also encourages dissipation and profligacy in the lower classes, which tend to the subversion of all order and good government.

During one of my excursions from London in a stage coach, I experienced the greatest extravagance and meanness, united in an Englishman, I had ever before seen. He was a genteel looking man, and, soon after we entered the coach, commenced a conversation with me. He asked a number of questions respecting India, particularly about the price of provisions, and was astonished at the cheapness of different articles; but, after a short pause, he said, "Probably the low price of provisions is owing to the scarcity of money, and the limited incomes of the inhabitants of that country?" I replied, he was much mistaken, that no country abounded more with wealth than Hindoostan, and that it was proverbial for making the fortunes of all adventurers. When we sat down to dinner, he called for the most expensive wines, and asked me to drink with him. As I had no inclination to do so, and was averse to the expence, I declined; but when the bill was brought in, he took it, and divided the amount equally to every person at table. I was surprized at his insolence; but as none of the other passengers chose to dispute the demand, although they all looked at him with astonishment, I was ashamed to appear more parsimonious than others, and for two days paid eight shillings for my dinner each day, being twice the amount usual for the passengers in a stage coach.

Should this spirit of extravagance ever pervade the Ministerial department, they will either commit frauds on the public treasury, or be open to bribery and corruption; than which nothing sooner brings a State to ruin.

It is said, that previous to the late revolution, the French Government expended immense sums on public buildings, gardens, illuminations, &c. and were parsimonious in the expences of the navy and army; that the nobles lived in a superb style, whilst the lower classes were reduced to the most abject poverty; that the patience of the latter having been exhausted, they readily joined the leaders of faction, and drove their inconsiderate and domineering masters from among them.

If the English will take the trouble of reading ancient history, they will find that luxury and prodigality have caused the ruin of more Governments than was ever effected by an invading enemy: they generate envy, discord, and animosity, and render the people either effeminate, or desirous of a change. To these vices may be ascribed the subversion of the Roman empire in Europe, and the annihilation of the Moghul government in India.

Their twelfth defect is a contempt for the customs of other nations, and the preference they give to their own; although theirs, in fact, may be much inferior. I had a striking instance of this prejudice in the conduct of my fellow-passengers on board ship. Some of these, who were otherwise respectable characters, ridiculed the idea of my wearing trowsers, and a night-dress, when I went to bed; and contended, that they slept much more at their ease by going to bed nearly naked. I replied, that I slept very comfortably; that mine was certainly the most decent mode; and that, in the event of any sudden accident happening, I could run on deck instantly, and, if requisite, jump into the boat in a minute; whilst they must either lose some time in dressing, or come out of their cabins in a very immodest manner. In answer to this, they said, such sudden accidents seldom occurred, but that if it did happen, they would not hesitate to come on deck in their shirts only. This I give merely as a specimen of their obstinacy, and prejudice in favour of their own customs.

In London, I was frequently attacked on the apparent unreasonableness and childishness of some of the Mohammedan customs; but as, from my knowledge of the English character, I was convinced it would be folly to argue the point philosophically with them, I contented myself with parrying the subject. Thus, when they attempted to turn into ridicule the ceremonies used by the pilgrims on their arrival at Mecca, I asked them, why they supposed the ceremony of baptism, by a clergyman, requisite for the salvation of a child, who could not possibly be sensible what he was about? When they reproached us for eating with our hands; I replied, "There is by this mode no danger of cutting yourself or your neighbours; and it is an old and a true proverb, 'The nearer the bone, the sweeter the meat': but, exclusive of these advantages, a man's own hands are surely cleaner than the *feet of a baker's boy*; for it is well known, that half the bread in London is kneaded by the feet." By this mode of argument, I completely silenced all my adversaries, and frequently turned the laugh against them, when they expected to have refuted me and made me appear ridiculous.

Many of these vices, or defects, are not natural to the English; but have been ingrafted on them by prosperity and luxury; the bad consequences of which have not yet appeared; and, for two reasons, may not be conspicuous for some time. The first of these is the strength of constitution both of individuals and of the Government: for if a person of a strong constitution swallow a dose of poison, its deleterious effects are sometimes carried off by the power of the nerves; but if a weak person should take it, he would certainly fall a victim. The second reason is, that their neighbours are not exempt from these vices; nay, possess them in a greater proportion. Our poet Sady has said,

"To the inhabitants of Paradise, Purgatory would seem
  a Hell:
But to Sinners in Hell, Purgatory would be a Paradise."[1]

From what I saw and heard of the complaints and dissatisfaction of the common people in England, I am convinced, if the French had succeeded in establishing a happy and quiet government, whereby the taxes could have been abolished, and the price of provisions reduced, the English would, of themselves, have followed their example, and united with them: for, even during the height of the war, many of the English imitated the fashions, follies, and vices of the French, to an absurd degree.

---

1 From Chapter 1, Story 7 of *The Gulistan* or *The Garden of Roses* by the Persian poet and Sufi thinker Sadi (1184-1291).

Few of the English have good sense or candour enough to acknowledge the prevalence and growth of these vices, or defects, among them; but, like the smokers of *beng* (hempseed) in Turkey, when told of the virtues of their ancestors, and their own present degeneracy, make themselves ready for battle, and say, "No nation was ever exempt from vices: the people and the governments you describe as possessing such angelic virtues were not a bit better than ourselves; and so long as we are not worse than our neighbours, no danger is to be apprehended." This reasoning is, however, false; for fire still retains its inflammable nature, whether it is summer or winter; and the flame, though for a short time smothered by a heap of fuel thrown on it, breaks out in the sequel with the greatest violence. In like manner, vice will, sooner or later, cause destruction to its possessor.

CHAPTER XX

The Author describes the Virtues of the English, under the following heads:—Honourable—Respectful to their superiors—Obedient to the laws—Desirous of doing good—Followers of fashion—Sincere in their dispositions—Plain in their manners, and hospitable. Peculiar ideas of the English of the meaning of Perfection. The Author censures some of the customs of London. Fires—Description of the fire-engines—Hardship of the owner of the property burned, being obliged to pay for the use of the engines. The Author dislikes English beds. He censures the custom of retaining handsome footmen to wait on Ladies.

I fear, in the foregoing Chapter, I have fatigued my Readers with a long detail of the vices, or defects, of the English: I shall, therefore, now give some account of their virtues; but, lest I should be accused of flattery, will endeavour to avoid prolixity on this subject.

The first of the English virtues is a high sense of honour, especially among the better classes. This is the effect of a liberal education, and of the contempt with which those who do not possess it are regarded. This sense of honour is carried to such a degree, that men possessing every terrestrial enjoyment, as wealth, estates, wife, and children, will, on the smallest imputation, sacrifice their lives, and the welfare of their families, to recover their reputation, or to wipe off an ignominious slander.

Their second good quality is a reverence for every thing or person possessing superior excellence. This mode of thinking has this great advantage—it makes them emulous of acquiring the esteem of the world, and thus renders them better men. In other countries, this respect is not paid to superior merit: people will therefore not give themselves any trouble on the subject: wisdom, knowledge, and virtue, are consequently banished from among them.

The third of their perfections is a dread of offending against the rules of propriety, or the laws of the realm: they are therefore generally content with their own situations, and very seldom attempt to exalt themselves by base or nefarious practices. By these means the establishments of Church and State are supported, and the bonds of society strengthened; for when men are ambitious of raising themselves from inferior to exalted situations, they attempt to overcome all obstacles; and though a few gain their object, the greater part are disappointed, and become, ever after, unhappy and discontented.

The fourth of their virtues is a strong desire to improve the situations of the common people, and an aversion to do any thing which can injure them. It may be said, that in so doing they are not perfectly disinterested; for that the benefits of many of these institutions and inventions revert to themselves.

During my residence in England, and at a time when coals were extremely dear, one of their philosophers invented a kettle, with a small furnace below, which required so little fuel, that a piece of lighted paper, or a burning stick, thrown into the furnace, would cause the water to boil long enough to dress a joint of meat. By means of such machines, and the various conveniences adopted in the fitting up of a house, so much time and labour are saved, that two servants in England will do the work of fifteen in India.

Their fifth good quality is so nearly allied to weakness, that by some worldly people it has been called such: I mean, an adherence to the rules of fashion. By this arbitrary law, the rich are obliged not only to alter the shape of their clothes every year, but also to change all the furniture of their houses. It would be thought quite derogatory to a person of taste, to have his drawing-room fitted up in the same manner for two successive years. The advantage of this profusion is the encouragement it gives to ingenuity and manufactures of every kind; and it enables the middling and lower classes of people to supply their wants at a cheap rate, by purchasing the old-fashioned articles.

Their sixth excellence is a passion for mechanism, and their numerous contrivances for facilitating labour and industry.

Their seventh perfection is plainness of manners, and sincerity of disposition: the former is evinced in the colours of their clothes, which are generally of a dark hue, and exempt from all tawdriness; and the latter, by their open and manly conduct.

Their other good qualities are good natural sense and soundness of judgment, which induce them to prefer things that are useful to those that are brilliant; to which may be added, their perseverance in the acquirement of science, and the attainment of wealth and honours.

Their hospitality is also very praiseworthy, and their attention to their guests can nowhere be exceeded. They have an aversion to sit down to table *alone*; and from their liberal conduct on this subject, one would suppose the following verse had been written by an Englishman:

"May the food of the misanthrope be cast to the dogs!
May he who eats alone be shortly eaten by the worms!"

It is said, that all these virtues were formerly possessed in a greater degree by the English, and that the present race owe much of their fame and celebrity to their ancestors.

The English have very peculiar opinions on the subject of *perfection*. They insist, that it is merely an ideal quality, and depends entirely upon comparison; that mankind have risen, by degrees, from the state of savages to the exalted dignity of the great philosopher NEWTON; but that, so far from having yet attained *perfection*, it is possible that, in future ages, philosophers will look with as much contempt on the acquirements of Newton, as we now do on the rude state of the arts among savages. If this axiom of theirs be correct, man has yet much to learn, and all his boasted knowledge is but vanity.

Having thus given my opinion freely on the vices and virtues of the English, I shall now take the liberty to point out a few of the customs of the metropolis which appear to me reprehensible, and might easily be amended. The number of turnpikes in the vicinity of London are a great grievance: they not only oblige the traveller to stop, but compel him to take bad copper money in exchange for his silver, and, very often, abusive language into the bargain. This, however, is not quite so disgusting as when a stranger, wishing to visit the House of God, or the Tombs of the Kings, (I mean the Cathedral of Saint Paul, and Westminster Abbey,) is obliged every ten minutes to take out his purse, and pay another and another fee. The same vile practice exists at the

Tower, and at most of the public buildings, and ought to be abrogated.

The number of fires which happen in London are a very serious evil, especially as most of them originate from the quantity of wood used in the construction of houses. It has been before mentioned, that the houses of this city are seldom lower than four stories, and join each other: all the floors, stairs, doors, and roof, are of wood; nay, many have great part of the walls supported by timbers, and some have the apartments lined with painted wainscot. In every room there is a fire-place; so that if, by the carelessness or malevolence of a servant, one of these houses is set on fire, it quickly communicates to the others, and before it can be extinguished burns down half a street.

I should be guilty of an act of injustice, were I not to give the English credit for their invention and adroitness in extinguishing fires. They have machines which, being placed upon wheels and drawn by horses, can be conveyed to any part of the town in a very short time. These machines are worked by a mechanical power, and will throw up water fifty yards high: and as there are pipes of running water under every street, the situation of which is perfectly known to certain persons, a hole is in a few minutes dug in the pavement, and a plug being drawn from one of the pipes, the water rushes forth and supplies the engine, which may then be worked for twenty-four hours, or longer if necessary.

To each of these machines a number of people are attached, who are paid by the parish. These persons are called *firemen*: they are remarkable for their courage and their honesty: they have been known to enter a house all in flames, and bring thence many valuable articles, which they have delivered to the proprietor.

The only complaint I have against this system is, that a considerable sum of money must be paid to the first engine that arrives, a smaller to the second, and so on: thus, if fifty machines should come to extinguish a fire, and all their efforts prove ineffectual, the sufferer, who is already ruined by the destruction of his property, is obliged to pay a large sum to the firemen, which doubles his loss, and adds to the anguish of his mind. Notwithstanding the assistance of these machines, there is scarcely a day in which fires do not happen, and cause much mischief; but no pains are taken to make the people rebuild their houses on a better or more secure plan.

The beds, and mode of sleeping, in England, are by no means to my taste. They have, in general, two or three beds, laid one over the other; and the upper one being composed of feathers, a person is immediately swallowed up in them, and finds the greatest difficulty in turning from one side to the other. In the very depth of winter, this is bearable; but as the weather becomes warmer, it causes pains in the back, and a general relaxation of the frame. Above them, they spread a sheet, two blankets, and a quilt; all of which are closely tucked under the bedding, on three sides, leaving an entrance for the person to creep in next the pillows; which always reminded me of a bear climbing into the hole of a large tree. The bed being broad, and the clothes stretched out, they do not close about the neck, and, for a long time, do not afford any warmth; and if a person turns about incautiously, the four coverings separate, and either fall off the bed, or cause so much trouble, that sleep is completely banished. All my other Indian customs I laid aside without difficulty, but sleeping in the English mode cost me much trouble. Our quilts, stuffed with cotton, and lined with muslin, are so light, and adhere so closely to the body, that they are infinitely more comfortable and warmer than blankets; and although it may be objected, that to sleep the whole season with the same quilt next the body is an uncleanly custom, I reply, that *we* always sleep in a night-dress, which prevents the quilt touching the skin; whereas the English go to bed nearly naked, and use the same sheets for a fortnight together. It also frequently happens, that a person, in travelling, is put into a bed with damp sheets, the moisture of which is quickly absorbed into the body, and infallibly brings on cold, surfeits, or a deadly fever.

VERSE OF MOULAVY ROUMY.[1]

"These people wandered about in quest of shade, and spread blankets to cover them from the Sun:

They could not see the branching trees loaded with fruit, because the thick veil of prejudice covered their eyes."

I cannot approve the custom of the nobility and gentry in London retaining a number of handsome footmen, and other male servants, to stand behind a lady's carriage, or to attend her

---

1   Mawlana Jalal ad-Din Muhammad Rumi (1207-73). His poems are extraordinarily influential on both Persian and Turkish literature, and his writings constitute a fundamental component of the teachings of Sufism.

when she walks out. These fellows are, in general, well-looking, and when smartly dressed have an engaging appearance. It should be recollected, that Cupid makes no discrimination between poor and rich, vulgar or noble, the beggar or the king; we are all his slaves, and the subjects of his power. Scandal and dishonour must sometimes be the consequence of such a system.

I think I have now fairly acquitted myself of my promise to describe minutely the character of the English, or at least such as it appeared to me. I shall, in the following Chapter, give an account of the war maintained for so many years by England, against France and the united Powers of Europe; and then hasten to the continuation of my Travels, after so long a sojourn in one place.

CHAPTER XXI

Of the Geography of Europe—its subdivisions into Kingdoms. Nature of the different Governments in Europe—Commencement of the French Revolution—Rise of Buonaparte—Confederated Armies invade France—History of Hanover—Confederates defeated—English retire from Toulon. Success of Buonaparte in Italy and Switzerland— sent to conquer Egypt. Account of the Naval Engagements which occurred in the course of the war—English Fleet sent in pursuit of Buonaparte—Description of the Battle of Aboukir.

As the affairs of this transitory world are intimately connected with each other, previous to entering on a detail of the wars of the English it becomes requisite to explain the present state of Europe, and its subdivision into various kingdoms. Be it known, that the branch of the ocean which bounds the north of Europe, is called the Baltic Sea, and encompasses four kingdoms; viz. Russia, Prussia, Denmark, and Sweden. These four kingdoms are, in general, united; but Russia is considered as the leading power. The sea which bounds Europe to the south, is called the Mediterranean, or Sea of *Roum*: this also encompasses four kingdoms, viz. Spain, Portugal, Italy, and Switzerland. Four other states are inclosed within the above-mentioned eight, viz. France, Germany, Poland, and Holland. The islands of Great Britain and Ireland lie considerably to the west of the Continent. It must however be understood, that Germany and Italy are subdivided into a number of petty states, each of which has its sovereign, and particular laws; and as long as the kings of Europe were restrained within the bounds of moderation, these princes were allowed to remain independent, and to support a certain kind of dignity and splendour.

The governments of the kingdoms of Europe are of various kinds. In some, the King alone bears despotic sway; in some, the nobles hold the reins of authority; in some, the common people preside; and in some there is a mixture of all the three species of government: but there are other countries which do not acknowledge any King. This subject has been particularly explained in a work called the *Lebbi Tuarikh* (Heart of History), which I compiled several years ago from a work written by Mr. Jonathan Scott,[1] for the information of the Nabob Assuf ad Dowleh of Lucknow, and renders any further detail here unnecessary.

The five most powerful sovereigns in Europe are, the Emperors of Russia and of Germany, and the Kings of Spain, France, and England. The four first rule their territories with despotic sway. The powers of the last have been already described. It is well understood, that although the monarchical form of government has some advantages, yet, if the sovereign be a weak or a wicked man, he may do much mischief, and ruin his subjects.

In the year of the Christian æra 1789, the people of France being disgusted with the tyranny of their government, sent petitions and remonstrances to their King, desiring a reform of the system, and expressing a wish to be placed on a footing with the English. The King and nobles did not, however, pay any attention to these complaints; till, at the end of two years, the people, finding their remonstrances ineffectual, broke out into a state of open rebellion, and drove away several of their governors. This circumstance aroused the King and the nobles from the lethargy into which they had fallen; and in order to quiet the people, a Parliament, somewhat similar to that of England, was summoned to assemble at Paris.

The discontented persons, being thus assembled together, felt their strength, and increased in their demands. They at length insisted that the French government should be changed to a Republic. It must be explained, that in a republican form of government the King becomes an useless member; and although the nobles are allowed to possess their wealth and titles, they are not

---

1 Orientalist scholar (1753-1829) who specialized in Mughal historical works and numerous popular works including a six volume translation of Edward Wortley Montagu's manuscript of the *Arabian Nights Entertainment* (1811).

permitted to have a greater share of power than any other of the representatives of the people, who are chosen and displaced annually: neither in a Republic are any pensions allowed to Princes, or salaries granted to any but the effective officers of the State.

As it was impossible for the King to yield to so unreasonable a demand, he not only refused compliance, but ordered the principal proposers of it to be imprisoned. This measure was opposed by the seditious, and many lives were lost on both sides; but the rebels proving victorious, the whole of the common people in the kingdom threw off their allegiance, and raised the standard of revolt. The nobles, alarmed at the danger, fled, with their families and what wealth they could carry with them, into the neighbouring countries. Many of them, in consequence, came to England.

The King, being thus left alone, took refuge in his castle; but the greater part of the army having espoused the cause of the rebels, he was obliged to submit, and was shortly after, with his wife, tried and put to death.

After this event, a complete revolution of affairs took place in France. The powerful were reduced to weakness, and the base raised to power. The common people elected representatives from the lowest classes; and appointed officers of their own choice, to defend their territories.

It was about the time above mentioned, that Buonaparte, now the despotic sovereign of France, and the most celebrated character in Europe, was promoted to the rank of Colonel, and appointed to the army in Italy.

This Buonaparte is not a Frenchman, but was born in one of the small islands dependent on Ancient Rome, called Corsica; the inhabitants of which are notorious for thieving and robbing. On his first entering the military line, he offered his services to the English; but having been rejected by them, he entered the Republican army, and, by his wisdom, bravery, and good fortune, has raised himself to the exalted situation he now possesses.

The common people of all the countries in Europe, hearing of the success of the French, shewed symptoms of revolt; according to the proverb, "One peach by looking at another becomes red": and even England was infected with the contagion.

About this time, the relations of the murdered King made application to all the Sovereigns of Europe to espouse their cause: and the English Ministers, thinking that some advantage might be reaped in assisting them, and that, at all events, a war against France would keep the people quiet at home, sent a large army, under the command of the Duke of York, the King's second son, to invade that country.

Several of the Kings of Europe, being of the same opinion as the English Ministers, entered into a confederacy also to invade France. The principal of these were, the Sovereigns of Spain, Holland, and Germany: the Emperor of Russia,[1] and the King of Prussia,[2] also promised to join; and the latter, under pretence of raising an army, received a subsidy of several millions of money from England, but never sent a man to their assistance.

When the Russians and Prussians found the confederated Powers were deeply engaged in the war against France, they invaded the kingdom of Poland, consisting of fourteen fine provinces, and divided it between themselves. This was the first act of treachery practised in Europe, by a powerful against an inferior State. This bad example was, however, soon repeated, in the partition of Hanover, the ancient territory of the King of England, by the Prussians, Russians, and Germans, each of which took an equal share.

Be it known, that the fourth ancestor of King George the Third was Sovereign of Hanover, and kept a standing army of 20,000 men, and also struck the coin in his own name. He was, notwithstanding all this greatness, dependent on the Emperor of Germany;[3] but owing to one of the revolutions in human affairs, and his relationship to the former Royal Family of England, he was chosen King of that country, though he still continued to govern his own territories by deputy.

Hanover was, as I have above related, taken possession of by treachery: and although King George could easily have retaken it, his Ministers and the Parliament, being of opinion that the possession of that country had always been a great injury to England, and that it had cost more to protect it than it was worth, would not give their consent to an army being sent thither for the purpose of recovering it; and it was thus left in the hands of the Prussians and others.

The army which England sent to assist the partizans of the murdered King of France soon captured the fort and harbour of Toulon. The confederate armies at the same time, having marched through Holland, advanced far into France, and took

---

1 Alexander I (1777-1825), czar of Russia.
2 Frederick William II (1744-97).
3 This was likely Leopold I (1640-1705), Holy Roman Emperor.

possession of many towns in the name of the young Prince,[1] then a prisoner in the hands of the rebels, and were daily joined by a number of the well-wishers of the royal family.

The affairs of the Republicans were at this time reduced to a very low ebb; and it was confidently expected that the Allies would in a few days gain possession of Paris: but the French having determined to try the event of a general engagement, collected the whole of their force at one place, and gained a complete victory over all their enemies.

The English were anxious to revenge this defeat; but the Spaniards and Hollanders refusing to co-operate any longer, the former found it requisite to retire from Toulon: they (the English) in consequence re-embarked their troops; and having burned sixteen of the French ships of war in the harbour, carried away with them the remainder, amounting to nine ships of the line, and several frigates.

The French, having thus driven all their enemies out of their own territories, advanced into Holland, and took possession of that country. They then turned their arms against the Germans and the Russians. During this time, the son of the murdered King was conveyed from place to place, and at length sent into the other world, in some manner never hitherto explained.

Buonaparte's fame continuing to increase, he was appointed, by the interest of M. Barras, to the command of the army in Italy. After his conquest of that kingdom, he proceeded to Switzerland, where, aided by his aspiring genius and invincible courage, he not only overcame all the obstacles of nature and season in that mountainous and cold region, but obtained a complete victory over the Germans, and in a short time got quiet possession of the whole of that country.

Although the French found themselves masters of the Continent, they durst not send an army to invade England, because of the superiority of the British navy: they therefore resolved, as they could not approach the stem or root of the tree, that they would endeavour to lop off the branches. They, in consequence, sent an army to take possession of and plunder Hanover. They also sent an army to assist the disaffected party in Ireland, who, on account of some religious differences, and the intrigues of the French, have frequently rebelled against their legitimate Sovereign.

---

1   Louis XVII (1785-95?), second son of Louis XVI and Marie Antoinette, and believed to have died in prison.

Whilst these events occupied the attention of the western world, Buonaparte was sent, with an army of 50,000 men and a numerous train of artillery, to take possession of Egypt; with instructions, that, after the conquest of that country, he should proceed to India, and, having united himself with Tippoo Sultan, drive the English both from the Dekhan and Bengal.

These schemes were quickly discovered by the English, who, trusting to the superiority of their navy, were not at all alarmed by these desperate undertakings of the enemy. They, in the first place, easily defeated the army sent to Ireland; and having subdued the rebellion in that country, they despatched a fleet in pursuit of Buonaparte.

Previous to entering on a detail of the operations of this expedition, I think it requisite to give some account of the different naval engagements which occurred in the course of this war. I shall not notice the battles which have been fought between a few ships of the contending parties, but confine my descriptions to the operations of their fleets. Of this kind there were six memorable battles fought during the late contest, in all of which the English were victorious, and convinced the French, that, *at sea*, they were not able to contend with the English. Their ships were therefore compelled, either to take refuge under their forts, or to remain unemployed in harbour; while the English ships roved over all the seas, and prevented the French generals from making use of the advantages they had gained by land.

The first victory gained by the English, during the late war, was by the fleet commanded by Lord Howe,[1] in the year 1794, on the coast of France. In this engagement the English had but twenty-five ships, and the French twenty-six: of these, six were taken, and one sunk: the remainder fled into one of their own ports.

The second battle was fought on the coast of Spain, by Lord St. Vincent. He had but fourteen ships, and the enemy twenty-seven: of these, four large Spanish ships were captured.

The third was fought on the coast of Holland, by Lord Duncan's fleet, in 1798. His lordship had twenty-four, and the enemy twenty-six ships: of these, nine were taken.

---

1 Richard Howe (1726-99), Earl Howe, was a distinguished naval officer who served in the Seven Years' War, the American War, and in the war against Revolutionary France. His engagement with the French on "the glorious first of June" 1794 was not decisive, but it was seen by the public as victory.

The fourth was Lord Nelson's battle of the Nile, in 1799, with the fleet which conveyed Buonaparte's army to Egypt. His lordship had thirteen ships, and the French seventeen: of these, nine were captured, three burned, and one sunk.

The fifth battle was fought by Sir James Saumarez,[1] against the united fleet of France and Spain, in the year 1801. In this engagement, although the English had but five ships, and the enemy nine, four of the latter were burned, and one taken.

The sixth engagement was when Lord Nelson attacked Copenhagen, the capital of Denmark; some account of which has already been given in this Work. In that instance, seventeen of the enemy's ships were burned or destroyed, besides much damage done to the town.

I shall now return to the pursuit of Buonaparte. When the English were informed of the great preparations making by the French, previous to the invasion of Egypt, they supposed that so formidable an army must be intended, either for the invasion of England, or to attack India; yet as these preparations were confined to the ports in the Mediterranean Sea, and it would be requisite for the French to pass through the Straits of Gibraltar (on one side of which the English possess an impregnable fortress) to attain either of these objects, Lord St. Vincent was sent with a fleet of twenty-five ships, to prevent their getting out; but, after his lordship had been cruizing for some time in the Straits, he received authentic information, that the French fleet had put to sea, and steered eastward. As, some years previous to this event, the Spaniards had joined the French, and *they* had also a fleet of twenty-four ships ready to put to sea, Lord St. Vincent deemed it imprudent to quit the Straits with his whole fleet: he therefore detached Lord Nelson, with thirteen ships, in pursuit of the French, and remained himself, with the other twelve, to watch the motions of the Spaniards. Whether it was owing to the latter not feeling any interest in the success of the war, or that, even with such a superiority, they were still afraid of the English, they did not quit their ports.

Lord Nelson having received some intimation that the French fleet were bound to Egypt, steered directly for Alexandria; but, on his arrival there, he could obtain no intelligence respecting them. He therefore returned towards Sicily; and, on his way thither, was informed that the French had been at Malta, and were then cer-

---

1 First Baron de Saumarez (1757-1836) who, along with Captain Richard Keats, was engaged in two separate battles on 6 and 12 July 1801.

tainly gone to Egypt. This news was joyfully received by Lord Nelson, who made no doubt of giving a good account of the French, whenever he should meet with them. He therefore summoned all his captains on board his own ship, and gave them directions for their conduct, according to the situation in which they might find the enemy.

The French having arrived safely off Egypt, immediately landed their troops, and drew up their fleet in the Bay of Aboukir: they also erected batteries, for its defence, on the shore.[1] On the 1st of August, 1798, Lord Nelson came in sight of the French; and, having attentively observed their position, resolved, instead of attacking them in the common mode, that is, by laying one of his own ships against each of the enemy's, to cut them off by detail: he therefore made the signal for six of his ships to get between the French and the land, and to cast anchor alongside the six windward vessels of the enemy; while he, with the remainder of his fleet, did the same on the outward side: by this means he got the French between two fires, and in a short time subdued their first division; he then proceeded to take or destroy the remainder. This mode of attack was quite unknown before, and totally unexpected by the French, who, in consequence of the batteries on the shore, and the little depth of water between them and the land, considered themselves perfectly unassailable on that side, and had, in consequence, drawn all the heavy guns of their ships to the opposite side. It was one of those measures which evince a great genius, and a manoeuvre that none but an English officer would have thought of: for although it was attended with some risk, on account of the shallowness of water, (and, in fact, one of the ships did run aground, and suffered much annoyance from the batteries on shore,) the advantages were so manifest, that when the plan was proposed, no brave man could object to it.

---

1 The British victory over the French at Abu Qir was of crucial importance not only in the war between Britain and France, but also for the future of the Middle East. By stranding the French expeditionary force in Egypt, Nelson foiled Napoleon's plans to make incursions on Britain's empire in Asia. The French then attempted a number of reforms while in Egypt which generated a desire for modernization among some Islamic communities and provoked fierce resistance to Western cultural imperialism among more traditionalist constituencies.

VERSE OF SADY.[1]

> "By the sword you may kill one in a thousand of your
>   enemies;
> But by good judgment you may destroy his whole army."

The most extraordinary part of this engagement was, its having
taken place at night, in so dangerous a situation. The battle commenced in the evening, and terminated with the blowing up of
the French admiral's ship at midnight. I saw an exhibition of this
engagement in one of the Panoramas (the nature of which I have
before described): the sight of it was really dreadful, and gave me
an idea of the horrors of the Day of Judgment.

CHAPTER XXII

*Conquests of the English by land, during the late war. Origin of the
war with Tippoo Sultan—Reflections of the Author on the events of
the contest. Invasion of Egypt by Buonaparte—Siege of Acre.
Second Confederacy against France. Buonaparte invited to return—
leaves Egypt, and arrives in France—dissolves the National Assembly—defeats the Confederates. A Turkish army, sent to expel the
French from Egypt, defeated—The English send an army, under Sir
Ralph Abercrombie, to their assistance, which lands at Aboukir—
Battle between the French and English—Indian army land at
Cosseir—The Turks advance to Cairo—joined by part of the English
army—Cairo capitulates—Alexandria capitulates. Buonaparte
threatens to invade England—Lord Nelson destroys some of the
French boats. Peace concluded.*

Besides the victories gained at sea, during the late war, by the
English, they made several conquests on land. Of these, the most
important was the Cape of Good Hope, which they took from the
Dutch in the year 1795. The circumstances of the capture of that
place have been already detailed: I shall only add, that if it had
fallen into the hands of the French, and they could have kept a
strong fleet there, the route to India would have been nearly
barred up. From the French they took the Island of Malta (a particular account of which shall be given in the sequel of this Nar-

---

1 See p. 218, note 1.

rative); the Island of Martinique; and an extensive country in America, called Surinam. From the Spaniards they took the Islands of Minorca and Trinidad; and from the Dutch, besides the Cape of Good Hope, the territory dependent on which is very extensive, they took the valuable Island of Ceylon, on which, it is said, they found stores of cinnamon and other drugs, worth two millions sterling. They also took possession of all the settlements of the French, Dutch, and Danes, in India.

The capture of Seringapatam, and the death of Tippoo Sultan,[1] are events so well known, that I should not have thought it requisite to mention them here, were it not to render the list of the English conquests complete, and to explain a few circumstances which are not generally understood.

After Buonaparte had gotten possession of Egypt, he privately opened a correspondence with Tippoo Sultan; and promised, that he would shortly send such a force as should enable him to drive the English from India. Some of these letters having fallen into the hands of the English, who were then at peace with the Sultan, irritated and alarmed them exceedingly: they therefore demanded, that he should make over to them, during the period the English continued at war with France, certain forts which covered the sea-ports of his dominions; promising that the forts should be returned to him, in the same state they were received, as soon as the war terminated. He was further informed, that if he did not break off all connexion with the French, the consequences would be fatal to him. Tippoo either was ignorant of the power of the English *nation*, and judged of their strength and ability by the wars in which he had formerly been engaged with them, at a time when the councils of the English were not united; or imputed their *moderation* on a former occasion to some less worthy motive: he therefore would not listen to this salutary exhortation, but boldly determined on hostility; and, led on by his evil destiny, instead of pursuing his father's mode of warfare, that is, by laying waste the country, and harassing the English with his cavalry and repeated skirmishes, he foolishly tried his strength in a general engagement; and when defeated, shut himself up in the fortress of Seringapatam; where he vainly hoped to resist people, who, by their contrivances, would scale the heavens, if requisite.

---

1   See p. 65, note 2.

The British army, under the command of General Harris,[1] invested his capital, and, in a short time, made an opening, by which a large body of them entered. The Sultan set his troops a good example, and fought at their head as long as he could: till, having received three wounds, he fell from his horse, under the arch of the gate leading to the inner fort, and shortly after expired. The fort having been taken, search was made for the Sultan's body, and, after several hours, it was discovered under a heap of slain.

By the capture of this single fortress, the English got possession of the whole of Tippoo Sultan's wealth and family, and, in fact, of all his dominions: never was so rapid a conquest known; for from the time the British troops were first put in motion, till the termination of the war, only four months had elapsed.

Had Tippoo acted with common prudence, he should have entrusted the defence of Seringapatam to one of his generals, and remained with his army outside; where, by cutting off the supplies of the English, and frequently harassing them, he might have prolonged the siege; and, at all events, could have retreated to some other part of his territories, and continued the war: but he had too much pride to leave his family and wealth in a fortress invested by the enemy, and resolved rather to die in defence of what he considered his honour. One of our Poets has well said:

VERSE.

"When Fortune turns away her face from a man, he does precisely that which he ought not to do."

In my account of Dublin, I mentioned having seen the principal events of *The Capture of Seringapatam* exhibited on the stage, by which I was very much affected.

The English have also to boast, among their conquests, the expulsion of the French from Egypt, and a temporary possession of that country. To explain this assertion, it becomes requisite to revert to the invasion of Egypt by Buonaparte. That celebrated general landed his troops in the vicinity of Alexandria; and as the

---

1   George Harris (1746-1829), first Baron Harris, saw extensive military duty in India, where he fought in both the Third and Fourth Mysore Wars. In the latter campaign he was commander of the Madras Army and defeated Tipu Sultan at Seringapatam on 4 May 1799.

Turks were not prepared to resist him, he got possession of that fortress in a few days. Thence he marched to Grand Cairo; and as that city, although the capital of the kingdom, was only defended by a mob, composed of Mamelukes, Turks, and Cophts, armed with bludgeons and slings, they were soon dispersed by the victorious troops of France, aided by muskets and cannon. Many of the Mamelukes also, disgusted with the Turkish government, joined the invaders: the remainder took refuge in the deserts, and the Turks fled towards Constantinople; thus leaving the French in quiet possession of the country.

Buonaparte, either terrified by the destruction of his fleet at Aboukir, or having some presentiment of the honour awaiting him at Paris, instead of pushing on his troops towards India, according to his instructions, resolved to secure the sea-coast on the east side of the Mediterranean; supposing that, when master of an extensive coast, he could more easily elude the vigilance of the British cruizers, and thus keep up his connexion with the mother country. In consequence of this determination, he marched with a large army into Syria, or Palestine, and laid siege to Acre, the seat of government of one of the Turkish Pashas. It fortunately happened, that Jezzar Pasha, the governor, was a man of consummate courage; but having little experience of European warfare, and but an undisciplined garrison, he was much alarmed at the approach of the all-conquering French, under their invincible general.

It so happened, that Sir Sidney Smith,[1] a captain in the British navy, was at that time cruizing in the Mediterranean Sea with three ships of war; and having learnt Buonaparte's intentions, offered his services, to assist in the defence of Acre. This proposal was gratefully accepted by Jezzar Pasha; and Sir Sidney, having anchored his own ship in a situation that flanked the fort, landed with a party of his sailors, and, pointing out to the Turks the weakest parts of the fortification, assisted in repairing them; after which he stationed his own people at the points most likely to be attacked. During this period, Buonaparte, full of confidence, and flushed with victory, made the requisite preparations for storming the fort. Eleven times he marched his troops up to the attack,

---

1 Sir (William) Sidney Smith (1764-1840), was celebrated for his service
   in the Royal Navy in the Mediterranean in the 1790s. He was an
   instrumental figure in the defeat of the French expeditionary force in
   Egypt, and gained great fame for his part in the siege at Acre. See p. 294,
   note 1.

and as often were they repulsed by the united efforts of the Turks and English sailors. In each of these attempts many of his men fell, from the well-served fire of the cannon, both from the fort and the ships; and, after losing upwards of 5000 men, he was compelled to make a hasty and disgraceful retreat towards Egypt.

This siege was also very well represented in one of the Panoramas. The portraits of the Pasha, of Buonaparte, and Sir Sidney, were said to be striking likenesses; and the spectator might imagine himself at once transported from London, into the midst of the horrid scene of confusion and slaughter.

The enemies of Buonaparte, in Paris, took advantage of this defeat, to slander him; and, for many months, the Republic never sent him any supplies of provisions, recruits, or money: this, however, may have been caused by the vigilance of the British navy.

About this period, a new confederacy of the Powers of Europe was formed against the French; and a large army of Russians and Germans prepared to invade that country. The Republic was, at the same time, torn in pieces by factions; and it was evident, without an able chief to direct them they must infallibly be ruined. Impressed with these sentiments, a strong party wrote to Buonaparte, that, if he could return to France, they would elect him First Consul, and place the reins of government in his hands.

In consequence of these despatches, Buonaparte made over the command of the army in Egypt to M. Menou, a very weak man;[1] and embarked privately on board a small, but quick-sailing vessel, which, in despite of all the English cruizers, landed him safe in France. The day after his arrival in Paris, the Representatives assembled in their Parliament-house as usual, without any arms or guard. They had scarcely begun their debates, when Buonaparte entered, surrounded by his partizans and twenty armed soldiers: some of the most forward of the opposite party he confined; and dispersed the remainder, by informing them their services were no longer required. He afterwards filled all the public offices with his own friends, and was, by their vote, pro-

---

1 Jacques François Menou (1750-1810) succeeded General Kléber as Napoléon Bonaparte's governor of Egypt in July of 1800. He converted to Islam in order to marry an Egyptian and changed his name to Abdullah. He declared Egypt a colony and attempted to institute a wide range of unpopular reforms. After the French capitulation to the Anglo-Ottoman forces at Cairo, he was forced to surrender at Alexandria in 1801. The French left Egypt shortly thereafter.

claimed *First Consul of the French Republic.* He soon after took the command of the army, and marched against the Confederates. It is astonishing with what facility he defeated these great Potentates; and having obliged them to sue for peace, he returned, victorious and triumphant, to Paris.

Some months subsequent to the conclusion of peace with the Germans and Russians, Buonaparte assumed the title of 'President of the Republic of Italy,' and persuaded the French to elect him 'First Consul *for life.*' Thus he daily increased in dignity and power, and, by degrees, usurped all the authority of the government. During the period that I resided at Marseilles, he ordered the coin to be stamped with his own image. He did not, however, at that time, venture to assume the title of King or Emperor.

After the departure of Buonaparte from Egypt, the Grand Signior (properly, Emperor of the Ottomans)[1] sent a numerous army, under the command of his principal Vizier, Yusuf Pasha, to expel the French from that country. But the Turks are now so ignorant of the art of war, that, although infinitely more numerous than their enemy, they received several very shameful defeats, and evinced to the whole world their weakness and want of courage.

This event drew aside the veil which had long concealed from public view the imaginary powers of the Turkish government, by which they had formerly made such extensive conquests in Europe, and the effects of which are still severely and impatiently felt by several of the neighbouring Christian sovereigns. The Germans and Russians, therefore, prepared to take advantage of the difficulties with which the Turks were now overwhelmed, in their contest with France.

In this dilemma, the English sent an army of 15,000 men, under the command of General Abercrombie,[2] (brother of the late Commander-in-chief in India,) to assist the Turks in expelling the French from Egypt. They also ordered another army to be sent from India, by the Red Sea and Suez, to co-operate in this undertaking. General Abercrombie landed his troops at Aboukir, though opposed by the French, who were drawn up with a numerous train of artillery on the shore, and compelled them to take refuge in the fortress of Alexandria.

---

1 Sultan Selim III (1761-1808).
2 Sir Ralph Abercromby (1734-1801) died in battle at Abu Qir. Sent to expel the French from Egypt, his mission was largely successful, though more than 4,000 soldiers were killed.

Some days after this event, General Menou having joined the French with a large reinforcement from Caïro, a general engagement took place between the two armies; in which, although Sir Ralph Abercrombie and four thousand of the English were killed, the French were completely defeated.

In this battle a celebrated corps of the French, who had ever accompanied Buonaparte in all his conquests, and were honoured with the title of 'The Victorious and Invincible Legion,' were totally routed, and their colours taken. After this disgrace, the French retreated to Alexandria.

In neither of these battles did the English receive the smallest assistance from their allies the Turks, but gained both victories by the prowess of their own arms; and convinced their enemies, that they were as formidable on shore as at sea.

It was about this time that the army from India, having landed at Cosseir in the Red Sea, prepared to pass the Desert, in order to gain the banks of the Nile.

The Turkish Vizier, encouraged by the success of his allies, again assembled a numerous army, and advanced towards Caïro. By his request, a detachment of the English army also moved in the same direction, and laid siege to that city.

As, at this time, discord prevailed amongst the French generals, and every hope of assistance from the mother country was cut off, they thought it advisable to capitulate; and gave up Caïro to the Grand Vizier, on condition of being sent home. The English soon after got possession of Alexandria, on the same terms. Thus the French were expelled from Egypt, and all their vain hopes of proceeding to India by that route completely annihilated.

After Malta and Egypt had fallen into the hands of his enemies, Buonaparte was secretly desirous of making peace; but, far from openly avowing his wishes, he affected a determination of prosecuting the war against the English with the utmost vigour. For this purpose he assembled an innumerable army at Calais, which is the nearest port to England, and is situated directly opposite to Dover. He also ordered an immense number of flat-bottomed boats, and gun-boats, to be assembled at the same place, for the purpose of conveying his army across the Channel, which, at this place, is only twenty-one miles over.

In order to oppose this invasion, the English stationed a large army, under the command of Lord Cornwallis, in the vicinity of Dover; and sent Lord Nelson, with a number of small vessels, to destroy the boats. In the first attack his lordship sunk several of the boats; but as they were linked together with chains, he was not so successful as he expected. In a subsequent attack, the French, having been aware of his lordship's intentions, posted a great number of soldiers below the decks of the boats, armed only with swords and daggers (in the use of which the French are said to excel all other Europeans), who waited quietly till the English had boarded, and were trying to cut away the chains; they then rushed out, and compelled Lord Nelson to retire, with the loss of seven hundred men.

After this event, both sides being equally anxious for peace, (Buonaparte with the hopes of recruiting his navy, and the English Ministers in order to satisfy the common people, who were very clamorous on account of the taxes and high price of provisions,) Lord Cornwallis was sent over to France as Plenipotentiary, to adjust all differences. After three months of continual discussion, his lordship concluded a treaty of peace,[1] on the following terms:

1. That all the conquests made by the French, in Italy, Switzerland, Germany, and Holland, should remain to them for ever.
2. That the Islands of Ceylon and Trinidad should remain in possession of the English.
3. That the Cape of Good Hope should be restored to the Dutch; Egypt to the Turks; and Malta, &c. to their former possessors.

This event gave great satisfaction to the inhabitants of London. For three days the streets resounded with festivity and rejoicing; and at night the moon was eclipsed by the splendour of the illuminations.

CHAPTER XXIII

The Author resolves to return to India—His purposed route—He quits London—Disgusted with Dover—Embarks for France—Account of his journey to Paris—Description of that city—Its Public Buildings—Hot and Cold Baths—Mode of washing clothes—Coffee-houses—

---

1   Abu Talib is summarizing the terms of the Treaty of Amiens of 25 March 1802, signed by Napoleon and Cornwallis, under which Britain recognized the French Republic.

French cookery—Houses—Lodging-houses—Lighting of the streets at night—Pavement—Description of the Boulevards—Palais Royal—Manufacture of China—Tuileries—Louvre—Public Gardens—Phantasmagoria—Public Library—Opera, and Playhouses.

As I had been for some time anxious to return to India, I determined to avail myself of the favourable opportunity of a general peace to do so; and, at the same time, to gratify my curiosity, by visiting several countries, the fame of which had excited my attention. The route I proposed to take was, through France, Germany, and Hungary, to Constantinople; thence through Turkey in Asia, either to Arabia or the Persian Gulf, whence to India the passage by sea is short.

After a residence of two years and five (Lunar) months in London, I bade adieu to my friends; and on the 10th of the month Suffur, A.H. 1217, corresponding with the 7th of June 1802, I set out in the stage coach for Dover.

As the distance was only seventy miles, we arrived at Dover the same evening; and as we did not stop to dine on the road, I meant to have regaled myself with a good English meal before I quitted that beloved country: but the inhabitants of Dover are so contaminated with French manners, that to my great disappointment all the dishes were dressed according to the rules of French cookery; and the people of the inn, seeing me a foreigner, would talk nothing but that language. In one particular they adhered to their English customs, which was in the extravagance of their bill, every article being charged even higher than the London prices. The custom-house officers were also, I thought, exceedingly troublesome, and objected to articles which I am convinced they had no right to do, merely to obtain fees.

The following day we embarked on board a packet, and in six hours were safely landed at Calais, a celebrated sea-port of France. It fortunately happened for me that one of my fellow-passengers in the stage coach was a gentleman of the most compassionate and liberal character. He was an Anglo-American merchant, named Neil, who was going to Paris to procure the liberation of his ship, which a year before had been unjustly seized by one of the French cruizers. He, seeing the impositions attempted to be put on me at Dover, and my total ignorance of the French language, on our arrival at Calais kindly offered to be my interpreter and bursar on the journey. These offices he faithfully and diligently performed; and it was with much difficulty I could prevail on him to accept of the sum he had expended on my account, when we arrived at Paris.

After supper we got into a heavy coach, called a *Diligence*, but which, from the tediousness of its motion, reminded me of a Hindoostany carriage drawn by oxen; and after three nights and two days of incessant travelling, we at length reached Paris. During the whole of this journey, the country was beautiful and highly cultivated; rich fields of corn were here and there divided by vineyards, or orchards of delicious fruit; rivulets of clear water crossed the road in various places, over which were constructed neat stone bridges; and every few miles we came to a populous town or village. In these respects it appeared to me superior to England. The cows and other animals were however thin and poor looking, and resembled those of India. The horses had the appearance of the Persian or Arabian breed, and better looking than the English, but I was informed were not near so good. It was on this journey I first observed oxen used in Europe to draw carriages. Many of the French dogs are exceedingly beautiful, and so small, that they are carried by ladies under their arms, to prevent their being fatigued.

The roads were very broad and level, and the sides were planted with rows of shady trees, which, in the summer, must be a great comfort to the traveller. Many of the towns are surrounded by walls, and have all the appearance of fortresses.

The villages in France are exceedingly mean, and do not at all resemble their towns. I thought the female peasants very disgusting, both in their manners and their dress: the attire of the village girls in India, in comparison with these, is infinitely superior. The inns on the road were also execrable, and filthy to such a degree, that I could neither eat nor drink in them with any pleasure.

As I had determined to remain only a short period in Paris, I lost no time in viewing every part of it; and shall here endeavour to give a description of that city, together with a short account of the character and customs of the inhabitants.

The capital of France is an extensive and noble city, and, in its exterior appearance, far surpasses London. Its public buildings are all of stone, and are seldom less than eight stories high; some houses have even eleven stories. A considerable river of fresh water, called the Seine, runs through it; from which several canals have been cut, to communicate with the different parts of the city: over these canals are many bridges; and over the river itself there are three handsome stone bridges, nearly as long as those of London.

Paris can boast of a great number of both hot and cold baths, which are much frequented by the inhabitants. I was particularly delighted with those which they have constructed on boats, and are moored in the river. The mode of constructing them is this: they first procure a large flat-bottomed boat, on which they build twelve or more cabins or apartments, which are painted, and neatly fitted up with the proper furniture: in each of these apartments there is placed a copper bath or cistern; and on the top of the boat are large boilers for the hot, and reservoirs for the cold water, which communicate, by pipes secured by brass cocks, with the cistern below; so that the bather can modify the temperature of the bath to any degree he likes. The reservoirs are filled, and the cisterns emptied, by means of pumps worked by the stream, by which there is a constant supply of fresh water, without any trouble or expence; and two or three persons are sufficient to keep every thing clean, and in good order. They have baths of this kind entirely appropriated to females, of which the servants are of course all women. This institution is well deserving of imitation. Some of these boats have covered steps, which communicate with the river, for the benefit of those who wish to swim. Others have a small deck near the stern, on which a table is generally laid out with refreshments, for those who may feel hungry after their ablutions, or may be inclined to sit and enjoy the cool air and prospect of the city. The mode of getting to these boats is by a long plank, two feet broad, which is extended from them to the shore, with a rail on each side to take hold of.

The people who wash clothes have boats also fitted up for the purpose: their boilers and tubs are below, and the deck is hung round with lines for drying. Owing to this simple invention, the clothes are much better washed and bleached here than in London, where the occupation is often practised either in a cellar or in a garret, amidst smoke and dust.

In Paris the coffee-houses are innumerable, but in general are very filthy; and as many of the French smoke *segars* or *cheroots* in them at all hours of the day, they smell shockingly of tobacco. A person is also much annoyed by beggars at these places: they follow a gentleman into the room, and sometimes even take hold of his hand, to move his compassion, or rather to tire him by their importunity: they are, however, content with a trifle, and will sometimes be satisfied by a piece of bread: to obtain this favour, they have frequently to contend with a surly rival, in the form of a large dog, whose filth is lying about in different parts of the room.

I had been so long accustomed to English cookery, that during the whole of my residence in France and Italy I could never relish their culinary process. Their roasted meats are burned up, and retain not a drop of gravy: the boiled meats were also overdone, and quite stringy. The French are exceedingly fond of mixtures, that is, meat stewed with vegetables, and a great quantity of garlic, spices, &c. On this account I have frequently risen hungry from a table of thirty dishes, on the dressing of which much pains had been bestowed, and principally on my account. The only good dinners I ever ate in these countries were at the houses of English or Americans, who had taken pains to instruct their servants in the proper mode. Neither could I relish their pies or tarts, &c. as an inspection of their pastry-cooks' shops had prejudiced me strongly against them.

During my residence in England, I often heard people railing against the exorbitant price of different commodities, and praising the cheapness of things abroad; but I declare, I found both France and Italy much more expensive than England, and the things not so good.

I have before mentioned that the exterior appearance of Paris is superior to London; so, in this respect, are their houses: they are very lofty, and have a great deal of gilding and finery about them; but, in the interior, they are not by any means so neatly or comfortably fitted up as the English houses.

The pleasures of this life depend much upon the attainment of three things:—1st, A clean, comfortable, and private house, to reside in. For such a situation, a stranger in Paris may seek in vain. 2dly, Good eating and drinking. Of this pleasure I was deprived by the badness of their cookery. 3dly, A facility of procuring those things which are requisite for our comfort. The better classes of inhabitants probably enjoy these means, but they are unattainable by a traveller.

A lodging-house in Paris, which is probably eight stories high, and contains fifty or sixty persons of both sexes, has only one entrance, and one yard. The noise and dirt made by such a crowd may be easily imagined. In these houses it is not customary to hang bells; and as the servants never think of visiting the rooms but once a day, that is, when they make the bed and bring up water, it becomes absolutely requisite for a person who wishes for any comfort, to hire a servant of his own, to whom he is obliged to pay a guinea a week. In France they seldom think of cleaning the grate, or fire-place; it is consequently a disgusting object: whereas, in England, I always thought it an ornament to the room, and a good coal fire more beautiful than a bouquet of flowers.

In some of the streets of Paris, there are, at night, a few lamps which yield a glimmering light, barely sufficient for a man of keen sight to find his way; and, as the shopkeepers do not light up their windows as in London, the city has then a very sombre appearance. In those streets which have not lamps, you frequently see a lantern suspended from the roof of a house by a long rope, which in the day-time has a disgusting and mean effect. The streets in Paris are not flagged on the sides, as in London; a rough pavement extends all the way across the street; and as the carriages drive up close to the doors, the foot-passengers are in constant danger of being driven over: on this account there is no pleasure in walking the streets of Paris, either by day or night.

In some measure to compensate for the above deficiency, there is a broad road, formed by the ramparts of the ancient city, which extends in a circle, for many miles, and is called the *Boulevards*. This road is properly divided into three portions: the middle, which is twenty-five yards wide, is allotted to horses and carriages, and the two sides are appropriated to the foot-passengers. Four rows of shady trees have been planted all along this road, which not only add to its beauty but to its comfort. Under the two exterior rows of trees, a number of tables are laid out with fruit, sherbet, pictures, toys &c. the property of petty tradesmen, who take their station here during the day, and return to their homes at night. As these people undersell the regular shopkeepers, their stalls are always crowded, either by persons wishing to purchase cheap bargains, or by passengers, induced from curiosity to look at their articles: in short, this walk is never empty.

A second favourite place of recreation of the Parisians is the *Palais Royal*.[1] This place, previous to the Revolution, was the residence of the King's Brother, but is now thrown open to the Public. The garden, which is surrounded by a wall, is an oblong square, five hundred yards long by two hundred wide; it is divided by a number of gravel walks, shaded by trees, into parterres of roses and other shrubs, flowers, &c.; at the ends are two lofty halls, sixty feet long by thirty wide, open in front, and supported by stone pillars; and within the inclosure there are not less

---

1 At the time of Abu Talib's travels, the Palais Royal's walled garden, originally part of the residence of Cardinal Richelieu, was Paris's first shopping arcade.

than twenty-five handsome coffee-houses, all of which are open to the garden. Morning and evening these rooms are crowded with persons of both sexes; especially one which is situated opposite the centre cross walk, and has a wide circular verandah. These gardens are the constant resort of thousands of people; who, when tired of walking, or meeting by chance with a friend, retire to the coffee-houses, and refresh themselves with wine, sherbet, fruit, or ice. I must here acknowledge that the French surpass the Persians, Indians, and English, in the manufacture of this latter article.

A place frequented by such a concourse of people must of course be the favourite resort of courtezans; hundreds of them are to be met in every walk; and the houses in the vicinity are filled with them. It is distressing to see a place, once the residence of Royalty, perverted to so ignoble purposes.

Near to the grand gate of the Palais Royal is an extensive and lofty building, converted into shops, in which are displayed some of the richest manufactures and finest productions of the country. I was particularly attracted by the jewellers' and china shops. It is requisite here to explain, that the French are celebrated all over Europe for the manufacture of china; it is difficult to say whether the beauty of the painting, the richness of the gilding, or the transparency of the material, is most estimable; in short, it is so highly prized, that, in England and other countries, it is either shewn as a curiosity, or only used when a guest of great consequence visits the house. The French are also famous for making very large mirrors.

A third place of resort for the luxurious inhabitants of Paris is the garden or pleasure-grounds of the *Tuileries*, a celebrated palace, now occupied by Buonaparte.[1] These grounds are divided into two portions: that next the palace is used as a parade for the troops; and, at times, five or six thousand horse are drawn up within the inclosure. On the side next the city, this garden is fenced in by a lofty iron railing, with two immense gates, such as in India are called *phateks*: on both sides of the gates are erected a number of stone pillars, on which are placed brazen statues of horses as large as life, part of the plunder brought from Rome by Buonaparte, and said to be the work of the most celebrated

---

1 The Tuileries Palace gardens were a fashionable site of leisure throughout the eighteenth century. During the French Revolution they were the site of numerous political events. When Napoleon came to power he made the Tuileries his imperial palace.

ancient masters. After passing through the square, you enter what are properly the Tuilerie gardens, which communicate with the city by various roads. These gardens are an oblong square, about two miles in circumference: in them are several rivulets of running water, and large fountains with lofty *jets d'eau*; also several gravel walks, shaded by umbrageous trees, under which stand a great variety of admired statues, all of which have been brought from the conquered countries. Tents are pitched in different places, in which they sell coffee, wine, sherbet, ice, fruit, &c. On the outside of the gardens there is an extensive park, adorned with shady trees and streams of water; the whole bounded by a deep wet ditch. From this park, on the right hand, is a beautiful view of the principal buildings of the city; and on the left hand there is an extensive prospect of the river, with its superb bridges. In this park a number of tents are also pitched, in which the people are either continually dancing to the sound of harmonious music, or exhibiting their skill in fencing to the surrounding multitude. It may be unnecessary to state, that in the vicinity of these tents abundance of refreshments are to be procured. In my opinion, this park is the pleasantest place about Paris, for walking and recreation.

The places I have hitherto described are better adapted to the taste and customs of the common people, than of the higher classes; but in the *Louvre*, all persons of science or liberal education may find an inexhaustible fund of amusement and information.[1] The Louvre is a repository of all the pictures, select statues, and other curiosities, plundered by Buonaparte and other French generals, from all the countries they have overrun; but the most valuable of them were brought from Rome. The sciences of sculpture and painting were formerly much better understood than they are at the present time. During the reigns of the Cæsars, these arts, especially the former, flourished to a great degree; but on the extinction of their power, the sciences were, for some centuries, totally neglected. Fortunately, the Popes, or Vicars of Jesus Christ, who succeeded to the government of Rome, and some of the Princes of Italy, collected a number of the statues, and a few pictures, which they carefully preserved. These have ever since served as models and copies for the artists of later times, who used to travel from all parts of Europe to Rome, to perfect themselves in their profession. When Buonaparte took possession of

---

1   The Royal Palace of the Louvre was first opened to the public as a museum on 8 November 1793, during the French Revolution.

that city, he scrupled not to plunder these venerable repositories, and ordered the most valuable articles to be selected, and sent to Paris.

The Louvre is a very extensive and lofty building. The whole of the lower story is filled with statues and heavy articles, the perfections of which I was not a competent judge of. On the first floor you enter a magnificent room, three hundred feet square, and one hundred and fifty high, lighted from the top by glass windows, in iron frames, laid in a sloping position, which not only give abundance of light, but keep out the rain and snow as well as a tiled roof. On the walls of this room, from top to bottom, are suspended many thousands of the most beautiful and valuable pictures the imagination can fancy. After passing this room, you enter a gallery ninety feet wide, and half a mile long: on the walls of this gallery are suspended a great variety of pictures, in gilt frames, and covered with glass to preserve them from the effects of the weather. The number of pictures in this collection is immense, and the value incalculable: some of them are seventy feet in length, and thirty in height. In short, after viewing the Louvre, I considered the pictures and other curiosities I had seen in Dublin and London merely as children's playthings. This place, as well as those before described, is supported at the public expence, and the people are admitted gratis: this serves to amuse them, and renders Buonaparte's government popular.

Besides the places of amusement already described, there is not a division of the city but has half-a-dozen public gardens, or other exhibitions: the principal of these are the Italian gardens, the Frescati and the Tivoli; in each of which there is an exhibition of fireworks, dancing, &c. every evening, and abundance of refreshments of all kinds to be procured.

I was particularly entertained in Paris by an invention called *Phantasmagoria*.[1] I cannot explain the principles of this art, further than it can only be exhibited in a dark room, and is effected by transparent paintings and shadows. A figure appears,

---

1 The most famous *fantasmagorie* was staged in Paris in 1797 by the Belgian inventor Etienne-Gaspard Robert. Under the stage name Etienne Robertson, he simulated hauntings in a Capuchin crypt by projecting images onto walls, smoke and semi-transparent screens with a series of movable magic lanterns. By 1801, a similar phantasmagoria was entertaining audiences at the Lyceum Theatre in London, but Abu Talib distinguishes this Paris production from the many projections he saw while in Britain.

apparently at a great distance, and sometimes as if coming from the roof of the house: it is at first very small, not larger than a star, but increases in size as it approaches. One of these figures represented a dead person in a shrowd, which approached by degrees, and, when it came close to us, opened the shrowd, and discovered a skeleton, horrid to behold. Many of the children, and even women, were alarmed, and cried piteously. The spectre then retired by degrees, and seemed to vanish through the roof; immediately after which, a sound, resembling thunder and rain, was distinctly heard, and added to the dismay. By means of this science, they can introduce on the stage the exact semblance of any hero of antiquity, or the likeness of any absent friend: and this art was formerly used by necromancers to deceive people, by leading them to suppose they possessed supernatural powers.

The Public Library of Paris contains nearly a million of books, in various languages, and upon all subjects. Its establishment is the most liberal I have any where met with, as the people are permitted to enter it gratis, and have not only permission to read there the whole day, but to make extracts, or even to copy any book in the collection.

In this city there are thirteen opera or play-houses, several of which I visited: and, upon the whole, I think the French operas are superior to those of London, both in respect to the singers and the dancers. There are also several places for equestrian performances; and the ball-rooms for dancing are innumerable.

CHAPTER XXIV

Character of the French. Anecdote of a Barber—of the hotel at Marseilles—Author's reflections. Observations on the appearance and dress of the French Ladies. He meets with several of his English acquaintances—Is displeased at his reception by Mr. Merry, the British Envoy. Anecdote of the people of Mazanderan. Author visited by a sharper— He forms an acquaintance with some of the French Literati—Is invited to Court.

The French in general, and especially the Parisians, are extremely courteous, affable, and flattering. They never make use of the simple words Yes or No, but have always some circuitous phrase ready, expressive of the honour you confer, or their regret. In pointing out the road, or explaining any thing to a foreigner, they are indefatigable, and consider such conduct as a proof of their

good-breeding and humanity. You may call on a French gentleman at any hour, and relate to him your whole story twice over:
he will listen with the greatest patience, and never betray a discontented look. How superior, in this respect, are they to the irritable and surly Englishmen!

Whilst travelling, or when dining at French ordinaries, I was
frequently surprised to see with what good-humour the gentlemen put up with bad food, and worse wine; and whenever I complained, they took great pains to persuade me the things were not
so bad, or that the master of the house was not in fault. The
French appear always happy, and do not vex themselves with
business; for immediately after dinner, they walk out, and amuse
themselves till midnight, in visiting the gardens, and other places
of recreation. To most of these places they have admission gratis,
the proprietors of them being content with the moderate profit
they can make by the sale of coffee, sherbet, ices, &c.; and at the
opera or play-houses, where admission is charged for, the prices
are not a fourth part what they are in London. It must however
be acknowledged, that some of the places of public amusement
are so confined and ill contrived, that none but a Frenchman
could tolerate them.

In some instances, I think the French have too much apathy
and want of exertion, and that the servants take advantage of the
forbearance of the better classes. I have often observed the servants neglect their duty, or, in order to avoid a little exertion at
first, bring on themselves double trouble in the end. I shall
content myself with quoting two or three trifling instances.

In a London coffee-house, if a gentleman calls for *breakfast*,
the waiter will at once bring him all the requisites on a tray, and
afterwards eggs or fruit, if called for. This he does to avoid
running backward and forward, to which the English have a great
objection. But in Paris, although the waiter perfectly knows by
experience what articles are requisite, he will first bring the
coffee, then the sugar, a third time the milk, and, before you can
possibly breakfast, he must have made half a dozen trips to the
bar. When a number of persons are assembled, such conduct
causes the greatest confusion, and a total want of all comfort.

My barber in Paris used to bring with him a large copper
basin, and a coarse cloth somewhat like the bags out of which the
horses in India eat their corn. Having tied the latter under my
chin, he then threw some water into the basin, and with a piece
of soap having made a quantity of lather, he daubed it all over my
face, neck, and breast, while he himself was wet up to the elbow;

after which he commenced his operation of shaving. Disgusted with this mode, I asked him one day if he had ever been in England. He answered that he had. "Then," said I, "you must have seen that there the barbers carry only a small box, which contains both soap and brush, and a couple of razors, with which they can shave fifty people in a morning, without daubing their customers, or dirtying their own clothes. Why do not you adopt their mode?" He replied: "Your observation is correct: I have both a box and brush at home; but as the French do not like them, and I cannot introduce the fashion, they have therefore never been used; but in future I shall bring them for your use."

During my stay at Marseilles, I resided some time at an hotel in which there was an ordinary, where twenty or thirty persons assembled every day. Unfortunately my sitting room was close to the ordinary, the door of which was allowed to swing backward and forward, and to make a horrid creaking noise, which rendered my room very uncomfortable. I frequently begged of the servants to shut the door after them, or to take some method of stopping the noise. It was all in vain; I might as well have talked to the wind. At length, losing all patience, I entered their apartment, and said: "Gentlemen, if you are not affected by the horrid creaking noise and flapping of this cursed door, what kind of feelings do you possess? and if it does disturb you, why do not you remedy the evil?" Some of them appeared surprised at my extreme delicacy, in being so easily annoyed; others, however, had candour enough to confess it was very disagreeable, but did not know what could be done. I replied: "Either insist on the servants shutting the door every time they go out or come in; or if you do not find it too cold, set the back of a chair against it, and let it remain always open." They complied with the latter suggestion, and thus relieved themselves and me from the disagreeable noise.

On beholding these inert qualities in the French, I was convinced, that notwithstanding their numbers, skill, and bravery, they will never gain the superiority over the English; who, although inferior in strength of armies, are persevering and indefatigable in resources and contrivances. It really astonishes me how the French, being so deficient in energy and perseverance, should have acquired so much fame and power.

The men in France are I think better looking than the English; their clothes are made to fit the body, and are of more lively colours; many of them also wear ear-rings and other ornaments.

The French women are tall, and more corpulent than the

English, but bear no comparison with respect to beauty. They want the simplicity, modesty, and graceful motions of the English damsels. Their fashion of dressing the hair was to me very disgusting, as it exactly resembled the mode practised by the common dancing-girls in India; that is, by dividing the hair into ringlets, two of which hung on the cheeks in an affected careless manner. They were also painted to an excessive degree, were very forward, and great talkers. The waists of their gowns were so short and full-bodied, that the women appeared hump-backed; whilst the drapery in front was so scanty as barely to conceal half their bosoms. Although I am by nature amorous, and easily affected at the sight of beauty, and visited every public place in Paris, I never met with a Frenchwoman who interested me.

In Paris I had the good fortune to meet with several of my English friends, and to form an acquaintance with some other gentlemen of that nation. The most distinguished of the former class were Sir Elijah and Lady Impey,[1] and their beautiful daughter. This gentleman was formerly Lord Chief Justice in Bengal; and it was during the time he presided that Rajah Nund-comar[2] was hanged for forgery. During the early part of the French Revolution, he placed a large sum of money in their funds, and was then endeavouring to procure payment from Buonaparte. He twice asked me to dine with him, and was very attentive to me.

I here also had the pleasure of again meeting my friend Colonel Wombell, from whom I experienced so much civility in Dublin. He was rejoiced to see me, and accompanied me to all the public places. From Mr. and Miss Ogilvy I received the most marked attention.

From General De Boigne, formerly Commander-in-chief of the armies of the Mahratta prince Mahdajee Scindia, of whose

---

1 Sir Elijah Impey (1732-1809) and his wife, Lady Mary (1749-1818; née Reade), were in France attempting to recover money they had lost during the French Revolution. Impey was appointed Chief Justice of Bengal in 1773, was recalled in 1782, but did not resign until 1787. His reputation was intimately connected to his handling of the trial and execution of Nandakumar.

2 Also spelled Nandakumar. He leveled charges of personal corruption against Warren Hastings in March 1775, was tried for forgery that same year, and was sentenced to death in August. His execution was a long standing source of controversy.

history I have taken some notice in my account of London, I also experienced much civility.[1]

I was much surprised to meet here my shipmate Mr. Grand. He had come to Paris to improve his fortune, through the interest of Madame Talleyrand,[2] to whom he once had the honour of being husband: and I understand she has since procured for him an appointment under the Dutch government, at the Cape of Good Hope.

To Mr. Merry,[3] the British Envoy at Paris, I carried a letter of recommendation from Lord Pelham, then one of his Majesty's Ministers: and although he procured me passports, and, like the Cashmirians, was remarkably courteous and polite, he was, I thought, very deficient in sincerity and friendship. His conduct on this occasion reminded me of an anecdote of the inhabitants of Mazanderan, who, being excessively lazy and indifferent about religion, neglected to attend divine service on the Sabbath. The superintendant having noticed this conduct, threatened to punish them: they however endeavoured to excuse themselves by saying, That if they spent the day in prayer, their children must go supperless to bed. The superintendant represented their case to the king, who, being a just and compassionate prince, ordered the treasurer to pay these poor people an allowance every Friday, that they might be then enabled to perform their spiritual duties, without injury to their temporal concerns. In consequence of this regulation, the people were obliged to attend the mosque at the hour of prayer; but it was noticed that they never performed the previous ablution, without which prayer has no efficacy. The superintendant was incensed at their conduct, and having summoned the seniors of them to his tribunal, said, "Now that his most gracious majesty has been pleased to give you an allowance sufficient for the support of yourselves and families for the Sabbath, how does it happen that although you attend at the mosque, you do not perform your ablutions, without which you must be sensible your prayers can be of no avail?" They replied: "The allowance made us by the king is for *prayer*: if his majesty is

---

1 Benoît Leborgne, comte de Boigne (1751-1835), fought for the powerful Maratha warrior Madhav Rao Sindhia (1727-94) at Patan and at the Battle of Marta in 1790. He organized Sindhia's forces along European lines and was a valued Maratha ally. Shortly after Sindhia's death in 1794, he returned to Europe with a vast fortune amassed while in India.

2 See p. 68, note 1, and p. 254, note 1.

3 Anthony Merry (1756-1835), a diplomat, was then minister *ad interim* in Paris.

anxious we should perform *ablution*, let him give us an allowance for *that* also." Thus Mr. Merry complied with the *letter* of Lord Pelham's recommendation, but overlooked the *spirit* of it; and had I not met with other friends in Paris, my journey through France would have been a very uncomfortable one. I must however acknowledge myself indebted to him for his *advice*, in consequence of which I relinquished my original plan of proceeding to Constantinople through Germany and Hungary, and was thereby four months and a half in performing a journey (to be detailed in the sequel) which Colonel Harcourt effected in twenty-one days, about the same period.

Shortly after my arrival in Paris, I was visited by a person who spoke Persian fluently, and, although dressed as a Turk, professed to be a Christian, and called himself Fertekulin. When we became better acquainted, I asked him what was his real history. He replied in a low tone of voice: "My proper name is Syed Mohammed. I was born in Persia, but have long resided in Constantinople. I have travelled over great part of the world, and can speak eleven languages; but I do not wish it to be known here that I am a Mohammedan." When I arrived at Constantinople, I made inquiries respecting this man's character; and learned that he was one of the owls (*sharpers*) of that city, and that his parents were Greeks of the lowest class.

In Paris I had the pleasure of forming an acquaintance with several of the French Literati, some of whom possessed a considerable knowledge of the Oriental languages, especially M. Langley and M. De Sacy.[1] These two gentlemen visited me daily: neither of them spoke Persian well; but as they had studied Arabic, and read a few poetical Persian books, they translated several of my odes into French verse with much facility; and I found them much quicker in comprehension than any Englishman I had met with. Perhaps the French language approaches nearer to the Persian idiom than English; or, that our poetical expressions are more congenial to their ideas than to those of the inhabitants of a colder climate. These gentlemen promised they would publish my compositions in their periodical papers.

About a fortnight before I left Paris, I received several messages from M. Talleyrand, requesting I would favour him with a

---

1   Antoine Isaac de Sacy (1758-1838), Baron Silvestre, was a leading
    French scholar in Arabic studies. His publications include *Grammaire
    arabe* (1810) and the unfinished *Exposé de la religion des Druzes* (1838).

visit.[1] I was also waited on by M. Jabere, the Government Oriental Interpreter, with an invitation from Buonaparte to attend his
levee. I was unfortunately unwell at that time, and afterwards had
not an opportunity of paying my respects to those two great men.

CHAPTER XXV

The Author sets out for Lyons—Account of his journey. Description of
the city of Lyons—Curious mode of building—Dyeing Manufactory.
The Author visits the house wherein the late General Martin was born.
He takes his passage on board a boat for Avignon—Account of his
voyage–Description of Le Pont de St. Esprit. He cultivates an acquain-
tance with M. Barnou—Arrives at Avignon—Sets out in a Diligence
for Marseilles—Description of that city—Hospitably entertained by the
Governor and his family—He forms an acquaintance with several
American gentlemen—Engages a passage to Genoa.

As I was anxious to pursue my journey, I made but a short stay
in Paris; and on the 1st of Rubby al Avul (1st of July) set out in
a *post-chaise* (probably *diligence*) for Lyons. As the fare charged for
this post-chaise was three guineas, I had flattered myself that I
should have been better accommodated, and travelled quicker,
than in the coach which brought me from Calais to Paris. I was
however much disappointed, when I got into the carriage, to find
that it was already occupied by two Frenchmen and a woman,
besides an Italian female as an outside passenger.

We travelled from sun-rise till nine o'clock at night, with the
rapidity of an English waggon, and then stopped to sup and sleep.
Of my companions inside, not one of them understood a word of
English; they were beside the most selfish and unfeeling people I
have met with in all my travels. They had secured the best places
in the carriage for themselves; and when I requested one of them
would exchange with me for a short time, according to the
English custom, they not only refused, but laughed at my distress.
Also when we stopped at night, they immediately ran and secured
the best beds; and the inn-keeper, finding I did not understand
French, and had nobody to take my part, put me into a shabby

---

1 Charles Maurice de Talleyrand-Périgord, 1st Sovereign Prince de
   Bénévent (2 February 1754-17 May 1838) served as a diplomat during
   the regime of Louis XVI, through the French Revolution and then
   under Napoleon I, Louis XVIII, Charles X, and Louis-Philippe.

dirty room. The third day, the Italian female, compassionating my situation, made me understand, partly by signs, that I should threaten, if they did not give me a good bed, that I would sleep in the carriage, and not pay them for a room. By following her advice, I afterwards succeeded in getting a tolerable apartment. We were five days performing a journey of two hundred and twenty miles; during which time my situation was very disagreeable and uncomfortable, and diminished the pleasure I ought to have enjoyed in travelling through so fine a country.

Lyons is one of the finest cities in France, and has a broad river (the Saone), resembling a canal, running through the middle of it; both sides of which are lined with stone: it is navigable for very large boats. On the side of this river is a broad walk, well shaded by trees. There is also, on the outside of the town, another large and rapid river (the Rhone), into which the former empties itself; and over both are several very handsome bridges.

There are in this city several magnificent public buildings, all of hewn stone. The gates also are very lofty, and have capacious apartments for the guards, or porters.

Many of the houses in the new town are built of clay, in a manner well worthy of imitation. A mould of planks is first formed, the length of the required wall, and about two feet high: this is placed on the foundation, and filled up with well-kneaded clay; after which it is allowed to stand for two or three days, till the clay is well dried: it is then taken to pieces, and placed on the wall, when a second layer of clay is put into it, which soon joins the lower one; and when it is dry enough, the mould is again removed, and continued in this manner till the wall is completed: the angles are then built up with unburnt bricks. By this means the walls are formed quite straight and perpendicular: they are afterwards plastered over with mortar, and look quite as well as if they were made of burnt bricks, and, if the top is preserved from rain, will last as long. These walls have two advantages over the mud walls of India: in the first place, they are much better looking, and, in the second, are more rapidly erected.

Lyons being famous for its dyeing manufactories, I gave them one of my turbans to dye, as an experiment: they brought it home the following day, a very beautiful purple colour, and so well done, that it lasted me several months, exposed to a hot sun, without fading, for which they only charged eighteen-pence: whereas in London I always paid four shillings for the operation, and notwithstanding the coldness of that climate, the colours vanished in ten or twelve days.

The vicinity of Lyons produces a variety of delicious fruits, especially cherries, which are the largest and finest I have ever met with: but, as every situation has its advantages and disadvantages, the heat of the climate, and the rivers which surround this town, breed millions of mosquitoes and other insects, which are so troublesome as to oblige the inhabitants to make use of gauze curtains for their beds.

It was a curious circumstance, that adjoining to the Hotel de Milan, where I resided, stood the house in which my old acquaintance, the famous General Martin,[1] of Lucknow, was born. It is still occupied by his nephew; and the General bequeathed a large sum of money to build a college in the vicinity. A friend accompanied me to see the house; and although the master was absent, we took the liberty of viewing every part of it.

I spent three days in Lyons, very much to my satisfaction: and as I was tired of travelling in a *post-chaise*, I now resolved to proceed by water to Marseilles. I accordingly engaged my passage, for a guinea, in one of the large boats which navigate the Rhone, and embarked early the following morning. These boats are made somewhat like the *budgerows* of Bengal; but the cabins are appropriated to the reception of bales and other merchandise, and the only accommodation left for the passengers is on the deck.

In this conveyance there was no want of society, there being, in all, twenty-five passengers of both sexes on board. Unfortunately it was the very height of the summer, and not a cloud could be seen in the whole hemisphere; the heat of the sun was therefore intense. Some of the passengers attempted to shelter themselves among the bales; others laid down on the deck, and spread blankets over them, preferring the heat of the wool to the rays of the sun; and a few got possession of a small carpet, which they tied to the shrouds, and formed an awning. As I had a silk umbrella with me, and had been well inured to the sun in India, I supposed I could brave its effects in France with impunity. I however lost the whole of the skin off my face the first day; and suffered so much distress, that I frequently wished myself in the *post-chaise* again.

Fortunately, the current was very rapid, and the boat went at the rate of seventy or eighty miles a day. Soon after noon we

---

1   Claude Martin (1735-1800), philanthropist and officer of East India Co., bequeathed money to schools in Lucknow, Calcutta, and Lyons which were subsequently each named La Martinière.

stopped at an inn on the banks of the river, to dine; and at night again stopped to sleep.

About the middle of the second day we passed under a bridge (aqueduct) which was built by order of one of the Cæsars, after the conquest of France by the Romans: it is called *Le Pont de St. Esprit*, and is celebrated throughout all Europe. Although it was built more than two thousand years ago, it appears quite modern; and contrary to the general mode of constructing bridges, with an elevation in the centre, this is nearly level: it contains twenty-one large, and eight small, arches: the former are all wide, but the center one is the largest I have ever seen. At this place the river is broader, and more rapid, than the Thames at London: and the bridge itself is more magnificent than any in England.

During the three days I was on board this boat, I endeavoured to forget the heat, in admiring the beauty of the country we passed through. I was also much entertained by a young couple, who thought of nought but love, and whose whole affections and attention were devoted to each other. They sat at one corner of the deck, and never spoke to any other person. Whenever they thought their fellow-travellers were either asleep, or intent upon any other object, the youth used to solicit a kiss; and the lady, under pretence of whispering in his ear, would sometimes, with timid looks, gratify his wish. They probably thought they were not perceived, as most of the passengers had their backs turned towards them; and as I did not wish to interrupt their happiness, I merely glanced at them through the corner of my eye.

To compensate for the inconveniences which I suffered during this journey, I had the good fortune to form an acquaintance, on board the boat, with M. Barnou, one of the most liberal and friendly gentlemen I have ever met with. He was nephew to the Governor of Marseilles, who had formerly held the office of *Vizier*, and was himself a captain in the French artillery. He was adorned with every perfection, and spoke English fluently. This amiable young man, perceiving my distress, did every thing he could to alleviate it: he was my interpreter on all occasions, and not only prevented my being imposed upon, but always procured for me, where we stopped, the best things, and the best bed in the inn.

On the evening of the third day we arrived at Avignon; where I learned that, as the course of the river does not approach nearer to Marseilles, I must pursue my journey to that city by land. I therefore quitted the boat, and returned thanks to God for my liberation from such thraldom. Being, however, anxious to get to the end of my journey, I went immediately, and engaged a place in the *diligence*, which I understood would set out in the morning, and for which I paid a guinea. I then returned to the inn, with an intention of eating a hearty supper, and of refreshing myself by a few hours of sleep, before I recommenced my journey; but scarcely was supper over, when the carriage drove up to the door, and the coachman called loudly for his passengers. I was therefore under the necessity of taking a hasty leave of M. Barnou, who had some business to detain him for three or four days longer at Avignon.

When I entered the *diligence*, I found there were three men in it before me, but, it being dark, I did not regard them; and as they soon fell asleep I did not experience any molestation from them during the night. In the morning, I discovered that they were three mean-looking Frenchmen. One of them was of a short stature, very much wrinkled, and sat in a bent posture. They attempted to enter into conversation with me; but as I did not understand their language, I scarcely made them any answer. About eight o'clock we were joined by another traveller, a handsome young woman, with remarkably fine eyes and long black hair. She was a native of Egypt, and, although born of Christian parents, spoke Arabic fluently. She had not been many minutes seated in the carriage, when the squalid little wretch I have before mentioned, having raised himself up, began to joke with her, and to take liberties both with his tongue and his hands: the others, encouraged by his example, attempted to do the same, and made signs for me to join with them; but I refused, with indignation. The courageous young woman, however, instead of crying at such brutal treatment, as a Hindoostany girl would, opposed them manfully, and abused them, in Arabic, most grossly: with this they seemed much delighted, and, although they did not understand the language, did all in their power to make her repeat the words again, and requested her to explain the meaning in French. They even snatched my cane, and struck her several severe blows with it. The scoundrel of a coachman, who ought to have protected her, seemed not only to enjoy the sport, but, when she was getting out of the carriage, had the impudence to lay his hand upon her bosom. When we again entered the carriage, I gave her my seat in the corner, placing myself between her and the most powerful of her adversaries, and was rejoiced to find she had sufficient strength to contend with the little wretch opposite her: they however continued to tease her the whole day, and, in fact, until we arrived at Marseilles, when we alighted, and all separated. I however met the young woman in the street, next day: she was grateful for my civility, and was of considerable service to me during my residence in that city.

Marseilles is a large and handsome town, and one of the most celebrated sea-ports of France. It is consequently resorted to by the merchants of all the countries on the shores of the Mediterranean Sea, especially of Italy, Turkey, Barbary, and Egypt. It is also famous for the manufacture of silks, satins, and gold stuffs; and I was informed, that its trade amounts annually to fifty-two crores of rupees (£.52,000,000).

The public buildings are all of stone. The houses are, in general, lofty, and have handsome porticoes over the doors. The streets are regular, well paved, very wide, and divided into three portions, as in London. One of the institutions of this city afforded me much satisfaction: In each of the squares, or principal streets, they have large reservoirs of water, which are supplied from some distant springs, and the water conveyed to them either through a cascade or *jet d'eau*. On one side of the reservoir, a place is constructed for the cattle to drink, which is filled from the overflowing of the reservoir. The water is then conducted to two small canals, which run on each side of the street, whence the people supply themselves with water for common use, or for sprinkling the roads to lay the dust; a measure which, if not indispensable in so hot a climate, is, at all events, a great luxury. Some of the roads in the vicinity of Marseilles are planted with shady trees, and are laid out in the same manner as the Boulevards of Paris.

The gardens in this neighbourhood produce a great variety of very fine fruits. The musk-melons are superior to any I have ever eaten, and much finer than those produced in the English hot-houses. Unfortunately, they do not continue in season for above a month.

I had taken the precaution to bring from Paris a letter of recommendation to Monsieur Samadite, one of the most opulent merchants of Marseilles; and the day after my arrival I waited on that gentleman. He received me in the most hospitable and friendly manner, and procured for me a handsome apartment in the hotel situated near his own house; but as in the coffee-houses of the south of France there is not any good butter or cream to be had, their breakfasts are very indifferent, consisting merely of coffee and dry toast. M. Samadite therefore requested, as I had been accustomed to good English breakfasts, that I would always eat that meal at his house, and also dine there whenever I was disengaged. This gentleman is by birth a Swiss, but was educated in France, and, although a merchant, possesses a most liberal and generous disposition. I dined with him frequently during my stay at Marseilles. His table was covered with the choicest viands and the finest wines. His parties generally consisted of fourteen or fifteen of the most respectable persons of that city. After dinner we adjourned to the play-house or opera, for which he always presented me with a ticket, and would by no means consent that I should pay for admission. During the fifteen days that I remained in Marseilles, he was constantly endeavouring to procure me a passage on board a good ship bound directly to Constantinople; but as he was unsuccessful, he requested I would continue with him till a favourable opportunity offered.

A few days after my arrival at Marseilles, my friend Monsieur Barnou called on me, and the same day introduced me to his uncle the Governor, M. Wilgrove, a person of noble deportment and friendly disposition. As at this period Buonaparte had issued a new coinage which bore his image, there were great rejoicings throughout all France. The houses of Marseilles were illuminated at night, and the Governor entertained the inhabitants by feasts and balls. He also requested that I would each day favour him with my company; with which I complied, and had an opportunity of seeing all the handsome women of that part of the country: none of them however pleased me, and they were certainly not to be compared with the English women.

As this was quite an unexpected pleasure, I spent my time very agreeably in Marseilles. The worthy Governor did me the honour also of asking me to several of his private parties; and introduced me to his lady, a most amiable woman, and to his son, one of the finest youths I have ever seen. This young man was studying English, and daily called on me to converse with me, and to shew me the curiosities of the city and its vicinity. In short, the whole of this family are so much respected and beloved in Marseilles, that there is not an inhabitant of the place who would not risk his life for their sakes.

In Marseilles you meet with persons of all nations, and there are a number of Greek and Egyptian families settled here. The women of these countries are very beautiful, and dress in the most becoming manner: in short, if they possessed the fine complexions of the English, they would be the handsomest women in the world.

In this city I had the pleasure of forming an acquaintance with Mr. Alderby, a young Englishman, who was pursuing his studies, and who was very useful to me on many occasions. I also received the most marked attention from the Society of Anglo-American Gentlemen: they did me the honour of giving me a public dinner at the Franklin Hotel: after which they pressed me much to give up my intention of proceeding to India over-land, and to embark on board one of their vessels bound to America, from the ports of which they assured me there were constantly excellent ships sailing to Calcutta. To this plan I would not accede, but promised, if I ever returned to Europe, to go by the route of America. Pleased with this declaration, each of them wrote his name and place of abode on a sheet of paper, which they gave me, and desired me, on my arrival in their country, to inquire for them.

After a residence of fifteen days in Marseilles, and finding there was no chance of procuring a direct passage to Constantinople, I resolved to proceed, with two American gentlemen, to Genoa; whence, I was informed, I should meet with many opportunities of continuing my journey. I accordingly engaged a passage on board a small French vessel bound to that port, for which I agreed to pay three guineas, and to find my own provisions.

CHAPTER XXVI

The Author embarks for Genoa. Description of the Mediterranean Sea. He arrives at Genoa—is hospitably entertained by the American Consul—His description of the city—Admiration of Italian Music—Courtezans—Cicisbeos. The Author embarks for Leghorn, with an intention of visiting Rome. He arrives at Leghorn—Description of that city—Scarcity of water—Distress of the Author, who is nearly assassinated—Account of the inhabitants. He cultivates an acquaintance with some Armenians. The L'Heureuse ship of war arrives at Leghorn with a tender—The British Consul promises the Author a passage in the latter—The Master refuses to take him—He applies to the Captain of the L'Heureuse, who consents to receive him on board. He quits Leghorn.

On the 25th of the month Rubby al Avul (the 25th of July), having taken leave of the Governor of Marseilles, of M. Barnou, and of my other friends, we embarked, and were soon under weigh. I had before given some account of the Mediterranean, or Sea of Roum, but shall now enter into a more particular detail. The Mediterranean is in length two thousand four hundred miles, and in breadth from twenty-six to six hundred. The narrowest part of it is called the Strait of Gibraltar, being a corruption of the Arabic name *Jebbal Tur*, the Promontory of *Toor*, a Moorish chief. From this sea there are two branches: one, which runs to the north, between the shores of Italy, and till it touches Trieste in Germany, is denominated the Sea of Venice: the other, which runs along the shore of Greece, is called the Ionian; from this a narrow arm extends to Constantinople, which is named the Sea of Marmora, and there forms a junction with the Black Sea. The proper boundaries of the Mediterranean (which is itself but a branch of the great Ocean) are, to the north, Spain, and other countries of Europe; on the east, Syria and Palestine; and on the south, Fez, Barbary, and other regions of Africa. Its western boundary is the strait above mentioned, which being commanded by the impregnable fortress in possession of the English, supported by several ships of war, gives that nation a great influence in the navigation of this sea, from which they appear to be entirely shut out by Nature.

During this voyage nothing extraordinary occurred; but as the vessel was very small, and much agitated by the waves, I was for two days very unwell, and perfectly indifferent about food. On the third day I recovered; and finding a keen appetite, inquired for the stock which I had brought on board, but it was nowhere to be found, the crew having no doubt stolen it. I was therefore obliged to live, for the remainder of the voyage, on bad biscuit, and vinegar mixed with water.

On the fifth day we arrived in the Bay of Genoa, and had scarcely anchored when a *health* boat came on board. This part of the world having been frequently visited by that horrid disease called *the Plague,* they never permit any person to land from a ship till it has been visited by a physician, who examines the countenance of every person on board, and makes such other inquiries as he may deem requisite. If he finds that any person has died during the voyage, or suspects that there is any one diseased on board, he orders the ship to anchor in a particular place, where she remains for forty days; and such of the passengers or crew who wish to get on shore are compelled to remain for the same period in an hospital called *the Lazaretto*; whence if any attempt to escape, the guards shoot them as they would a mad dog. The physician who came on board our ship was a meagre, sallow-looking person, who appeared as if just risen from the bed of sickness; whilst our crew were handsome healthy fellows. Having first looked at us, and then at himself, he seemed as if ashamed of the comparison, and, without examining our certificates, granted us permission to land.

I immediately accompanied Mr. Shoolbred and Mr. Jolly, the American passengers, to the Red Lion Hotel. We afterwards paid our respects to Mr. Wilson, the American Consul, to whom I brought a letter of introduction from M. Samadite, and met with a most gracious and friendly reception. We dined with the Consul the three days we remained in this city, and were entertained in an hospitable and sumptuous manner.

The situation of Genoa is beautiful, and the city itself very superb. It is built round the bay, which is circular: and had I not visited the Cove of Cork, I should have thought it the handsomest harbour in Europe. The public buildings and most of the houses are constructed of hewn stone, very lofty, and adorned with pillars, porticoes, &c. Some of the streets are very wide and regular; others are so narrow that the sun never shines on them; but as the town is built on an acclivity, and the streets are well paved, no mud or filth is ever to be seen in them. The town, which is constructed in the form of a crescent, is entirely surrounded by strong fortifications, both on the land side and towards the sea, so that they are well prepared to resist all their enemies.

The interior parts of the houses are richly fitted up; but painted in such gawdy colours, that I, who prefer plain fashions, could not approve their taste. I must however acknowledge, that Genoa is, on the whole, the handsomest city I have ever seen.

The inhabitants of Genoa are all proficients in the science of music, and possess a greater variety of instruments than I have seen elsewhere. One night I was reposing on my bed, when I was roused by the most charming melody in the street I had ever heard. I started up, and involuntarily ran down stairs to the street door, but found it was locked, and the key taken away: I therefore hastened again to my room, and felt every inclination to throw myself out of the window; when, fortunately, the musicians stopped, and my senses returned.

I had frequently been informed, in London, that the Italians excelled all the world in their skill in music; and I here acknowledge, that the Indian, Persian, and Western Europe music bears the same comparison to the Italian that a mill does to a fine-toned organ.

The regulations of Genoa respecting courtezans are of a most extraordinary nature. These women never appear in the streets, either in the day or night, but have smart-dressed footmen stationed at every corner, to invite gentlemen to their lodgings.

A still more extraordinary custom in this country is, that every woman of fashion has two husbands, between whom she equally divides her time. The first husband is obliged to pay all her expences, and provide her with a house and accommodations of every kind; for which he has the privilege of sleeping with her, and of being called the father of all her children. The business of the second husband is, to attend her during the day, to escort her to all public places, and, in short, implicitly to obey all her orders, and to comply with all her whims and fancies. If, during the day, the first husband is by chance engaged with his wife, and the second should knock at the door, the former immediately retires. These second husbands are called *Cicisbeos*: they are, in general, well-looking young men that have no legitimate wife of their own; but it sometimes happens, that elderly men, regularly married, become *Cicisbeos* to the wives of some of their acquaintance.

The vicinity of Genoa produces very delicious melons of both kinds; also abundance of peaches, plums, grapes, and other fruits.

On the second day after my arrival, Mr. Wilson informed me that there was an opportunity of proceeding immediately to Leghorn, which he advised me to embrace, and, by all means, if I wished to see the *greatest wonder of the world*, to proceed thence, by the route of Florence, to Rome; and, after having satisfied my curiosity at that place, to travel to Naples, whence I should find no difficulty in procuring a passage to Malta. I approved highly of his advice, and, accompanied by Mr. Jolly, went immediately and engaged a passage to Leghorn, on board an English ship commanded by Captain Royston.

We embarked early next morning; and during the voyage the Captain behaved in the most friendly manner, entertained us with the greatest hospitality, and resigned to me his own cabin and bed. In two days we reached Leghorn; and, upon producing our certificate of health, we were immediately permitted to land, and proceeded to the Guiny Hotel. I shortly after waited upon Mr. Grant, the British Consul, to whom I had a letter of introduction: he received me politely, and informed me that an English ship of war was daily expected from Malta, upon which he would procure me a passage for that island. I inquired whether I could not proceed to Florence, as it was my intention to visit Rome, and thence to go to Naples; but learned that the journey, at this hot season of the year, was considered very dangerous, on account of an epidemical fever which raged with great violence through the interior of Italy. I was therefore obliged to relinquish my intention of seeing the most celebrated city in Europe, although Mr. Wilson had furnished me with letters of recommendation to persons of consequence, in Florence, Rome, and Naples.

Leghorn, though a very celebrated port, and resorted to by all the nations on the shores of the Mediterranean, is a small city. A person may stand in the middle of it, and with great ease see the four principal gates. It is however surrounded with strong fortifications, and the houses are, in general, four or five stories high. The town is extremely confined, and the houses very inconvenient, dreadfully hot, and swarming with mosquitoes, bugs, and other vermin. Good water is scarce; and the squares in which the public fountains are situated are very confined. The water runs so slowly from the artificial fountains, that one person is half an hour filling his vessel; and I have often seen the people stoop, and suck the cock, to open its vent. During this time, a crowd of people are waiting in the square till it is their turn to approach the pipe, and they often quarrel and fight about it. As it was impossible to get a draught of cool water in their houses, I frequently went to the fountain, but seldom succeeded in being able to quench my thirst.

The heat being at all times excessive in the house, I generally walked out early in the afternoon, and sometimes sat down under the shade of a wall, or wandered into a coffee-house, to pass away the time. At night, I used to go and sit in the porch of a large church which is situated in one of the squares about the middle of the town, in order to catch a little fresh air. May the curse of God light on such a city! and on such people! who, notwithstanding their boasted wealth, are such avaricious knaves, that they would plunder a stranger of his last penny.

One night I was sitting, according to custom, on the steps of the church, when a fellow came behind, and snatched off my turban. By the merest chance, one end of the muslin was loose, which I laid hold of; and rising up, I attempted to catch the fellow: but, as he had a knife in his hand, he immediately cut the turban in two pieces, and ran off with the half of it. When I related this circumstance to my English acquaintances, they cautioned me never to sit there again, nor to go out alone at night; as the Italians frequently, from bigotry or other prejudices, assassinate foreigners, by stabbing them with a knife or dagger. It is thus also that the Italians revenge an affront, or supposed injury.

In Leghorn there is a great variety of fruit to be met with; but their *water-melons* are superior to any I have ever seen, and are twice the size of those produced at Allahabad or Mainpoory, which are esteemed the best in India.

The greater number of the inhabitants of this city are Jews, Greeks, and Armenians, all of whom are of a covetous and parsimonious disposition. One of my English acquaintances, thinking it would be gratifying to me to meet with a person who understood the Persian language, took me to the house of an Armenian merchant, who was born at Julfa, a suburb of Ispahan, in order to introduce me to him. When we arrived at the Armenian's house, he was at dinner, but sent out his son in a great hurry, with instructions to say that his father was very unwell, and had quite forgotten the Persian language.

I frequently met, in the coffee-houses, with another Armenian, named Khojeh Raphael,[1] who was also born at Julfa, but pretended to be ignorant of the language of that city. He was a complete old scoundrel, who had seen a great deal of the world, and understood a number of languages. He had left Persia when a young man, and went by sea to Surat: thence he proceeded across the Peninsula to Bengal: after residing there for some time, he made a voyage to England, and from that country went to Russia; and after travelling over great part of the continent of Europe, at length settled, as a merchant, at Leghorn. He called on me several times, but was never of the smallest service; and was so over cautious, that he would not even assist me with his advice, respecting the route I should pursue.

To compensate for the want of friendship in the Armenians, I had the pleasure of forming an intimacy with Mr. Darby, an English merchant, who had been long settled in this city. He frequently carried me with him to his country-house, situated six miles from Leghorn, where I enjoyed the fresh air, and every luxury he could procure. To this gentleman I related all my grievances; and as I had lost all patience at my detention in so disagreeable a place, I fear I often tired him with my complaints: he however said, and did, all in his power to comfort me.

---

1 A Persian merchant who purportedly sold the 'Orlov Diamond' to Grigori Orlov, lover of Russia's Catherine II, for £90,000.

At the end of a fortnight, the *L'Heureuse*, an English man of war, with a tender, arrived from Malta. This circumstance gave me much joy; and I lost no time in requesting Mr. Grant, the Consul, to procure me a passage; but instead of adhering to his original promise, he never mentioned my name to Captain Richard: and having sent for the master of the tender, desired him to take me on board. As I was anxious to get away from Leghorn in any way, I did not object to this arrangement; and having hired a small boat, I rowed out several miles, to where the tender was at anchor. When I got on board, the master informed me, that, without Captain Richard's permission, he dared not take me with him, but that he would go on board the L'Heureuse, and ask his leave to do so. He returned in a very short time, and told me, that Captain Richard had positively forbidden him to take me. I replied, that he had behaved very ill, in not informing the Consul how he was circumstanced, before he gave me the trouble of coming to his ship.

After some consideration, I resolved to go myself to Captain Richard, and explain to him my uncomfortable situation. When I reached the L'Heureuse, I was politely received; and having introduced myself to the Captain, requested he would permit me to embark on board the tender for Malta. He replied: "I have not any other objection, but that, if this tender falls in with any other ship of war, the captain may take away all her stores, and order the master to proceed to England: in which case you will have the pleasure of paying a second visit to your friends there." I was much distressed at this intelligence; but, taking courage, said, "Sir, your ship, at all events, is not liable to such an accident; and if you can feel for a traveller in distress, allow me to come on board here." Captain Richard was touched with sympathy, and said, "Sit down, and dine with my officers; after which, return to the tender, and bring your luggage on board the L'Heureuse; whilst I, in the mean time, go and settle some business on shore."

When I returned to the tender, the master gave me such an account of Captain Richard's irritable temper and other supposed bad qualities, that I was alarmed, and resolved to go back to Leghorn, there to wait for some other opportunity. Having put my trunks into the boat, I rowed to the shore, and again took possession of my lodgings.

When Captain Richard returned to his ship, and found that I had not come on board, he sent for the master of the tender; and having learnt from him that I had gone back to Leghorn, he instantly ordered his barge, and came on shore. On his way to my lodgings, he called on my friend Mr. Darby; and having brought him along with him, they both insisted upon my immediately taking my luggage on board the L'Heureuse. To this I consented; and early next morning, being the 21st of Rubby Assany (about the 20th of August), we quitted Leghorn.

End of Vol. II.

CHAPTER XXVII

Polite conduct of Captain Richard to the Author. Account of the voyage to Malta—Description of the island—Characters of the Governor, Admiral, Commander-in-chief, and Commissary-general. The Author lands, and is hospitably entertained by all the public officers—His reflections on this subject—He discovers a great affinity between the Maltese and Arabic languages. Account of the invasion of Malta by the Turks—Climate of that island. The Author re-embarks, on board the L'Heureuse, for Smyrna. The ship puts into the port of Miletus—Short description of that place—Proceed on their voyage—pass by Athens— arrive at Smyrna. The author well received by the Consul—visits Osman Aga. The ship quits Smyrna—arrives at the Hellespont— Description of the Sea of Marmora—arrives at the Dardanelles.

As soon as I had an opportunity of shewing to Captain Richard the letters of his Majesty's Ministers to the English Consuls and Ambassadors at the different courts, and he was thereby convinced of my attachment to, and connexion with, the British nation, he conducted himself to me with brotherly affection, and anticipated every wish of my heart. This voyage was therefore one of the pleasantest I had ever undertaken.

In a few days we passed by the Island of Corsica, the birth-place of Buonaparte; and, shortly after, by Sardinia, a large island, which has an independent sovereign of its own. We also passed by Sicily, the largest island in the Mediterranean, but dependent on Naples, the king of which is the monarch of both countries. It is from Sicily that the inhabitants of Malta obtain all their supplies of provisions; the former being one of the most fertile countries in the world, and Malta the most barren. This voyage was not attended with any occurrence worthy of note; and on the 1st of September we cast anchor in the harbour of Malta.

This island is well known in Arabian history, and several of the antient Philosophers were born there. After the expulsion of the Christians from Jerusalem, it was made over by the Pope and the kings of Europe, to a society of military monks, the chief of whom is called the Grand Master. As these monks were, in general, men of family and fortune, who had retired from the world, they devoted the whole of their wealth to erect churches and fortifications on this island. As immense sums were thus annually expended, it is now become one of the strongest fortresses in the world. Some parts of these works are said to have been constructed a thousand years ago, and yet appear quite fresh; and are so massy, that, in all probability, nothing but an earthquake will overturn or demolish them. To a person not perfectly conversant with the science of fortification, it would be a vain attempt to explain the nature of the works which defend Malta: suffice it to say, that they are considered as the masterpiece of theory and practice united. This island fell into the hands of the French by *treachery*; and was taken from them by the English, by means of *starvation*, after having in vain essayed to take it by force. By one of the articles of the late treaty of peace, this island is to be restored to the Grand Master: it is however at present occupied by a garrison of six thousand British troops.

The public officers, at the time of my visiting Malta, were, First, Sir Alexander Ball,[1] Governor. This gentleman possesses every quality requisite to render him esteemed and beloved; he is, in consequence, adored by all the inhabitants, whether English or Maltese.

Second, General Vandeleur, Commander-in-chief of the Land Forces, an officer highly respected.[2]

Third, Sir R. Bickerton, Admiral of all the ships in the Mediterranean: a command of the greatest trust and importance.[3] With these officers the Governor consulted upon all military affairs.

Fourth, Mr. Macauly, Deputy Governor.

Fifth, Mr. Wilkie, Commissary of Supplies, and Commissioner of the Docks. These gentlemen acted with the utmost unanimity, on all occasions; and, except at the Cape of Good Hope, I have never witnessed so pleasant a society.

Soon after we had cast anchor in the harbour, Captain Richard went on shore, and reported my arrival to the Governor.

---

1   Sir Alexander John Ball (1756-1809), was governor of Malta from 1803 until his death.
2   Sir John Ormsby Vandeleur (1763-1849) went on to become a principal figure in the Marathas campaigns from 1803 to 1805.
3   Sir Richard Hussey Bickerton (1759–1832), second baronet, commanded the Mediterranean fleet during the Peace of Amiens. He played a prominent role in the naval operations against the French forces in Egypt and later in the blockade of Toulon.

His Excellency was pleased to give orders that I might land whenever I chose, and requested the favour of my company at dinner on that day. Captain Richard had the goodness to return on board with this polite message; and advised me to deliver his Majesty's letter, addressed to the British Ambassador at Vienna, to the Governor, who he doubted not would act, in consequence, as if it had been addressed to himself, and probably order the L'Heureuse to proceed with me to Constantinople; by which I should avoid the risk of going in a ship commanded by one of the *owls* of the Levant.

In compliance with the advice of Captain Richard, I carried my letters of recommendation on shore, and fortunately found the Governor and the Admiral together. When I presented the letters, I addressed myself to both, and informed them, that, in consequence of the advice of the English *Chargé d'affaires* at Paris, I had been induced to deviate from the route I originally purposed, and, instead of going by Vienna, was arrived so far on my way to Constantinople; that as the letters I had now the honour to deliver were of a public nature, I hoped they would consider them as addressed to themselves, and afford me such assistance as should be in their power.

These illustrious officers listened to my address with great condescension, and assured me of their willingnesss to comply with my solicitations, but hoped I would allow them the pleasure of my society for a short time at Malta. We shortly after sat down to an elegant dinner, and I spent the day with the greatest happiness. Before we broke up, the General asked me to dine with him the next day, the Admiral the day following, Mr. Macauly the third day, Mr. Wilkie the fourth day: and such was the hospitality of these gentlemen, that, during the fortnight I remained at Malta, I was never a single day disengaged.

I had a very good apartment at the Hotel de Soter, where I was visited by all the principal officers: but as the tea and butter were very indifferent at the hotel, the Governor and the General requested me to breakfast alternately with them.

How different was their conduct to that of Mr. Merry, at Paris. To that gentleman I carried a letter of introduction, dictated by the orders of his Majesty, and backed by the recommendation of Lord Pelham. He received me only with dissimulation and flattering speeches; and although he complied with the Royal orders, in procuring me passports, he sent me by a route which involved me in a labyrinth of difficulties. At Malta I landed as a perfect stranger, and furnished only with a letter of introduction to a person *at Vienna*; notwithstanding which, I was received with hospitality and kindness, and all my wishes complied with.

VERSE OF HAFIZ.

> "I am become the slave of the seller of wine; be not therefore angry, O shaikh.
> From you I received nought but promises: he has conferred on me real benefits."

On the second evening after my arrival, the Governor, as the representative of the Grand Master, gave a ball and supper to the principal inhabitants of the island. There was, of course, an assemblage of all the beauty and fashion of the place; and I thought some of the women very handsome. The supper was elegant, and the music excellent.

I was much surprised to find that the Maltese language contained a great portion of Arabic: the pronunciation is very similar; and the letters *S, Z,* and *T*, were exactly the *Saad, Swaad,* and *To,* of the Arabs. The remainder of the language is a mixture of Greek, Italian, and French. I however met with several of the well-educated Maltese, who spoke Arabic fluently.

I omitted to mention before, that at Marseilles, Genoa, and Leghorn, the language of the Arabs was understood by a number of the sea-faring people. This circumstance is no doubt owing to the great power which the Moorish chiefs of the Merwan dynasty possessed in Spain for many centuries; who had colonies, or factories, established on all the shores of the Mediterranean. Many of the buildings, and even whole cities, in this part of the world, bear evident marks of their having been founded by the followers of Mohammed.

Several hundred years ago, one of the Turkish Emperors of Constantinople sent an army to invade Malta. As the fortifications were not then completed, they succeeded in getting possession of half the island, and besieged the remainder for a very long period; but after losing an immense number of their men, they were compelled to retreat. The remembrance of this event is kept up by the Maltese celebrating the anniversary of the Turkish retreat with great rejoicings.

The climate of Malta is very warm, and the houses abound with mosquitoes, fleas, &c. to such a degree, that I seldom slept more than two or three hours in any night. I was also much annoyed by the droves of hogs, which are constantly ranging the streets, and defile every place they can approach. The inhabitants are so partial to these animals, that they rebelled against one of their Grand Masters who ordered the hogs to be confined, and compelled him to rescind his order. Since that period they have had free access to every part of the town, except the square opposite the palace.

At the expiration of a fortnight, his Excellency the Governor, and the Admiral, were pleased to order Captain Richard to convey me, on board the L'Heureuse, as far as Smyrna, which is only five days' journey short of Constantinople; and furnished me with letters of introduction to the British Consul at that port, desiring he would facilitate the remainder of my journey.

On the 16th of September, I again embarked with my friend Captain Richard. For three days the weather was delightful; but on the fourth there arose a dreadful storm, which lasted all that day, and the whole of the night. We lost one of our masts, and several of the yards; the sails were all blown to pieces, and our rigging much damaged. These circumstances did not cause Captain Richard much alarm; but, as the Mediterranean Sea comprehends a great number of small islands and hidden rocks, he was fearful lest we should be driven on some of them. We were however fortunate enough to escape these dangers: and the wind having shifted early next morning, we ran a hundred and fifty miles in twenty-four hours, and on the sixth day anchored in the harbour of Milo, a very celebrated port. We afterwards learned that eleven ships had been lost in this gale; and such was the extent of our damage, that the Captain thought it advisable to put into this port, to refit.

During the storm, we passed the Island of Candia, and several other islands, denominated by Arabian geographers, the Ionian Islands.

In this neighbourhood there are several large towns, all of which are situated on the tops of hills. The Governor and military men are all Turks: but the rest of the inhabitants are Greeks, who, in consequence of the despotic and tyrannical government of their oppressors, are the most abject poor wretches I have ever seen; even the most oppressed subjects in India are princes, when compared with these. The Turks adhere strictly to the Mohammedan regulations, of exalting the subjects of their own religion, and of depressing those of any other. The spirits of these Greeks are entirely broken, and they appear to have given themselves up to despair. Melancholy and want are so strongly depicted on their countenances, that I could not help feeling for their deplorable condition.

We were detained at Milo by the requisite repairs of the ship, till the 3d of October, on which day we again set sail. Two or three days afterwards, we passed along the shores of Athens, the birth-place of Plato, of Diogenes the Cynic, and of several other cele-brated Philosophers. By the aid of our glasses, we could plainly perceive the ruins of some famous temples, the roofs of which have long since fallen in; but the marble columns are still stand-ing, and glittering in the sun. Athens is not an island, as is gener-ally supposed, but a part of the continent of Greece, and is included in the Turkish government of Natolia. After a pleasant voyage, we cast anchor on the 5th, at Smyrna.

As soon as Captain Richard had given his orders respecting the ship, we went on shore in his barge, and proceeded to the house of Mr. Vesey, the British Consul. That gentleman received us with the utmost politeness, and invited us to stay dinner and to sleep at his house. After dinner, we walked out, and proceeded to the residence of Hajy Osman Aga, the Custom-master of the port, which was situated in the middle of a handsome garden, a little distance out of the town. We were fortunate enough to find the Aga at home, and just preparing for dinner. He received us in the most courteous manner; and although we had dined, insisted upon our again sitting down with him, and regaled us afterwards with *hookas* of the Cullian kind, and coffee. When we broke up, he made me promise to dine with him on the following day.

Previous to the hour appointed, he sent some of his retinue with a handsome caparisoned horse for my conveyance. I soon mounted, and proceeded to the garden. The Aga again embraced me with much cordiality; and we sat down to a sumptuous enter-tainment, in the Turkish style. As I had been four years without tasting any good Oriental cookery, I was much gratified by this feast. After dinner, we had ices, sherbet, and the Cullians, and continued to converse till near midnight. As I had some intention of leaving Smyrna the next day, he kindly gave me a letter of introduction to a friend of his, who was one of the inferior Viziers at Constantinople; but requested, if I should prolong my stay, that I would favour him with my company every day. I returned him many thanks for his obliging invitation, but made an excuse for not accepting it, stating, that I was the Consul's guest, and could not possibly leave him. He acknowledged the propriety of my excuse, and, having ordered his boat to be got ready, directed some of his officers to accompany me home.

The Consul and Captain Richard having deliberated on the best mode of conveying me to Constantinople, and finding that I should be put to much inconvenience if I journeyed by land, determined that I should proceed thither in the L'Heureuse. Although the Captain had not the Admiral's sanction for this measure, yet as the ship was in want of a top-mast and some yards, which could only be procured at Constantinople, he thought himself justified in proceeding to that port. Preparations were therefore made for continuing the voyage, which delayed us a short time longer.

Smyrna is a large city, pleasantly situated, and inhabited by Greeks and Mohammedans: there are also a number of Christian merchants settled here, and it is a place of resort from all the ports in the Mediterranean. It is well supplied with all kinds of provisions, and a great variety of fruits: melons are in such quantities, that they pile them up in heaps, like mountains: there is also a great abundance of grapes, pomegranates, and a species of quince which I had never before seen.

The third day we dined with Mr. Price, one of the principal merchants; and on the fourth, the Aga called on me, and took me with him to his garden, where he entertained me as on the former occasion. We sat till midnight; and when we were breaking up, he ordered one of his servants to convey on board the ship, for my use, a hundred melons, a load of grapes, fifty cakes of bread, two goats, and a calf. He then accompanied me as far as the outside door, and ordered his deputy to go with me in his boat, to see me safe home.

On the 13th of October we again set sail, and soon after reached the Island of Mitylene, celebrated for being the birthplace of several of the ancient Philosophers. As it was nearly calm when we were opposite the city (Castro), we went on shore to look at it, but were much disappointed. All the towns in these countries are built on the slope of a hill; and the houses, being white, look very well at a distance, but, when examined, are far from being neat or handsome. The streets of the bazars are covered over with vines, which, although pleasant in the hot season, render them in wet weather very dark and dirty: they are also very badly paved, and filthy. The inhabitants are Greeks, but subject to the Turks.

On the fifth day we were opposite the Isle of Tenedos; and, as the winds are very changeable in the Ionian Sea (Archipelago), we were obliged to cast anchor. We went on shore, and paid our respects to Omar Aga, the Governor, who was very civil, and pressed us to stay dinner: but as our departure depended entirely on a change of wind, we deemed it imprudent to stop, and therefore requested he would excuse us. The next day the wind favoured us a little, and we got as far as the entrance of the Sea of Marmora (Strait of Gallipoli); which, branching off from the Archipelago, passes by Constantinople, and joins the Black Sea. But, as at this place there is always a rapid current running from the Black Sea into the Ionian Sea, it is impossible to enter this strait without the assistance of a strong westerly wind; and we found here not less than fifty ships, of different nations, waiting for a favourable opportunity, some of which had been delayed for nearly two months.

It is requisite to be known, that the Sea of Marmora separates *Ajem,* the ancient Persian empire, from *Freng;* called by the English, Asia and Europe. This sea is 120 miles long, and of a considerable breadth in the middle; but at the ends it is reduced to two narrow channels, two or three miles broad, called the Straits of Gallipoli and of Constantinople. All the countries lying to the north-west of this sea are included in Europe, and those to the south-east are comprehended in Asia.

Loharasp, called by the Arabs *Bukht al Naser,* was the first Persian monarch who subdued the countries constituting the Asiatic frontier. This conquest was originally attended with much bloodshed, and was the cause of continual warfare between the Greeks and Persians.

When the Romans had supplanted the Greeks, and extended their dominion over all Europe, they also engaged in endless wars with the Persian kings of the Ashcanian and Sassanian dynasties, for these Asiatic provinces. The events of these early periods are not well described in *our* histories, as we have no *authentic* records prior to the time of Mohammed: but the Greeks, who have histories which extend back two thousand years, have minutely detailed all the circumstances of these wars.

After the Turks had taken possession of Constantinople, and extended their dominion over several of the European provinces, the Ottoman Emperors assumed the title of *Sultan al Bereen, wa Khacan al Bihereen,* "Emperor of the Two Continents (Europe and Asia), and Lord of the Two Seas" (the Archipelago and Black Sea); which they still retain.[1]

Near to the mouth of the Hellespont, on the coast of Natolia, is a place called Troy, once the residence of a celebrated philoso-

---

1 This title is still stamped on all Turkish coins. (Translator's note)

pher and poet, named Homer, whose works are still extant in the ancient Greek language, and are much read and admired in Europe. Along this shore there are a number of hillocks to be seen, which they say are the graves of the kings and heroes who fell in the battles described by that poet.

After waiting here two days, we again got under weigh, and, having a light breeze in our favour, proceeded nearly as far as the Dardanelles; when the wind failing us, and the current being very strong, we were obliged to cast anchor. At this place the strait is very narrow, and strongly defended by two forts, mounted with cannon of an enormous size, which could with ease sink any enemy's ship that might attempt to pass up the strait, even aided by a strong and favourable wind. It is on this account that the Dardanelles are famous all over Europe, and not from there being any city of that name.

On the strait above Constantinople, which joins the Black Sea, there are also two very strong forts, to guard that passage. The Turks consider these forts, and the difficulty of entering the Straits, as a very great security to Constantinople, and the bulwark of their empire. I am however of a very different opinion; for if ever the Turks are so reduced as to shut themselves up in Constantinople, and trust to its walls for their defence, I am convinced it will not stand a fortnight's siege against a victorious army.

CHAPTER XXVIII

The Author arrives at Constantinople—is graciously received by the British Ambassador. Description of Constantinople—Of the climate—Population—Coffee-houses—Inns—Hot Baths—Useful institutions—Dress of the Turks—their indolence—great smokers.—Anecdote of Nadir Shah. Turkish luxury, and its effects. Account of the Post-office—Turkish mode of living—Houses of Constantinople—Frequent fires—Furniture—Mosques—Description of St. Sophia—Bazars—Derveishes

We were detained fourteen days at the Dardanelles, waiting for a favourable wind: at length, on the 5th of the month Rejeb (2d of November), our wishes were accomplished: and a strong westerly wind springing up, nearly one hundred vessels, of different sizes and various nations, got under way at the same time. As this was a scene I had never before witnessed, having made all my former voyages in a single ship, I was much delighted at the view of a whole fleet under sail, and the attempts of the ships to get before each other. In a very short period we passed the forts, and had a beautiful view of the country on both sides the strait; and on the third day we anchored opposite the city of Constantinople. I immediately sent intelligence of my arrival to Lord Elgin, the British ambassador, and requested his lordship would procure a proper habitation for me.[1] The next morning I received a message from his lordship, that a house was ready for my reception, and that he should be happy to see me as soon as convenient.

After breakfast I quitted the L'Heureuse with regret; and Captain Richard, resolving to omit no mark of attention or friendship, accompanied me to the shore, and ordered a salute to be fired as soon as I got into the boat. By this means my arrival was made known to all the inhabitants of Constantinople, from the Janissary to the Grand Signior.

The city of Constantinople, like London, consists of three towns. That in which all the Christian ambassadors reside is on the opposite side of the harbour, and is called *Galata*: thither I repaired, and, immediately on landing, paid my respects to Lord and Lady Elgin.[2] As I had been for several years intimately acquainted with his lordship's brother, the Hon. Mr. Bruce, I was received in the most gracious and friendly manner.[3] His lordship is descended of a very ancient and noble family, possesses an amiable and liberal disposition, and supports the dignity of Ambassador with great lustre. He is also invested with very great powers; all the English Consuls, and subjects of every description settled in Turkey, as far as Bagdad and Bussora, being subject to his authority.

---

1   Thomas Bruce, (1766-1841), 7th Earl of Elgin, was the ambassador to Constantinople from 1799 to 1803. Operating with great latitude under a firman (or imperial order) from the Sublime Porte, he gained access to and eventually arranged for the removal of key sculptures and arte-facts, now in the British Museum, from the Parthenon in Athens. Abu Talib's contact with Elgin is contemporaneous with these controversial events.

2   Mary Bruce (1778-1855; née Nisbet), first wife of Thomas Bruce (see p. 142, note 6). She was divorced for adultery in 1807-08 amidst much scandal.

3   The Bruce family had close ties to both Pitt and Dundas. Abu Talib's prior association with Dundas no doubt facilitated his relationship with the family.

Lady Elgin possesses great elegance of manners, a smiling countenance, and a sweet disposition; her ladyship is also endued with a lively wit, and sound understanding, which she has much improved by study and travel. During the month which I resided in Constantinople, I passed the greater part of my time in their society, in the most delightful manner.

The house which his lordship had procured for me was in the vicinity of his own; it was remarkably clean, neat, and well furnished. The servants belonging to it were four handsome Greek women, who appeared to take a pleasure in waiting on me, and not a little contributed to my comfort.

The city of Constantinople is composed of three towns, situated on the shores of the Propontis. The principal of these is where the Emperor, the nobles, and all the opulent Mussulmans reside, and is called *Istanbole*. The second town is on the opposite side of the harbour, and is called *Galata*: it is principally inhabited by Christians; and if a Mohammedan settles there, he plants a cypress-tree opposite his door, that his house may be known to belong to one of the *Faithful*; no Christian being allowed to plant the cypress in his grounds. By riding round the head of the harbour, a person may go by land from Galata to Istanbole; but the road is very bad. The third town is across the strait, on the Asiatic shore, and is called *Scudari*: it can only be approached from Istanbole by water. Constantinople, being situated on an acclivity, appears a regular and magnificent city when viewed from the strait; and while in the boat, I thought it the grandest place I had ever seen; but when a person enters the streets, he feels much disappointed.

The climate of Constantinople is, in general, cold; and in winter there falls much rain and snow. Notwithstanding the principal Turks have fire-places in their rooms, they never light a fire in the day; and although, in the evening, they permit it to be done, they always place a screen before it when they say their prayers, lest they should be suspected of paying adoration to that element: therefore, in order to keep themselves warm, they are obliged to wear a load of clothes, which incapacitates them from exertion, and, in the summer months, serves as a hot-bed for the production of all kinds of vermin, and, I have no doubt, perpetuates the plague. This bad habit prevails all through the Turkish dominions, even in the hot countries, as at Aleppo, Caïro, and Bagdad.

It is impossible to ascertain the number of inhabitants, or the extent of Constantinople; for the gardens, hamlets, &c. are continued on both sides of the strait, as far the Black Sea; and if the length of the city was to be calculated in this manner, it would not be less than thirty miles. It is a common saying of the Turks, that their capital is three days' journey in circumference.

A Turk of the smallest consequence never thinks of walking; and to save this trouble, there are 100,000 small boats plying about Constantinople. These are all open, but handsomely painted, carved, and gilded, with soft cushions to sit on: they are rowed by one, two, or three men, and are procurable at all hours. On the quays, and in that part of the town which is not accessible to boats, there are a number of horses standing ready saddled for hire; so that a person may travel all over the city without walking twenty yards. The streets are narrow, badly paved, and, in winter, up to the horses' knees in mud: the concourse of people is, notwithstanding, so very great, that a stranger has much difficulty in getting along.

The coffee-houses and barbers' shops in this city are innumerable. The Turks, though very indolent, are not fond of retirement or solitude: they therefore, immediately after breakfast, go to one of these places, where they sit, smoking, drinking coffee or sherbet, and listening to idle stories, the whole day. Their conversations are carried on in a loud tone of voice, and sometimes eight or ten persons talk at the same time; it is therefore impossible for a foreigner to understand what they are saying; and, in short, the societies in these coffee-houses are little better than an assembly of brutes. The rooms are also exceedingly dirty, and seldom afford any thing but thick coffee, and tobacco cheroots or pipes.

The inns of Constantinople are horrid places; and the only good accomodation for a traveller in this city is at the French and English hotels in Galata.

The hot baths are also innumerable, but very filthy, and common to both sexes. The men use them from day-light till ten o'clock, and the women from that time till after noon.

The only praise-worthy institutions I could observe in Constantinople, were, first, the boats; secondly, the horses kept for hire; and thirdly, the public fountains; for in every street there is a reservoir of water, with a cock fixed in it, to which is attached a small copper vessel, fastened by a chain; so that, whenever a person is thirsty, he may help himself to a draught of cool water,—a luxury very desirable, after struggling through a crowd, in the narrow streets, on a hot day.

To the above may be added, the custom of having a separate

bazar for every kind of merchandise; by which means a person is certain of procuring the article he wishes for, without much difficulty, if it is to be had. The staple commodities of Constantinople appeared to be, sable, ermine, and other skins, which are all remarkably fine of their kind, and sold at a reasonable price.

The Turkish dress is more expensive than that of any other people in the world, and is composed of the choicest manufactures of various nations. They use a great quantity of European broad-cloths and satins. From India they are supplied with muslins, and from Persia with shawls and embroidered silks. The trowsers of the higher classes are made of fine broad-cloth, but so wide, that the skirts of half-a-dozen coats are with ease inclosed in them, and a person unaccustomed to wear them cannot move in them. Their caps, which they call *cavuk*, are also made of broad-cloth, and do not weigh less than twelve or fourteen pounds. They wear four or five coats, made after the Arab fashion, over each other: the upper one of broad-cloth, lined with fur; and over all they throw an immense long cloak: in short, their dress would be a heavy load for an ass: on this account they avoid moving as much as possible, and consequently are deprived of taking exercise, or enjoying themselves in the fresh air, both of which would contribute greatly to their health and happiness.

During my travels in Turkey, I spent several days at the houses of the Pashas; and I invariably observed, that, at an early hour of the morning, they entered the hall of audience by a small door which communicated with the *haram* (women's apartment), and that they remained there till midnight, after which they retired into the haram by the same door. During the whole day, they never even looked into the garden, much less thought of going out to walk or refresh themselves.

From the time they rise in the morning, till they go to bed at night, the pipe is never out of their hands; and the common people are such slaves to this habit, that even while walking, or on horseback, they continue smoking. They always carry a steel and tinder-box about them, and even while riding at a brisk pace will strike fire and light their pipes. If by any accident they are obliged to desist from smoking, they put the pipe into a leather case, which is suspended, like a quiver, to their saddles. It was in consequence of this habit that Nadir Shah (the Persian usurper),[1]

---

1 Nadir Shah (1688-1747), King of Persia from 1736 to 1747 and a formidable military leader. A Shiite of Turkic descendent, he successfully rebuffed both Ottoman and Afghan attempts conquer Persia.

when encouraging the Persians to attack the Turks, said, "You need not have any fear or anxiety respecting this nation: for God has given them but two hands; one of which is absolutely requisite to keep on their caps, and the other to hold up their trowsers; and if they had a third, it would be employed to hold their pipes: they have therefore none to spare for a sword or shield."

The cavuk, or high-crowned cap, is only worn by the higher classes; but as the rank of a person in Turkey is known by his cap, there is a great variety of them, none of which weigh less than the cavuk, and some much more. The Syeds, or descendants of the Prophet, wear a green turban folded round the cap, and all other Mohammedans wear white; but no Christian is permitted to wear either of these colours.

The Turks are a very luxurious people: they assume a great deal of state in their dress and equipage, and retain a number of servants and women. They are also very extravagant in their entertainments. These habits are not confined to the great officers, but extend to the lowest clerk in office, and pervert the revenues of the State to improper uses: these, however, do not suffice to support their extravagance; they have therefore thrown open the doors of bribery and corruption; and these practices are now so common, that they are not considered as disgraceful or criminal; and, in fact, no business can be accomplished in this country without a bribe. Even the Government departments are ruined by this nefarious system. The army is without discipline, the ordnance unfit for use, the regulations of the post-office totally neglected, and the clerks in the offices without employment. The persons at the head of all these departments are only anxious to procure money, and to deceive the Government.

As the nature of the post-office differs considerably in Turkey from any other country, I shall endeavour to explain what it was, and what it now is. The regulation on this subject directs, that at the end of every nine *fersukh* (thirty-six miles) there shall be a *Bam Khana* (post-house) erected, with convenient stables; that at each of these houses there shall be stationed a landlord, a cook, a hostler, and a farrier; that there shall be an allowance of 30,000 *kurush*[1] paid monthly by Government for the support of each of these houses; and that all persons proceeding on the business of Government shall be accomodated therein. It shall be the business of the landlord to keep beds prepared, and the house in good order; the cook to provide provisions (coffee is only mentioned);

---

1 A *kurush* is 1s.10 1/4 *d*. English. (Original note)

and the hostler to have always in readiness, one, two, or more good horses; all of which were to be provided out of the Government allowance. Formerly, all the principal officers in the army made use of their own horses; after breakfast they mounted one of the post-horses, and rode to the next stage, where they dined; after which they rode a third stage, and stopped for the night. No delay was ever admitted; and it was quite optional with the officer, whether he should make the contractors a small present, or not; and if he experienced any difficulty, or want of attention, it was his duty to report the circumstance to the postmaster-general. In this manner all the despatches of Government were conveyed throughout the empire.

At present, the post-house is the resort of all the poor wretches of the village who cannot afford to burn a fire at home. As they are allowed to sit there all day, and even sometimes to pass the night, the furniture of the house swarms with fleas and lice; and the appearance of the beds repels every idea of sleep. When the traveller demands a fresh horse, they amuse him for an hour with some idle excuse; after which they produce a horse without a shoe on his feet, and of course he must be sent to the farrier to be shod; but as this will occupy a couple of hours, the traveller is induced to order some food to be dressed, which when produced, is abominable. A horse is at length reported to be ready: when inspected, he is found to be blind, lame, and galled. If the traveller is irritated at this treatment, they say they cannot help it, so many persons have lately passed that way, that their horses are lamed or dead, and that for many months they have not received the Government allowance. The traveller being about to depart, they make an exorbitant demand on him for his entertainment; and if he does not comply with it, they abuse him grossly, and sometimes even beat him.

The ruin of these post-houses is owing to two circumstances: first, the irregular payment of their allowance; and secondly, the institution was only intended for the use of the Sultan's *actual* messengers, or officers sent to join the army; but in the process of time, every person who could bribe the postmaster-general received an order for his horses, and thus defeated the intention. The *actual* royal messengers now put up where they please, and oblige the head man of the village to supply all their wants gratis.

The Turks eat three times in the day: their breakfast consists of bread and sweetmeats, or fruit; at noon they take a slight repast of bread, *kibobs*, and vegetables, all of which are to be had of a superior quality at the cooks' shops; but their principal repast, and the only one to which they invite company, is after evening prayer.

The Turkish mode of cookery is a bad imitation of that of Persia and Hindoostan: it consists of pulaws, curries, kibobs, forcemeats, stews, and a number of sweetmeats, &c. Their mode of serving up dinner differs, however, very much from the practice of either of the above countries, and in the latter would be considered very derogatory to the greater number of the guests.

In Turkey, if a party consists of eighteen persons, there are three cloths laid in different parts of the room, on each of which are placed six cakes of bread. The master of the house, with the five superior guests, take their places at the upper table; the six next in rank take the second table; and the others the inferior one. A large tray is then brought in, containing a single dish, which is placed on the upper table: the master of the house and his guests immediately take two or three mouthfuls with their hands; the dish is then changed, and carried to the second table; when the party having helped themselves in the same manner, it is carried to the bottom table, and thence in a few minutes taken out. In this mode, a succession of thirty dishes are frequently produced; but before a person can tell whether he likes any particular dish, it is taken off, and perhaps replaced by a much inferior one. For soups, custards, rice, milk, &c. they make use of wooden spoons, which being very shallow, and quite round, scarcely hold any thing, and only serve to dirty the table-cloth, and spoil a person's clothes.

The Turkish mode of living is, upon the whole, very disgusting; and I never could make a comfortable meal with them. In the first place, the single dish being placed upon a wide tray, round which six people are sitting, it requires the arm to be stretched out at full length: then the servants are so inattentive to the guests, or so rapid in their motions, that they frequently snatch away the dish when a person is in the act of helping himself; and, as all the dishes are brought from the kitchen at the same time, and laid down in an adjoining apartment till wanted, those which are produced last are frequently cold. The Turks, on account of their taking no exercise, and constantly indulging themselves in smoking and drinking coffee, have seldom any appetite for their dinner, and appear always anxious to get it over, that they may return to the pleasures of the pipe again. Owing to all these causes, I have frequently risen very hungry from table. The only article in which the markets of Constantinople excel those of other cities, is fish: of these they have a great variety, some of which are very delicious.

The houses in Constantinople are, in general, constructed of wood, either plastered with mortar, or painted to resemble brick.

They neither possess the solidity and grandeur of the habitations of India, nor the comforts and conveniences of those of Europe; but the greatest defect of these houses is, the constant danger of their catching fire; and whenever it does happen, many hundreds of them are consumed before the fire can be extinguished. There is scarcely a street in the town that has not been burned down, three or four times within the last fifty years. They however continue to rebuild them with wood; and assign as a reason their apprehension from earthquakes: this, however, is a mere idle excuse; and the real fact is, that they do not wish to expend such a sum of money as would be requisite to build a brick or stone house; not considering that the rebuilding a wooden one, with the loss of furniture, &c. is, in the end, more expensive. Besides, although several earthquakes have happened in this city, they have not destroyed the mosques or other public buildings, all of which are built of brick or stone.

In the houses of the higher classes, there is always a large room, either for business or for the reception of guests; the entrance to which is in the long side. Opposite the door is the seat of the master of the house; and along that side of the room there is a row of heavy, gloomy windows. All round the room, except at the entrance, is placed a seat, a foot and a half high, on which are laid cushions stuffed with wool, three or four inches thick, and covered with broadcloth. When a person sits down on one of these cushions, in the Oriental fashion, he sinks into it, and finds it difficult to alter his position. The middle of the room is covered with a thick carpet; which, with the cushions, are not taken up once in six months, and are, consequently, well inhabited by fleas and bugs. These creatures do not seem to annoy the Turks, but are sure to pay their respects to a stranger.

In Constantinople there are twenty-five public mosques, all of which are built in a handsome style, and highly ornamented; but the great Mosque of *Sufyeh* (Sophia) excels, in grandeur and elegance, any building I have ever seen.[1] The boasted cathedral of

---

1 The Hagia Sophia mosque, a former patriarchal basilica constructed between 532 and 537AD, is considered the finest example of Byzantine architecture in the world. It was converted into a mosque under the orders of Sultan Mehmed II after the Ottomans conquered Constantinople in 1453. Abu Talib's dating of the building seems to apply to the first church built on the site, which was constructed in 360 AD and was destroyed in 404 AD. The building's celebrated dome became the model for many Ottoman mosques.

St. Paul's, the superb domes of Paris and Genoa, were all obliterated from my memory by the sight of this sanctuary: in short,
nothing in the world is equal to it. The centre of the building,
immediately under the great dome, is one hundred yards square;
this is surrounded on all sides by lofty aisles, forty yards wide,
supported by massy, but highly ornamented, pillars of porphyry.
All round the upper part of the building there runs a gallery,
capable of holding an immense number of spectators.

This mosque is built of various kinds of stone, and was erected
by order of Constantine, the founder of the city, and the first of
the Cæsars who was converted to Christianity. It was finished in
the year of the Christian æra 314; that is, 1488 years ago; and was
for many years sacred to Christianity. But when Sultan
Mohammed took Constantinople, he sanctified it to the Mussulman religion. It is constructed of such excellent materials, and
the workmanship is so well executed, that, notwithstanding its
antiquity, it has all the appearance of a modern building.

The mosques next in celebrity to St. Sophia, are those built by
the Sultans Ahmed, Mohammed Fateh, Bajazet, Mahmood, and
Mahmood Pasha.[1] The exterior architecture of all these is very
fine: they are also handsomely carved and gilded. In front of each
of these there is an extensive court, in the centre of which is a
large reservoir, containing a *jet d'eau*, for the purpose of purification. There are also, round the court, several other reservoirs for
this purpose; and on the outside of the court-wall is an extensive
range of buildings, containing shops, coffee-houses, &c. Some of
the mosques have also colleges attached to them, where the students are instructed gratis.

The private mosques in Constantinople are innumerable; but
these are, in general, mean buildings; and, except the door, and
the minars, on which the Mauzins stand to call the people to
prayer, there is nothing handsome about them.

Several of the bazars in this city are handsome; but the most
celebrated one is a square, encompassed with a wall, extending a

---

1 The Sultan Ahmed Mosque, or the Blue Mosque, was built between
1609 and 1616 during the rule of Ahmed I. The Fatih Mosque was built
over the ruins of the Church of Apostles between 1463 and 1470 and
bears the name of the Ottoman conquerer of Istanbul, Fatih Sultan
Mehmet. The mosque is the site of his mausoleum. The Bayezid
Mosque is part of a large Islamic complex built by Sultan Bayezid II
between 1501 and 1505. The Mahmud Pasa Mosque was completed in
1464 and thoroughly renovated during the rule of Osman III in 1753.

mile each way. It has several large gates, and is laid out in the interior with gravel-walks, covered at top with an arched roof lighted by glass windows, which may be opened or shut by means of ropes and pulleys. On each side of these walks there is a range of shops, containing a great quantity of valuable merchandize. Each profession, or trade, has its particular walk; but the most extraordinary regulation of this bazar is, that the shops are never open after twelve o'clock in the day; and on Friday there is not a single person to be seen in it.

I had heard a number of Persians speak in raptures of this bazar; but as, in the course of my life, I have been often disappointed in my expectation from the exaggerated descriptions of other people, so, in this instance, I was completely mortified. In the first place, the shops are so dark, that it is impossible to distinguish colours; and although I put on my spectacles, and held my bargain up to the light, I bought a blue turban instead of a green one. Secondly, the air is so confined, that disagreeable smells are engendered; and, thirdly, as the sun can never penetrate the shops, or the streets between them, the former are excessively damp; and in the latter, the mud is ancle deep during the whole winter.

In Constantinople there is a great variety of fruit to be procured: they have abundance of both musk and water melons; also apples, quinces, mulberries, pomegranates, lemons, and grapes. Their dried fruits are all excellent, especially their raisins, prunes, almonds, pistachios, nuts, and dates.

In one of my peregrinations through the city, I met, at the Mosque of the Emperor Bajazet, with an Afghan of Candahar, who spoke Persian fluently, and said he was a student in the college; and further informed me, that many Mohammedans came yearly to Constantinople, from Candahar, the Punjab, Sinde, and other places of India, to study the sciences in the numerous colleges of this city;—that a little distance from where he resided, there was a monastery of three hundred Indian Fakeers, and that, if I wished it, he would introduce me to them; but as I concluded they were an assemblage of low, ignorant people, or smokers of opium, I declined his offer.

It may be necessary to explain, that, in Turkey, derveishes are treated with great respect, and the common people are strongly impressed with an idea of their sanctity. There are several sects of them, each of which is distinguished by a peculiar cap. They exhibit a number of sleight-of-hand tricks, and pretend to work miracles: they turn round and dance to the sound of a drum, till they are quite giddy, and will then rush into the fire, or attempt any other mad action. The Turks are partial to the derveishes of their own country, but tolerate those of any other nation.

CHAPTER XXIX

Character of the Turks—Limited power of the Emperor—Authority of the Viziers, and of the Cazies—Freedom of the Women—Female Slaves—Hard fate of the Princesses. The Author introduced to the Viziers—presented to the Emperor—not visited by any of the Nobility—forms an acquaintance with the East-India Company's Agent, and the Interpreter to the English Embassy, also with the Interpreter to the German Embassy—obtains a second audience of the Emperor. Passports. A public Mehmandar, or Conductor, appointed to attend the Author to Bagdad—his character, and an account of his conduct.

The Turks are, in general, persons of strict honour, intrepid, liberal, hospitable, friendly, and compassionate; and their government is conducted with greater attention to justice than any other of the modern Mohammedan States. I had not a sufficient opportunity of judging correctly of their jurisprudence; but I learned that their Emperors have not the power of shedding blood unjustly, nor can they follow the bent of their own inclinations or passions with impunity. On all affairs of consequence they are obliged to consult their nobles, who are kept in proper subjection by the hope of promotion or the fear of punishment; and although the nobles seldom transgress, either against the laws or the regulations of the State, they are always trembling for their lives; as it frequently happens, that, on mere suspicion, they are summoned to the Ministers' tribunal, and there condemned to suffer death, without knowing of what, or by whom, they are accused.

The authority of the Viziers is also so very despotic, that the governors of provinces, or generals of armies, seldom dare to harbour an idea of insurrection or rebellion; but if an instance of the kind ever does occur, and the Ministers do not feel themselves sufficiently powerful to punish it immediately, they compromise the affair, and wait till the disaffected chief is either carried off by death, or falls into their snares. By these means the Ottoman Government has flourished for six hundred years, without experiencing any open rebellion, though symptoms of insurrection have been frequently manifested.

The *Cazies* (judges),[1] although in general illiterate, and open to bribery, are nevertheless very arbitrary in their decisions; and whether these decisions are correct or otherwise, they are irrevocable, and must be obeyed by the governors or commanders. The Cazies are appointed and displaced by the *Sudder Aazim* (Lord Chancellor), who is always one of the principal Viziers. Their nomination is only for one year, at the expiration of which period they return to Constantinople; and if their conduct has been approved, they are again appointed to some other district; but if condemned, they are dismissed, and compelled to retire in disgrace. On this account they are always very circumspect, and do not connive at the malconduct of the governors and collectors, but administer justice with more impartiality than might be expected from such characters.

The Turkish women are allowed a much greater degree of freedom than those of Persia or India. The wives of the noblemen and higher classes are permitted to go out, and visit each other, either entirely unveiled, or with a small veil over their faces. They are also allowed to walk out in the streets, bazars, and gardens. Male slaves, and young men from fifteen to twenty years of age, if nearly connected, are permitted to enter the women's apartments, and converse with their relations. By these means, the Turkish women acquire some knowledge of the world; and being constantly accustomed to see men, behold them with more indifference than the ladies of India. If, notwithstanding these advantages, they are sometimes guilty of impropriety, they are not so liable to be discovered as in India, and the husband's honour is thereby preserved.

In India, it is reckoned disgraceful for a woman to marry a second time; but a Turkish woman may marry again, within a few months after the death of her husband, without any scandal or reproach.

Although the opulent Turks keep a number of women, they are seldom married to more than one wife at a time: the remainder consist of Georgian and Circassian slaves, who are celebrated throughout the world for their beauty and accomplishments. These are permitted to dress and live equally well with the wife; but they are, in every other respect, subject to her authority and command.

Besides the Georgian and Circassian women, every *haram* contains a number of Ethiopian, or other female slaves, who

---

1 A Cazi or Qadi is a judge and interpreter of Islamic law or Sharia.

perform all the menial offices. These are sometimes permitted to share their master's bed, but are generally given in marriage to the male slaves, or some man dependent on the family. When tired of their concubines, they dispose of them in the same manner.

One of the most peculiar and reprehensible of the Turkish customs, is their marrying the sisters and daughters of the Emperor to different noblemen; on condition, that if they have any male issue, the child shall immediately be put to death. The origin, or reason of this regulation, is unknown, and appears quite unaccountable. If it was occasioned by an apprehension that those children should ever lay claim to the throne, and thereby cause dissension in the State, why is not the same rule enforced on the Princes? but on the contrary, they are allowed to increase and multiply their species, on condition of the children remaining in the Seraglio (*Serai Aaly*, Imperial Palace) till summoned to the throne. Whatever may have been the origin of this absurd custom, the fact is, that the Emperor's midwives always attend the *accouchement* of every Princess; and if the child proves a boy, they immediately dispatch him to his forefathers.

The better classes of the Turks are very religious, and say their prayers regularly five times in the day: they also scrupulously observe all the ordinances of the ecclesiastical law, and fast every day during the whole month of Ramzan, or Mohammedan Lent, whether at home or on a journey.

The day after my arrival in Constantinople, Lord Elgin, the British Ambassador, sent intelligence of it to the *Reis Effendi* (Minister of Foreign Affairs), who requested to have the pleasure of seeing me on the following day. At the hour appointed I waited on his Excellency, and was graciously received. He entertained me with coffee, and the hookah: but as he did not understand Persian, and seemed an illiterate man, I requested he would introduce me to the Prime Minister, Yusuf Pasha. He immediately assented, and sent a message to that nobleman, explaining my wishes.

The offices of all the Viziers are in the same court or division of the palace; the entrance to which is through a lofty gateway, called the *Babi Homayon* (Imperial Gate), translated by Europeans, the *Sublime Porte*.[1] Here all the business of the empire is transacted, and the public letters are dated from this spot. All the

---

1 The term, derived from the French, was used by Europeans to denominate the seat of Ottoman government and its various offices of state.

Viziers assemble at an early hour at the Prime Minister's apartment; and having consulted with him on the state of affairs, repair to their own offices, where they remain the whole day. The vicinity of these offices to each other much facilitates business, and is deserving of imitation.

The messenger of the Reis Effendi soon returned, accompanied by a servant of Yusuf Pasha, who informed me, that his master was anxious to have the pleasure of seeing me. Having taken leave of the Effendi, I immediately proceeded to the apartments of the Prime Minister. I found him seated in a magnificent hall, lighted by glazed windows, and handsomely furnished with couches and rich carpets; and attended by above fifty slaves, or servants. He received me with much politeness, and we conversed for a considerable time in Persian. As his Excellency's beard was very long, and mine had been lately cut, he rallied me much on this subject, and made me promise never again to let the scissars touch it.

After I had taken my leave of the Prime Minister, I received a message from Ahmed Effendi, commonly called *Kija Beg*, the Vizier for the Home Department, to request I would honour him with my company: I immediately waited on him, and experienced much pleasure from this visit. His Excellency has the most intelligent and handsome countenance I have ever seen: his manners are elegant, and his conversation lively and agreeable. When I was about to depart, he ordered one of his servants to attend me to the Mosque of St. Sophia, and to shew me all the sacred places, and other public buildings of Constantinople.

Some days afterwards, I had the honour of being introduced to the Emperor, Sultan Selim,[1] (May his prosperity endure for ever!) and presented his Majesty with a complete Persian translation of the *Camoos* (a celebrated Arabic Dictionary), in two volumes. As it is a very scarce work, and had cost me a large sum of money, and much pains to correct it, and as all the well-educated Turks are admirers of the Persian language, I requested that his Majesty would have the goodness to order it to be

---

1 Sultan Selim III (1761-1808) ruled the Ottoman Empire from 1789 to 1807. A reformist, he attempted to westernize Turkish society and instituted widespread re-organization of the military and the taxation system. Despite attempts to engage with Europe diplomatically, his tenure was marked by a series conflicts with European powers and by rebellion within the Empire itself. He was Britain's ally against Napoleon during this period.

printed, as a book which would prove exceedingly beneficial to his subjects. I also stipulated with his Majesty, that, in the preface of the printed edition, it should be recorded by whose means the book became known in Constantinople. The Emperor condescendingly acquiesced in my request; and, having ordered it to be committed to writing, signed the paper with his own hand, and delivered the book to the librarian. He then commanded that I should be clothed in a dress of honour, and a sum of money be given me. The latter I begged leave to decline; and informed his Majesty, that my only motive for bringing the book to Constantinople was for the benefit of mankind; that for this pious action I hoped for a reward in the *next* world, and therefore would not give up my expectation for the vanities of *this*. The Emperor smiled, and desired to see me again, before I left his capital.

As the period of my residence in Constantinople was only twenty-eight days, my acquaintance with the Turkish nobility was very limited, and I only visited the Viziers and Officers of State in their public capacity; the reasons for which were briefly these. In the first place, as the winter was fast approaching, and the road to Bagdad is frequently obstructed by snow, I was only anxious to pursue my journey. Secondly, as the Turks have a great enmity to the Persians, on account of their ancient wars and difference of religion, and even consider the shedding of their blood as lawful, they used to look on me with aversion. It perhaps would have been prudent in me to have changed my dress; but as I intended to remain among them only a short time, and had a great abhorrence to their cumbrous garments, I would not yield to their prejudices. Thirdly, as I prided myself on being a descendant of the Prophet, (on whom, and on his descendants, be the blessing of God!) I expected that they should first visit me; and they, being proud of their offices and wealth, thought it my duty to wait on them.

To compensate for the inattention of the Turks, I had a very extensive society of Persians, Indians, and Armenians. The two former were, in general, well-informed, or religious men, who had come to Constantinople for the purpose of study. The latter reside in Galata, and are mostly engaged in trade: they come hither from Aleppo, Tokat, Amasia, and other cities in subjection to the Turks. Their language is a mixture of Armenian and Turkish. Many of them have acquired great wealth; but, as their national vice is avarice, I never experienced any degree of hospitality or liberality from them. Once or twice I was asked to their evening parties, and had an opportunity of seeing a number of their young women, many of whom I thought handsome.

Mr. Tooke, the East-India Company's Agent, who had resided forty years in Turkey, and had, in consequence, nearly forgotten the English morality, behaved to me with much politeness, but, I suspect, with very little sincerity; for when I requested him to procure for me a *Chupur* (conductor), to guide and assist me in my journey, at the current rate of the country, which, I have since learned, is only one hundred and fifty, or two hundred kurush, he assured me that no respectable person of that kind could be had for less than 1500 kurush; that the requisite expences amounted to 1000; and that the man could not expect less than 500 for his trouble. It was in consequence of this statement, and his hypocritical conduct, that I applied to the Viziers for one of the public conductors, who behaved excessively ill to me, and cost me much more than I could have hired one for, who would have paid implicit obedience to my commands. This subject will be further explained in the sequel.

I had frequent opportunities of becoming acquainted with Mr. Pozany, the Public Interpreter to the British Embassy. This person is a Greek, and has acquired an immense fortune by his employment, independent of the great emoluments he derives from the business of his office. All the English who travel this road are entirely at his mercy; and from not understanding the language of the country, they are obliged to employ him, or one of his deputies, in all their transactions: they are, in consequence, completely pillaged. I know not whether it was from his having been disappointed in his expectations of plundering me, or that it was owing to the antipathy the Greeks bear to all Mohammedans, that he became my enemy, and, previous to my setting out, whispered something in the ear of my conductor which effaced from his recollection the solemn injunctions and positive commands he had received, both from Lord Elgin and Ahmed Effendi (the second Vizier), as will hereafter be explained.

From the society of Mr. Himrou I derived much satisfaction. He is a young man of a most amiable disposition and enlightened understanding: he is by birth a German, but speaks the Latin, French, English, Greek, Turkish, Arabic, and Persian languages. He was formerly employed as interpreter by Sir Sidney

Smith,[1] and was his constant companion during the siege of Acre. He is now in the service of the Emperor of Germany, who constantly retains a splendid embassy at the Turkish Court. This gentleman translated several of my odes, into English, French, and German; and sent them to London, Paris, and Vienna. He visited me daily, and introduced me to his Excellency the German Ambassador. By means of this introduction, I had an opportunity of seeing, at his Excellency's routs, not only all the ladies belonging to the different European embassies, but also a great number of Greeks and Armenians. The Ambassador and his lady are very highly esteemed in Constantinople; and, judging from their conduct, and that of some others of their countrymen whom I have met with in the course of my travels, I conclude that the Germans stand very high in the scale of polished nations.

Having seen every thing that was worthy of observation in Constantinople, and being anxious to pursue my journey before the winter set in, I solicited my audience of leave, which was immediately granted: and the Emperor, on this occasion also, behaved to me with the greatest condescension and kindness.

In obedience to the Royal orders, a *Mehmandar* (conductor) was appointed to attend me from Constantinople to Bagdad, whose duty it was to provide me with horses, and every other requisite, on the road. I was also furnished with three *firmauns* (orders, or passports). The first of these was general, and addressed to all the Pashas, Governors, and Commanders, wherever I should halt, to be attentive to me, to take me into their *own* houses, and to supply all my wants: it also directed the postmasters to furnish me, at every stage, with two riding horses, and four horses for my servants and baggage. The second firmaun was addressed to Abdullah Aga, Governor of Mardine, directing him to send a party of cavalry to escort me safe over the desert which is situated between Mardine and Mousul, a place said to be replete with danger. The third was directed to Aly Pasha, Viceroy of Bagdad, commanding him to yield me every assistance in his

---

1   Sir Sidney Smith (1764-1840) served as a naval officer in numerous campaigns in the Mediterranean and famous for his role in the defense of Acre in 1799. See Abu Talib's account of Acre on p. 235. Smith's actions were rewarded by Sultan Selim III and by British parliament. His brother Spencer Smith was minister-plenipotentiary at Constantinople and a key rival of Thomas Bruce in the Ottoman court during the time of Abu Talib's travels.

power, to entertain me in his own house, to facilitate my pilgrimage to the shrines of the Martyrs (Hussein, grandson of Mohammed, and his family) who fell at Kerbela, and to escort me safe to Bussora.[1]

As an additional proof of the Emperor's esteem, the sum of six hundred kurush were paid from the treasury to my *Mehmandar*, whose name was Hajy Aly, to furnish me with provisions on that part of the road where there were not any towns or public officers.

When I took leave of my friend Ahmed Effendi, he ordered the Mehmandar into his presence; and told him, in my hearing, that he was, in every respect, to conform to my wishes; to permit me, if I chose it, to make three days' journey in one, or *vice versa*; and, in short, to act as if he, the Effendi, was the person under his charge. He also informed him, that if he conducted himself with propriety, and brought back from me a certificate to that effect, he should be promoted. The scoundrel kissed the hem of the Effendi's garment; and said he would willingly forfeit his eyes and his head, if he deviated, in the smallest degree, from his commands.

The next morning, however, he came to Lord Elgin, and said the money entrusted him by Government was insufficient for the purpose, and solicited a further sum. His lordship generously gave him a hundred kurush in addition, and conferred on him a *khelaat*, or dress of honour, with an exhortation to take the greatest care of me, which he most solemnly promised.

As it would be an endless task to enumerate all the villainies of this scoundrel on the road, I shall here give a compendium of his conduct. In the first place, the money which was given him for my use he appropriated to himself, and during the whole journey did not expend one hundred kurush on my account. Secondly, instead of conducting me to the houses of the Pashas or Governors, he took me, during the first part of the journey, to the post-houses, where I was so bit by fleas and bugs, that I could not sleep an hour during a whole night. When I demanded why he did not carry me to the house of the Governor, he told me some gross falsehood, as an excuse. However, after the first three or

---

1 The *firmans*, or imperial orders, described in this paragraph guarantee passage to Mosul and Karbala and thus enable Mirza Abu Talib's pilgrimage. Karbala is the most holy city in present day Iraq and of particular importance to Shiites because it was the site of the Battle of Karbala (680 AD) where the grandson of Muhammad, Husain ibn 'Ali and his associates were killed. His tomb is a preeminent Shia shrine.

four days, having discovered his character, I myself waited on the Pashas, or Governors, whenever we arrived at the end of our journey before midnight; and having shewn them the Sultan's order, I was immediately received into their houses, and treated with much respect. Thirdly, contrary to his instructions, he frequently obliged me to ride three or four long stages in one day; but when it suited his own convenience better, he would not go more than one or two stages in a day. His chief object in this conduct was, to avoid the towns in which the Pashas resided, and to oblige me to pass the night in the post-houses, where, in consequence of my passports, he was supplied with every thing gratis. During our journey we fell in with a caravan, and for several days he obliged me to keep company with it, under pretence that the road was infested with robbers. His conduct was, in short, so disgusting, that I hated the sight of him; and on my arrival at Diarbekir, I entreated the Governor, Ahmed Effendi, to furnish me with another conductor as far as his authority extended. This request he obligingly complied with, and ordered one of his own servants to accompany me to Mardine: thence I was escorted by one of the servants of Abdullah Aga Pasha as far as Mousul; and from Mousul to Bagdad by an officer in the service of Mohammed Pasha.

Although I had dispensed with the attendance of the cursed wretch (the *Mehmandar*), and told him he might return to Constantinople, he would not quit me, fearing he should be called to an account for the sum of money advanced to him for my use: and, upon our arrival at Bagdad, he had the impudence to demand from me a certificate of his good behaviour, and that I was in every respect satisfied with his conduct.

CHAPTER XXX

The Author leaves Constantinople. Account of his journey. History of the city of Amasia—Gold and Silver Mines in its neighbourhood. Account of Sewas, or Sebaste. Anecdotes of the inhabitants of Hussen Buddery. Occurrence at Malatia. Description of the Euphrates. Account of a salt-water lake. Description of Diarbekir—Author hospitably entertained by the Governor. Description of Mardine—Panegyric on the Governor. Account of Nisibes.

On Sunday the 4th of Shaban 1218, (2d of December 1802,) having taken leave of my kind friends, Lord and Lady Elgin, I crossed the harbour from Galata, and passed the night at an inn, near the mosque of Mahmood Pasha, in Constantinople. The following day I crossed the strait, and passed that night at Scudari, a handsome town on the Asiatic shore.

On Tuesday, after breakfast, I commenced the most toilsome and dangerous journey I had ever undertaken: but, as it was a part of the world I was anxious to see, and led towards home, I was in good spirits. We stopped the first night at Keza, twelve fersukh from Scudari. This journey is not performed by the caravans in less than twelve hours, as they seldom travel at a quicker rate than a fersukh in the hour. A fersukh is equal to two Hindoostany coss, or four English miles.

The following day we reached Azmut, pronounced, by Europeans, Azmus, being only thirty-six miles. It is a very ancient and extensive town, inhabited chiefly by Christians. Its bazars are well supplied with provisions and merchandise.

On the 8th (Shaban) we mounted our horses at daylight, and, after travelling twenty-eight miles, refreshed ourselves, and changed horses, at a mean, dirty village, called Tebanche: thence we proceeded forty miles, to Khunduk, a pretty village, with a stream of clear water running through it. As the posthouse was here tolerably clean, and the people civil, I passed a pleasant night. The weather now began to be very cold, and we had several showers of hail, with some frost. On the 9th, we again set out at day-break, and, having changed horses at Dozjeh, arrived, some hours after dark, at Bely. This day's journey was ninety-six miles; and the latter part of it was over a very steep mountain, of nearly twenty miles ascent. The road is excessively narrow, and cut, in a zigzag form, up the side of the mountain, resembling the path-way made by ants over a mole-hill.

As the weather was very cold, I was so loaded with clothes and furs, that I could not walk; and although it was quite dark while we were descending, I was obliged to trust entirely to my horse; but if he had either stumbled, or gone six inches out of the road, I must inevitably have been dashed to pieces. It was therefore very bad management in my conductor to come on this second stage, at such a season of the year; and I strongly advise all persons who shall travel this road, to stop during the night at Dozjeh, and commence this stage with the morning light. I must however observe, that the inhabitants of this village have the character of being savages, thieves, and robbers.

On the 10th, we proceeded to the village of Karadah, forty-eight miles, and intended to have gone on another stage that evening; but the postmaster being an acquaintance of my conductor, he insisted upon entertaining all our party. He gave us an excellent dinner; and the ducks at this place were superior to any I have ever eaten.

On the 11th, we mounted early in the morning, and changed horses at Baynder, thirty-two miles: thence to Kerajile thirty miles. Here we again obtained fresh horses, and proceeded to Carajuran, twenty-two miles; making, in all, eighty-four miles. It was midnight before we arrived at the last stage, and were therefore obliged to put up at the post-house, among fleas and bugs. This place is famous for good honey and fine butter; and both these articles are carried to a great distance.

On the 12th we reached, at an early hour, Kubbeh Hissar, a dirty village. The people of the post-house were great knaves, and detained us two hours, under pretence of shoeing their horses, and preparing dinner for my attendants. After repeated entreaties, they brought our horses; but, in consequence of this detention, it was late at night before we arrived at Tosieh. The journey this day was about eighty miles. Tosieh is a very large town, but the post-house was the filthiest place I had ever seen; the keepers of it were also the most avaricious and troublesome people I ever met with. In consequence of their impositions and altercation, it was nine or ten o'clock on the 13th before we could proceed. Our first stage was to Hajy Humze, thirty-six miles; and the second to Osman Jok, thirty-two miles: total, sixty-eight miles. The whole of this day's journey was over steep mountains and dreadfully bad roads.

The 14th we dined at Mersuan, distance fifty-six miles; and at midnight reached Amasia, thirty-two miles: total, eighty-eight miles. Mersuan is a large village, situated in an extensive plain, and contains an excellent post-house, the people of which were exceedingly attentive, moderate in their charges, and readily supplied us with horses. At Amasia, though a considerable city, well inhabited, and abounding with both water and wind-mills, every thing was the reverse. The streets were narrow, and full of mud; the post-house filthy in the extreme, and the landlord a great cheat; the provisions were also bad, and the servants inattentive. During this journey I had occasion to observe, that the accommodations in the villages were always superior to those in large towns.

Be it known, that after the defeat and captivity of Sultan

Bajazet by the Emperor Timour (Tamerlane),[1] at Sewas, all the Ottoman princes and nobles having dispersed themselves in various quarters, Sultan Mohammed (the son of Bajazet) took refuge at Amasia, and by the strength of its fortifications was enabled to repel the attacks of a detachment of the Tartars which was sent against him.

When Timour returned to Samarcand, Sultan Mohammed declared himself Emperor of the Ottomans, and for twenty years made Amasia his capital. During this period he was constantly engaged in war with his relations, many of whom had taken possession of certain districts, and assumed independence. He finally conquered them all; and, having crossed the Strait of Constantinople, got possession of some of the European provinces, and, in fact, regained all the authority and dominion of his father.

On the 15th, I chose to stop at the village of Terkhal, but was obliged to feed the horses at my own expence; it being contrary to the Turkish regulations to stop any where but at the regular stages. This village was however clean, and the people very civil.

On the 16th we reached Tokat, being a journey of eighty-eight miles. This is a very ancient and celebrated town of Armenia; it produces the largest and finest grapes I have ever seen, and in great abundance; but the post-house is one of the worst on the road: we were however detained at it for three days, for want of horses. At length the Governor compelled one of the public carriers to supply me with two horses and some mules; and threatened the master of the post-house in such a manner, that he and all his dependants absconded.

The country between Amasia and Tokat is exceedingly mountainous, and the road very circuitous and difficult. In these mountains there are mines both of gold and silver, which are worked on account of Government, and the metal sent to Constantinople to be coined. We slept the night of the 20th at a village called Carkhan.

On the 21st we reached Sewas. The distance between it and Tokat is ninety-six miles, and is generally performed in one day; but, on account of the badness of the weather, and the fear of being lost in the snow, I took two days to do it. During these two

---

1   Also known as Timur Lenk or Timur the lame and thus in English as Tamerlane (1336-1405). Turkish conqueror of vast regions from India and Russia to the Mediterranean. His conquests were widely held to be extremely brutal, but his dynasty was also revered for its cultural achievements.

days it snowed very hard, and blew with such violence, that two of the mules, which were heavy laden, fell down precipices, and were dashed to pieces.

Sewas (the Sebaste of the Romans) is an ancient and large city, and is frequently mentioned in history. It is, however, a very dirty town, and our horses sunk up to their knees in the streets. At this place I had the honour of being entertained by the Pasha: but as even his house was very dirty, and infested with fleas, how abominable must the post-house have been!

The country between Tokat and Sewas is a continued range of mountains, and at this time was entirely covered with snow. Tokat, Sewas, Diarbekir, and Mardine, are all reckoned in Turkish Armenia. The cities of Kariz, Erzeroum, Van, and Errvan, lay at some distance on our left hand, and are considered as belonging to Persian Armenia. On the 22d we stopt at Olash, and on the 23d reached Dilkuldash, distant from Sewas forty-eight miles. This place is famous for its raisins and currants. The town is situated on the top of a mountain, which, being covered with snow, was exceedingly difficult of ascent.

The 24th we halted at Aljekhan, and the 25th at Hussen Chelebi. The distance of these two stages is sixty-four miles.

The 26th we only travelled forty-four miles, and stopped at Hussen Buddery. The country between this and Tokat is, on account of its elevated situation, excessively cold; but as we were travelling south, it gradually became warmer.

Hussen Buddery is inhabited by Soonies, (followers of Abubeker, Omar, and Osman,) whose ancestors fled from Daghistan, in consequence of the cruelties of Nadir Shah.[1] They are a stupid and savage race,[2] and so avaricious, that they will not put their provisions to the fire till the traveller has paid twice the value: and when the dinner is laid out, they sit down without being asked, and thrust their hands into the dish without ceremony. Their women bring fruit and other articles for sale, and are very abusive if you do not purchase of them. The post-house is surrounded by beggars, who are very clamorous: they are also accused of being highway robbers. As I was apprehensive of being plundered by these people, and afraid of being lost in the snow, I made short journeys through this part of the country, and gener-

---

1 See p. 281, note 1.
2 As a Shiite, Abu Talib is typically disdainful of Sunni Muslims; this remark is directed specifically at the residents of Hussen Buddery.

ally contrived to arrive at the end of the stage by four o'clock in the afternoon. Although by this method I avoided all danger, it subjected me to disagreeable company, who, out of curiosity, used to come and smoke their pipes where I was.

On the 27th, after a journey of thirty-two miles, I reached Malatia early in the day. When we approached this city, we found the fersukhs marked by stones, which custom is certainly a great comfort to the weary traveller.

Malatia is a large town, but very dirty, owing to the streets in this country not being paved; and as the post-house was excessively filthy, I took up my residence at the house of a Mutusullum (a pretend Mussulman). The old gentleman had a most reverend-looking white beard, a foot and a half long, and was very austere. During our conversation, his children, who were very beautiful, gathered round us, and began to laugh at my appearance and mode of talking. The old man got into a passion, beat some of them, and drove them all away. I was much vexed with him for his conduct, as I preferred their innocent prattle and playfulness to his musty conversation. During this day it rained very hard; and I was informed that snow very seldom falls here, though it is to be seen on the mountains between this and Mardine; but at Mousul and Bagdad it is never seen.

On the 28th we left Malatia, and, after travelling twenty-eight miles, arrived on the banks of the Euphrates. At this place the river rushes from between two mountains, with great violence and considerable depth. A little further down the stream we came to a ferry, where we crossed, and halted at Aiz Ougly. This is a Kurd village; and its Chief was one of the proudest, stupid fellows I have ever met with: and as at this place there is not any post-house, he entertains all travellers of rank gratis; but he makes up for this expence by the exorbitancy of his charges for horses. Notwithstanding this village is situated on the banks of the river, I found the greatest difficulty in getting water, and was absolutely obliged to set out in the morning without washing my face or hands.

We mounted our horses at an early hour on the 29th, and, after travelling sixteen miles, were again obliged to cross the river. We then struck into a very mountainous country. The steepness of several parts of the road was such, that our saddles slipped backward and forward, and I lost a very valuable surtout coat which was buckled on the back of my saddle; in consequence of which I suffered severely, for several days, from the rain and cold.

In the evening we arrived at Hizpote, distant from Aiz Ougly forty-eight miles. Here we found an excellent post-house, and got a very good dinner. It was my wish to have stopped here for the night, but my brutal Mehmandar insisted upon my proceeding another stage: we therefore travelled on till midnight, through shocking roads, and were obliged to put up at a ruined caravanserai, in the midst of the mountains. During this part of the journey we passed by a salt-water lake, which is forty-eight miles in circumference, and in many places unfathomable. As the road lay along the shores of this lake, and the rocks often projected into it, we were frequently forced to ride up to our horses' bellies in the water: and if these animals had not been much superior to those with which we were generally furnished, they must have sunk under the fatigue. Two loaded mules, belonging to some persons who accompanied us, were lost during the darkness and storm.

The last day of Shaban,[1] after travelling thirty-two miles, we arrived at Arganeh. The distance between this place and Hizpote is sixty-four miles. The whole of the road is over mountains, difficult of access. One of these, on account of its height, is called the Arched Mountain: it contains several valuable mines of copper; and in it is the source of the river Tigris. During the course of this morning's journey, we were obliged to cross the river four or five times. The water in it was very shallow, but ran with great rapidity, and was of a yellow colour, being strongly saturated with mud. This river increases quickly in size, as you descend the stream. At Diarbekir it is of considerable breadth. At Mousul they are under the necessity of having bridges over it, at all seasons of the year; and at Bagdad I have seen it, at times, as broad as the Ganges.

Arganeh is situated on the side of a mountain; which is not cut into terraces to render the ascent easy, but the streets are absolutely so steep, that it is with much difficulty a stranger can clamber up them. This is considered as the first town, on the road from Constantinople, in the Jezireh or country between the rivers Tigris and Euphrates. As the post-house was, as usual, dirty, I took up my lodgings at the house of a pretended Mussulman; and, as the road was considered very dangerous, in consequence of the inhabitants of Diarbekir having revolted against the Turkish Government, I halted the 1st of Ramzan (28th December),[2] in order to accompany a caravan which was to leave Arganeh the next day.

---

1 Sha'aban is the eighth month of the Islamic calendar.
2 Fasting during Ramadan, or the ninth month of the Islamic calendar, is
   one of the five pillars of Islam.

On the 2d we set out at an early hour, and, after travelling fourteen hours, halted at a ruined caravanserai, the only shop remaining in which was that of a seller of wood; but, as it had rained the whole day, and was excessively cold, even that shop afforded a great comfort, as we were thereby enabled to light large fires, and to dry our clothes and blankets over them.

On the 3d, although it continued to rain very hard, we proceeded on our journey, and at noon reached Diarbekir, sixty-eight miles distant from Arganeh.

Diarbekir is the handsomest and most populous city on this road. It is situated on the bank of the river, and is surrounded by hills: these, however, are of an easy ascent, and covered with verdure. The tops of them are level, and contain some neat villages, surrounded by gardens and groves. In short, the appearance of this place was quite delightful, after the rude and rugged scenery through which we had lately passed.

The city is surrounded by a wet ditch, and a good rampart with stone bastions: it contains several handsome mosques and caravanserais, also the tomb of the celebrated Khaled Ben Valed, Generalissimo of the first Khalif, who conquered Syria.[1] Notwithstanding it rained very hard, I immediately waited on Ahmed Effendi, the Governor, who received me with much hospitality and kindness, and insisted upon my staying with him two or three days. When I complained to him of the villainy of my conductor, he regretted it was not in his power to punish or exchange him, as he was a public servant of the Government, but kindly ordered one of his own officers to accompany me to Mardine, and to supply all my wants. He also made me a present of a large surtout coat lined with fur, which I found of the most essential use to me during the remainder of the journey.

On the 6th I took leave of this worthy man, and, after travelling fifty-six miles, halted at a caravanserai in the mountains; but as it had no chimney, and we were obliged to light a fire in the middle of the room, I was kept awake all night by the smoke.

Between Arganeh and this place, we several times saw horsemen, who appeared to be robbers; but as we were a numerous party, they did not venture to attack us.

On the morning of the 7th we found it had snowed very hard

---

1   Commonly referred to as the "Sword of Allah," he was a distinguished Arab military leader who converted to Islam in 620 and served Mohammad's successor Abu-Bakr in the campaign to wrest Syria from the Byzantine empire.

during the night: and as we were apprehensive that the roads would be impassable if we remained at the caravanserai any longer, we mounted our horses during a heavy fall of snow, and pushed on to Mardine, sixteen miles. It was fortunate we escaped; as I afterwards learned from Mr. Jones,[1] that when he made that journey, nineteen horses out of twenty-one which accompanied him perished in the snow.

Mardine is situated on the side of a steep hill, and is surrounded by a good rampart and stone bastions. On the top of the hill there is a strong citadel, built by Soleyman Pasha, Governor of Bagdad; and as the approach to this city is over mountains and rugged roads, it is esteemed one of the strongest fortresses in this part of the world.

The language of the common people of Mardine is a mixture of Arabic and Kurdish; but the higher classes understand Turkish and Persian also. On the road from Constantinople to Malatia, Turkish only was understood: from the latter to Diarbekir, many of the inhabitants spoke Arabic; and between Diarbekir and Mardine I met with several persons who could converse in Persian: but between this and Bagdad, all four languages are understood.

Soon after my arrival at Mardine, I paid my respects to Abdullah Aga, the Governor, who invited me to take up my residence at his house.[2] This officer is one of the most intelligent of the Turkish noblemen; and although well known to the Emperor, and on the best terms with the Viziers, is still but the deputy of the Viceroy of Bagdad. He was formerly Governor of Bassora, as the deputy of Soleyman Pasha, and has left there many monuments of his fame. He was beloved by all the inhabitants, both rich and poor, who relate many anecdotes of his justice and wisdom. As he spoke Persian fluently, and was an entertaining companion, I passed my time very pleasantly with him. He pressed me much to remain with him all the month of Ramzan (the Mohammedan Lent); but as I was anxious to pursue my journey, and the weather was very cold at Mardine, I declined his obliging offer.

---

1   This is likely Sir Harford Jones Brydges (1764-1847), first baronet. He worked for the East India Company in Basra from 1783 to 1794 and then in Baghdad from 1798 to 1806. He added Brydges (a maternal family name) to his own in 1826.

2   Abdullah Agha was an Ottoman general and related by marriage to two Grand Viziers, Ali Pasha and Ibrahim Pasha.

I remained at Mardine four days; and as the Governor did not feel himself authorized to send away the public Mehmandar, he obligingly ordered one of his own servants to accompany me, to whom he gave positive orders to comply with all my wishes. And as the road to Mousul, across the Desert, is considered as replete with danger, on which account the Emperor had ordered Abdullah Aga to furnish me with a proper escort for this part of the journey, he therefore proposed to me to join a large caravan which was proceeding by that route; and having sent for the chief of the caravan, he recommended me to his peculiar care.

On the 12th we quitted Mardine; and after a journey of forty-eight miles, reached Nisibis. During this day's march, I had the good fortune to form an acquaintance with the new Cazy (judge) of Bagdad, who was proceeding to his station, with a retinue of several led horses, a *Tukht ruan* (a litter), fifteen troopers, and twenty musketeers, and, of course, was considered as a person of great consequence. He did me the honour to request I would be his companion during the time we travelled together; and I found considerable advantages in this association.

Nisibis[1] was, several hundred years ago, a very extensive and celebrated city; and, at one period, was the residence of the Roman Emperor. It was also, for a time, the capital of the Mohammedan empire, but is now fallen into decay, and retains no traces of its former grandeur, except the tombs of two Mussulman Saints. It however possesses a good post-house, the landlord of which was very civil, and supplied us with excellent horses. For this last act of kindness we were particularly obliged to him; as between Nisibis and Mousul, which is 200 miles, there is not any place to change horses; the whole country being, in fact, a desert, and much infested by robbers. It was therefore necessary that all our troop should be able to keep together, as any one falling behind would doubtless have been plundered and murdered.

---

1 Or Nusaybin, a centre of Nestorian Christian education throughout the fourth and fifth centuries even as the city went back and forth between the Persians and the Romans.

CHAPTER XXXI

The Caravan enters the Kurd country, on the borders of the Desert.
Description of the Desert. Caravan detained. Account of the Tribe of
Senjar, a race of mountaineers. Journey over the Desert. Author arrives
at Mousul—Panegyric on the Arabian horses—Courteously received
by Mohammed Pasha—Visits the tomb of St. George of England.
Description of Mousul and its inhabitants. Author complains against
his conductor—He quits Mousul—is hospitably entertained by some
Christian Arabs. Description of Kirkook and Karutapa. The Author
arrives at Bagdad. Computation of the distance from Constantinople
to Bagdad.

On the 13th we entered the country occupied by the Kurds, and
halted at a village twenty-four miles from Nisibis, in the vicinity
of which the Chief of the clan resided. He sent his sons to visit
us; but obliged the caravan to pay a heavy duty, for permission to
pass through his territories, of which he seemed to consider
himself the sovereign, and perfectly independent of the Turkish
Government. I accompanied the Cazy to the house of a Kurd
carpenter, who gave us an excellent dinner, and comfortable
beds.

On the 14th, after a march of twenty-four miles, we arrived at
the village of Abareh, the residence of Hyder Aga, the chief of a
tribe, who entertained us in an hospitable manner.

The reason of our making such short journeys these two days,
was, first, that the established duties might be regularly collected
from each person in the caravan; and, secondly, as we were about
to enter an uninhabited desert, that the carriers and camel-
drivers might have time properly to arrange their loads, and make
the requisite alterations.

The generality of the Kurds I met with understood Persian,
and, supposing me to be their countryman, behaved with great
kindness and attention.

These two days' journey are considered as forming part of the
Desert; but no portion of the road from Constantinople is better
inhabited, or more abundantly supplied with water; and the
whole of the two hundred miles, from Nisibis to Mousul, which
had been represented as terrible, is, in my opinion, the pleasantest part of the whole journey; for from Constantinople to Nisibis
the country is so mountainous, that we were constantly ascending or descending, and never met with a plain of a dozen miles in
extent. The Desert, on the contrary, is quite level, and resembles

Persia, or Hindoostan; and although water is not very plentiful, yet we crossed a rivulet every five or six miles. It must however be recollected, that I passed it at the most favourable season of the year; and that, as there is nothing to shade travellers from the sun, it must be very distressing in the hot weather. The most astonishing circumstance attending this region is, that, notwithstanding it adjoins the countries of Syria and Arabia, both of which abound with woods, and in many places it produces fine pasture, yet there is not to be found in the whole of the Desert, which is a thousand fersukhs[1] in circumference, a tree of a yard high. The inhabitants are therefore obliged to dress their food, and warm themselves in the winter, either with the dung of their cattle, or to bring wood and coals, at a great expence, from other countries. On this account they are very sparing of their fuel; and suffer as much from cold in the winter, as they do from the violent heat of the summer.

In the Desert there are scarcely any villages to be found; but the stages, and residence of the Chiefs of the tribes, are marked by mounds or hillocks.

We halted two days at Abareh, waiting for Shaikh Shellal, chief of the tribe of Ty, who had promised the Governor of Mardine to escort us safely across the Desert; but as he did not come, the leaders of the caravan, which consisted of two or three thousand men, among whom were several hundred musketeers and horsemen, agreed with Hyder Aga, of the above-mentioned tribe, to accompany us. The reason of their taking this precaution was, that, at a little distance to the right of our route, there is a range of hills occupied by the tribe of Senjar, commonly called Kurds of Yezid, who are said to be infidels, and sworn enemies to the followers of Mohammed. But they themselves say, that they are descended from the Arab tribe of Beni Yezid, or Beni Omieh, who, in consequence of a dispute with the tribe of Beni Abass, were obliged to emigrate from Arabia, and take refuge in these mountains. In the course of time, having increased in numbers, they have rendered themselves formidable to the Turkish Government by their depredations.

After the most minute inquiry on the spot, I am induced to believe they are orthodox Mohammedans, and that their conduct has not been so reprehensible as the people of Constantinople represent. The name of their chief was Hussein; and during the course of this year he had only plundered one caravan, which had

---

1 A unit of measure roughly equivalent to thirty-six miles.

neglected to send him his tribute, and attempted to pass the Desert unknown to him. Some stragglers of this tribe have also at times entered the adjacent territories, and committed highway robberies.

The hills of Senjar produce remarkably fine figs and prunes, which they dry, and carry to the markets of Mardine, Mousul, and Bagdad. The prunes are the largest I have ever seen, and I think were superior to any fruit I have ever tasted.

During our passage across the Desert, a number of these people visited us, and brought with them a quantity of figs, raisins, prunes, walnuts, &c. which they disposed of for money, or exchanged for cloths or other goods. Their dress and language were both Arabian.

On the 15th we travelled fifty-two miles; and as there are no villages or groves on this route, we halted at a spot called *Tul al Hua* (the Hillock of Eve). As this place was not far distant from the Senjar Hills, we were under some alarm; but, fortunately, Shaikh Shellal, with one hundred select horsemen, with large turbans, well armed, and mounted on fleet Arabian mares, joined us at this place. As we were only to halt a few hours, we did not unload the camels, but lay down on the ground without any covering, while the horses and camels ate their corn, and rested a little.

At one o'clock of the morning of the 16th, we again mounted, and, after travelling fifty-two miles, arrived at Hookteh, the residence of Shaikh Shellal, which was nothing more than a castle built on a hillock, for the security of the women and children, in case of any sudden danger. The Kurds always live in tents made of black blankets or hair cloth; and we here found encamped about two hundred families of the tribe of Ty. The remainder of the clan, which, we were informed, consists of fifteen or sixteen thousand families, were dispersed in the Desert, at the distance of one or two days' journey, under the command of a brother of our conductor, named Shaikh Faris; but who, with the whole tribe of Ty, acknowledge Shaikh Shellal as their chief. This person, in fact, assumed all the importance of a sovereign, and, with true Arabian hospitality, kept a constant table for fifty persons. I had the honour of dining with him several times; but although his table was plentifully supplied, his cookery was wretched.

At a very early hour on the 17th, we re-commenced our march, and, after a short journey of thirty-six miles, reached Homideh, the residence of Shaikh Faris. This place is distant from Abareh (the first stage in the Desert) thirty-five fersukhs; and, except the encampment of the tribe of Ty, there is no other intermediate habitation.

As our conductor was to be relieved at this place by his brother, the caravan was again laid under contribution; and each person was obliged to pay his proportion, according to the value of his property, or number of his camels and horses. I took the opportunity of the delay occasioned by this circumstance, to go into the village, where I was hospitably entertained, by an Arab, with some excellent bread and butter, and fresh dates; and, as I had not slept for three nights, I also enjoyed a sleep of several hours: after which, as we were only distant twelve miles from Mousul, I ventured to quit the caravan, and in two hours safely reached that city.

As we ought to be grateful to every person or thing that has been useful to us, I must, in this place, express my admiration of the spirit and perseverance of the Arab horses. That on which I rode across the Desert was, in appearance, little better than a poney; and, on the first day, his groom, having been unwell, left me, and returned to Nisibis: on the second day I lost his bag of corn; in consequence of which he had nothing to eat, during the five days' journey, but the little grass which he was enabled to pick up while we halted. During this time he never had his saddle taken off, or even his girths loosed: notwithstanding which, when I rode into Mousul, he appeared quite fresh, and was playing with the check of his bridle. In short, there are no horses in the world equal to them.

Soon after my arrival at Mousul, I paid my respects to the Viceroy, Mohammed Pasha: he received me in the most courteous manner, and invited me to remain with him for some days. Mohammed Pasha is descended from one of the former Sultans, is a man of great dignity, and one of the most respected of the Turkish nobility. He never associates with any of the inferior officers; but conversed freely with me, and even dispensed with my kissing the hem or skirt of his garment, and some other humiliating ceremonies of his Court. He also regaled me with coffee and a pipe; and then gave in charge to his son, Mahmud Beg, who is also his deputy, to carry me home, and take care of me.

Mahmud Beg is a very handsome and well-informed young man, and blessed with an amiable disposition. He mounted me every day on one of his finest horses, and took me to see all the places worthy of observation in the vicinity of Mousul: on these occasions we were always attended by a party of horsemen. By his assistance, I visited the tombs of the Prophet Jonas, and of Saint George the champion and tutelary saint of England.

Mousul is situated on the banks of the Tigris, in what is called the *Jezireh*, or 'country between the rivers.' It is fortified, like Mardine, with a deep ditch, a good rampart, and stone bastions; and has a stone bridge across the river.

In this city they have the finest bread and meat I have ever eaten. They have also a great abundance of dried fruits; but, notwithstanding these advantages, the climate is unhealthy, and the people were as desirous of a physician as a person in a high fever is for a draught of water. As I possessed a small degree of knowledge in the science of physic, and had the good fortune to cure one or two persons, I had innumerable applications made to me; and as my fame preceded me, I was annoyed at every stage during my journey to Bagdad, by having all the sick of the village brought for my advice.

In consequence of the attention paid to me by the Viceroy, I was visited by all the public officers, and by the principal inhabitants of Mousul. These, in general, I found to be well-informed, sensible men, of sociable dispositions and lively imaginations, and much superior to the Turks of Constantinople. In short, since leaving Paris I had not met with such witty and clever people; and if the Viziers of the Sultan had but a tenth part of any one of their abilities, I should be under no apprehension for the fate of the Turkish Government. The principal of these were Ahmed Effendi and his brother, both of whom were secretaries to the Pasha. Also Selime Beg, the late Governor of Kurdistan, a sensible and entertaining man, who spoke Persian fluently, and who had in his suite some of the best officers in the Turkish service. He had, some years ago, rebelled against Aly Pasha, the Viceroy of Bagdad, and endeavoured to depose him; but having failed in the attempt, he was obliged to fly, and take refuge in Mousul.

At this place I also met with Nejif Khan, a Persian nobleman, and formerly Governor of Baba, who had fled from the tyranny of Futteh Aly Shah, the king of Persia. He was a well-looking young man, dressed well, and had his attendants dressed and mounted in a very superior style.

I remained at Mousul five days; and during this time made a formal complaint to the Pasha against my Mehmandar, and requested to have him exchanged. My reason for again resuming this subject was the behaviour of the officer belonging to the Governor of Mardine, who, instead of obeying the instructions of his master, in attending to my wishes, leagued with the Mehmandar against me. Upon my representation of the case, the Pasha ordered the Mehmandar instantly to quit Mousul, and to proceed whither he pleased. He also directed Casim, his *Khojehdar* (confidential servant), to attend me to Bagdad.

This communication was very disagreeable to the Mehmandar; who, in consequence, left Mousul, but, instead of returning to Constantinople, as I wished, proceeded, as I afterwards learned, to Kirkook, a town on the road to Bagdad, where his family resided, and where, I was informed, he meant to rejoin me as I passed, in order to obtain from me a *Razy Nameh* (approval of conduct). In this, however, I disappointed him; and laid my plans so well, that I did not see his detested face again till after my arrival at Bagdad.

On the 23d of Ramzan I left Mousul; and, having crossed the river Tigris over the bridge, halted at Kerakoosh, distant sixteen miles.

On the 24th we proceeded to Ankueh, a journey of forty-eight miles. About half way we crossed the river Zab, upon a raft composed of reeds. This river is the boundary between the Governments of Mousul and Bagdad. During these two days' journey I was escorted by ten troopers, belonging to Mohammed Pasha; not on account of any danger on the road, but as a mark of respect, and as a proof of his friendship. The country we passed through, both days, was inhabited by Arab Christians, of the tribe of Beni Ghussan; and as the post-houses were very mean, my new conductor, the Khojehdar, carried me to the houses of the Chiefs, who entertained me very hospitably.

On the 25th, after travelling forty-eight miles, we reached Altin-kupri. This is a large village; and its name, in Turkish, signifies 'Many bridges,' there being no less than eight bridges over the river at this place. These, in general, have only one arch, which is consequently very high, and its passage as difficult as the Jebbal Mehrab, formerly mentioned.

Our journey on the 26th was to Kirkook, only thirty-six miles. The reason of my making such slow progress was, that the constant and heavy rain impeded our travelling over this level country, as much as the snow had formerly done in the mountains of Sewas and Tokat.

Kirkook is a large town, surrounded with a good rampart and stone bastions, but falling into decay. The houses within the fort are all built of stone or brick; but those in the suburbs are constructed of mud. As this town stands in the middle of an extensive plain, it makes a good appearance, and is seen at a considerable distance.

On the 27th we travelled thirty-six miles, and entered the village of Taoukh an hour before sun-set. The post-house at this place was a very comfortable one, and the people civil: but as I was apprehensive, if I stopped at this town, that Aly Hajy, my Constantinople Mehmandar, whose house was at Kirkook, and who must have heard of my passing, would follow and overtake me, I changed horses, and proceeded another stage of twenty-eight miles, and slept at Khermaty.

The 28th I rode thirty-six miles, to Kiffery; and having changed horses, proceeded to Karutapa, twenty-eight miles further on. This town is situated at the bottom of a range of hills, from which there is a plain extending all the way to Bagdad. This place is memorable for a complete victory gained by Nadir Shah over the Turks; and even now the field of battle may be easily traced, by the remains of the redoubts, and lines, which were thrown up by both armies on that occasion.[1] Kirkook was also the scene of one of his victories.

The post-house at Karutapa, and all the others through this district, being miserable hovels, Mustapha Beg, the Collector of the province, compels the farmers to lodge and provide for travellers, and pockets the allowance granted by Government for this purpose. As the farmers dare not disobey his orders, they reluctantly receive strangers into their houses, but give them very poor accommodations, and worse food, to which they frequently add abusive language. The horses supplied by them are also miserable starved brutes, and not of the genuine Arab breed. Before I quitted Karutapa, I insisted upon seeing this worthy Collector, (may the curse of God light on him!) and abused him for his meanness. He was excessively angry; and said I ought to be ashamed to complain of the badness of food which was given to me gratis. I replied, "I do not complain on my own account, but for the sake of future travellers; and it is you who ought to be ashamed, to deprive the people of the post-houses of their livelihood, by appropriating to yourself the allowance granted by Government, and obliging the farmers, either to ruin themselves, or to act in a rude and inhospitable manner to strangers."

The 29th I travelled thirty-six miles, and halted at Dilabass. As it rained the whole of this day, I put up at the post-house, which

1 See p. 281, note 1.

was a miserable place; but the people were civil, and worthy of a better Governor.

The 30th I travelled forty-eight miles, and passed the night at Dokhelah, a poor village; and on the 1st of Shual (27th of January 1803) entered Bagdad. This stage is reckoned only thirty-two miles, but, in my opinion, it is at least forty. However, as my horses were very bad during these last four stages, and could scarcely carry me, and as it rained most of the time, I possibly thought the road longer than it really is.

Between Dokhelah and Bagdad the country is an open plain; not a house, nor even a tree to be seen; and the roads very bad. Although I had six horses with me, two for riding, and four for my luggage, they were all so completely tired, that I was obliged to walk the last eight miles, with the wind, accompanied by rain, blowing in my face. All these circumstances contributed to render this day's journey the most fatiguing and disagreeable I had ever experienced. Fortunately, close to the gate of the suburbs there was a post-house, at which I changed my horses, and then proceeded to the house of Mr. Jones, the English Consul.

It is very extraordinary, that in the neighbourhood of so large a city as Bagdad, the road for forty miles should be without the least accommodation for a traveller. And I am convinced, had I attempted this journey at night, and lost my way, I should have sunk in the mire, and have perished of cold. A year seldom passes that some unfortunate travellers do not fall a sacrifice to this inhospitable track, which neither furnishes shelter to man or beast in the winter, nor a drop of water in the summer. In short, the journey from Constantinople to Bagdad is such, that none but a person in good health and vigour should attempt it.

This route was formerly well known to the Romans, but has been seldom travelled by Europeans for some centuries. The distance is estimated at 475 fersukhs, being 950 coss of Hindoostan, equal to 1900 English miles. There are fifty post-houses or stages on the road: and the caravans, at the most favourable season of the year, do not perform it in less than three months. I was fifty-six days on the road, fifteen of which I halted, but it has been rode by an active *courier* in twelve days; and, had I not met with impediments, I think I could have performed the journey in five or six weeks.

N.B. The whole of this route may be easily traced in any correct Map of Turkey in Asia. (Translator's note)

CHAPTER XXXII

Description of the city of Bagdad—inferior to the cities of India. The Author's object in taking this route. Account of the Mausoleum of Kazemine—its peculiar privileges—Oppressive conduct of the Turks— Description of the Tombs of Mohy Addeen and Abdal Cader. The Author sets out for Samerah—Account of his journey. Anecdote of the Khalif Moatisim. Description of the Mausoleum of Samerah. Author returns to Bagdad.

Bagdad is situated on the banks of the Tigris, and consists of two towns, one on each side the river, which are distinguished by the names of the New and Old Town. The former is on the eastern side, and contains the residence of the Pasha, and of all the principal officers: the latter is in the *Jezireh* (island), on the western side of the river, and contains very few good houses: and between the two there is a good stone bridge. Both towns are fortified, and have each a very deep and wide ditch; the bottom of which, during peace, is cultivated, but, in case of any alarm, can easily be filled with water from the river. This city is about eight miles in circumference. The fortifications of the New Town were built by Sultan Oubus Keran, commonly called Sultan Saujy. Those of the Old Town were constructed by order of the late Soleyman Pasha, as a defence against the Vahabies.[1]

Bagdad, being situated on the skirts of the Desert and in an extensive plain, when viewed from the exterior, has a very grand appearance; but in the interior it is a dirty filthy town, especially the Old Town, which, during the winter, is fully as bad as Moorshedabad, or any other city in Bengal. Although the principal bazar is built of brick and mortar, and has an arched roof, it is, nevertheless, a confined, dark, and stinking place.

The houses of the principal people are constructed with bricks and mud; the walls of which are not stronger than those of India.

---

1   Muhammad ibn Abd al-Wahhab (1703-87) advocated a form of fundamentalist Islam which rejected both Sufi beliefs and Arabian folk practices. Wahhabism was a puritanical doctrine which began to make significant political inroads during Abu Talib's lifetime. In 1773 the Saudi-Wahhabi alliance proclaimed Riyadh to be its capital. Between 1803 and 1805, the alliance seized both Mecca and Medina and destroyed many tombs and shrines, including that of the Prophet Muhammad. Abu Talib discusses these desecrations in the next chapter.

The wood-work and the ornaments of the rooms are, however, much inferior, and give the whole of the building a mean appearance. In short, the palace of the Pasha, and the best buildings in this city, are not equal to the houses of the middling classes of people in Lucknow; much less to be compared with the palaces of the Nabob Assuf ad Dowleh, or of his late Minister, Hussen Reza Khan.[1]

The fame of the cities of Bagdad, Bussora, Nejif, and other places of Persia, with which Hindoostan resounds, is like the sound of a drum, which is thought best at a distance: for I declare, that from my quitting Constantinople till I arrived at Bussora, I never saw a house that a person of moderate fortune in Lucknow would have considered respectable, or could live comfortably in, except that of Aga Jafeir at Kerbela; and even that was only calculated for a small family.

Bagdad abounds with coffee-houses, and rooms for smoking tobacco; but they are even darker and dirtier than those of Constantinople. The markets are well supplied; and the pomegranates, lemons, and *Aloo Bokhara* (dried plums), are the best I have ever eaten.

As the principal object of my taking this route was to worship at the shrines of the Martyrs and Saints of our religion (Shyâ Mohammedans), and to visit the tombs of some of my pious ancestors, descendants of the Prophet, I devoted the greater part of the time I remained at Bagdad to this sacred duty.[2]

The most celebrated of these shrines is that of the seventh and ninth *Imams* (pontiffs), both of whom were surnamed Kazem; on which account the mausoleum, as well as the village, is called

---

1   Muhammed Reza Khan (c.1717-91), a Bengal administrator, was often referred to in British papers as "the minister" or "the prime minister."

2   Abu Talib identifies himself as a Shiite. Shiites believe that the true imam must be a descendent of the Prophet Muhammad's daughter Fatima and his cousin Ali ibn Abi Talib. The Imami or Twelver Shiites recognize twelve imams directly descended from Ali who guide the community in spiritual matters. The twelfth imam is in hiding and will return at the end of time as the mahdi or messiah. In the meantime, the community is guided by scholars. The subsequent account of Abu Talib's pilgrimage signals a religious awakening and he appears to have been scrupulous in following in the footsteps of Ali and the Alid imams.

Kazemine.[1] It is situated in the Jezireh,[2] four miles to the north-west of Bagdad, and contains better houses than those of the city. It is chiefly inhabited by strangers from Persia and India, and is surrounded by a mud rampart. As the intercourse between the city and the mausoleum is very great, hundreds of asses and mules, ready saddled, are always standing on the western side of the bridge, and may be hired for five half-pence; and when the rider arrives at the gate of Kazemine, he finds a person ready to take charge of the animal.

The dome of this mausoleum, as also that of Kerbela, was some years ago rebuilt, and covered with *golden tiles*, at the expence of Mohammed Khan Kejar, king of Persia.[3] The court-yard, walls, gates, and bazar, have also lately been rebuilt and ornamented, at the expence of the late Nabob Assuf ad Dowleh, Vizier of Hindoostan.

This bazar is not very extensive, but in cleanness and beauty it stands unequalled; and the mausoleum, although not equal to that of Kerbela and Nejif, is still very extensive and magnificent. The cupola, being covered with gold, may be seen, when the sun shines on it, at the distance of five fersukhs; and the inside of the mau-soleum is lined with *painted tiles*. These tiles are very beautiful, and are an invention peculiar to this part of the world, and have not yet been introduced either into Europe or India; at least I have never met with them, but think them superior either to painting or gilding. On these tiles are pourtrayed flowers, and other various devices; also pieces of beautiful writing, in the Nastalik, Niskh, and Togray characters; and, in short, every thing that the pencil of the limner can delineate. They are also so nicely joined, as to appear one perfect piece, and are never affected by the weather.

In the court-yard there is a second dome, under which are buried two of the children of the Imams, at whose tombs it is also customary to offer up prayers.

---

1   Musa al-Kazim (745-99) was the seventh Shia Imam. He was Imam during the Abbasid dynasty and was persecuted by the Caliph Harun al-Rashid. He was rumoured to have been poisoned by the Abbasid ruler and was buried in the town of Kazimain. His grandson Muham-mad al-Taqi is also buried at this site and the shrine is an important pilgrimage site for Shiites.

2   Mesopotamia. (Translator's note)

3   Mohammed Khan Kejar (1720-97), Shah of Persia from 1794 to 1797. After a protracted civil war he overthrew the Zand dynasty and founded the Kejar dynasty.

This mausoleum is under the charge of a superintendant, and several servants of different degrees in rank; and notwithstanding it is so near Bagdad, Turkish bigotry is excluded from its walls, and the pious Shya may pray here according to his own fashion. The fact is, that at this shrine, and in the vicinity of Samerah, Nejif, and Kerbela, there are so many Shyas settled, that the Turks, who are Soonies, and everywhere else abuse and spit on the Shyas, dare not, at these places, make use of any abusive language.

The reason assigned for this toleration is, the vicinity of the Persian Monarch, who might take revenge for any insult offered to persons of his own faith. But the real fact is, that the number of pilgrims who visit these sacred places bring a great quantity of money into the country, and yield a considerable revenue to the State: the Princes of Hindoostany, and the Kings of Persia, also, often send valuable presents to these shrines: so that it is to Turkish avarice we are indebted for the freedom here enjoyed.

The Turks, so far from paying any respect to these holy places, frequently pillage and oppress the poor pilgrims, and throw every obstacle in their way. For instance, some years ago there was a ferry over a very narrow part of the Tigris, opposite to a considerable village, the inhabitants of which thought proper to complain to the Pasha of Bagdad that they suffered much inconvenience from the great concourse of pilgrims who came that road, and requested the boats might be stationed at some other place. The Pasha, blinded by bigotry, listened to this unreasonable complaint, and stationed the ferry-boats at the very broadest part of the river, and at a place where there was not any accommodation within eight miles for the poor travellers: in consequence of which, the boats can only make one passage in a day, and the pilgrims are obliged to wait on the sands for many hours, and sometimes days, before they can cross the river. Pious Shyas have, at various times, built caravanserais on this road, for the accommodation of the pilgrims; but the Turks, by their oppressions, have driven away all the shopkeepers and tradesmen who used to attend them, so that the buildings are of very little use.

I know not whether it is owing to the oppression of the Turks, or to the neglect of the superintendant, but none of these shrines are properly lighted at night. Those of Kazemine, Nejif, and Kerbela, have a few glimmering lamps; but at Samerah the doors are locked at sun-set, by which the devotees are prevented from going to the mosque, to say their prayers at the stated hours. On beholding this state of things, I could not help shedding tears; and was mortified to think that the tomb of one of our spiritual guides is not supported with half the splendour that is constantly exhibited at the mausoleums of the *pseudo* Saints of Hindoostan, Musaoud Ghazy of Gorruckpore, and Shah Mudar of Canouge.

In the vicinity of Kazemine is situated the tomb of Abu Hanifa,[1] commonly called the Imam Aazem (Superior Pontiff), the dome of which is covered with painted tiles, but it has scarcely any gilding about it.

The mausoleum of Abd al Cader Jilany,[2] one of the most celebrated Soofies (mystics), is situated in the middle of Bagdad, and has several rich estates appertaining to it, the income from which enables the superintendant to live in a handsome style, and to support a number of dependants. There were not less than one or two thousand pilgrims and students, principally from India, residing within the inclosure, while I was there, who daily received an allowance of food from the funds of the shrine. The superintendant, who is dignified by the title of Shaikh al Mushaikh (Chief Prelate), having heard of my arrival, invited me to take coffee with him. I accordingly waited on him; but, as I found him a *great bear*, I made my visit very short.

In the middle of the city is also situated the tomb of Shaikh Shahab Addeen Sheherverdy. It is built in the centre of a delightful garden, and has a mosque and several other buildings dependent on it.

On the outside of the city walls there are several handsome mausolea of celebrated personages: the chief of these are, the tombs of Shaikh Ahy Kuzat, and of Zybindeh, the queen of the Khalif Haroun al Rashid. Here is also the Christian Hermitage, celebrated for the miraculous discovery of a fountain or spring by the Khalif Aly.[3]

Having made the tour of all the sacred places in the city or its precincts, I resolved to make a pilgrimage to the superior shrines

---

1   Abu Hanifa (699-765), an important Islamic scholar and founder of the Hanifi school of fiqh or Islamic law. He is revered by Shiites for his resistance to the Abbasid caliph al-Mansur's attempt to name him chief judge of the state. He died in prison for his refusal to submit to the caliph.

2   Abdul Qadir Jelani (1077-1166) was a renowned mystic and legal scholar revered by Sufis. After 25 years of self-imposed seclusion he returned to Baghdad in 1127 and his preaching had a wide ranging impact.

3   See Ockley's History of the Saracens, vol. ii. p. 41. (Translator's note). See p. 322, note 1 below.

of Samerah, Kerbela, and Nejif. In consequence of this determination, I hired horses, and on the 15th of Shual (February 11th, 1803) we crossed the Tigris, and, retracing a considerable part of my three last days' journey from Constantinople, reached Samerah on the fifth day, before sun-set. If I had made inquiries on this subject when I arrived at Karutapa, I might have saved myself much fatigue, as Samerah is only distant from that town twenty-four miles, and might easily have been taken in my route to Bagdad. But, as it was decreed I should have the merit of making a toilsome journey, purposely to worship at this holy place, I passed within a short distance of it without knowing the circumstance, and, in consequence, suffered much fatigue of body and distress of mind on this occasion; for from the moment I left Bagdad till I returned it never ceased raining; and the conductor sent with me by the Pasha of Bagdad, being a bigoted Soony, oppressed and harassed the Shyas wherever we passed: the people of the villages therefore fled whenever we approached, and cursed me for coming near them.

The first night we slept under a tent, belonging to an Arab Chief, of the tribe of Beni Tumeem, in the vicinity of a hillock denominated the Mound of Nimrod, whence, it is said, that monarch made the mad attempt to climb the heavens.

The second night we reached the town of Dilujil, on the borders of the sacred territory, and took our abode with a Mutusellum (a pretended Mussulman, i.e. a Soony).

On the third day, during the journey, I paid my respects at the tombs of Ibrahim Malik Ashter (a celebrated General of Aly the son-in-law of Mohammed), and of Mohammed the son of Imam Aly al Hady, who is so much reverenced in this neighbourhood, that the people swear by him.[1] It was therefore late before we reached the Tigris, which, at this season of the year, is always full, and runs with great rapidity. As it was requisite we should cross the river, we embarked in an old crazy boat, the crew of which appeared quite ignorant of their profession: but as it rained and blew very hard against us, all our attempts to cross were fruitless; and after toiling for an hour, we returned to the shore. We were then obliged to return twelve miles, to the village of Balbud, and with much difficulty procured uncomfortable beds, at the house of a Shaikh of the tribe of Beni Saad.

---

1   Malik al-Ashtar was one of Ali's most important generals. He, along with Abu Bakr, was a crucial figure in the wars against Syria and became governor of Egypt in 658. Imam Ali al-Hadi was the tenth Shia Imam.

On the fourth day we returned to the bank of the river, and with much toil and considerable danger effected our passage. We arrived on the opposite shore a little before the setting of the sun, and passed the night in the tent of a wandering Arab Chief. This Shaikh was a great flatterer and hypocrite; but being indisposed with a violent cold and rheum, he was anxious to benefit by my medical skill, and therefore pressed me to remain some time with him. As I declined his invitation, he contrived to have my mule, and the conductor's horse, stolen during the night, and pretended they had run away. By this scheme, he hoped not only to detain me, but to obtain a reward for the recovery of the animals. I was not a little vexed at this treatment; and told him that his complaint was in the socket of his eye, which could not be cured without a deep incision; and that as I had not any instruments with me, I could render him no assistance. He was at length convinced by my reasoning; and about the middle of the day produced the horse and mule, which we immediately mounted, and proceeded on our journey. Before we had travelled many miles, we came to Naherwan, a village celebrated for the victory gained by the Khalif Aly over his enemies the Kharegites.[1] After passing this place, we travelled for some time through broken grounds and ravines, till about three o'clock in the evening, when we reached a ruined caravanserai, situated on a hill called the Serai of Mirza Kujy. This is the second station where the pilgrims perform the prescribed ceremonies. When at the distance of four fersukhs from Samerah, our eyes were illumined by the sight of the holy shrines of the tenth and eleventh Imams, on whom be the peace of God!

A little to the right of Samerah is a considerable hillock, which the people of that district call the *Tul al Mukhaly*. In Arabic, *Tul* signifies a mound, and *Mukhaly* a small bag for holding four or five pounds of corn, such as are used in London to feed the hackney-coach-horses. There is a tradition, that Moatisim, one of the Abbasy Khalifs, wishing to make a display of his power before

---

1   The Kharijites were one of the first dissenting sects in Islam. They acknowledged the first two caliphs but refused to recognize Uthman, Ali, and subsequent imams revered by Shiites. Ali antagonized the Kharijites when, following the Battle of Siffin in 658, he agreed to submit his dispute with the Umayyads to arbitration. The conflict was decided in favor of the more powerful party, the Umayyads. Ali was assassinated by the Kharijites in Kufa in 661 and buried in Najaf, which became a major shrine for Shiites.

Hussein Askerry (the eleventh Imam), ordered his army to be reviewed in this plain;[1] and after the review was over, to commemorate this event, he directed each of the troopers to fill his bag with earth, and to empty it on this spot. Such was the number of his army, that by this means a hillock was shortly raised. After seeing this, the Imam said to the Khalif, "If you will give me leave, I will now shew you my army." He then pointed to a particular quarter; where the Khalif beheld in the air an immense host of men and horses, advancing against him; the former all clothed in armour, and the latter terrific-looking creatures. The Khalif was frightened at this vision, and requested forgiveness. The Imam graciously pardoned him, and assured him of his forgiveness. It was from this event that Hussein got the title of *Askerry* (the Leader of Armies).

In the evening we entered Samerah, sometimes called *Sermenrai* (Rejoicing the beholder), distant from Bagdad ninety-six miles. It is said, that, during the prosperity of the Khalifs, these two cities were so nearly joined together, that a cock could fly from house to house, the whole distance; and even now there are vestiges of buildings all the way.

Samerah is situated on the western bank of the Tigris: and the direct road to Bagdad would be nearly a straight line; but on account of the plundering Arabs and other impediments, travellers are obliged to make the circuit I have detailed.

In this city is situated the mausoleum of Aly al Hady (the tenth Imam), built by Ahmed Khan Dunbely. This building is higher and more solid than any of the domes of Kerbela, Nejif, or Kazemine, but is not guilt [sic], nor of so handsome a construction as the mausolea of those places. Within the building there is a large wooden chest, or coffin, which covers the tombs of four saints; viz. Aly Hady; Hussein Askerry; Narjiss Khatun, the mother of Mehedy the twelfth Imam; and a daughter of Aly Hady the tenth Imam. At the distance of a bow-shot from the mausoleum, is the cave whence Imam Mehedy disappeared, whose return is still looked for by all pious Shyas. No alteration has been made in the cave, but a dome has been erected over it.[2]

The day after my arrival, Syed Kheleel, the superintendant of

---

1 Hasan al-Askari was the eleventh Shia Imam. Al-Mutasim was the Abbasid caliph from 833 to 842.
2 Imam Ali al-Hadi was the tenth Shia Imam. The Al-Askari mosque, which houses his mausoleum, was one of the most holy shrines for Shiites. It was destroyed by a bomb in February 2006.

the mausolea, called on me; and although by religion a Soony, he paid me great attention.

The following day, being much annoyed by the crowd of beggars, and the tyranny exercised by my conductor over the Shyas, I resolved to shorten my visit; and as soon as I had performed all the required ceremonies, set out to return to Bagdad. Before we had travelled many miles, it recommenced raining, and never ceased till we arrived in that city. This journey, going and returning, is generally performed in six days; but, owing to the badness of the roads, and the inclemency of the weather, I was twelve days in effecting it.

N.B. Persons desirous of information on the subjects of this and the subsequent Chapter, are referred to any of the following books:

Ockley's History of the Saracens.[1]
Universal History.
Gibbon's Decline and Fall of the Roman Empire.[2]
Bibliothèque Orientale.[3]

See the titles, *Mohammed, Ali, Hussein,* &c. (Translator's note)

CHAPTER XXXIII

The Author sets out on a pilgrimage to Kerbela and Nejif—Hospitably entertained at the house of a Syed, and by the Governor of Kerbela—meets with his Aunt. Description of the Mausoleum, and of the town of

---

1 Simon Ockley, *The History of the Saracens. Containing the lives of Abubeker, Omar, ... and Abdolmélick, the immediate successors of Mahomet* (London, 1718). Ockley (1679-1720) was an extremely influential orientalist. The two-volume *History of the Saracens*, republished in 1757, was the primary source of information in English on the Umayyad caliphate.

2 Arguably the greatest work of history in the eighteenth century, Edward Gibbon's *The History of the Decline and Fall of the Roman Empire* (1776-88) runs to twelve volumes.

3 Barthélemy d'Herbelot de Molainville's *Bibliothèque orientale, ou dictionnaire universel contenant tout ce qui regarde la connoissance des peuples de l'Orient* was completed by Antoine Galland and published posthumously in 1697. It is based on a vast bibliographical dictionary of Arabic works by the Turkish scholar Haji Khalifa or Kalfa (1609-57) entitled *Kashf al-zunun'an asami al-kutub wa al-funun.*

Kerbela—Account of its capture by the Vahabies—Plundered a second time by the Arabs. History of the Vahabies—Letter of their Chief to the King of Persia.

After resting myself for a week at Bagdad, on the 4th of Zykad (1st of March 1803) I again set out on a pilgrimage for the shrines of Kerbela and Nejif Ashru. On this occasion I did not acquaint the Pasha, lest I should be again annoyed by a Soony conductor. I therefore privately hired some horses and mules from a carrier, and bargained that he should accompany me. By this contrivance, I performed this journey with great satisfaction to myself; and the people on the route, not being alarmed by the presence of a Turk, paid me the utmost attention.

In the course of my first day's journey, I had the good fortune to fall into company with Mulla Osman, the Judge of Kerbela, who was returning home; and who, although a Soony, was a man of liberal mind, and unbiassed by prejudices. He expressed great happiness at meeting me, and requested I would be his guest during the journey.

On the road from Bagdad to Nejif, there are, at every eight miles, good caravanserais, built of brick and mortar, in the form of forts, which are called *khans*, but few of them are inhabited.

On the first day we travelled forty miles, and passed the night at the khan of Mirza Keejy; and on the second day, about three o'clock, we arrived at Kerbela. I put up at the house of Syed Khemzeh, whose nephew, Syed Ahmed, was well known to me while I resided at Moorshedabad in Bengal, and whom I hoped to have embraced again at Kerbela; but this worthy man had, unfortunately, died a few months before my arrival: his relations were, however, very hospitable and attentive, and assisted me in performing all the ceremonies of the pilgrimage. The Governor, Ameen Aga, was also very civil, and invited me twice to dine with him. He also procured me horses and mules to continue my journey to Nejif, the hire of which he wished to pay; but as his doing so would have deprived me of the merit of the pilgrimage, I requested he would excuse my accepting this proof of his friendship.

I had the happiness of meeting at this place with my aunt, Kerbelai Begum, and several of her female servants and slaves, who, in consequence of the misfortunes of our family, and my quitting home, had retired from the world, and come to end their days in the sacred territory. As this meeting was unexpected, it afforded us much mutual gratification. As they had been plundered of all their property by the Vahabies, I assisted them as far as lay in my power.[1]

The mausoleum of Kerbela, and the court-yard, were repaired, not many years ago, at the expence of Mohammed Khan Kejar, king of Persia.[2] The dome is entirely covered with plates of gold, and the inside highly gilt and ornamented; the most celebrated goldsmiths, painters, and engravers, having been sent from Persia for that purpose. The tomb of the Prince of Martyrs (Hussein, son of Aly, and grandson of Mohammed) is in the centre of the building, and is covered with a steel case, inlaid with gold, highly ornamented; and in the courtyard are the tombs of the seventy-two martyrs who fell with their prince.[3]

At the distance of a quarter of a mile from the mausoleum is a cave, which has been excavated under the spot where the martyrs were murdered. It is from this cave that the holy earth of Kerbela is brought away, and carried to all parts of the world, as a sacred relic.

Near this place is the spot on which the tent of the Imam Zien al Abadeen (son of Hussein) was pitched on the day of the battle; over which a handsome cenotaph has been erected, at the expence of the wife of the late Nabob Assuf ad Dowleh of Lucknow; and in the vicinity the lady had also commenced building a caravanserai, but was obliged to relinquish the undertaking in consequence of the Nabob's death.

At the distance of eight miles from Kerbela is a magnificent tomb of one of the martyrs, which is generally visited by pilgrims; but, in consequence of the depredations of robbers who assume the dress of Vahabies, it is now neglected, and I durst not approach it.

The town of Kerbela is surrounded by a mud wall, and was formerly the residence of a number of wealthy merchants; but since it was plundered by the Vahabies, it is falling into decay, and

---

1 See p. 314, note 1.

2 See p. 316, note 3.

3 Karbala is the fourth holiest city for Shia Muslims. At the centre of the old city is the Masjidu l-Husayn, the tomb of Husayn ibn Ali, grandson of the Prophet Muhammad by his daughter Fatima and Ali ibn Abi Talib. Husayn was the third Shia Imam and his tomb is a place of pilgrimage for many Shia Muslims, especially on the anniversary of the battle, the Day of Ashura. Mirza Abu Talib also makes the typical Shia pilgrimage to al-Makhayam, traditionally believed to be the location of Husayn's camp, where the martyrdom of Husayn and his followers is publicly commemorated.

has been forsaken by many of its opulent inhabitants. This event occurred only eleven months previous to my arrival, and was effected in the following manner.

On the 18th of the month Zilhige (April 1802), the greater part of the respectable inhabitants of Kerbela having gone to pay their devotions at the shrine of Nejif, 25,000 Vahabies, mounted on Arab horses and swift camels, made a sudden incursion from the Desert, and, being in league with some persons inside the town, shortly made themselves masters of the place.[1] After having massacred and plundered the inhabitants for many hours, they attempted to break off the gold plates from the mausoleum; but the metal was so strongly riveted, that they could not effect their purpose. They however very much injured the tombs and other parts of the building; and, without any apparent cause of alarm, retreated at sun-set.

The Governor, Omar Aga, being a bigoted Soony, was suspected of carrying on a correspondence with the Vahabies, and of having been bribed by them. So much is certain, that, on the first alarm, he fled to a neighbouring village, and did not make the smallest opposition. He was, in consequence, tried by Soleyman Pasha, and condemned to death.

During the short time the Vahabies remained in the town, they murdered 5000 persons, and wounded twice that number. They also plundered all the inhabitants, of their gold, silver, and every thing that was valuable.

As this event had so recently occurred, the people could talk of nothing else; and their description of the cruelties practised by these wretches made my hair stand on end. It however appeared, that the murdered persons acted in a very unmanly manner, and did not attempt to defend themselves, but submitted to be slaughtered, like sheep by the hands of the butcher.

When the Vahabies had retired, the Arabs of the neighbourhood, taking advantage of the general despondency, entered the town, and carried off the copper and other heavy articles, which the Vahabies had not thought worth the carriage. They also murdered many of the inhabitants, and retained possession of the place for two nights and a day.

---

1 Their signal of attack was: "Kill the Associators! Cut the throats of the Infidels!" (Translator's note). After the Wahhabi invasion the city operated as an independent republic until the reimposition of Ottoman rule in 1843.

During my residence at Kerbela, I endeavoured to collect as much information respecting the laws and religion of this new sect, as I could procure: but, as the inhabitants of Kerbela are of an indolent disposition, and do not trouble themselves with what does not immediately concern them, my knowledge on this subject is still very limited.

I learned, that the founder of this sect was named *Abd al Vehab* (The servant of the Bestower of all Benefits).[1] He was born in the neighbourhood of Hilla, on the banks of the Euphrates, but brought up, as an adopted son, by a person of some consequence, named Ibrahim, of the tribe of Beni Herb, in the district of Nejid. During his youth he was considered as superior to all his contemporaries, for his ready wit, penetration, and retentive memory. He was also of a very liberal disposition; and whenever he received any money from his patron, he distributed it immediately amongst his inferiors. After having acquired the common principles of education, and a little knowledge of the law, he travelled to Ispahan, late the capital of Persia, where he studied, for some time, under the most celebrated masters of that city. He then travelled to Khorassan, and thence to Ghizni; whence he proceeded to Irac; and after sojourning there some time, he returned home. About the year of the Hejira 1171 (A.D. 1757-58), he began to publish his new doctrines. At first, the fundamental principles of his religion were the same as those of the celebrated Imam Abu Hanifa, but in his exposition of the text he differed considerably. After a short time, he drew his neck from the collar of subserviency, and promulgated doctrines entirely new. He accused the whole Mohammedan church of being associators (giving partners to God), infidels, and idolaters. He even accused them of being worse than idolaters: "For these," said he, "in the time of any calamity, forsake their idols, and address their prayers directly to God; but the Mussulmans, in their greatest distress, never go beyond Mohammed, or Aly, or some of the saints. The common people, who worship at the tombs of the Prophet and his descendants, and who solicit these persons to be

---

1 See p. 314, note 1. Abu Talib discusses the rise of Muhammad ibn Abd al-Wahhab, his doctrines and the ensuing political turmoil in the following paragraphs. His disappointment at the failure of the Ottoman and Safawid dynasties to effectively deal with Wahhabism is symptomatic of the political decline of both imperial orders. By this time the Mughal empire was in no position to defend itself against these religious and political developments.

their mediators with God, are, in fact, guilty of idolatry daily: for no nation was ever so stupid as to address an image as their God, but merely as the representation of one of his attributes, or of one of their intercessors with the Deity. Thus the Jews and Christians, who have pictures and images of Moses, and of Jesus Christ, never associate them with God, but occasionally address their prayers to them, as mediators."

By these arguments he, by degrees, collected a number of followers, and proceeded to plunder and destroy the tombs and shrines of the Prophet, and of all the saints. By these means he acquired much wealth and fame, and, previous to his death, was possessed of great power and authority.

He was succeeded by his son Mohammed, who, being blind, remains always at home, and has assumed the title of Imam, and Supreme Pontiff of their religion. He employs, as his deputy, a person named Abd al Aziz, who was an adopted brother of his father's, and who is of an immense stature, with a most powerful voice. This man is eighty years of age, but retains all the vigour of youth, and predicts that he shall not die till the Vahaby religion is perfectly established all over Arabia. This person waits on Mohammed twice every week, and consults with him on all points of religion, and receives his orders for detaching armies to different quarters. Their power and influence is so much increased, that all Arabia may be said to be in subjection to them; and their followers have such reverence for them, that, when going into battle, they solicit passports to the porters at the gates of Paradise, which they suspend round their necks, and then advance against they enemy with the greatest confidence.

Although the Vahabies possess great power, and have collected immense wealth, they still retain the greatest simplicity of manners, and moderation in their desires. They sit down on the ground without ceremony, content themselves with a few dates for their food, and a coarse large cloak serves them for clothing and bed for two or three years. Their horses are of the genuine Nejid breed, of well-known pedigrees; none of which will they permit to be taken out of the country. The whole of their revenue is expended in the support of this army, which enables them to maintain innumerable forces, the whole of which are ready to undertake any exploit, however distant, either for the sake of extending their religion, or of acquiring plunder.

Except the cities of Muscat, Mecca, and Medineh, the Vahabies are in possession of all Arabia. For many years they refrained from attacking the holy cities: first, on account of their respect for the house of God; and, secondly, from their attachment to the Shereef of Mecca, who professed to be of their religion; and the emoluments derived from the pilgrims who passed through their dominions. But lately, at the instigation of the Turks, Abd al Aziz sent a large army, under the command of his son Saoud, into the sacred territory; who, after burning and laying waste the country, entered Mecca, and broke down many of the tombs and shrines; after which he proceeded to Jedda, and laid siege to it. The Shereef immediately took refuge on board a ship anchored in the Red Sea; and the people of the town having agreed to pay a large sum of money, the Vahabies proceeded to Oman. Soon after their arrival in that province, they were joined by a brother of the Sultan of Muscat, who embraced the Vahaby religion, and assumed the title of Imam al Mussulmeen (Pontiff of the Mussulmans), and soon compelled all the inhabitants of the open country to follow his example, and embrace the new faith. They have, in consequence, thrown off their allegiance to the Sultan, whose authority is now limited to the city of Muscat and its environs; and Saoud, being convinced that it must fall into his hands some day, does not at present press the matter.

The people of Bussora and of Hilla are in such apprehensions of a visit from the Vahabies, that they cannot pass a night in comfort; and the inhabitants of Nejif and Kerbela, having sent all their valuable property to Kazemine for security, tranquilly smoke their pipes, till the day breaks, and they are assured of safety.

As the depredations of the Vahabies have frequently been carried to within a few miles of Bussora, it is very probable they will shortly render themselves masters of that city. They have lately conquered the tribe of Outub, who are celebrated for their skill in the art of ship-building and of navigation, and have already commenced to form a maritime force. Whenever they have effected this point, they will soon be masters of Bussora; after which they will easily capture Bagdad: and I have no doubt, but that in a few years they will be at the gates of Constantinople.

The sacrilegious plunder of the holy cities of Mecca and Kerbela, by the Vahabies, ought to have roused the vengeance of the Turkish Emperor and of the King of Persia, and to have induced them to unite their forces for the extirpation of this wicked tribe, whose insolence is now arrived at that pitch, that, not content with the sovereignty of Arabia, they have, in imitation of the Prophet Mohammed, written to both those monarchs, inviting them to embrace their religion. The following is a copy of the letter of their General, or Vice-regent, to the King of Persia.

"We fly unto God for refuge against the accursed Satan. In the name of God, the Compassionate, the Merciful. From Abd al Aziz, Chief of the Mussulmans, to Futteh Aly Shah, King of Persia.

Since the death of the Prophet Mohammed, son of Abd' Allah, polytheism and idolatry have been promulgated amongst his followers. For instance, at Nejif and Kerbela, the people fall down and worship the tombs and shrines, which are made of earth and stone, and address their supplications and prayers to the persons contained therein. As it is evident to me, the least of the servants of God, that such practices cannot be agreeable to our Lords Aly and Hussein, I have used every exertion to purify our holy religion from these vile superstitions, and, by the blessing of God, have long since eradicated these pollutions from the territory of Nejid, and the greater part of Arabia; but the attendants on the mausolea, and the inhabitants of Nejif, being blinded by covetousness and worldly interest, encouraged the people to a continuation of these practices, and would not comply with my exhortations: I therefore sent an army of the Faithful (as you may have heard) to punish them, according to their deserts. If the people of Persia are addicted to these superstitions, let them quickly repent; for whosoever is guilty of idolatry and polytheism, shall in like manner be punished.

Peace be to him who obeys this direction!"

CHAPTER XXXIV

The Author continues his pilgrimage to Nejif. Account of the canals of Husseiny and Assuffy. Panegyric on the late Nabob Assuf ad Dowleh. Description of the cities of Hilla and Nejif. Account of the Mausoleum of Aly. Anecdote of an Arab. The Author devotes his mind to religious contemplation—Returns to Bagdad. Reasons why he first went to live with the British Consul—bad consequences thereof. Author disgusted with Mr. Jones's mode of living. Manner of travelling in Irac. Author embarks on the Tigris.

As soon as I had finished all the ceremonies of the pilgrimage at Kerbela,[1] I set out for Nejif by the route of Hilla, and arrived at

---

1 These places are marked, in some maps, Mejid Hosein, and Mejid Aly, (the Mausolea of Hussein and Aly). (Translator's note)

the latter city the first day, the distance being only sixteen fersukhs. During the course of this day's journey, I crossed two bridges built over canals. The first of these canals, which is called the Niher Husseiny, is only a few miles from Kerbela, and was dug by order of Sultan Murad, one of the Turkish Emperors, to convey water from the Euphrates to Kerbela; which pious work has obtained for him the blessings of the inhabitants of that district. The other is named the Niheri Hindue, or Assuffy, having been cut at the expence of the late Nabob Assuf ad Dowleh of Lucknow:[1] it is much larger than the canal of Husseiny, and is as broad as a tolerable-sized river. The intention of this aqueduct is to convey an ample supply of water from the Euphrates to Nejif, the burial-place of Aly. Ten lacs of rupees (£125,000) have already been expended; but, owing to the duplicity of the Pasha of Bagdad, and malversation of the superintendant, who, instead of cutting it in a direct line, have made it wind round by Cufa and other towns, it does not yet approach within four miles of its destination. The work is, however, still carrying on, and, when completed, will convey the waters of the Euphrates into the ancient bed of the river Ny, now dry, which formerly ran under the walls of Nejif, and was nearly as wide as the Tigris; and which, after making a considerable circuit, will again unite with the Euphrates.

This pious work of the Nabob Assuf ad Dowleh has not only given present employment to the poor of that neighbourhood, but will confer permanent comfort on the inhabitants in general, and give fertility to the soil, which has been long parched up, for want of water to irrigate the fields. In short, if the blessings of millions, and the prayers of the righteous, can benefit the souls of the departed, or can give consolation to the friends of the deceased, no man ever possessed a better claim to them than that Prince. Nor are the people of Irac ungrateful, but daily offer up prayers and supplications for his eternal salvation, and never mention his name but with rapture and enthusiasm.

Hilla is a very ancient and celebrated city, and was for a long time the capital of the Sultans of the tribe of Beni Muzyd, during the Kalifat of the house of Abassy, and is situated on both sides of the river Euphrates.[2] The residence of the Pasha and principal

---

1   See p. 66, note 2. Abu Talib honors Asaf ud-Daula throughout this chapter as a protector of Shia holy sites despite the waning influence of the Mughal empire.

2   Al-Hillah was a major site of Shia learning and an important administrative centre during Ottoman rule.

officers is on the western side, next the Desert; but they have numerous gardens and buildings on both sides of the river. The most celebrated of the buildings are, the Mosque of the Sun, and the Minar (turret) of Aly. The former is built on the spot where Aly performed his devotions while the Prophet commanded the sun to stop its course. If a person mounts the latter, and says, "In the right of Aly," the turret shakes; but if he repeats, "In the right of Omar," it is perfectly motionless. Of the anecdote respecting the former we have no authentic evidence; but with respect to the latter miracle, I have conversed with persons who declare they have witnessed it, and that they have placed a man on the line of the shadow previous to the operation, and that when the turret began to shake, the shadow moved backward and forward two yards.

I passed the night at Hilla, and early next morning proceeded on my journey. During the course of the day, I visited, on my route, the tomb of Zu al Kuffel (Master of the Lock), and the well and station of Imam Mehedy, not far distant from the fort of Nejif.[1] The former is situated in the middle of a village, surrounded by a wall, the inhabitants of which are all Jews; and which, next to Jerusalem, is held in the highest respect by all the people of that sect settled in Arabia, numbers of whom come annually on a pilgrimage to it.

The country in the vicinity of Nejif is an open plain. The soil is clay mixed with sand, which produces a fine vegetation, and such a variety of spontaneous flowers and shrubs, that, in my opinion, it stands next to the Cape of Good Hope for fertility and variety of productions.

In the neighbourhood of this city there arises a very strong vapour from the soil, especially from the dry beds of the rivers, which, at the distance of a hundred paces, has all the appearance of a fine river, and is of that nature which has so often deceived weary and thirsty travellers in the deserts of Arabia and Tartary.

The city of Nejif is surrounded by a rampart, with bastions at the angles, but till very lately had no ditch. At the period that the inhabitants were under great apprehensions of an attack from the Vahabies, the late Nabob Assuf ad Dowleh remitted a large sum

---

1 Imam Mahdi is the twelfth Shia Imam. Both Sunnis and Shia believe that the Mahdi is the ultimate savior of mankind and redeemer of Islam. But Shiites believe that Muhammad al-Mahdi was born in 688 and remains alive but in hiding until his reappearance at the end of days. Sunnis do not believe that he is the Mahdi.

of money, to be distributed amongst the poor and pious persons of this city. On the receipt of the remittance, the Governor assembled the poor inhabitants, and proposed, that, instead of expending it in the usual manner, they should apply the amount to digging a good ditch, to defend them against their enemies. This suggestion was readily complied with, and during my residence at Nejif the work was carrying on.

The mausoleum of Aly (the son-in-law of Mohammed and first of the Imams), with the apartments surrounding the courtyard and the gate, are all of the finest order of architecture.[1] The dome and the turrets, which are covered with golden tiles, were rebuilt by one of the favourites of the Persian usurper, Nadir Shah. The interior of the dome, and the walls of the surrounding houses and gateway, are cased with the painted tiles before described; and in front of the mausoleum, there is an extensive sofa or platform of white marble, for the pilgrims to rest on. The doors of the mausoleum, the tomb, and small cupola over it, are all of solid silver; and although great part of the precious articles belonging to this shrine have been sent to Kazemine for security, yet there are many rich carpets, silver lamps, sconces, and other valuable furniture, remaining.

After worshipping at the tomb of Imam Aly, the devotees are instructed to turn their faces to one of the corners of the building, and repeat a prayer for Imam Hussein,[2] whose head, they say, was brought from Syria by his son Zein al Abadeen, and buried in that spot. After this ceremony, they go to the foot of the tomb, and make two prostrations, one for Adam, and the other for Noah, both of whom, the attendants on the shrine affirm, were buried in this place.

On the outside of the mausoleum, near the door, and under the path-way, are deposited the remains of Shah Abbass, of Persia:[3] and on the other side of the building, adjacent to the

---

1 Najaf is the third most holy city of Shia Islam because it is believed to be the burial site of the first Shia Imam Ali ibn Abi Talib. It was beseiged by the Wahhabis in the late eighteenth century, but the famous Imam Ali Mosque remained a major pilgrimage site. As Abu Talib indicates, Najaf was also the burial site of many important Muslim leaders.

2 See p. 324, note 3.

3 Shah Abbas I (1571-1629), the most important ruler of the Safawid empire, brought military and economic reform to Iran and fostered a great efflorescence of art and culture.

platform on which prayers are said, is a small apartment, in which is the tomb of Mohammed Khan Kejar, late king of Persia,[1] formed of a single block of white marble, on which they constantly burn the wood of aloes, and every night light up camphire tapers in silver candlesticks; and, during both the day and night, several devout persons are perpetually employed in chanting the Koran. All this pomp and state at the tomb of Mohammed Khan is highly improper in the vicinity of the holy shrine, and can only be attributed to the ignorance and rusticity of his descendants.

Upon entering the holy shrine, I was so impressed with religious awe, that, although supported by four of the attendants, I trembled like an aspen leaf, and it was with the utmost difficulty I could perform the prescribed ceremonies. During this time, a Bedouin (Arab of the Desert), with a white beard descending to his middle, which seemed as if it had never been disturbed by a comb, his body covered by a coarse and dirty shirt, and, in place of trowsers, a piece of cloth girt about his loins; his heels, from much walking, as hard as the hoof of a horse, and full of cracks; and who, in short, appeared as if just arrived from a long and toilsome journey, entered the sanctuary. He took no notice of the attendants, but immediately began to walk round the tomb; and instead of repeating the prescribed prayers, he called aloud: "Ya Abul Hussein (O Father of Hussein), peace be to you!" and, notwithstanding his apparent want of respect and decorum, he was so much affected by his faith and sincerity, that the tears trickled from his eyes. Seeing him treat the illustrious sepulchre with so little ceremony, I at first supposed that Abul Hussein was one of his companions or intimate friends, who had fallen asleep in the mausoleum, and that he was endeavouring to awake him; but after observing him attentively, and reflecting on his sincerity and purity of heart, and on my own unworthiness, I was convinced his vows were more deserving of acceptance than mine, and envied him his zeal and happiness.

At a little distance from the great mausoleum, there are two cenotaphs erected to the memory of Zein al Abadeen (son of Hussein), and Suffeh Suffa: but as the army of Mousul, which had lately arrived for the defence of Nejif against the Vahabies, was encamped in their vicinity, the brutish Turks had defiled those sacred places with all kinds of impurity.

The hereditary superintendant of the mausoleum, who was also Governor of Nejif, was named Moola Mahmood. He was a

1 See p. 316, note 3.

respectable, learned, and religious man, and, in consequence of a recommendation from the Pasha of Bagdad, behaved to me with the utmost attention. He allotted me an apartment in the court-yard of the mausoleum, and sent servants to wait on me: he also invited me to live with him during my stay; and as he kept both Persian and Hindoostany servants, his table was better supplied, and served with more elegance, than I ever before experienced among the Turks. Although a Soony, he regularly said his prayers in the mosque of the mausoleum; and as he understood Persian perfectly, I had much pleasure in his conversation.

Ever since quitting Constantinople, I had given up my mind much to religious contemplation; and during the journey I com-posed two elegies in praise of Hussein and Aly. Whilst at Bagdad, I had them beautifully transcribed, on gold paper, and suspended them near the tombs of those illustrious saints, at Kerbela and Nejif. These elegies were much approved by both the superinten-dants; and they promised me to take care they were not removed, but that they should be preserved, as a testimony of my zeal.

After having performed all the prescribed ceremonies at the shrines of Nejif, I set out upon my return to Bagdad; but as parties of the Vahabies were patroling the country, I found it req-uisite to return by the route I came, although there is a more direct road.

Between Nejif and Hilla I offered up my devotions at the Mosque of Cufa and the Dome of the Camel. To persons acquainted with Mohammedan history, Cufa is too well known to require any description of it here.[1] The Dome of the Camel was built to commemorate the event of a hill bending forward to salute the camel which bore the corpse of Aly, and which still remains in that position. The first night I slept at Hilla, the second at Kerbela, and on the third day returned safe to Bagdad.

---

1. After the assassination of Uthman the second caliph in 656, Ali based his forces in the garrison city of Kufa for what would become the first civil war. Of his chief rivals, Talha and al-Zubayr were quickly defeated, but Muawiya, the governor of Syria, was a more formidable opponent. Ali and Muawiya fought at the battle of Siffin in 657 and the resolution of the conflict resulted in the murder of Ali by the Kharijites (see p. 320, note 1). Throughout the Umayyad era Kufa's inhabitants would go on to support caliphal claimants from Ali's descendants and thus it plays a vital role in the history of Shia. Kufa became the capital city of the Abassid Caliphs and was an important centre of both legal and theological scholarship.

Having thus narrated my adventures and toils in pursuit of my spiritual welfare, I shall now return to my temporal concerns. When I was about to take leave of Mohammed Pasha, the Governor of Mousul, whose kindness I shall ever gratefully remember, he put into my hands a letter of recommendation, addressed to Aly Pasha, the Governor of Bagdad; and gave me strict injunctions, that, on my arrival at that city, I should immediately proceed to the house of the Pasha. He added, "You have already in your possession the Emperor's passport, or order, directed to the Pasha; that, in all probability, will insure your receiving from him every mark of public attention; but this letter will procure for you his private friendship, by the aid of which you will be expeditiously and safely conveyed to Bussora, whence, assisted by his interest, you will find no difficulty in obtaining a passage in one of the Arab ships to Bombay."

I promised the Pasha that I would punctually comply with his directions, and left Mousul with that determination; but, during the journey, when I reflected on the uncomfortable mode of living of the Turks, and the filth of the Pashas' houses, and called to mind the hospitable reception I had always experienced from the English, and the superior comforts of their dwellings, I felt more inclined to take up my residence with Mr. Jones, the British Consul,[1] than to trouble the Pasha. When I entered Bagdad, it was late in the day, I was dreadfully tired, and all my clothes completely drenched in rain. I therefore preferred present ease and comfort to the prospect of future advantages, and directed my guide to take me to the house of Mr. Jones.

This conduct of mine gave great offence to Aly Pasha, who, having been apprised of my approach, had prepared a house for my reception, had hired a Hindoostany interpreter to attend me, and was in hourly expectation of my arrival. All the other Mohammedan officers, to several of whom I had recommendations, also took offence at my preferring the society of a Christian to theirs. In consequence of this false step, when I sent the Emperor's order to the Pasha by Mr. Jones, he declined seeing me for some days, under pretence that he was busily employed in

---

1 Sir Harford Jones Brydges (1764-1847) was an assistant and factor for the East India Company at Basra from 1783 to 1794 and its president in Baghdad from 1798 to 1806. Under Robert Dundas's patronage he was appointed envoy-extraordinary and minister-plenipotentiary to the court of Persia, where he remained from 1807 to 1811. Later in life he published historical and political texts on Persia.

fitting out an army to send against the Kurds: and when I visited him, he kept me waiting two hours in a tent, before he granted me an audience; and then received me with much formality, but with little respect. This, I was afterwards informed, was all owing to my connexion with Mr. Jones, with whom he was on bad terms.

Although the Pasha thus declined giving me any proofs of his private friendship, he was under the necessity of complying with the Imperial orders; and, in consequence, supplied me with passports, letters, and conductors to the superintendants of the sacred places, as I have already described.

The only persons who would visit me at the house of Mr. Jones, were, Hajy Hussein, and three other merchants of Ispahan. But as these gentlemen had long resided at Bagdad, they had forgotten their Persian manners, without having acquired the Turkish ones: they were therefore like the crow in the fable, who in vain attempted to learn the gait of the partridge, and forgot his own. They were, consequently, very stupid companions; but, as I was sensible I owed all the neglect I experienced to my own imprudence, I did not vent a complaint or murmur on the subject.

I should have borne this neglect of the Mohammedans with more stoicism, had I not been grievously disappointed in the expectations I had formed of the comforts of Mr. Jones's house. But that gentleman, either owing to his long residence among the Turks, or want of regularity in his domestic economy, did not take any pains to keep his house clean, or in good order. Some days he breakfasted at nine, and other days at twelve: his hour of dinner was equally irregular, and his provisions consequently badly dressed. The conversation at his table was always dull and insipid, and never enlivened by wit or gaiety; and symptoms of disgust and aversion to his guests, whether Asiatics or Europeans, were evident on his countenance. He was also of a jealous disposition, and would not allow me to accept of any assistance from the Turkish officers; saying, that as I had placed myself under his protection, he would not permit any other interference. But, as he was too great a personage to attend to my business himself, he committed me and my affairs to his steward, an Armenian of Ispahan, who was an arrant scoundrel, and in consequence of whose contrivance I suffered the greatest distress, and had nearly lost my life.

The general mode of travelling from Bagdad to Bussora is by water, especially in the rainy season, when the Tigris being full, the current runs with great rapidity. It was therefore my intention to have joined with one or two respectable persons, who might be travelling that way, to hire a comfortable boat, fitted up with apartments, which could have been done at a moderate expence, and to have proceeded at my leisure. But on the day that I returned from Nejif, the Armenian informed me that a fine large boat, loaded with goods belonging to the East-India Company, under charge of a guard commanded by one of Mr. Jones's conductors, would depart for Bussora in a few hours, and that I had better embrace that opportunity of proceeding, free of expence, and well secured against the dangers of the voyage.

As I concluded that the boat was properly fitted up, I consented to go, without taking the precaution of first inspecting it, and desired him to send my luggage on board. When I arrived at the bank of the river, I found a large flat-bottomed, dirty, and old boat, loaded with chests, without any roof, and manned with a savage-looking crew; in short, just such a boat as is used to convey wood from the Sunderbunds (forests) to Calcutta. At the sight of such a conveyance, I drew back, and was about to return to the house; but when I reflected on the whole of Mr. Jones's conduct, and the aukward predicament in which I was placed at Bagdad, I resolved to brave all the hardships I might suffer, and jumped on board. The period of my residence in Bagdad, and excursions to the sacred places, was forty-four days.

I had nearly forgotten to mention, that, soon after my arrival at Bagdad, Hajy Aly, my Mehmandar, demanded from me a certificate of his good conduct: and when I refused to give him one, he got Mr. Jones's Armenian to speak in his favour to his master, who had the weakness to solicit I would forgive the wretch, and grant him the certificate: but, as I thought my doing so would be an injustice to future travellers, I positively refused.

CHAPTER XXXV

The Author quits Bagdad—Arrives at Sook al Shyukh—description of that village. The Author taken ill of a fever—Arrives at Mâkul, or Markile, the English factory at Bussora—obliged to proceed to the city. Character of the inhabitants of Bussora—Description of that city— Character of the Governor. Author invited to the house of Mr. Manesty: His opinion of that gentleman. The Author disappointed of a passage to Bombay, and detained at Bussora. Extraordinary occurrence in that city—Conduct of Mr. Manesty on this occasion. The

Author regrets his long detention at Bussora. He embarks on board the grab Shannon.

I quitted Bagdad on the evening of the 16th Zykad (10th March); and as the boatmen rowed night and day, we arrived on the 20th at Sook al Shyukh (the market of the Shaikh), the distance to which is calculated to be about 150 miles, and half-way to Bussora.

This place is the principal residence of the Arab tribe of Muntefakh, who inhabit the Desert between the two cities. It is a tolerable good market, and yields all the necessaries of life. The Chief of this tribe is named Shaikh Anfiteleh: he is a person of great consequence, and can collect an army of forty or fifty thousand men, principally cavalry. For many years he gave great annoyance to the Government of Bussora; but he is now considered as the defender of that city against the Vahabies. The market is surrounded by a rampart constructed of mud; but its principal defence is its low situation on the banks of the Tigris, by cutting away a small portion of which, they can, at the approach of an enemy, inundate the country for many miles around. Thus, when the Persians, under the command of Kerim Khan, not long ago captured Bussora, they sent an army to take this place. The Arabs allowed them to approach near the town; and during the night, having cut the embankment, the Persians were surrounded by water before they were aware of their danger. The Shaikh then advanced against them, and killed Aly Murdan Khan, their General, and the greater part of his army.

During this voyage down the Tigris, I lived very abstemiously: but as I had nothing to shade me from the heat of the sun during the day, or to shelter me from the rain or dew during the night, I was on the fourth day attacked with a violent fever, which confined me to my bed for nearly a month after my arrival at Bussora.

On the 22d we arrived at the town of Korna; under the walls of which the rivers Tigris and Euphrates unite, and form a very broad stream, nearly twice the size of the Ganges, which is then named Shat al Arab (the Arabian River), and continues its course till it falls into the Persian Gulf.

On the 23d, which was the seventh day of this disagreeable and tedious journey, we arrived at Mâkul, pronounced by Europeans Markile, two fersukhs distant from Bussora. Here the English East-India Company have a small Factory, in which the Consul resides. The house is surrounded by a mud wall, and is therefore called Kote Frengy (The European Fort); *Kote* signifying, in Arabic, a small fort.

The sight of this place afforded me much pleasure; as I had no doubt, from the general character of Mr. Manesty,[1] the Resident, that I should meet with a hospitable reception, and quickly recover from my disease, which by this time had very much reduced both my strength and spirits.

Unluckily for me, a short time previous to my arrival at Bussora, some persons, to answer a particular purpose, the nature of which it might be deemed invidious to relate, had invented a story, that symptoms of the plague had made their appearance at Bagdad; in consequence of which, Mr. Manesty, who is of a timid disposition, and very careful of himself, would not permit any person arriving from Bagdad to enter the Factory; but when informed of my arrival, he came to the river side, and, saluting me at a distance, requested I would proceed to Bussora, where he had provided a house for my reception.

Knowing the falsity of the report, and the authors and motives of the contrivance, I was hurt at his conduct; but, in compliance with his desire, I proceeded to the city, and found apartments prepared for me at the house of Aga Mohammed Abdal Nubby, a merchant of Bussora, and a particular friend of Mr. Manesty's, whom the Persian Monarch had lately summoned to his court, to dignify with the rank of Ambassador to the Governor-General of India, in the room of Hajy Kheleel Khan, who was killed accidentally by the soldiers of his guard at Bombay, and whose body was sent, at the expence of the East-India Company, to be buried with much state and public mourning at the holy shrine of Nejif.[2]

The house was under charge of a tall one-eyed man, whose proper name was Fiez Aly, but to whom the people of Bussora had given the nick-name of Hajy Ferzeen (the Queen of Chess), from his impudence and interfering disposition. This fellow was very neglectful and inattentive to my wishes; which conduct, at a time when I was very unwell, quite depressed my spirits, and made me very anxious to quit Bussora. Often did I regret that I

---

1 Samuel Manesty, wealthy English agent residing at Basra; was active c. 1780-1802. He is listed as Resident at Bushire in 1804 with 'self-appointed' in parenthesis after his name. See "Samuel Manesty and his Unauthorized Embassy to the Court of Fath Alī Shīh." *Iran: Journal of the British Institute of Persian Studies* (1986): 24, 153-60.

2 See Asiatic Annual Register, A.D. 1803. Bombay Occurrences for November. (Translator's note)

had not remained in England; and the only consolation I had during my confinement, was calling to mind the many happy days I had passed there, and thinking of the many friends I had quitted, perhaps for ever.

Bussora is inhabited by a number of Persians of good family, who have been obliged to fly their country, in consequence of the various revolutions which have long desolated that kingdom. Many of them visited me, and invited me to their houses. I found them, in general, agreeable men, and much superior to the natives of Bussora, the majority of whom are low minded, and of avaricious dispositions, though so very punctual in all their commercial dealings that they never require bonds from each other. They are all perfectly convinced of the reality of the Philosopher's Stone; and frequently questioned me, whether I had not learned the art of making the Elixir during my residence in Europe.

Bussora is a much larger city than Bagdad, and is the resort of merchants from all parts of the East. It is well fortified by good rampart, and a deep ditch, which is filled from the river. Within the fort there are several groves of date-trees, extensive gardens, and some vineyards; which are well watered by a canal cut from the river that runs through the town. The buildings are, in general, formed of mud, and very irregular in their construction; they are, in fact, little better than huts. As the climate is very hot, and the town surrounded by marshes, it must be a very unhealthy place. During the four months of the rainy season, the river often overflows its banks, and inundates the country; and the Arabs frequently cut deep trenches in the bank, to let the water run into the Desert: the consequence is, that when the river falls, many pools of stagnant water remain, the exhalations from which are very pestiferous; and if the disease generated by these causes is not the plague, it is something nearly as bad. The Arabs call this season of the year *Maa al Mouj* (The overflowing of the waters), which the English translate 'The waters of death.'

The inhabitants of Bussora were formerly so much annoyed by the Wandering Arabs, that they entered into an engagement with the tribe of Munafekh, to pay them half the produce of their fields, to defend them against the other tribes; but, notwithstanding this agreement, the wild Arabs frequently approach the city during the night, and plunder every thing they can find.

In order to protect the farms and country-houses, the Governor, Abdullah Aga, has lately built a wall towards the Desert, sixteen fersukhs in length, which encompasses a number of the estates and farms, and has placed guards at all the gates. This worthy man has used all his exertions to render the people under his charge happy and contented; and has so well succeeded, that all the inhabitants of Bussora are lavish in his praise.

At the distance of eight miles from Bussora are the tombs of Taleha and Zobeir (two of the companions of Mohammed); but as parties of the Vahabies and Wandering Arabs were patroling in the vicinity of the town, I durst not visit them.

At the termination of twelve days, the Consul being convinced that I was not infected with the plague, did me the honour to invite me to his house. For this mark of his attention I was indebted to a letter of recommendation from Lord Pelham, and to the orders of the Court of Directors, desiring Mr. Manesty to give me every assistance in his power. As I was very much hurt at his conduct, the only request I made of him was, to procure me a passage in the first ship that should sail for Bombay; and even in this he disappointed me.

This gentleman, being the representative of the East-India Company at Bussora, is considered by the inhabitants of that city as a person of great consequence; they therefore never address him but in an adulatory and flattering manner: he is, on this account, puffed up with pride and vanity, and could not bear my plain and blunt *English* style, which he considered as bordering on insolence: he was therefore resolved to humiliate me, and to make me sensible of his importance.

One part of the Consul's employment is, to forward the overland packets and despatches from and to India, for which purpose he is allowed to charge a considerable sum of money. For some years he either contracted with the mercantile Arabs of the tribe of Outub, to convey the despatches in their vessels, called *grabs*, to Bombay, or sent them by any English ship that chanced to be at Bussora when the packet arrived: but being a man of a speculative turn of mind, he discovered that it would be more advantageous to have small vessels of his own, which he might freight with the merchants' goods, and at the same time convey the despatches without any additional expence. He therefore built or purchased six or eight of these vessels, which now nearly monopolize all the traffic of Bussora. The masters and crews of them are all his private servants, and of course must be obedient to his orders.

Some days after I had been at Mr. Manesty's house, he informed me that a ship was about to sail for Bombay; but that I must myself settle with the master for my passage, as it was a perquisite of office with which he did not interfere. I immediately went to the master, who demanded five hundred rupees (£.62. 10s.) for my conveyance. I thought this an exorbitant sum; and being much more than was paid by the inhabitants of Bussora, I concluded he was imposing on me. I therefore refused to give it, and returned to the Consul, who, having heard my story, said he could not interfere.

The following day I went again to the master, and offered him three hundred rupees (£.37.10s.), which he agreed to take but said I must embark immediately, as the wind was fair, and he was just going to weigh anchor. I told him my heavy baggage was at Bussora, but that, if he would wait an hour or two, I would bring it on board: he refused, alleging, that in two hours the wind might change, and perhaps detain him for ten days longer in the river. I thereby lost this opportunity.

A few days afterwards Mr. Manesty despatched another vessel, without giving me any intelligence of her departure; and when I reproached him with this procedure, he replied, "You wish to see the beauties and curiosities of Bombay, and that ship is gone to Bengal." A third ship was sent off, and still there was some idle excuse for not granting me a passage. I was therefore much irritated, and told him he had resided so long in the East, that he had entirely forgotten all his English principles: I also wrote a satirical poem on him, and occasionally repeated some of the lines in his hearing. He replied, that I had been spoiled by the luxuries and attention of the people in London, and that it was now impossible to please me. These altercations and bickerings were however carried on in apparent good humour, or half joke, half earnest. In every other respect I passed my time pleasantly at his house, as he was very hospitable, and our society was enlivened by the presence of Capt. Spens and Doctor Mills.

During my residence at Bussora, an event occurred which caused much confusion at the time, and it was apprehended might be attended with serious consequences. A Captain White, master of one of the Consul's ships, who rented a house in the city, kept an Armenian woman. One day a poor Arab was passing his door, and found a letter, written in Arabic, lying on the ground, the contents of which were as follow:

"People of Bussora, I demand your protection. I am a Mussulman, born in Egypt, and, during the invasion of that country by the French, fell into the hands of this Christian, whom I abominate: therefore, I pray you, deliver me from him."

The Arab immediately carried this letter to the tribunal of justice, and swore that the letter was thrown to him from the top of Captain White's house. Other witnesses also appeared, and declared that they had frequently been in Captain White's house, and heard the woman declare all these circumstances. On this evidence, the Cazy was under the necessity of sending an officer to summon the woman to his tribunal. The circumstance was so novel, that a great crowd assembled, and a number of the mob accompanied the officer. The Captain refused to deliver up the woman, and, having barred his doors, sent intelligence of his situation to the Consul. As that gentleman, in consequence of his wealth and public station, possesses great influence with all the Turkish officers, he sent a messenger to the Governor, requesting he would postpone the trial till next day, when he himself would attend the tribunal; and if the woman was a Mussulman, or wished to become one, he would order her to be delivered up. The Governor immediately complied with this request, and sent some soldiers to disperse the mob.

It happened, that the master of another ship, which was taking in freight for Bombay, lived in the same house with Captain White, and, being alarmed at what was transacting, began to send some treasure and other valuable articles on board the ship: in consequence of which a report was quickly circulated, that the oppressed Mussulman female had been sent on board the ship, and would be shortly out of the reach of justice.

The mob re-assembled, and, having forced their way into Captain White's house, took hold of the woman, and led her to the tribunal. When questioned by the Cazy, the woman declared that the whole story was a gross falsehood; that she and all her family were Christians; and that she had not the smallest inclination to change her faith, or to leave her master. On hearing this declaration, a number of witnesses stepped forward, and swore that she was guilty of falsehood, for that they had heard her repeat the Mohammedan Creed. The Cazy was much astonished at this business; and said to the woman, "By the evidence of these Mussulmans, you are proved to have once belonged to our faith; and, by denying it, you acknowledge that you are now a renegado. By so doing, you are liable to the punishment of death: and if, in three days, you do not abjure your heresy, I must pass the sentence of the law on you." He then ordered her to be carried to the Moofty's house, and confined in the Haram (female apartments).

The second night the woman found an opportunity to escape, and proceeded towards the English Factory. She was however re-taken, and brought back. Next morning, being again brought before the Cazy, he gave her the option, to abjure Christianity and marry a Mohammedan, or suffer death. The poor woman, not being prepared to die, consented to become a Mussulman. A subscription of a thousand kurush was immediately collected for her dower, and she was next day married to one of the soldiers, who carried her home in triumph.

This circumstance hurt the feelings and pride of the Consul, who sent a message to the Governor, that, as the woman was beyond all doubt a Christian, and under his protection, if she was not immediately returned to him, all friendship must cease between them, and he might have cause to repent his conduct. He at the same time ordered the gates of the Factory to be shut, and no person from Bussora to be allowed to enter them.

The Governor expressed his regret on the occasion, and laid the blame on the mob, whose actions he could not controul: but as the woman was now married to a Mohammedan, and had embraced the Mussulman religion, he could not possibly reverse the sentence of the law.

As Mr. Manesty's pride and overbearing conduct had given offence to many of the principal inhabitants of Bussora, of which they related numerous instances to me, it was generally supposed that the whole of this business was a scheme, laid by some of his enemies, to mortify him. If such was really the case, they had, in the sequel, reason to repent their conduct.

The business was not settled when I left Bussora; but I have since learned, that Mr. Manesty, having first appealed to the Pasha of Bagdad, and afterwards to Constantinople, had not only procured the sentence of the Cazy to be reversed, but had him turned out of office. The Governor was also severely censured, and several of the leaders of the riot banished. I have since seen the woman in Calcutta, who corroborated all I had heard. This circumstance shews, that the English possess nearly as much power in Bussora as they have in India, and ought to render people cautious how they interfere or quarrel with them.

Had I been aware, when I first entered Bussora, that I should have been delayed there so long, I would have proceeded by land to Suster, and thence to Shiraz, whence I could have travelled to one of the Persian ports, and there embarked for Bombay; by which means I might, without a greater loss of time, have travelled through a country I was very anxious to see, and escaped from the pride and tyranny of Mr. Manesty.

At length, after remaining fifty-five days at Bussora, I procured a passage in one of the Consul's grabs, named the Shannon, and embarked, on the evening of the 19th Mohurrem 1218, (May l0th, 1803).

CHAPTER XXXVI

The Author sails from Bussora—Account of his voyage, and description of the Persian Gulf—Enters the Sea of Oman, and the Indian Ocean—Arrives at Bombay—Hospitably received by the Governor. Description of Bombay. Account of the Parsees, and other native inhabitants. Description of the Fort. Account of the Mohammedan inhabitants. Marked attention of the Governor to the Author, who procures him a passage on board the Bombay frigate. The Author embarks for Bengal. The ship arrives in Balasore roads—anchors in the Ganges. Author proceeds to Calcutta.

Immediately on my going on board, we weighed anchor; and, as the wind was strong and favourable, by twelve o'clock the next day we arrived at the mouth of the river, which is distant from Bussora ninety miles, and entered the Persian Gulf.

This gulf is an arm of the Sea of Oman, which is itself a branch of the Indian Ocean. The course of the Persian Gulf is N.W. and S.E. It is nearly 500 miles in length, and in some places 150 in breadth, but at the entrance is only thirty-six wide. The distance from Bussora to Bombay is computed at 1500 miles.

On the 20th we were opposite the island of Kharek. This island is about nine miles long, and three miles broad. The Dutch formerly got possession of it, and built thereon a strong fort; but it was taken from them by the Arab Shaikh of Bundarick.

On the 21st we passed Abu Sheher, one of the most celebrated ports of Persia. It soon after fell calm, and we remained for several days in its vicinity. I very much regretted that the wind had not ceased sooner, that I might have had an opportunity of going on shore, and of seeing one of the Persian cities.

On the 25th we passed the island of Abu Shayib, said to be

150 miles long; and on the evening of the same day we anchored at the island of Kies, to take in a supply of fresh water.

The 27th brought us opposite the Isle of Hormuz (Ormus), which is only six miles long, and three in breadth.

On the 28th we passed Kisshimy, the largest island in the Persian Gulf, being sixty miles long, and twenty broad; and on the 30th we entered the Sea of Oman. At the entrance to this sea, the shores of Persia and Arabia are both to be seen.

In the Persian Gulf are a number of uninhabited islands. One of these is called by the English the Tomb of Zoom, from a tradition that one of the Generals of Alexander the Great was buried there. Another is a barren rock, called Mamma Selma, round which there runs so strong an eddy, that if a ship comes within its vortex it is infallibly dashed to pieces.

One of the greatest curiosities found in this sea is a fish which the English call *Star-fish*. It is circular, and at night very luminous, resembling the full moon surrounded by rays. When touched, it is as soft as jelly, and appeared to me to be of a species between the vegetable and animal creation. If any part of it touches the human body, it causes a blister, which often turns into a very troublesome sore. Frequently, during the voyage, I sat upon the deck at night, for several hours, to admire these extraordinary phænomena.

Soon after we entered the Sea of Oman, a contrary wind arose, which amounted nearly to a gale; but as it was not accompanied by rain, it did not much distress us.

It is worthy of remark, that, during the course of my travels, I sailed through the Indian, Southern, and Atlantic Oceans, and over the Mediterranean, Italian, Ionian (Grecian), Marmorean, Persian, and Oman Seas; in all of which I experienced storms, but, by the blessing of God, did not sustain any injury.

On the 5th of Suffer we passed by Muscat, but not sufficiently near to see the land; and the following day we again entered the Indian Sea, which completed the circle of my navigation; as the Bay of Bengal, whence I set out, is considered a part of this ocean. At this place we had a view of the Eastern promontory of Arabia, which is called Rasalgat, and is 120 miles distant from Muscat.

On the 10th of the month Suffer, corresponding with the 3d of June, at one hour after sun-rise, we cast anchor in the harbour of Bombay, being within four days of a year from the time of my leaving London.

In justice to the captain of the grab, I must say, that, notwithstanding the vessel was very small, we had every comfort on board, and that I passed my time very pleasantly.

Soon after the ship had anchored, I went on shore, and proceeded immediately to the Government House, having had the honour of being well known to Mr. Duncan[1] in Bengal. As it was so early an hour, the Governor was not risen; but his servants were extremely attentive, shewed me into a room, and asked if I wished for a hookah, or any other refreshment.

At eight o'clock I was informed that the Governor was dressed, and waited breakfast for me. I immediately paid my respects to his Excellency, and was received in the most gracious and friendly manner. He congratulated me on my safe return to India, and requested I would favour him with my company during the time I resided at Bombay. As his own house was full of guests, he directed his steward to go and hire one for me in the neighbourhood; and before breakfast was finished, I was informed the house was ready for my reception: he then ordered his servants to supply me with every thing I wanted; and concluded with saying, he should expect to see me every day at breakfast and dinner, when I was not otherwise engaged. The contrast between this reception, and that I had experienced at Bussora, was so great, that my feelings quite overcame me.

During the course of the day, my friend, Abd al Lutief Khan, (whom may God preserve!) having heard of my arrival, called on me, and insisted upon my immediately accompanying him to his house, a little way in the country. As my chief object in coming to Bombay was to visit this illustrious friend, I could not refuse him, but was afraid of giving offence to the Governor. I however again waited on his Excellency, and explained to him my situation; when he most graciously said, "By all means, go and enjoy the society of your friends; but whenever business or pleasure calls you into town, come and occupy your house, and eat with me." I returned his Excellency many thanks for his kindness, and accompanied my friend; but, as I had many engagements in the town, and some business to transact, I found the Governor's house of great service. From Mr. Lechmere, Member of Council, and Colonel Gordon, Commander of the troops, and many others of the Bombay gentlemen, I also experienced much attention and kindness.

---

1 Jonathan Duncan (1756-1811) was then the governor of Bombay and worked to combat infanticide at Benares.

The Island of Bombay is situated between the eighteenth and nineteenth degrees of northern latitude, and is remarkable for the purity of its air, and the excellence of its water. Its neighbourhood produces all the fruits and grains of the other parts of India; but there are some groves of mango-trees on the island which bear fruit of a very superior quality.

The city in which all the English reside is situated within the fort, the houses of which are three or four stories high, and built of brick and mortar, with painted doors and windows; but they have all sloped roofs, covered with tiles, in the European fashion; and there is not a house in the town to be compared with the worst of those at Chouringhy (part of Calcutta). The inhabitants are chiefly English, Parsees, Indian Portuguese, and Hindoos.

The Parsees are descended from the ancient Guebres, or worshippers of fire. About eleven hundred years ago, many of them fled from Persia, on account of the excessive zeal and oppressions of the Mussulmans, and settled at Surat, Bombay, and other places on this coast. They are now so much increased in numbers, that most of the artificers and servants at Bombay are of that sect. Several of these are respectable merchants; and a few are possessed of very great wealth. They all understand, besides their own language, English and Hindoostany; but few of them can converse in the Persian of the present day.

As they never intermarry or cohabit with any other tribe or people, they are all very similar in features and colour, and are supposed not to have altered, in the smallest degree, since their ancestors first emigrated.

Many of the English philosophers contend, that distance from, or proximity to the sun, does not at all affect the human colour; and quote, in support of this argument, the two instances, of the Parsees at Bombay, and the Armenians at Julfa (suburbs of Ispahan), who, in the course of many centuries, have not in any degree changed their colour: but if this axiom is true, I cannot comprehend why Europeans should be fair, Ethiopians black, and Indians of swarthy complexions.

The Parsees affirm, that they possess altars, and some of their sacred fire, both of which were brought from Persia eight hundred years ago. They worship two Deities; one, the principle of all good, whom they call *Yezdan*; the other, the principle of evil, named *Aherman*: but as the human mind is always governed more by fear than by gratitude, the Parsees are much more assiduous in their devotions to the latter, than to the former Deity.

They are exceedingly jealous of the reputation of their women; and if they even suspect a female of impropriety, they secretly make away with her. They are not however possessed of a spark of liberality or gentility: none of them ever came to visit me during my residence at Bombay, much less to invite me to their houses. This possibly may have proceeded from an idea, that my rank was so superior to theirs, I would have refused their invitations.

The only Parsee I was ever acquainted with who possessed a liberal education, was Moola Firoz,[1] whom I met at the house of a friend. He was a sensible and well-informed man, who had travelled into Persia, and had there studied mathematics, astronomy, and the sciences of Zoroaster. He spoke Persian very fluently; but I did not think much of his poetry in that language.

Two miles to the north of the fort there is another town, entirely inhabited by the natives of India, in which is an excellent bazar, from which the market of the fort is supplied. In the vicinity are a number of gardens and orchards, belonging to various persons of opulence in the island; also several groves of cocoa-trees, which are planted so very thick, that there is scarcely any circulation of air between them.

The lower classes of people at Bombay are the worst-looking of any I have seen in India: they are of a small stature, very black, and nothing but skin and bone. Some of the Parsee women are, indeed, large, fat, and fair; but they have very coarse features, and bold disgusting manners. I had often heard that the inhabitants of Surat, which is only a few days' journey north of Bombay, were remarkably handsome, but I cannot believe it: the idea has, I suppose, originated from the fair complexions of the Parsees; but, in my opinion, the women of Bengal have much more life and vivacity about them, and are in every respect preferable.

Between the town and the fort there is an extensive plain, which is always covered with a fine verdure, and is kept for exercising the troops, and for the inhabitants to enjoy the fresh air. From the western side of this plain is an extensive prospect of the sea; and on the eastern side there is a very delightful view of the woods and mountains of the Concan.

The fort of Bombay is stronger and larger than that of Calcutta: it is defended on one side by the sea, and encompassed on the three others by a deep and wide ditch, which is filled from the

---

1 This is likely the Zoroastrian scholar Mulla Firuz (d. 1833), whose library is held at the K.R. Cama Oriental Institute in Mumbai.

sea. The ramparts and bastions are all constructed like those of Calcutta; but all round the interior of the rampart there is a brick wall, to prevent the earth from being washed away by the rains. There are several gates, the entrances to which are defended by draw-bridges and portcullisses. This fort was originally constructed by the European Portuguese, when they possessed very extensive power in India; and was given to one of the Kings of England,[1] as the marriage portion of a Princess of Portugal: since that period it has been in the possession of the English, who have much strengthened and improved it.

The most respectable and worthy of the Mohammedans who resided at Bombay during my visit to that place, were, first, Abd al Lutief Khan, a gentleman descended from a very ancient Persian family, and distinguished, amongst the learned, as the author of the *Tohfit al Aalum* (The Rarity of the World). From him I received the most solid proofs of friendship and kindness, and was his guest during a great part of the time.

Secondly, Aga Hussein, the nephew of Hajy Kheleel, the unfortunate Persian Ambassador, who was killed (on the 20th of July 1802) during the affray between the Persians of his suite, and the Sepoys of his guard of honour. He was a sensible and genteel young man, and had not quite recovered from the effects of five or six wounds which he received in the contest; but was waiting at Bombay, in expectation of being appointed Ambassador, in the room of his deceased uncle, and, in consequence, received a liberal pecuniary allowance from the Company. He lived in a handsome style, and frequently invited me to his parties. He asked me a number of questions respecting Europe, and was particularly anxious to learn the history of the Freemasons. A short time before I quitted Bombay, he received intelligence, that Aga Abd al Nubby, the Bussora merchant, was appointed to fill the station of his uncle; which very much mortified him, and he was obliged to return to Persia.

Thirdly, Mirza Mehdy Khan: he was by birth a Persian, and came to seek his fortune in India. He first visited the Court of the Nizam, at Hyderabad: he then came to Lucknow, where, by the interest of Mr. R. Johnson, he obtained an appointment; but being of an expensive turn of mind, he got into difficulties, out of some of which I extricated him. He afterwards went to Benaras, where he was noticed by Mr. Duncan; and when that gentleman

---

1   King Charles II (1630-85) received this fort as part of the marriage
     dowry of Princess Catherine of Braganza.

was appointed Governor of Bombay, he followed him to that place. As Mr. Duncan had a very high opinion of his abilities, he sent him, as the East-India Company's Agent, to Abu Sheher in Persia. But this appointment not meeting with the concurrence of the Governor-General, he was recalled, and rewarded with a pension of eight hundred rupees per month. He was, however, very much dissatisfied; and so far from evincing any gratitude or friendship for me, he was envious of the civilities I received from the Governor. There were, besides these, several respectable and opulent Mohammedan merchants, but none of them persons of consequence.

During the forty-five days I remained at Bombay, I dined once or twice each week with Mr. Duncan, and every Monday evening attended his balls at the Government House, where I had an opportunity of seeing all the ladies and principal inhabitants of the settlement.

I frequently expressed to Mr. Duncan my wish to proceed to Bengal, and requested he would procure me a passage: but he would not agree to my leaving him so soon, and kindly said, he was convinced I was not sufficiently recovered from the fatigues of my journey, to commence another voyage; but that I might be assured he would procure me a passage in a good ship.

At length the Bombay frigate, a very fine vessel belonging to the Company, having been ordered round to Calcutta, he informed me, that if I was tired of Bombay, he would direct the Captain to take me on board, and to pay every attention to my accommodation and comfort. I replied, I could never tire of any place where his Excellency resided, but that I was very anxious to see my family, from whom I had been separated for several years: I would therefore embrace his kind offer. He immediately sent for Captain Hayes, the commander of the frigate, and, having introduced me to him, commended me to his care and protection. By this means I was conveyed to Calcutta free of expence; whereas, if I had taken my passage in a merchant ship, I should have been obliged to pay 2000 rupees (£250). In short, the kindness of Mr. Duncan was such, that I am at a loss for words to express my obligations to him.

On the 26th of Rubby al Avul (16th of July) I embarked on board the Bombay frigate; and, as the wind was favourable, we were soon under weigh, and, after a very quick passage of eleven days, arrived, without any particular occurrence, in Balasore Roads, at the mouth of the Ganges. During this voyage, Captain Hayes and his wife (who was on board) behaved to me with the greatest politeness and attention; and, as the ship was very roomy and in fine order, I had every comfort that is procurable at sea.

We were detained some days, waiting for a pilot: at length one came on board, and in two days carried the ship up the river to Fulta, where I got on board a small boat; and on the evening of the 15th Rubby Assany 1218, corresponding with the 4th of August 1803, after an absence of four years and six months, I landed safely in Calcutta, and returned thanks to God for my preservation and safe return to my native shores.

End of the Travels.

Appendix I

Ode to London

See Vol. I. p. 130
Turned into Verse by a Young Gentleman.[1]

No more in gardens, rivers, fields,
The wearied eye can find delight;
Henceforth each joy that London yields
Be ours—where Beauty charms the sight.

We thirst no more for golden fruits
That deck the trees of Paradise,
Content to rest from life's pursuits
Where these dark groves of cypress rise.

Let Mecca's Shaikh offended frown,
And curse us for apostate slaves;
Still may eternal blessings crown
These temples, while the bigot raves.

Fill up the goblet! welcome wine,
Which bids the convert ne'er return;
His faith he gladly will resign,
His breast with raptures high will burn.

What though life's prime and blooming spring
Confest an Indian Cupid's wiles,
Maturer years more blessings bring;
In British beauties, sweeter smiles.

Fair creatures, hail! with flowing tress
Of jet, of auburn, or of gold:
Ye sure were form'd my soul to bless
I gaze—and die as I behold.

---

1 This may be George Swinton who also translated "Poem in Praise of
Miss Julia Burrell." See Appendix A1.

Your ruby lips might animate
The marble block, or torpid clay:
Could I reverse the laws of fate,
Yours should be each devoted day.

Oh TALEBA! these wounds, so deep,
Are not of chance the offspring weak;
Love bids thy heart th' impression keep,
As Nature tints the tulip's streak.

Appendix II

Translation of an Elegy on Tufuzzul Hussein Khan,[1] Envoy from the Nabob of Oude to the Governor-General of India.

Written by Mirza Abu Taleb Khan (2d May 1802) in the Persian Language, and presented by him to Lady Elford. Turned into Blank Verse by the Rev. R.H.[2]

O Universe! in primeval order
Still holds thy form compact, extinct the life
That seem'd the centre of thy orb, and pois'd
In balance intellectual thy laws.
Alas! no more shall the enraptur'd ear
Stay on that tongue, delighted; whose sweet sound
Of eloquent philosophy, sweeter
Than note of nightingale tho' sweet, would charm
Coy Nature to disclose her hidden reign,
As we together through the garden fair
Of knowledge studious walk'd, in search of truth,
That amaranthine flower so rarely cull'd.
That sound so sweet, alas! no more is heard:
Through all the groves of science, silent now,
Devious I wander, and alone, nor cheer'd
With Nature's secret lore, celestial song.
Alas! he's fled; who the heaven's expanse,
With truer ken than the Pelusian Sage
Survey'd; or than that other, Grecian born,
Tho' Egypt's boast. Unopen'd, unexplain'd,
Again obscure, the Almagestum[3] lies.
Alas! the zest of Learning's cup is gone;
Whose taste ne'er cloy'd, tho' deep the draughts;
Whose flavour yet upon the palate hangs
Nectareous, nor Reason's thirst assuag'd.

---

1 For a further account of *Tufuzzul Hussein Khan*, see Character, No. I. in the *Asiatic Annual Register* of 1803. (Translator's note)
2 This may be Bishop Reginald Heber (1763-1826), the Anglican hymnographer who would eventually become Bishop of Calcutta and who reviewed the *Travels* for *The Quarterly Review* (Appendix B1).
3 The title of the Arabic version of the works of Ptolemy. (Translator's note)

But yes!—rent is the garment of the morn;
And all dishevell'd floats the hair of night;
All bath'd in tears of dew the stars look down
With mournful eyes, in lamentation deep:
For he, their sage belov'd, is dead; who first
To Islam's followers explain'd their laws,
Their distances, their orbits, and their times,
As great Copernicus once half divin'd,
And greater Newton proved: but, useless now,
Their works we turn with idle hand, and scan
With vacant eye, our own first master gone.

    Alas! that tongue, defence of Jaffier's faith,
Potent as the sword of God to cut short
All opposition vain, forsakes the world.
And thou, O earth! dost moisture still supply
To feed the lily's freshness; when that tongue,
Parch'd as the lips of thirsty traveller
When southern blasts low o'er the desert sweep,
Now stiff, no more shall eloquence distil.

    But still some joy, CANOPUS![1] still is thine:
If fainter, yet it's joy: if set the sun,
Whose excellence through heaven shot far its beams;
Fitting thy pensive walk, at solemn hour,
Reflecting soft, fraternal light,
The morn shall guide thy melancholy way.

    But ah! faded now is that lively face,
Where wisdom bloom'd superior, and outshone
All faces in intelligence divine,
Where friends congenial learned converse join'd;
As all flowers besides, the rose excels,
Tho' bright they spread their colours to the sun.
Ah! faded is the rose-bud's elegance,
Unrivall'd in its bloom: ah! clos'd the eye,
That aw'd presumption mute: but mild the ray
It shed on humble merit, as it watch'd
The fire of genius playing in its beam.
O heart! melancholy alone fills up
Thy dreary waste of life. Ah! throb no more.

---

1   Brother of the deceased. (Translator's note)

Exulting at blithe pleasure's call, to thee
Jocund no more, since he, belov'd, for whom
Thy warmest pulse was wont so oft to beat
In concord of sweet friendship, from thee torn,
Is fled,—and with him flies from thee all joy.
Behold that corse, how fall'n! that body, rob'd
But yesterday in silks of richest dye,
And furs the hunter's rarest prize, now wrapp'd
In coarse sepulchral weeds, all beauty gone,
In kindred dust deep cover'd, mouldering lies:
Prostrate the date tree now, whose stately crown,
At once the garden's glory, and defence
From high noon's sultry ray, low fallen, lies
Cumbering the ground.—In pensive mood,
At foot of cypress or of yew outstretch'd,
We weeping lie, and court funereal shade.

    Tho' long the way, and arduous, old age
Forgot its stiffness; with new vigour brac'd,
Agile it moved its limbs, and urged their speed,
On anxious thoughts intent, to view his form,
And hear new wisdom falling from his tongue.
But now, how sad the change! our youth weigh'd down
With grief's oppressive load, or helpless sit,
Or feeble grown, as feeble worm that creeps,
Their limbs drag slowly on their care-worn frame.
Behold that head, for whose far-stretching thought
The universe appear'd too small a bound,
In close and narrow grave finds room enough!
If thou, O rose! when drooping Nature mourns,
Thoughtless, in pride of beauty laugh'st, pluck'd off
By some rude hand, thy blushing honours torn,
The sport of winds unheeded may they fly!
Ah! see'st thou not, that e'en the vaulted sphere,
Hard hearted as she is, unwont to melt
At other's woe, at this distressful hour,
In sign of grief, her deepest azure spreads?

    O TALEB! learn from this a dear-bought truth;—
Nor dignity, nor form, nor talents rare,
Nor rarer knowledge, o'er the fated hour
Man's short abode on earth prolong, nor keep their
Frail possessor from the destin'd tomb.

Appendix III

See Vol. I. p. 138.

COLONEL SYMES[1] returned to India in the year 1801, and early in the following year was again sent, by Marquis Wellesley, as Ambassador to the Court of Ava, between which and the British (Indian) Government a very serious misunderstanding had taken place: which circumstance, added to the intrigues of the French at that Court, rendered this negociation still more difficult than his former mission.

Such was the nature of this dispute, that his Birman Majesty was pleased to say, in public Court, that no other man but Colonel Michael Symes could have reconciled him to the English.

The abilities and zeal manifested on this occasion induced Marquis Wellesley, some time after the return of the Embassy from Ava, to appoint Colonel Symes to a very high and important situation at the Court of Dehly; but severe illness obliged him to relinquish these flattering prospects, and to embark, in the end of 1803, for Europe.

When the unfortunate expedition under Sir John Moore was planned, Colonel Symes, who was then one of the assistants in the Quarter-master General's department, and in a bad state of health, relinquished his situation to take the command of the 76th regiment. He soon after embarked for Spain, under the command of General Baird,[2] by whom Colonel Symes was employed to inspect the state of the Spanish armies. His reports on this subject have appeared in the account of that expedition. In the performance of this duty, Colonel Symes rode eighty miles post, over bad roads, in one day; which event, being followed by the harassing retreat to Corunna, so completely exhausted his constitution, that he died two days after the troops had re-embarked.

It was during the interval between Colonel Symes's return from Ava, and his being appointed to Dehly, that Mirza Abu Taleb arrived in Calcutta. The latter lost no time in visiting his friend, and was for several months a frequent guest at his table;

---

1 Michael Symes (1761-1809) was sent to the court of King Bodawpaya of Burma in 1795 to improve diplomatic relations and prevent French incursions in Burma. His *An Account of an Embassy to the Kingdom of Ava Sent by the Governor-General of India in 1795* (1800) is one of the earliest and most extensive accounts of Burma in English.

2 Sir David Baird (1757-1829), first baronet.

where the Translator of this Work had often the pleasure of meeting him, and of hearing him relate a number of anecdotes respecting his travels.

When the Colonel was appointed to Dehly, Abu Taleb requested to accompany him, and to be appointed his assistant: but this scheme having been frustrated by the Colonel's illness, he proceeded up the country, to his friend Mr. Augustus Brooke, at Benares, through whose interest and recommendation he was appointed Aâmil of one of the districts of Bundlecund; and died in that situation, in the year 1806.

As he left but little property, the East-India Company have generously settled a pension upon his wife and family.

P.S. His son, Mirza Hussein Aly, is now employed in the College of Fort William; and, in the year 1812, edited the Printed Copy in the Persian language, of these Travels.

Appendix IV

See Vol. II. p. 174.

The following Tract, on the Liberties of the Asiatic Women, was written by Mirza Abu Taleb Khan, during his residence in England, and was translated by his friend and shipmate, Captain David Richardson, who, it is to be feared, has perished in one of the missing ships from India. It was published by the intelligent author and compiler, Mr. Dundas Campbell, in the Asiatic Annual Register of the year 1801.

Vindication of the Liberties of the Asiatic Women.
By Mirza Abu Taleb Khan.

One day, in a certain company, the conversation turned upon LIBERTY, in respect of which the ENGLISH consider their own customs the most perfect in the world. An English lady, addressing herself to me, observed, that the women of Asia have no liberty at all, but live like slaves, without honour and authority, in the houses of their husbands; and she censured the men for their unkindness, and the women, also, for submitting to be so undervalued. However much I attempted, by various ways, to undeceive her, (and in truth, said I, the case is exactly the reverse, it is the European women who do not possess so much power,) yet it did not bring conviction to her mind. She however began to waver in her own opinion; and falling into doubt, requested of me to write something on the subject, the purport of which she might comprehend at one view, and be enabled to distinguish the truth from falsehood. Since the same wrong opinion is deeply rooted in the minds of all other Europeans, and has been frequently before this held forth, I considered it necessary to write a few lines concerning the privileges of the female sex, as established, both by law and custom, in Asia and in Europe; omitting whatever was common to both, and noticing what is principally peculiar to each, in the manner of comparison, that the distinction may be the more easily made, and the real state of the case become evident to those capable of discernment.

It must be first laid down as a general maxim, that, in social order, respect to the rules of equity and politeness, and forbearance from injury, is a necessary condition; for, otherwise, the liberty of one would be destructive of the liberty of another: thus, if a person be at liberty to do with his own house what may endanger the safety of his neighbour's, this must be in direct opposition to the liberty of that neighbour; or if, in order to free himself from the inconveniences of the hot weather, he should visit his friends in his dressing-gown or night-shirt, although it would be ease and liberty to him, yet it would be sowing the seeds of ill-breeding: therefore the observance of these rules is essential.

Those things which make the liberty of the Asiatic women appear less than that of the Europeans, are, in my opinion, SIX.

The *first* is, "The little intercourse with men, and concealment from view," agreeably to law and their own habits: and this is the chief of these six; for it has been the cause of those false notions entertained by the European women, that the inclination of the Asiatic women leads them to walk out in the streets and market-places, but that their husbands keep them shut up, and set guards over the door. It may be here observed, that the advantages of this *little intercourse*, which prevents all the evils arising from the admittance of strangers, and affords so much time for work and useful employments, are so very manifest, that they need not be enlarged upon; and besides, the practice in London, of keeping the doors of the houses shut, and the contemptible condition of the Dutch at the Cape, are sufficient proofs. Notwithstanding this, the custom of the intercourse of the sexes is allowed in England; and it is owing both to the force of virtue and good manners generally to be found in the English, and to the apprehension of other greater inconveniences, the chief of which are four, as here mentioned, and whose effects are not felt in Asia. *One of these* is, the high price of things, and the small number of servants and rooms; for were there a separate house and table and equipage for the wife; the expence would be too great to be borne; and therefore, of necessity, both husband and wife eat their food, with their guests, in one place, sleep together in the same chamber, and cannot avoid being always in each other's company; contrary to the custom in Asia, where, by reason of the cheapness of work, the women have separate apartments for themselves, and have not to make their time and convenience suit that of their husbands; and when their particular friends are with them, they do not desire their husband's company for several days, but send his victuals to him in the murdannah (or male apartments); and, in like manner, when the husband wishes to be undisturbed, he eats and sleeps in the murdannah.

A second cause is, "The coldness of this climate, which requires exercise and walking, and the husband to sleep in the same bed with his wife: but concealment from view is incompatible with walking: and as for the second case, another cause is the want of room; for, otherwise, it is the natural disposition of mankind, when under distress and affliction of mind, to wish frequently for privacy and unrestraint, and sleep in a room alone."

A *third cause* is, "The people here being all of one kind;" for, in this kingdom, placed in a corner of the globe where there is no coming and going of foreigners, the intercourse of the sexes is not attended with the consequences of a corruption of manners, as in Asia, where people of various nations dwell in the same city; and to allow the women such a liberty there, where there is such danger of corruption, would be an encroachment upon the liberty of the men, which (as shewn in the beginning) is contrary to justice; and that a corruption of manners must ensue, where various kinds of people mix together, is too evident to require demonstration. Before the Mussulmans entered Hindoostan, the women did not conceal themselves from view; and, even yet, in all the Hindoo villages it is not customary: and it is well known how inviolable the Hindoos preserve their own customs, and how obstinately they are attached to them; but now so rigidly do the women in the great towns observe this practice of concealment from view, that the bride does not even shew herself to her father-in-law, and the sister comes but seldom into the presence of her brother.

A *fourth cause* is, "The necessity which the European women have to acquire experience in the affairs of the world, and in learning various arts, on account of the duty that belongs to them to take part in their husband's business;" which experience could not be obtained by keeping in concealment: whereas the duties of the Asiatic women consisting only in having the custody of the husband's property, and bringing up the children, they have no occasion for such experience, or for laying aside their own custom of concealment. What has been just said, was to shew that the Asiatic women have no necessity to expose their persons; but it must also be observed, that they have many reasons for preferring privacy. One is, the love of leisure, and repose from the fatigue of motion: a second is, the desire of preserving their honour, by not mixing with the vulgar, nor suffering the insults of the low and rude, who are always passing along the streets; a feeling in common with the wives of European noblemen, who, to preserve their dignity, are never seen walking in the streets; and also with ladies in private life, who when walking out at night, and even in the day, are always attended by a male friend or servant to protect them. The notions which the European women have, that the women of Asia never see a man's face but their husband's, and are debarred from all amusement and society, proceed entirely from misinformation: they can keep company with their husband's and father's male relations, and with old neighbours and domestics; and at meals there are always many men and women of this description present; and they can go in their palankeens to the houses of their relations, and of ladies of their own rank, even although the husbands are unacquainted; and also to walk in gardens after strangers are excluded; and they can send for musicians, and dancers, to entertain them at their own houses; and they have many other modes of amusement besides these mentioned.

The *second* is, "The privilege of the husband, by law, to marry several wives." This, to the European women, seems a grievous oppression; and they hold those very cheap who submit to it. But, in truth, the cause of this law and custom is the nature of the female sex themselves, which separates them from the husband, the several last months of pregnancy, and time of suckling; and besides these, the Asiatic women have many other times for being separate from their husbands. This privilege not being allowed by the English law, is indeed a great hardship upon the English husbands: whereas the Asiatic law, permitting polygamy, does the husband justice, and wrongs not the wife; for the honour of the first and *equal* wife is not affected by it; those women who submit to marry with a married man not being admitted into the society of ladies, as they are never of high or wealthy families, no man of honour ever allowing his daughter to make such a marriage. The mode in which these other wives live is this: they who are of a genteel extraction, have a separate house for themselves, like kept-mistresses in England; and they who are not, live in the house of the equal wife, like servants, and the husband at times conveys himself to them in a clandestine manner. Besides, these wives cannot invade any of the rights of the equal wife; for although they and their children are by law equally entitled to inheritance, yet, since the equal wife never marries without a very large dowry settled upon her, all that the husband leaves goes to the payment of this dowry, and nothing remains for his heirs. The opinion that the men of Asia have generally three or four wives, is very ill founded, for in common they have only one; out of a thousand, there will be fifty persons, perhaps, who have from one to two, and ten out of these who have more than two. The fear of the bad consequences of polygamy makes men submit with patience to the times of separation from the equal wife, as much the better way; for, from what I know, it is easier to live with two tigresses than two wives.

The *third* is, "The power of divorce being in the hands of the husband." This is ordained by law, but not practised; for if a great offence be the motive to divorce a wife, and if it be proved against her, she receives punishment by the order of the magistrate, or from the husband, with the concurrence of all her relations; and if the offence be of a trivial nature, such as a difference of temper and unsociability, the husband punishes her by leaving the female apartments, and living in his own. But the reason for divorce being at the will of the husband, lies in the very justice of the law, and the distinction of the male sex over the female, on account of the greater share they take in the management of the world; for all the laborious work falls to their lot, such as carrying heavy burthens, going to war, repulsing enemies, &c. and the women generally spend their lives in repose and quiet. Nevertheless, if the wife establishes a criminal offence against the husband, such as an unfair distribution of his time among his wives, or a diminution of the necessaries of life, she can obtain a divorce in spite of him.

The *fourth* is, "The little credit the law attaches to the evidence of women in Asia;" for, in a court of justice, every fact is proved by the testimony of two men; but if women be the witnesses, four are required. This does not arise from the superiority of the one over the other, but it is founded upon the little experience and knowledge women possess, and the fickleness of their dispositions.

The *fifth* is, "The Asiatic women having to leave off going to balls and entertainments, and wearing showy dresses and ornaments, after their husband's death." This is owing to their great affection for their husband's memory, and their own modes and habits; for there is nothing to prevent a woman's doing otherwise, or marrying a second husband, but the dread of exposing herself to the ridicule and censure of women of her own rank.

The *sixth* is, "The Asiatic daughters not having the liberty of choosing their husbands." On this head nothing need be said; for in Europe this liberty is merely nominal, as, without the will of the father and mother, the daughter's choice is of no avail; and whatever choice they make for her, she must submit to; and in its effects, it serves only to encourage running away (as the male and female slaves in India do), and to breed coldness and trouble amongst the members of a family. But granting that such a liberty does exist in England, the disgrace and misery it must always entail is very evident. The choice of a girl just come from the nursery, and desirous by nature to get a husband, in an affair on which the happiness of her whole life depends, can neither deserve that respect nor consideration which is due to the choice of her parents, who have profited by experience, and are not blinded by passion.

But what the Asiatic women have more than the European, both by law and custom, may be ranked under EIGHT heads.

First, "Their power over the property and children of the husband, by custom;" for the men of Asia consider the principal objects of marriage, after the procreation of their species for the worship of God, two things,—the one to have their money and effects taken care of, and the other to have their children brought up; so that they themselves, being left entirely disengaged of these concerns, may turn their whole endeavours to the attainment of their various pursuits. The chief part, therefore, of whatever wealth they acquire, they give in charge to their wives; and thus the women have it in their power to annihilate in one day the products of a whole life. Although this seldom happens, yet it is often the case, where the husband having amassed a large fortune in youth and power, has delivered it in charge to his wife, and requires it back in his old age and necessity, she does not allow him more than sufficient for his daily support, and lays the rest up, in a place of security, for the sake of her children. And so great is the power they possess, as to the disposal of their children, that frequently they are brought up without any education, or die in childhood; for the women, on account of their little sense, are never pleased to part with their children, by sending them to school, and to acquire experience by travelling; and when they fall sick, they give them improper medicines, by the advice of their own confidants, or, from their softness of heart, indulge them in whatever it is the nature of the sick to take a longing for, and thus they cause their death.

Second. "Their power, by custom, as to the marriage of their children, and choice of their religious faith;" for if the husband wishes to give one of them in marriage to a person the wife disapproves of, the match does not take place: but the other way, it generally does. All the children, both male and female, from being mostly in the company of their mother, and looking upon her as their protector against their father, whom, on account of his wishing to have them educated, they consider their tormentor, follow the religious tenets of their mother, and remain perfect strangers to those of their father. It often happens where the wife is a Shya, and the husband a Soony, the children, having been Shyas from their own natural disposition and the instructions of the mother, speak disrespectfully of the chiefs of the Soony sect in their father's presence; and he, who all his life never bore such language from any person, but was even ready to put the speaker of it to death, has no redress, but patiently submitting to hear it from them, as, on account of their want of understanding, they are excusable; and thus, by frequent repetition, his attachment to his faith is shaken, and, in the course of time, he either entirely forsakes it, or remains but lukewarm in it.

Third. "Their authority over their servants;" for the servants of the male apartments, the keeping and changing of whom are in the hands of the husband, through fear of exposing themselves to the displeasure or complaints of the wife, when she finds a proper opportunity, by their committing some fault, which servants are continually doing, are more obedient to her than to their own master; and the servants of the zenana, whom the wife has the care of retaining or turning off, stand so much in awe of their mistress, that many of them pass their whole lives in the zenana, without ever once coming into the presence of the husband: some of them never perform any service for him at all; and others, who do, enter not into discourse with him: and the women are so obstinate in this respect, their husbands never can turn off one of these servants, but his very complaint against them is a recommendation in their favour; and his recommendation has the effect of complaint, by subjecting them to their mistress's resentment. Contrary to this is the manner of the European ladies, who have not their own will with their children and servants, but live more like free and familiar guests in their husbands' houses: and the household establishment and equipage being in common to both, if any part, as the carriage for example, is previously employed by the one, the other has to wait till it is disengaged. Of this there is no doubt, that if a quarrel ensues between an English husband and wife, the wife has to leave the house, and seek her dinner either at her father's or a friend's: whereas in Asia, it is the husband that has to go out; for frequently the utensils of cookery are not kept in the male apartments.

Fourth. "The freedom, by custom, of the Asiatic women from assisting in the business of the husband, or service of his guests;" whereas this is generally the duty of European wives, whether their husbands be of a genteel business, such as jewellery, mercery, or perfumery, or the more servile ones. I have seen many rise from their dinner, to answer the demands of a purchaser: and although all these duties are not required of the ladies, yet some, especially the entertaining the guests, carving and helping the dishes at table, and making the tea and coffee, are generally performed by them. Now the Asiatic ladies have no such duties at all, but live in the manner before described.

Fifth. "The greater deference the Asiatic ladies find paid to their humours, and a prescriptive right of teasing their husbands by every pretext," which is considered as constituting an essential quality of beauty; for if a wife does not put these in practice, but is submissive to her husband's will in every thing, her charms very soon lose their brilliancy in his eyes. Thus, when a wife goes to visit her father, she will not return to her husband, till he has come himself several times to fetch her, and been as often vexed by her breaking her promise: and every day when dinner is served, by pretending to be engaged at the time, she keeps her husband waiting, and does not come till the meat has grown cold; and in the same manner at bed-time;—for returning quickly from her father's house is considered as a sign of fondness for the husband, which, in their opinion, looks very ill; and coming soon to dinner they think betrays the disposition of a hungry beggar. In these, and such like, the husband has nothing for it but patience; nay, it ever pleases him. I have known of many beautiful women, constant in their affection, and obedient to their husbands night and day, whom, for not having these qualities, the husbands have quickly tired of, and unjustly deserted, for the sake of plain women who possessed them.

Sixth. "The greater reliance placed by the Asiatic husbands on their wives' virtue, both from law and custom." For as to the European ladies, although they can go out of doors and discourse with strangers, yet this is not allowed, unless they have a trusty person along with them, either of the husband's or the father's; and sleeping out all night is absolutely denied them,—contrary to the way of the Asiatic ladies, who, when they go to the house of a lady of their acquaintance, though their husbands be entire strangers, are not attended by any person of the husband's or father's, and they spend not only one or two nights in that house, but even a whole week; and in such a house, although the master is prohibited entering the apartments where they are, yet the young men of fifteen, belonging to the family or relations, under the name of children, have free access, and eat with and enter into the amusements of their guests.

Seventh. "Their share in the children, by law." For if a divorce happens, the sons go to the father, and the daughters to the mother; contrary to the custom here, where, if a divorce takes place, the mother, who for twenty years may have toiled and consumed herself in bringing up her children, has to abandon all to the father, and full of grief and affliction, leave his house.

Eighth. "The ease, both by law and custom, with which the wife may separate herself from her husband, when there may be a quarrel between them, without producing a divorce." Thus the wife, in an hour's time after the dispute, sets off with the children and her property to the house of her father or relations; and until the husband makes her satisfaction she does not return: and this she can always do, without a moment's delay.

Besides these eight, as above noticed, of the superior advantages the Asiatic women enjoy over the European, there are many others, here omitted for brevity's sake.

What has been said is enough for people of discernment. Farewell!

Finis.

Appendix A: The Social Context

1. Mirza Abu Talib Khan, "Poem in Praise of Miss Julia Burrell," trans. George Swinton (1807)

[Julia Burrell is referred to a number of times in the text, but this poem was not a part of *Masir-i-Talibi*, but rather is collected in *Diwan-i Talib*. The text below was translated by Abu Talib's student George Swinton and published as *Poems of Mirza Abu Talib Khan* (London, 1807). It gives some sense of the verse in praise of various women that Stewart left untranslated either out of a sense of propriety or simply because he could not render the verse.]

No one has seen beauty to compare with Julia;
God has created her with his own hand.
By her formation, he has shown his master-piece,
And his skill in the knowledge of painting.
If he had not brought her into the world,
The perfection of mental and corporeal beauty would have
    remained unveiled.
By her disposition, she is the lady of ladies
By her charms, enchantress of the sagest enchanters.
She is sovereign in the European kingdom of beauty:
Other beauties resemble liars, she the moon.

Praise of the Beauty of her Person.

From her freshness and transparency, you would think
Life and beauty breathed from every pore.
Her countenance is the morning burst into light,
Scattering salt upon wounded hearts by garden in blossom,
Fresh and verdant as the bower of youth.

Praise of her Lips.

Her lips resemble the smiling rose-bud;
Laughter cannot re-enter from the smallness of her mouth.
The rose-bud withers with jealousy of her mouth;
Wisdom itself is perplexed by her waist, slender as a hair.

Her lip demands tribute from sugar-candy;
It demands plunder from the ruby of Kundoong.[1]
The blood of wine is its only nourishment;
The ruby abashed creeps into a stone.
Pearls are but as pebbles compared with her teeth;
The soul of the pomegranate with envy melts into blood.
Her eye is not an eye, it is a doe in the wilderness of tulips,
From its excessive modesty, in shyness like the fawn.
Misfortune sleeps in the curls of her ringlets;
Many hearts are distracted with love of those locks.
Her eye-brow shoots not alone destructive arrows;
Her eye-lashes also stand with drawn daggers.

Praise of her Mole.

Although her mole, by its charms, prove[s] fatal to lovers;
Her beauty, like the Messiah, recalls them to life.
Say not, that it is a cypher to increase the beauty of her lip;
For it is a robber that lurks by a river's banks.
Not only have remained unshut the eyes of men, on account of
   that mole;
The pupil of her eye is also its constant attendant.
Although the European be ruler over a part of India;
Yet behold an Indian who is sovereign of all Europe.
What a mole! the essence of a hundred caskets of ottar makers;
What a face! the cure of a hundred diseased cities.
Her chin is not an apple of the garden;
It is a well full of the water of life.

Praise of her Neck and Bosom.

From the transparency of her neck, when she drinks,
The wine appears as in a goblet of crystal.
The bottle has exalted its neck,
From the false comparison with it by the poets.
Her bosom, fragrant as the lily, is of pure silver;
But within is all iron, and flinty stone.

---

1   The kundun method of setting stones in pure gold was perfected by
    artisans in the Mughal period. Here, substances were fused at room
    temperature so that the jewels were flush with the surrounding precious
    metals.

Beware that its outside deceive you not;
The lion flies with terror from the hardness within.
When they washed pearls and the moon pure
With bird's milk, they have modelled the globes of her breast.
Behold, the fingers of her hands are reeds,
Which write indelible characters of love on the heart,

Praise of her Gait and Stature.

From the extreme fineness of her waist,
The shadow of her ringlets is a burden to her stature.
Her stature is a cypress when she walks,
But it bears, however, the fruit of seedless pomegranates.
She moves more gracefully than the water of life.
Like me, the pheasant and partridge are lost in astonishment.
Although she should tread on the pismire at her feet,
Its smallest hair would receive no injury.
Yes, it is for this that she treads so lightly,
Under every step lie a hundred souls.

Praise of her Cap.

Her cap of white straw placed on her head,
Appears like a halo surrounding the moon;
In roundness and whiteness like the full moon,
Under what heaven are two moons?
From the circumference of her cap two violet bands
Hang down, and are tied under her chin.
Who has seen a band around the neck of the moon?
Or ringlets playing on the face of the sun?
They are more graceful than any ornament you can conceive;
They are more ensnaring than the ringlets themselves.

Praise of her Veil.

If she had not concealed the sun of her face by a veil,
The world would have been consumed by the splendour of her
    cheeks.
And although that cloud appears as a shade,
Yet it augments our fever by the desire of seeing through it.
Think not, that under that shade you can enjoy repose;
The very obstacle it opposes to our sight, increases tenfold our
    curiosity.

Like the dew on the rose, it is sometimes of white lace;
And she has chosen it to strain the too[1] powerful odour of
   the rose.
The looks of men, like flies, are in it entangled:
If it be compared to the spider's web, it deserves it.
It increases her beauty and our raging madness to behold,
As a picture appears to more advantage behind glass.
But should she be acquainted with its effect,
When would she show her face unveiled?
Like a garland of roses, from both sides of her neck;
She has crossed around her waist a silken kerchief.
The white amongst the green appears like the milky way;
Or it is the striped Indian serpent carrying poison in its bag.
If the idols of India had ever beheld it,
They would have cast away their necklaces of pearls and
   emeralds.

Praise of her Gown.

Her gown in length is like the life of the prophet Khizir;[2]
It sports with the wisdom of philosophers:
Its train, when she moves, sometimes sweeps along the ground;
Like her commands, passing over the souls in her way,
Sometimes like the waning moon, the skirts are tucked up;
You would think the splendour of the moon had been expedient
   in the weaving;
And that from the leaves of the lily they had spun the threads.
Yes; for had its texture been of cotton,
Its coarseness would have lacerated her delicate skin.
The colour is sometimes green as the field of the careful
   husbandman;
And lilies blossom in it as in a flower garden.
Or rather they are the eyes of lovers which have been ensnared,
And placed there for ornament, like the spots in the peacock's
   tail.
No; I am mistaken, it is the cultured field of the heavens;
And in the place of flowers, they are brilliant stars.

---

1   This has been corrected from "two" in Swinton's text.
2   Al-Khidr or al-Khidir is a notable figure in Sufi literature and Middle
    Eastern folklore more generally. An immortal being, often equated with
    Elijah, he travels across space and time to assist those in need and to
    instruct Sufi novices.

Behold, her white girdle is the milky way;
And in front Jupiter and Venus are in conjunction.
When her immaterial waist thus becomes substance;
Well it deserves to be reckoned a miracle.

Praise of her Ornaments.

Upon this ear hangs a cloud surcharged with lightning;
Or it is Venus sits enthroned in her ear-ring.
On that ear, behold Jupiter augments her beauty;
In one morning whoever saw both constellations.
Since the lobe of the ear is the polar star of the world of
    elegance;
Her ear-rings are the Greater and Lesser Bears which revolve
    around.

Praise of the Bunch of Flowers in her Cap.

The bunch of flowers hath increased the beauty of her cap;
The moon appears in the constellation of the Pleïades.[1]
This nosegay composed of leaves, and buds, and flowers,
Art hath endued with the very smell and texture of nature;
It far surpasses every flower of the garden;
Maany[2] himself would wonder how to paint it.
You would think that the buds were in the act of blowing;
And that from their freshness, the leaves and branches were
    ready to break.
Its leaf has never felt the autumn;
Its flower enjoys an eternal spring.
You would declare, that it is fed with the water of life;
Or, that it is in the neighbourhood of that capital of youth.

---

1   A prominent star cluster with extensive mythological significance in a
range of cultures across the globe. In Greek mythology, Zeus immortal-
ized the Seven Sisters who committed suicide out of sadness for the
death of Atlas by transforming them into stars. They surface in both
Arabic and Persian literature under the names al-Thurayya and Pervin
respectively.

2   The founder of the ancient Persian gnostic religion Manicheanism, who
lived in present day Iran during the third century AD. He was reputed
to be an extraordinary painter and his writings, now lost, were heavily
illustrated.

Bezhad[1] is lost in astonishment at its colour and delicacy.
O God! may the hand that made it never decay!
In this bunch of flowers of many pleasing hues,
There is an ear of corn green as the emerald;
Excepting in that envy of the royal crown,
When did the Pleïades ever dwell with Virgo?
The stone in her breast pin is not for fattening her robes;
It is a sun-beam from the heart of the morning.
Or, it is rather the soul of one of her base lovers,
That is dragging her by the neck to expiate his blood.

Praise of her Bracelet.

A black ribbon is upon her silver wrist,
To which the hair and eyes of lovers pay obeisance;
Than this ornament there is nothing more heart attracting,
Nor a stronger fetter to enchain souls.
If her hand even in those bonds, is so long,
Were they not around it, what would become of our hearts?
Should those hands be freed from their chains,
I know not what cruelties they would commit.
Sometimes her bracelet is of white and green ribbon;
Coiled like the snake, with its tail around its head.
Or like the striped Indian serpent fitting upon her sleeves.
At the sight of that serpent many have their souls ready in their
    sleeves.

Praise of her Unaffectedness.

Since she is unaffected in her disposition as in her beauty,
She little adorns her person with colours and ornaments.
Yes, twould be a pity ornaments upon such a body.
The jeweller considers as blemishes every spot in a precious
    gem.
The whiteness of her neck is of the milk of the morning;
A necklace of pearls near it would appear to disadvantage.
The crown of the sun never was bedecked with ornaments.

---

1   Kamal al-din Bihzad or Kamaleddin Behzad (c. 1450–c. 1535) was the
    most famous painter of Persian miniatures and the head of the royal
    workshops in Herat and Tabriz, which produced extraordinary illumi-
    nated manuscripts during the late Timurid and early Safavid periods.

The hand of Venus never was bound with bracelets.
The designer would not consider it as proper
To form any figures upon crystal that is pure.
The very want of ornaments to her person
Is with her equal to a thousand jewels.

Praise of her good Qualities.

In her nature she is inflexible and difficult to please;
Yet from the sweetness of her disposition, she sympathizes with
  others.
The humble alone are the objects of her regard;
The mighty she treats with indifference.
Her heart melts at the woes of the afflicted;
She is anxious to relieve the pain of an ant.
Like the dew-besprinkled rose, when she speaks,
Her roses become moistened by modesty.
Sweetness and her voice are twins;
Her words are nourishment to the soul,
From her excessive modesty she seldom speaks;
From her sense and understanding she expresses herself slowly.
Like the Virgin Mary her virtue is immaculate,
She is deeply versed in the ways of Christ,
In the night she sleeps like the humid narcissus;
In the morning she rises pure in heart as the rose-bud;
None but the purest thoughts enter her mind;
No actions occupy her but study or play.

Mention of her Loves.

From the hearts her admirers have left behind them,
There is no getting access to her abode.
Thousands iie slain and wounded;
Many in pain are languishing as her eye.
One of those helpless beings is the heavens,
Which are revolving around her night and day.
The Zephyr is another, who, by his good fortune,
Is permitted to touch her ringlets in perfuming them with ottar,
If the sun is not enamoured of her face,
Why does he look pale, and dart his beams into her house;
And if the full moon is not captivated with her love,
What flame is it that consumes him every night.

Disputation.

Although the heart be impatient to behold her,
Yet justice commands respect and politeness.
She fears that if her delicate colour should be beheld;
The rays of sight might, by their warmth, cause it to fade.
Wisdom also on another account refrains himself,
Lest tears be the fruit of beholding her.
Where is the wise man who would approve seeing that
Which would shut his eyes to every thing besides?
Madness says that her sight is easy to be borne.
What are the ties of religion, and self existence, and prudence?
They are of no weight in the balance of beholding her.
Time passes quickly; seize the opportunity.
Although much argument was used by both;
Yet much remained to establish their opinions.
At last wisdom had to yield to madness;
That it was impossible to abstain from her sight.

2. The Duchess of Devonshire's Gala Breakfast (*Morning Post and Gazetteer*, 7 and 8 July 1800)

[The following two-part article gives an account of breakfast at Chiswick house discussed by Abu Talib in Vol. 2 Ch. 15 (p. 190). Comparison gives some sense of the complex sexual negotiation that underlies Abu Talib's observations.]

The Fashionable World

Duchess of Devonshire's Gala[1]
   On Saturday her Grace gave a grand *Fete* at Chiswick to a large party of fashion, amounting to at least five hundred personages. From two to three o'clock the roads from London were continually enveloped in dust. Curricles, chaises, coaches with four and six horses, out-riders, &c. passed in one regular cavalcade. Four hundred carriages at least were on Saturday at the magnificent villa of her Grace of Devonshire. On the lawn the scene of festivity took place. Flowers of all kinds, orange and lemon trees, were placed in regular rows around the house and in the apartments,

---

1   See ch. 15, p. 189, note 4.

the refreshing coolness and fragrance of which were delightful. Marquees were erected on the lawn, near the canal, and bands of music played on the water, the bridge, and other parts of the gardens. Bands of music also played on the Thames.

This rural fete was what is called a *public breakfast*. It consisted of feasting, music, and dancing, from two o'clock till dusk; but the most brilliant period of the day was from three to six. Lady Georgiana Gordon was among the best of the dancers. A more splendid and agreeable scene has not been witnessed this season. [The article goes on to list the prominent guests by rank.]

From the *Morning Post and Gazetteer*, 8 July 1800

The Fashionable World

The news from France yesterday prevented us from giving so full an account of the Duchess of Devonshire's public breakfast at Chiswick, as the elegance of the entertainment and the gaiety of the scene require. Her Grace provided various amusements for her guests, and some of them brought *voluntary contributions* to the general stock of entertainment. The Prince brought the band of his regiment from Guildford, and it was stationed opposite his Royal Highness's tent on the lawn. It consists of twenty-four in number and they performed charmingly. The Lord Mayor brought the band of the West London Militia, which also played well. Four bands of Savoyards and one Organ were also stationed in different parts of the garden, so that wherever you turned, you were saluted by a concord of sweet sounds, as well as the refreshing perfumes of the finest flowers and shrubs.

Among the amusements, besides that of viewing in all parts a crowd of beautiful women, elegantly dressed; and besides the good cheer, the most important part of the Gala with John Bull, there were cricketting for the athletic youths, and dancing for the lively Misses.

Cricket was played in the Great Park.... A band of music performed the whole time in this part of the ground; and the cricket players had an opportunity of catching the ball, *Piano*, or bowling out to *quick time*. A table was laid for twenty-four, furnished with cold meats, jellies, wines, &c. to heighten the agility and increase the strength of the combatants; among whom Mr. T. Sheridan made a distinguished figure.

The dances commenced with Lady Mary Ramsey and Lord Dalhousie, a medley, by

Lady Georgiana Gordon,	Marquis of Lorne.
Lady Georgiana Cavendish,	Mr. Skellington.
Lady Mary Bentinck,	Sir Watkin Williams Wynne.
Lady Stewart,	Lord Ossulstone.
Miss Thompson,	Col. Cooper.
Miss Fordyce,	Lord Brooke.
Lady Arabella Annesley,	Mr. T. Sheridan.
Miss Milner,	Mr. Tho. Hope.
Lady Charlotte Primrose,	Lord Morpeth.
Miss C. Fordyce,	Sir Hugh Montgomery.
Miss Maxwell,	Rev. Mr. Grosvenor.
Lady A. Bennett,	Lord Milsington.

The next dance was "Neel Goaw, and this is not my house," a medley; then succeeded reels and strathspeys out of number. At last fatigue began to overpower the most alert, and the heat to incline them to take refreshment; one more dance being called for, they concluded with "The Devil among the Tailors."

Until the Prince came, at four o'clock, no one sat down to breakfast; but immediately on his arrival the company retired from the lawn to the tents, &c. In the Roman Temple adjoining, 30 covers were laid; the cold meats, fruits, jellies, &c. were laid out with great taste. It was here that the Prince, the Duchess, the Duke of Bedford, Mr. Sheridan,[1] &c. took refreshments; but there were many tents in various parts of the extensive and beautiful grounds, and several parties took refreshments in the house.— The company appeared all to be in high spirits, quite delighted with the scene, to which the lovely Lady Georgiana Cavendish added greatly by her attentions and elegant appearance; and many of the guests were reminded of the chorus of *The Deserter*;[2]

> And be what it will,
> Our wish shall be still,
> Joy and Health to the Duchess wherever she goes.

---

1 Thomas Sheridan (1775-1817), was the son of playwright and Whig parliamentarian Richard Brinsley Sheridan (1751-1816). Through the influence of his father, Thomas, at this time, was being sponsored by the Prince of Wales for a variety of patronage posts. He was eventually elevated into a position of command in the Prince's regiment.

2 Charles Dibdin's popular adaptation of Pierre-Alexandre Monsigny's eponymous *Opéra Comique* was first staged at Drury Lane in 1773. The cited passage is from the play's first chorus.

3. The Lord Mayor's Feast (*Oracle and Daily Advertiser*, 11 November 1800)

[As discussed at length in Vol. 2, ch. 16, p. 197-99, Abu Talib was present at the Lord Mayor's Feast described in the following extract. Close comparison of the two accounts of the tribute paid to Lord Nelson following his victory over the French at Abu Qir reveals a great deal about how Abu Talib negotiates with political topics of direct consequence to himself.]

LORD MAYOR'S DAY

The Lord Mayor[1] proceeded from Guildhall, accompanied by his Predecessor in Office, the Recorder, Mr. Sheriffs Perring and Cadell, Aldermen Boydell, Skinner, Anderson, Eamer, Herne, Price, and Perchard, to Westminster Hall, in the usual precession, attended by all the City Officers. The City Barge, in which they embarked, was followed by those of seven or eight companies;....

After the party had landed as usual at Blackfriars, they were joined by the carriage of Lord Nelson,[2] who was waiting to receive them. But as soon as the populace discovered the vehicle which was to convey the Hero of the Nile, they unharnessed the horses, and drew him in triumph to Guildhall, while another party of them did the same by the carriage of the Old Lord Mayor.

Between four and five thousand Ladies and Gentlemen then sat down to a very excellent Dinner, consisting of the choicest Wines and all the rarities of the season. After several toasts had been given Lord Nelson was requested to come forward, that he might receive the Sword lately voted to him on account of his very extraordinary service.

---

1 Harvey Christian Combe (1752-1818), a brewer with radical Whig politics, was Lord Mayor during 1799-1800; his wife, the Lady Mayoress, was Alice Combe (d. 1828; née Christian).
2 Viscount Horatio Nelson (1758-1805), the most renowned naval officer of his generation and a much decorated hero. In this context, he is being celebrated for his epochal victory over the French fleet at Abu Qir on 1 August 1798. Nelson's tactical innovations routed the French line and stranded the French expeditionary force in Egypt. This had profound effects not only on the course of the war with France, but also on the history of intercultural relations between Europe and the Islamic peoples of the Middle East.

The gallant Hero of the Nile then presented himself to an admiring assemblage, taking his situation, as requested, under a triumphal arch, when he was thus addressed by Mr. Chamberlain Clarke, supported by Mr. Crowther, the comptroller and Vice Chamberlain;—

"Lord Nelson,
In cheerful obedience to an unanimous resolution of the Right Hon. Lord Mayor, Aldermen, and Commons, the City of London, in common Council assembled, I present to your Lordship with the Thanks of the Court for the very important Victory obtained by a Squadron of His Majesty's Ships under your command, over a superior French Fleet, off the Mouth of the Nile, on the 1st of August 1798—a Victory splendid and decisive—unexampled in Naval History—and reflecting the highest honour on the courage and abilities of your Lordship and your Officers, and the discipline and irresistible bravery of British Seamen, and which must be productive of the greatest advantages to this Country, and every part of the Civilized World, by tending to frustrate the designs of our implacable Enemy, and by rousing other Nations to unite and resist their unprincipled ambition!

And, as a further testimony of the high esteem which the Court entertains of your Lordship's public services, and of the eminent advantages which you have rendered your country, I have the honour to present to your Lordship This Sword!

The consequences of the action I am thus called on to applaud, are, perhaps, Unequalled in the History of Mankind! A numerous army, which had triumphed in *Europe* over brave and veteran troops commanded by Officers of the most established reputation, landed in *Egypt* under the command of him who now sways the Gallic Sceptre, with designs of the most ambitious and extensive nature. One of their objects, as acknowledged by themselves, was to annihilate, by degrees, the English East India Trade, and finally, to get into their possession the whole commerce of *Africa* and *Asia*.

Such were the gigantic views of our implacable foe; and such confidence had they in the fleet which conveyed them, and in the station it took on the coast of the devoted country, that it bade defiance to the whole Navy of *Britain*. But, at this momentous period, the Almighty directed your Lordship, as his chosen instrument, to check their pride, and crush their force, as a maritime power, during the present contest.

The circumstances attending this grand display of Providential Interposition and British Prowess, must interest the feelings of every Englishman. Had a space been chosen to exhibit to the World a struggle for superiority in nautical skill, and personal valour, between the two greatest naval powers of the Globe, none could have been more happily selected. The three grand divisions of the Antient World were witnesses; and the shores which had beheld the destruction of the Persian Navy by the Greeks and the heroic acts of Sesostris, now resounded with the echo of British Thunder![1] To your Lordship belongs the praise of having added Glory to such a scene! The heroes we applaud would themselves have applauded us! And he, who ages since led his three hundred against an almost countless host, might, on that proud day, have wished himself a Briton.

The thanks of your Country, my Lord, attend you; its honours await you; but a higher praise than even these imply is yours. In the moment of your unexampled victory, you saved your Country—In the next moment you did still more—you exemplified that virtue which the heathen world could not emulate; and in the pious "*Non nobis, Domine*" of your modest dispatches, you have enforced a most important truth, that the most independant Conqueror felt, in the most intoxicating point of time, the influence and protection of Him, whom our enemies, to their shame and their ruin, had foolishly and impiously defied.

May that same Power, my Lord, ever protect and reward you! May it long, very long, spare to this Empire so illustrious a teacher, and so potent a champion!"

After which Lord Nelson, amidst the plaudits of some thousands of Ladies and Gentlemen, addressed Mr. Chamberlain Clarke in the following short but impressive Speech—

"Sir,

It is with the greatest pride and satisfaction that I receive from the Honourable Court this testimony of their approbation of my conduct; and with this very sword—(*holding it up in his left and remaining hand*)—I hope soon to aid in reducing our implacable and inveterate enemy to proper and due limits—without which

---

1 Clarke is comparing the defeated French fleet to the decimated Persian navy at Salamis and to the Palestinian peoples subjugated by Sesostris. See Herodotus's *Histories* (8:70-94) for the account of the battle of Salamis and (2: 110) for an account of Sesostris's conquest of Syria/Palestine.

this Country can neither hope for, nor expect, a solid, honourable and permanent peace!"

His Lordship's Address was received with the most rapturous applause; and the whole assemblage was seemingly animated by one grand impulse of gratitude and sensibility for the most signal and most wonderful achievement recorded in any age, or in the history of any nation!

The Sword is of admirable workmanship, cost 200 guineas, but when in possession of the renowned Hero of the Nile, may be said to be immediately enhanced to an incalculable value. It is richly ornamented; the handle gold, with blue enamel, studded with diamonds. The crocodile appears as emblematical of the Grand Event; and the guard is supported with anchors....

The Lady Mayoress conducted herself with uncommon affability and attention; and the commencement of the new Mayoralty—which was superb in decoration, and abundant in the choicest viands and wines—was distinguished by the presence of a Hero who will be the favourite and admiration of the latest posterity! So emulous were the Spectators in their attentions to Lord Nelson, that he shook by the hand more than 2000 *en passant*!....

Dignum, Sale, and other excellent Singers assisted in the festivity of the evening. The first air was *Non Nobis, &c*; the second, *God save the King!* And the third, after Lord Nelson's brief but memorable speech, was *Rule Britannia!*

The Ladies were all dressed in the most elegant style; and the Ball, as usual, attracted the most expert at the "light fantastic toe."

Appendix B: Contemporary Reviews

1. *The Quarterly Review* (August 1810)

[There were a number prominent reviews of Stewart's translation of *The Travels of Mirza* published shortly after its publication. The reviews in the *Annual Register* 52 (1810): 749-57, the *Critical Review* (January 1811): 20-38, the *British Critic* (September 1810): 270-77, and the *Monthly Review* (June 1813): 182-93, simply excerpt snippets of the text and give little sense of reception beyond their approbation. However, Reginald Heber's essay in the *Quarterly Review* (August 1810): 80-93, offers a sustained engagement with the text.[1] Heber's references are to the 1810 edition.]

It is difficult to imagine any character whose first impressions would excite more natural curiosity, than an Asiatic traveller in Europe. There is so much value in even the most common knowledge, that the pride of man is secretly gratified by the surprise of a stranger at objects which are familiar to us, even where that familiarity confers no merit on ourselves; and this is perhaps the secret charm, which, fortunately for travellers, makes their society courted in foreign countries, and which constitutes in no small degree, what all of us have sometimes felt,—the pleasure *of shewing the lions*.[2] There is, too, a vivid shrewdness which generally accompanies the observations of a sensible man on objects which are new to him, altogether unattainable by those whose perceptions already are deadened by habit. We may hope then for instruction, as well as entertainment, in such society; and it is not irrational, except in the extreme to which it has been sometimes carried, that an Omai,[3] a

---

1 Reginald Heber (1783-1826) was trained at Oxford, ordained as an Anglican minister in 1807 and eventually appointed the Bishop of Calcutta in 1823. He wrote many essays for the *Quarterly Review* on works of literature and history.

2 Richard Grose's 1785 *Dictionary of the Vulgar Tongue* defines this phrase as follows: "To shew the lions and tombs; to point out the particular curiosities of any place, to act the ciceroni: an allusion to Westminster Abbey, and the Tower, where the tombs and lions are shewn."

3 Mai, popularly known as Omai, travelled from Raitea to England on the second voyage of Captain Cook. While in England from 1774-76 he was introduced into the highest echelons of British society by Sir Joseph Banks and became a celebrity. He was the subject of important paintings by both Sir Joshua Reynolds and William Hodges.

Bannelong,[1] or any other far-fetched curiosity in human form, should be feasted by the great, courted by the fair, and attended to public places by crowds of gaping observers. After all, however, on a mere savage, the wonders he witnesses are too many and too unintelligible to make any distinct impression. To him, a paper kite and a balloon are equally miraculous; every step he takes is on enchanted ground; and, like a child who reads a fairy tale, he soon ceases to be surprised at wonders; because he expected to meet with nothing else, and because in such a place, such wonders are only natural. Again, people care little for what is totally above their comprehension, and a savage would be more interested in an ironmonger's shop, than in all the curiosities of the British Museum, or all the magnificence of St. Paul's or Blenheim. With the Asiatic, however, the case is different; he brings with him a sufficiently cultivated judgment to distinguish between our customs and his own; a mind to which the objects he meets with are not so new as to be incomprehensible, though they are so differently modified in form and circumstance from those to which he is accustomed, that another planet could hardly produce a greater variety; it is a variety which he understands and feels, and it is the same in kind (though from evident reasons, much greater in degree) as that which an European, prepared as he is by hundreds of precursors, and tens of hundreds of descriptions, must ever experience on entering for the first time, a Mahommedan or Hindoo country.

Accordingly, as no real oriental traveller had yet appeared, his place and character were eagerly assumed by European writers, who, under the names of Turkish Spies, Ambassadors of Bantam, and Chinese or Persian Tourists, endeavoured to instruct, as impartial spectators of our European feuds and follies; or to amuse, by ridiculous oppositions of our manners and character with their own. That the experiment succeeded, is evident by the number of imitators which every generation has produced; but still, amusing as they were, these Turks and Persians wanted the charm of reality. They were Brigg's 'French beads, and Bristol stones,'[2] in comparison with the

1   Bennelong (1764?-1813), an Australian Aboriginal, was captured in November 1789 and brought to the settlement at Sydney Cove by order of Governor Arthur Phillip. He was quickly integrated into the society of the colonists and he traveled with Phillip to England in 1792, and like Mai, was introduced to George III. He returned to Australia in 1795.
2   Heber is referring to the masquerade scene in Book 2, ch. 3 of Frances Burney's novel *Cecilia* (1782) in which Cecilia's miserly guardian Mr. Briggs ridicules the fake jewels of Sir Robert Floyer's Turkish costume. Another of Cecilia's guardians, Mr. Harrel, attempts to marry her to his creditor Sir Robert, in spite of the fact that she dislikes him, in return for the cancellation of his debts.

genuine treasures of Golconda;[1] and the difference in interest was almost the same, as between a view of the Great Mogul himself, and the well-bred Sultan of a French tragedy, or an English masquerade.

The reality, however, prefigured by so many types, has at last made his appearance. A bonâ fide Mahommedan has produced a tour; and, as luck would have it, this tour has appeared at a time, when all the world, or at least all the idle part of it, was still on the stretch of curiosity, respecting His Excellency Mirza Abdul Hassan.[2]

Now, when the ladies had once ascertained, by actual experiment, the length of a Persian's beard, and the texture of his skin and clothing; when their minds were pretty well made up what to think of their formidable guest, it was surely no unnatural desire to know that guest's opinion of them. And as His Excellency's sentiments are not yet to be expected in English, it will no doubt be, in the mean time, acceptable to learn what was thought and said under almost similar circumstances, by a man, who was every inch of him, as true a mussulman (as 'catholic a devil,' as Sancho Panza[3] hath it,) as if, like his aforesaid Excellency, he had borne credentials from the King of Iran and Touran, and excited by his presence and supposed intrigues, the jealousy both of the eastern and western Cæsar. This lucky coincidence has, we are afraid, even made the reality of our tourist suspected, and many have too rashly classed him, without examination, with the Anacharsis[4] of our continental neighbours, or our own ingenious Hidalgo Don Manuel de Espriella.[5] In this, however, they have

---

1 In the 16th century, Golconda was the capital and fortress city of the Qutb Shahi kingdom, near Hyderabad. The city was home to one of the most powerful Muslim sultanates in the region and was the center of a flourishing diamond trade. During the early modern period the name became synonymous with vast wealth.

2 See Introduction, p. 11.

3 Squire to the eponymous hero of Miguel de Cervantes's 1602 novel *Don Quixote* who was famous for his ironic proverbs.

4 In 1788 Jean Jacques Barthelemy (1716-95), a highly esteemed classical scholar and Jesuit, published *The Travels of Anacharsis the Younger in Greece*, a learned imaginary travel journal, one of the first historical novels. It was widely translated and generated fascination with antiquarian topics, especially those pertaining to ancient Greece, across eighteenth-century Europe.

5 Heber is alluding to Don Manuel Alvarez Espriella's *Travels in England* (1807) which was written by the Romantic poet Robert Southey (1774-1843). Southey, writing under this pseudonym, articulated his increasingly Tory politics, and famously argued that revolutionary insurrection would never take root in England.

done Abu Taleb a great injustice; though not so learned as the first, nor so entertaining as the last of these gentlemen, he is, or rather was, a more substantial personage than either. Under the name of the Persian Prince, he was seen and known in fleshly form in the several countries which he has undertaken to describe, and was generally allowed, in the words of Massinger's Borachia,[1]

> '——— as absolute a Turk
> In all that appertains to a true Turk,'

as any former candidate for public notice.

And it will be owned that few inhabitants of east or west, have gone over so large or so interesting a tract of earth and sea. Reduced in his circumstances by events which he himself very modestly and briefly relates, and deprived, though by no fault of his own, of an appointment which he held under our East India Company, an opportunity was thrown his way of undertaking a journey, which, to an oriental, must have appeared desperate; and which he began, as he informs us, in the comfortable hope, that in a voyage so replete with danger 'some accident might cause his death; and thus deliver him from the anxieties of this world, and the ingratitude of mankind.' Accidents, however, and elements were kinder than he expected; and after visiting the Cape, St. Helena, and many parts of Ireland and England, he returned by France, Italy, Constantinople, and Busserah, to his native province in India, where he was appointed once more collector of a district in Bundelcund, and died in that situation in the year 1806.

During the latter years of his life, he prepared and digested his journal, in which he styles himself 'the wanderer over the face of the earth, Abu Taleb, the son of Mohammed of Ispahan, who associated with men of all nations, and beheld various wonders both by sea and land;' and which he commences with true oriental piety, by thanksgivings to God, the Lord of all the world, and 'to the chosen of mankind, the traveller over the whole expanse of the heavens, (Mohammed,) and benedictions without end on his descendants, and companions.'

---

1   Heber is referring to Philip Massinger and John Fletcher's tragicomedy *A Very Woman, or The Prince of Tarent* (1655) in which Antonio, the eponymous prince, is misrecognised as a Turkish slave by a court functionary's wife named Borachia. The cited passage is from Act IV, scene 3.

The first misfortune which befel him on his expedition, was embarking on board a Danish vessel, manned chiefly by indolent, and inexperienced Lascars, of whose filth, confusion, and insubordination he complains most bitterly.

'The captain was a proud self-sufficient fellow. His first officer, who was by birth an American, resembled an ill-tempered growling mastiff, but understood his duty very well. The second officer, and the other mates were low people, not worthy of being spoken to, and quite ignorant of navigation.'—vol. i. p. 22. [68]

After many days of suffering from the united plagues of stinks, bad provisions, and a cabin, 'the very recollection of which makes him melancholy,' he arrived at the Nicobar Islands, where the usual phenomenon of refraction, by making a flat shore visible to the eye, though not to the telescope, and the usual solution of it by a ring in a bowl of water, excited his surprise. The explanation, however, does not, in his opinion, solve the phenomenon. Sixteen of the Lascars deserted here, and Abu Taleb himself was so much captivated with the mildness of the climate, the beauty of the plains and rivulets, and the kind of life which the men enjoyed, that he had nearly resolved to 'take up his abode among them.' The passage of the equinoctial line, and the ceremony of dipping are next described, and he saw what he had never before believed, numerous shoals of flying fish. He was disappointed at not finding a southern polar star, nor any constellation which exactly corresponded with the Ursa Minor or Major, and was astonished that the month of May, so hot in Bengal, should be so extremely cold in the Antarctic hemisphere.

'On the 24th of May, we had a view of part of the continent of Africa, about 200 miles to the north of the Cape of Good Hope; and although we had not the most distant intention of going on shore here, yet the sight of land brought tears into my eyes. While sailing along the coast, we had frequent opportunities of seeing one of the wonders of the deep. Several *fish, called whales*, approached so close to the ship that that we could view them distinctly. They were four times the size of the largest elephant, and had immense nostrils, whence they threw up the water to the height of fifteen yards.' vol. i. p. 44. [76]

His voyage to the Cape was a dismal one; he had repeated storms to encounter, and his cabin was placed between those of a corpulent and surly gentleman, who when the ship rolled, rolled also, and of three crying and ill-tempered children; to whom, if he had known the poetry of Simonides, he would doubtless have exclaimed with Danäe in a similar situation 'ευδει βρειροç."[1] As it was, he thought of the verse of Hafiz, which did just as well:

'Dark is the night, and dreadful the noise of the waves and whirlpool,
Little do they know of our situation, who are travelling merrily on the shore.'[2]

The miseries of a voyage he classes under four genera, subdivided into many distinct species, of which we shall only mention 'the impurity of being shut up with dogs and hogs, the necessity of eating with a knife and fork, and the impossibility of purification.'On the whole, however, he had ample reason to complain, and to advise his countrymen never to undertake a voyage, unless they have money to purchase every comfort; nor to embark, except in an English vessel. At the Cape, he was highly delighted with the neatness of the houses, the pavement of the streets, the shady trees, and the benches for smoking a pipe in summer evenings; a custom which 'appeared to him excellent.'

'In short, the splendour of this town quite obliterated from my mind all the magnificence of Calcutta, which I had previously considered as superior to any thing to be found between India and Europe. In the sequel, I changed my opinion respecting the Cape; and indeed I may say, that from my first setting out on this journey, till my arrival in England, I ascended the pinnacle of magnificence and luxury the several degrees or stages of which, were Calcutta, the Cape, Cork, Dublin, and London; the beauty and grandeur of each city effacing that of the former. On my return towards India, every thing was reversed, the last place being always inferior to that I had quitted. Thus, after a long residence in London, Paris appeared to me much inferior; for although the latter contains more superb buildings, it is neither so regular, so clean, nor so well lighted at night, as the former, nor does it possess so many gardens and squares in its vicinity; in

---

1 Heber is alluding to the poem "Danae and Perseus" by the Greek lyric poet Simonides of Ceos (c. 556 BCE-468 BCE). In Greek mythology, Danae, after bearing Zeus's child Perseus, is cast with her child into the sea in a chest. The cited passage has Danae, in despair, encouraging her son to continue sleeping in spite of their danger. The allusion simultaneously elevates and infantilizes Abu Talib.

2 This is a translation of the fifth couplet of Hafiz's first ghazal in the Diwan.

short, I thought I had fallen from Paradise into Hell. But when I arrived in Italy, I was made sensible of the beauty of Paris; the cities of Italy rose in my estimation when I arrived at Constantinople; and the latter is a perfect Paradise, compared to Bagdad, Mousul, and other towns in the territory of the *Faithful.*' vol. i. pp. 64, 65. [83-84]

Of the Dutch, both male and female, Abu Taleb formed no favourable opinion. He describes the men as low-minded and inhospitable, and more oppressive to their slaves than any other people in the world. The women he stigmatizes at once as vulgar and immodest; but here we must allow a little for the prejudices of a Persian. The girls, who so much offended him, were perhaps only laughing hoydens, who would have been heartily frightened, had they known how he interpreted their airs and glances. It may however be an useful hint to some females nearer home. Lord Valentia[1] imagines that Mahommedans confound all European ladies with *nautch girls*,[2] and it must be owned, that recent oriental travellers have had tolerably good reason for their mistake.

Among the various inhabitants of the Cape, he found 'many pious good Mussulmans, some of whom possessed considerable property;' with these, and in the hospitable society of the English officers, (whose ladies, it is pleasing to observe, he excepts from the general scandal, and compares to the elegant reserve of Indian Princesses,) he passed his time pleasantly, though expensively. At length, being heartily tired of his Danish captain, who had cheated him in every possible manner, he submitted to the loss of his passage money, and embarked the 29th of September, on board an English South Sea whaler. The superior comforts of this ship, he praises highly, though he still seems to have had some apprehensions; 'it being the practice of Europe, that whenever the ships of two enemies meet at sea, the most powerful carries his adversary with him into one of his own ports, and there sells both ship and cargo for his own advantage.'

Of St. Helena he gives one of the best descriptions we have yet seen; and relates a fearful battle, which his captain had, in a

---

1 Heber is referring to George Annesley, Viscount Valentia's *Voyages and Travels to India, Ceylon, the Red Sea, Abyssinia, and Egypt, in the years 1802, 1803, 1804, 1805, and 1806* (1809).

2 Nautch was a style of popular dance performed by young girls in Northern India during the late Mughal period and through the nineteenth century under British rule. For Britons it had connotations of lasciviousness.

former voyage, sustained with a number of marine animals, 'of a size between a horse and an ass, which they call sea-horses.' He notices in his course, 'the Fortunate Isles, whence the Mahommedans commence their longitude;' and the 'entrance into the Mediterranean Sea, which runs east as far as Aleppo.' And being driven by unfavourable winds from the English Channel, (the meaning of which term he explains, as well as that of 'bay and sea,') he anchored on the 6th of December in the Cove of Cork.

'We found here not less than 40 or 50 vessels of different sizes, three of which were ships of war. The Bay resembles a round basin, sixteen miles in circumference. On its shore is situated the town, which is built in the form of a crescent, and defended at each end by small forts. On one side of the bay, a large river, resembling the Ganges, disembogues itself; this river extends a great way inland, and passes by the city of Cork. The circular form of this extensive sheet of water, the verdure of the hills, the comfortable appearance of the town on one side, and the number of elegant houses and romantic cottages on the other, with the formidable aspect of the forts, and so many large ships lying securely in the harbour, conveyed to my mind such sensations as I had never before experienced; and although in the course of my travels, I had an opportunity of seeing the Bay of Genoa, and the Straits of Constantinople, I do not think either of them is to be compared with this.' vol. i. pp. 94, 95. [95]

Nor, though the Cove on a nearer view disappointed him, did he fail to be delighted with the fertility of the neighbourhood, and the hospitality of the mistress of the Post-Office, whose mature charms (for though the mother of 21 children, she had still the appearance of youth,) astonished the inhabitant of a country, where a woman is old at five and twenty.

It is a pleasing circumstance in this Persian's journal, that in every part of our United Kingdom, he met with hospitality and kindness. He here left his vessel, and was proceeding to Dublin to wait on Lord Cornwallis, when he received a visit from an officer whom he had known in India, and who conducted him to his house in the neighbourhood of Cork, where, on an estate of a few hundreds a year, he was enjoying, as Abu Taleb assures us, more comfort and plenty than an English gentleman could in India, upon an income of a lack of rupees.[1] At Cove, he had seen

---

1   At the time, approximately £12,500.

a spit turned by a dog, but here the machinery for roasting was moved by smoke, and together with the dressers for holding china, and the pipes and arrangement of a steam kitchen, excited his warmest admiration. This officer had two nieces, who, 'during dinner,' says the Mussulman, 'honoured me with the most marked attention.'

'After dinner, these angels made tea for us, and one of them having asked me if it was sweet enough, I replied, that having been made by such hands, it could not be but sweet. On hearing this, all the company laughed, and my fair one blushed like the rose of Damascus.' v. i. p. 103. [98]

We shall not follow him minutely through his journey by Dublin and Chester, to London; we must however observe, that in the former place, where he spent some time, he first beheld the phenomenon of a fall of snow, which greatly delighted him by its novelty, and that he was quite reconciled to the coldness of the climate, by the power it gave him to bear fatigue, and by the many advantages which it confers on the inhabitants; making, as he asserts, the men vigorous, the women handsome, and both sexes open-hearted and sincere. 'Boys and girls of fifteen years of age, are here as innocent,' in the Persian's opinion, 'as the children of India of 5 or 6, and have no wish beyond the amusement of play-things, or the produce of a pastry-cook's shop.' Nay many grown persons of wealth and rank are, as he assures us, in an almost similar predicament!

'What I am now to relate, will, I fear, not be credited by my countrymen, but is, nevertheless, an absolute fact. In these countries, it frequently happens, that the ponds and rivers are frozen over; and the ice being of sufficient strength to bear a great weight, numbers of people assemble thereon, and amuse themselves in *skating*.' vol. i. p. 147. [115]

On the whole, he seems more delighted with Ireland than with any other place which he visited, and manifests a very natural preference of the urbanity, good-nature, and intelligence of these, his first European friends, over all other nations. Some of the traits which he mentions are indeed really national, and shew in a strong light the peculiar character of that hospitable and good-natured race; but it must not be forgotten, that here every thing was new, and that consequently all the amusements of which he partook were more attractive in his eyes. Here, for instance, he was first at a theatre, where he received the greatest entertainment from the adventures of an *Ethiopian magician called Harlequin.* Mr. Astley's horsemanship,[1] and the Panorama of Gibraltar, gave him great delight; but he was rather scandalized than pleased with the estimation, approaching to idolatry, in which statues of lead and marble are held.

'It is really astonishing that people possessing so much knowledge and good sense, and who reproach the nobility of Hindostan with wearing gold and silver ornaments like women, should be thus tempted by Satan to throw away their money on useless blocks.' vol. i. p. 129. [105]

Of the meanness of the hot-baths he bitterly complains; and though he expresses a pious hope that the flesh-brush was composed of horse-hair, yet a doubt seems lurking in his mind, that its bristles were shorn from a less holy animal. He noticed, on his road from Holyhead, Conway, with its ancient walls resembling those of Allahabad; and Chester, with the *verandahs* which line the principal streets; and on the 25th of Shaban, corresponding to the 21st of January, 1800, arrived safe in London, being five days short of a lunar year from the period of his leaving Calcutta.

In London he appears to have chiefly remained during the rest of his stay in England. He made indeed an excursion with some friends to Windsor, Oxford, and Blenheim; and at the second of these places was greatly delighted with the 10,000 Oriental manuscripts in the Bodleian, and the different specimens in the Anatomy school. The public buildings, he observes, are 'of hewn stone, and much resemble, in form, some of the Hindoo temples.'

But not all these wonders, nor even the charms of Mr. Hastings' dairy and farm-yard, could long detain him from London, where, with a naïveté almost equal to that of Mr. Ker Porter,[2] 'Cupid,' he observes, 'had planted one of his arrows in his bosom;' and whose 'heart-alluring damsels' he celebrated in a Persian ode, in which he asserts,

'We have no longing for the Tubah, or Sudreh, or other
    trees of Paradise,

---

1   See p. 110, note 1.

2   Robert Ker Porter (1777-1842) was a painter, writer and diplomat. Heber does not seem to be referring to Ker Porter's spectacular paintings of military campaigns in India and Egypt, but rather to his travel writings. *Travelling Sketches in Russia and Sweden during the Years 1805-1808* and *Letters from Portugal and Spain, Written during the March of the Troops under Sir John Moore* were both published in 1809 roughly contemporaneous with this review.

We are content to rest under the shade of these terrestrial *cypresses.*'

Abu Taleb seems, indeed, notwithstanding his horror of hog's bristles, to have been very soon completely reconciled to the habits and liquors of infidels, and, 'according to the advice of the divine Hafiz,' to have given himself up to love and gaiety.

It may be well imagined, that the head of a man, who had been so far elated by the attentions of the provincial beauties of Cork, would be completely turned by the blandishments of rank, fashion and luxury which surrounded him in London; and it is truly amusing to observe the complacency with which he relates how much his society was courted, while his 'wit and repartees, with some impromptu applications of Oriental poetry, were the subject of conversation in the politest circles.'—Poor Abu! he little suspected that all the while he was only entertaining from the Caftan outwards.

In the middle, however, of dissipation, more serious studies were not neglected: he saw the Tower, and the Freemasons, and the Eidouranion, and the Irish giant; and amidst all the curiosities of the British Museum, selected, as most worth notice, the good woman whose forehead was decorated with horns. And though the slight mention of the joys of Paradise, and his ready compliance with the use of wine, may be considered as blots in his character among the True Believers, yet, on the other hand, he takes care to inform those of his own faith, that, in a conversation with an English Bishop, he stoutly maintained the divinity of Mohammed's commission, and almost, as he imagined, persuaded his right reverend friend to embrace the tenets of Islam. There are, however, many better things in his book, and which really evince an active and curious mind, bent on acquiring knowledge, and, when acquired, able to digest it. The following observation would not be, perhaps, unworthy of the most civilized and philosophic describer of the effects of English mechanism.

'On entering one of the extensive manufactories in England, the mind is at first bewildered by the number and variety of articles displayed therein; but after recovering from this first impression, and having coolly surveyed all the objects around, every thing appears conducted with so much regularity and precision, that a person is induced to suppose one of the meanest capacity might superintend and direct the whole process. Whatever requires strength or numbers, is effected by engines; if clearness of sight is wanted, magnifying glasses are at hand; and if deep reflection is necessary to combine all the parts, whereby to insure a unity of action, so many aids are derived from the numerous artists employed in the different parts of the work, that the union of the whole seems not to require any great exertion of genius.' vol. i. pp. 244, 245. [167-68]

In his miscellaneous observations on the English character, education, and form of government, we are often forcibly reminded of the Spanish worthy to whose travels we lately alluded; and it is no slight praise to the author of that entertaining work, that the sentiments which he gives to his hero are so nearly the same with those of a traveller to whom all was new. The praise which he lavishes on all the higher powers, however deserved, is not perhaps free from suspicion, since at the time of publishing his Persian journal, he was still subject to British governors, and still a candidate for British patronage. But the detail is curious; and though he taxes us pretty smartly with pride, philosophy (meaning atheism) and laziness, (for which last vice he recommends, as a cure, shorter meals and longer beards,) yet the impressions which he evidently feels are most flattering to our nation.

It is of course impossible that his views of every subject should be just; and we find, accordingly, that many misconceptions relating to laws, juries, and government, are to be found in every part of his work; and when he compares a certain honourable house to two parties of parroquets, scolding on opposite mango trees, it is evident that he describes from fancy. But though he is often misinformed, he is seldom absurd; and, in truth, we are not sure whether his journal would not be more entertaining, if it had more of the Oriental leaven. The following observation, however, may be excepted from this stigma. He is speaking of an unfortunate class of females, whom he considers as more numerous in London than the truth, we believe, will warrant.

'The conduct of these women is rendered still more blameable, by their hiring lodgings in, or frequenting streets which, from their names, ought only to be the abode of virtue and religion;—for instance, "Providence-street," "Modest-court," "St. James's-street," "St. Martin's-lane," and "St. Paul's Churchyard." The first of these is one of the epithets of God, the second implies virtue, and the others are named after the holy apostles of the blessed Messiah. Then there is "Queen-Anne-street," and "Charlotte-street;" the one named after the greatest, the other after the best of queens. I, however, think that the persons who let the lodgings are more reprehensible than the unfortunate women themselves.' vol. ii. pp. 45, 46. [215-16]

His summary of the last war, and of the politics of Europe, though not free from error, is really, considering his situation, extraordinary; and we rejoice that such an account, from an impartial quarter, of British heroism by land and sea, exists in the universal language of the East. It would be, in our opinion, an object worthy of an enlightened policy, by the aid of the press, to give currency in every possible manner to the original, both in Persia and Hindostan. There are some few things which are offensive to English nationality; but we may well endure that, where so much is said in our favour, some blame should be mingled; and, at any rate, a clear and sensible view of the manners of Europe, as it may tend to reconcile the nations of the East to a preponderance, which must be chiefly supported by opinion, is of the greatest advantage to the country which has the greatest stake there.

Of Paris, which the author next visited, as compared to London, we have already given his sentiments; but it is fair to own, that he expresses, in pretty strong terms, his preference of French to English politeness. He had complained before of our aversion to taking any trouble, even for a friend; and in this respect he says our neighbours are very superior 'to the irritable and surly Englishman.' On the whole, however, he did not like a residence among them, and complains heavily of their idle, slovenly, and trifling habits, which he thinks will effectually prevent their gaining a superiority over their insular neighbours. The women, too, he does not like; 'they were painted to an excessive degree, were very forward, and great talkers.' Amorous as he confesses himself by nature to be, and easily affected at the sight of beauty, he never met with a French-woman who interested him. In the English chargé des affaires then at Paris, he seems, if his report is correct, to have had a tolerable specimen of the indolence, nonchalance, and utter want of information, which too often characterize the young men who fill that important office. By his advice he was persuaded to abandon the usual road to Constantinople, through Germany and Hungary, for the more tedious course of Italy and the Mediterranean. The ever-waking eye, which is turned so wistfully towards the East, did not overlook our tourist; the sçavans, Langlais and De Sacy, were employed to cultivate his acquaintance; and he received repeated invitations from Talleyrand, and at length from Buonaparte. Indisposition, however, prevented his accepting them, and he passed on by Lyons and Avignon to Marseilles. During this journey he noticed the famous bridge of St. Esprit, as having been built by order of one of the Cæsars; and in the diligence, between Avignon and Marseilles, witnessed a kind of brutality in his fellow passengers to a handsome Egyptian girl who was in the coach, which it is painful to conceive possible in any country, and which may be safely pronounced peculiar to France. Not content with the most licentious freedoms, they even snatched his cane, and struck her several severe blows with it. Surely this was enough to make Abu Taleb recall his assertion of the superiority of French politeness and delicacy.

Genoa, Leghorn, and Malta, are in their turn described; at the first of these places he gives us a natural testimony in favour of Italian music; Leghorn he did not like, and prays that 'the curse of God may light on such a city and such a people.'

At Constantinople he only found four praiseworthy institutions; 'the boats'—'the horses kept for hire'—'the public fountains'—and 'the several bazars for merchandize.' Of the Turks he says but little; his stay in Constantinople was short, and they and the Persians have no liking for each other. He allows them, however, many amiable qualities; and, what is singular, does not consider the power of their Sultan as absolute.

The relation of his journey by Amasia, Diarbekir, Mousul, and Bagdad, is very brief, and not particularly interesting:—he was now among nations whose manners and faith were familiar to his countrymen; and the only things which he appears to consider as worth their notice, or his own, are the shrines and tombs of saints on the road. Perhaps he was a little anxious to efface, at the sepulchre of Ali, the guilt of his compliances with infidel customs, on the banks of the Thames and the Liffey. He curses the Turks heartily for heretics and soonys; and notices a minaret which shakes and trembles at the name of Ali, while it remains immoveable by all possible mention of Omar. There are, however, many particulars in this part of his work, worth the attention of future travellers, who may take this little frequented route; and we have not yet seen a more satisfactory account than is here given of the Vahabies. The founder of this powerful sect, Abdul Vechab, it is well known, forbad all worship of Mohammed, and all reverence to tombs and shrines as idolatrous, and giving partners to God. He was, like the original impostor of Arabia, a warlike fanatic; and though his son Mohammed, to whom he transmitted his authority, is blind, he is ably supported by an adopted brother of his father's, named Abd al Aziz, an extraordinary man of gigantic stature; and, though eighty years old, possessing all the vigour of youth, which he predicts he shall retain, till the Vahaby religion is perfectly established over Arabia.

'Although the Vahabies have collected immense wealth, they still retain the greatest simplicity of manners, and moderation in their desires: they sit down on the ground without ceremony, content themselves with a few dates for their food, and a coarse large cloak serves them for clothing and bed, for two or three years. Their horses are of the genuine Nejid breed, of well-known pedigrees; none of which will they permit to be taken out of their country.' vol. iii. pp. 332, 333. [372]

The successes and sacrilege of this 'wicked tribe' grievously offend Abu Taleb, and he calls on the Sultan and the Shah to unite in repressing them. Both Sultan and Shah, however, have need, as it should seem, themselves to tremble before them; and 'the least of the Servants of God' (so this Eastern Pontiff styles himself) has written to both these monarchs, denouncing, 'in the name of God the compassionate and merciful,' fire and sword, and destruction on them and their impenitent subjects.

What part they may yet be destined to perform, is only known to that wisdom, which seems to have set apart the portion of the world where they are placed, as the theatre of the most important scenes and the most singular revolutions. At Busserah, Abu Taleb quarrelled with the English resident, and took a singular method of revenge, by 'writing a satirical poem on him,' and repeating some of the lines in his hearing. On the other hand, the English-man retorted, perhaps with reason, that Abu Taleb was spoilt 'by the luxury and attentions of London, and that it was now impossible to please him.' These bickerings, after being carried on between jest and earnest some time, were terminated by his departure for Bombay. After a pleasant residence of some months in that island, and an agreeable voyage in one of the Company's vessels, 'on the evening of the 15th Rubby Assany 1218, corresponding with the 4th of August, 1803, he landed safely in Calcutta, and returned thanks to God for his preservation and safe return to his native shores.'

We have been hitherto so much engrossed with Abu Taleb himself, as to have no opportunity of mentioning Mr. Stewart, to whom we are obliged for these Travels in their English dress. He assures us, in the Preface, that they are as literally translated as the nature of the two languages will allow, and that he has only omitted some part of the poetry, and two discussions, one on anatomy, and the other on the construction of a hot-house, which, though full of information to Abu Taleb's Oriental readers, he rightly judged would be tedious to those who peruse him in Europe. To this merit of fidelity, which, from Mr. Stewart's character, we are fully disposed to take for granted, may be added the praise of an easy natural English style, which makes on the whole the Travels of Abu Taleb Khan not only a curious, but a very agreeable present to the Western world, for which we owe no trifling obligation to his ingenious translator. To the work itself, indeed, we cannot help attaching a stronger interest, than the apparent abilities of Abu Taleb claim; it is the first description of European manners and character, which has, as far as we know, appeared in an Oriental language; and if sufficient circulation be once given to this production of a Persian, and a descendant of Mohammed, (Vol. ii. p. 245. [253]) it is impossible, from the novelty, and peculiar interest of the subject, that it should not become a common and fashionable study among the polite and learned of those climates. We have already hinted, that to England this must be advantageous; but we do not stop here. When we consider the other circumstances of the East, it is probable that the improvements and knowledge thus revealed in part,—no longer coming under the suspicious garb of the report of an enemy and a conqueror,—will excite a spirit of imitation among those, who before considered the Europeans as a race of warlike savages. One effect will perhaps speedily follow,—that other orientals will pursue the example of Abu Taleb in visiting countries, where, though there are 'Giants,' there are no man-eaters; where, though the sheep are without 'broad tails,' the mutton is confessedly tolerable; and though the men are 'sellers of wine,' the women are stately as the trees of Paradise. From such intercourse, good-will must follow, and where an European is now considered as accursed, he will not, in future, want protectors or imitators. There is a possibility of even greater advantages. When we witness, as in the present tour, the reverence with which a Mussulman has learnt to regard the founder of our religion; and ·when we consider that internal divisions are, at this moment, weakening his attachment to his own peculiar tenets; there is a chance, which (if not spoiled by indiscreet zeal on the one hand, or selfish indifference on the other,) will grow stronger every day, that the cause of religion, as well as that of civilization, may profit by our connexions with Asia.

2. *The Eclectic Review* (August 1811)

[In contrast to Reginald Heber's review in *The Quarterly Review* (Appendix B1), the following excerpt from the *Eclectic Review* (August 1811): 72-84 gives a sense of a more skeptical, and ethnocentric, trend in the reception of the *Travels*.]

It is too obvious to need a remark, that the exhibition, in London, of a Persian manuscript, actually brought from the East, can be no proof of its being a copy of a work of Abu Taleb, or of his ever having written such a work. It is obvious too, that the course of transmission here related [see Translator's Preface], admits the possibility of fabrication, unless, (not to look any lower down) it were certified that Captain Taylor understood Persian, and had collated the copy said to have been given him by Abu Taleb with that written by the Moonshy. If the work were a thing of material importance, a much stricter mode of authentication would evidently be required, than that under which the public now receive it, and under which they may without any very serious scruples receive it. The history given by the translator, may be allowed to carry with it a sufficient degree of probability: and the reader fancies, rather frequently in the course of the work, that he descries signs of an author who both was really an Asiatic, and actually passed through the adventures he relates. There are various *minutiae* strongly evocative of reality in both these respects.

We have been so thoroughly saturated with the European travels of fictitious Asiatic personages,[1] of all ranks and religions, that the present work must be indebted for what attention it obtains to the presumption of its being what it purports to be. On that presumption it may seem to pretend to some considerable importance. We unthinkingly let ourselves imagine it may be very instructive to listen to the remarks made on us by a native of some place on just the other side of the globe. But

---

1 These would include most notably Giovanni Paolo Moranna, *The Eight Volumes of Letters Writ by a Turkish Spy* trans. William Bradsaw (1687-94), Montesquieu's *Persian Letters* (1721), Oliver Goldsmith's *The Citizen of the World* (1762), and Elizabeth Hamilton's *Translations of the Letters of the Hindoo Rajah* (1796). See Ros Ballaster, *Fables of the East: Selected Tales 1662-1785* (New York: Oxford UP, 2005) for a useful array of eighteenth-century examples.

how is this advantage to arise? What do we want to know that, for instance this Mahometan of Lucknow can tell us? Is it impossible to be satisfied, without his testimony, whether we have advanced beyond the Asiatics in the sciences, and the other parts and accompaniments of civilization; whether the art of thinking has been tolerably exemplified by our most distinguished reasoners; whether our art, poetry, eloquence, and criticism, have any conformity with the ascertainable principles of universal truth; or whether, perhaps, the Newtonian philosophy is founded in demonstration? Or shall we doubt of the truth of the Christian religion unless Abu Taleb becomes a convert? Or is it only from an Asiatic there could be any possibility of becoming apprised, that there is a melancholy discrepancy between our words and our practice? Is there no discovering, without the help of a sagacity brought all the way from the banks of the Ganges, that there are among us a prodigious number of rogues, both in the upper ranks and the lower; or that our great towns are haunted, through every part, with abandoned and miserable females; or that ridiculous and pernicious follies mingle with almost all our customs and fashions? After the nice discrimination of almost numberless modes and shades of the follies, are our moralists and satiric poets to receive from an eastern adventurer a sort of second sight for the perfection of the ridiculous in human society? In truth, after all the cant we are accustomed to repeat, about the advantage attending to the remarks of a stranger from a distant country who contemplates our manners in another point of view than by the nature of things we can have done, there is really nothing that we expect, or would even submit to learn, from a deputed instructor from a foreign and perhaps but half-civilized country. All we are in fact expecting is the mere amusement of often laughing at his simplicity, and now and then perhaps wondering at his shrewdness, or luckiness, when he hits on some observation, which in our self-complacency believe we have made a hundred times before.

These remarks do not deny that a person of very extraordinary faculties, brought up in a barbarous or semi-barbarous nation, visiting any part, even the most enlightened part, of the whole world, would there make observations highly worthy of attention, and which, though they contained no new truth might yet reflect some points of our own knowledge with such a vividness, and such a novelty of association, as should seem to give us in those points a stronger intelligence and conviction. If the king of Cochin

China[1] for instance, or Tamahama,[2] the king of the Sandwich islands, could visit and pass some months in this country, there is no society, and there are no volumes, that might not be for a while advantageously relinquished, to observe the operation of one of these powerful minds on a new field of subjects. It would be most interesting to see in what manner their intelligence would, we may so express it, cut in; to observe how many general principles they were in possession of, through native power of understanding; with what directness and decision of thought he would glance back from effects to their causes; how promptly and keenly he would advert from our professed principles, and how pointedly he would signify his vivid perception of the inconsistency; with what earnest inquisition he would speculate on each part of our national economy, often striking on the truth as with intuitive rectitude of understanding, and evincing his penetration even when he judged wrong. From such a man, coming from *any* country, the very wise men of any other country might derive the direct advantage of aids in thinking, as well as the pleasure of observing the operations of a strong mind in a new situation. But our Persian Prince was not a man of this order. He appears to have been a reasonably sensible personage, somewhat above, indeed perhaps considerably above, the majority of his countrymen of similar education; but by no means one of the persons we should be inclined to invite from distant regions as embodying the concentrated intelligence of a large portion of mankind, living under a moral system as different from ours as their locality is remote. He was not the man to be brought across half the globe to sit in council with our philosophers, moralists, and legislators, as the representative of natural reason and social institutions opposite to our own.

---

1   The reviewer appears to be referring to Cochinchina, a term used for various southern regions of present day Vietnam, and not to any particular ruler.

2   Kamehameha I (1737 or 1758 to 1819) conquered the Hawaiian Islands and formally established the Kingdom of Hawai'i in 1810.

Appendix C: Persia: Orientalist Translations and Essays

1. From Sir William Jones, "A Persian Song of Hafiz," *Poems consisting chiefly of translations from the Asiatick languages* (Oxford: Clarendon Press, 1772)

[Hafez was a fourteenth-century Persian poet and Sufi mystic. He is widely considered the preeminent practitioner of the *ghazal*, and the focus of much interest among orientalist scholars in the late eighteenth century. This translation was widely admired for capturing the spirit of the original. Each six line stanza corresponds to Persian verses of four short (or two long) monorhymed lines.]

Sweet maid, if thou would'st charm my sight,
And bid these arms thy neck infold;
That rosy cheek, that lily hand,
Would give thy poet more delight
Than all Bocara's vaunted gold,
Than all the gems of Samarcand.[1]

Boy, let yon liquid ruby flow,[2]
And bid they pensive heart be glad,
Whate'er the frowning zealots say:
Tell them, their Eden cannot show
A stream so clear as Rocnabad,[3]
A bower so sweet as Mosellay.[4]

O! when these fair perfidious maids,
Whose eyes our secret haunts infest,
Their dear destructive charms display;
Each glance my tender breast invades,

---

1 Samarkand, the capital of Tamerlane's empire, and one of the key stops on the Silk Road.
2 Hafez frequently writes of wine, which, to some eighteenth-century readers, seemed to contradict the Islamic prohibition against drinking. Interpreters of Sufism have frequently insisted that intoxication figures for devotion or religious rapture in the verse.
3 A famous stream of Shiraz, the Persian city of wine, poets and flowers.
4 Celebrated gardens of Shiraz.

And robs my wounded soul of rest,
As Tartars seize their destin'd prey.

In vain with love our bosoms glow:
Can all our tears, can all our sighs,
New lustre to those charms impart?
Can cheeks, where living roses blow,
Where nature spreads her richest dyes,
Require the borrow'd gloss of art?

Speak not of fate; ah! change the theme,
And told of odours, talk of wine,
Talk of the flowers that round us bloom:
'Tis all a cloud, 'tis all a dream;
To love and joy thy thoughts confine,
Nor hope to pierce the sacred gloom.

Beauty has such resistless power,
That even the chaste Egyptian dame
Sigh'd for the blooming Hebrew boy:[1]
For her how fatal was the hour,
When to the banks of Nilus came
A youth so lovely and so coy!

But ah! sweet maid, my counsel hear
(Youth should attend when those advise
Whom long experience renders sage):
While musick charms the ravish'd ear;
While sparkling cups delight our eyes,
Be gay; and scorn the frowns of age.

What cruel answer have I heard!
And yet, by heaven, I love thee still:
Can aught be cruel from thy lip?
Yet say, how fell that bitter word
From lips which streams of sweetness fill,
Which nought but drops of honey sip?

Go boldly forth, my simple lay,
Whose accents flow with artless ease,
Like orient pearls at random strung:
Thy notes are sweet, the damsels say;
But O! far sweeter, if they please
The nymph for whom these notes are sung.

---

1   Jones is referring to the love story of Yusuf (Joseph) and Zulaika as ren-
    dered by Firdowsi.

2. From Sir William Jones, "Essay on the Poetry of the Eastern Nations," *Poems, consisting chiefly of translations from the Asiatick languages* (Oxford: Clarendon Press, 1772)

[This important essay argues in no uncertain terms that the poetry of Arabia and Persia was not only of great aesthetic value, but also had the potential to reinvigorate contemporary European poetry, which according to Jones was mired in classicism. As Michael J. Franklin has observed, "Jones's consideration of the influence of climate upon the fertility of the Oriental imagination, and his description of Persian and Arab cultures of poetry ... reflect an eighteenth-century Enlightenment relativism. In his emphasis on the primacy of the imagination, however, Jones is a true precursor of the Romantics."[1] The extract below is Jones's account of the urbane sophistication of Persian verse.]

The great empire, which we call PERSIA, is known to its natives by the name of *Iran*; since the word *Persia* belongs only to a particular province, the ancient *Persis*, and is very improperly applied by us to the whole kingdom: but, in compliance with the custom of our geographers, I shall give the name of *Persia* to that celebrated country, which lies on one side between the *Caspian* and *Indian* seas, and extends on the other from the mountains of *Candahar*, or *Paropamisus*, to the confluence of the rivers *Cyrus* and *Araxes*, containing about twenty degrees from south to north, and rather more from east to west.

In so vast a tract of land there must needs be a great variety of climates: the southern provinces are no less unhealthy and sultry, than those of the north are rude and unpleasant; but in the interior parts of the empire the air is mild and temperate, and, from the beginning of May to September, there is scarce a cloud to be seen in the sky: the remarkable calmness of the summer nights, and the wonderful splendour of the moon and stars in that country, often tempt the *Persians* to sleep on the tops of their houses, which are generally flat, where they cannot but observe the figures of the constellations, and the various appearances of the heavens; and this may in some measure account for the perpetual allusions of their poets, and rhetoricians, to the beauty of the heavenly bodies. We are apt to censure the oriental style for

---

1 Michael J. Franklin, *Sir William Jones: Selected Poetical and Prose Works* (Cardiff: U of Wales P, 1995), 319.

being so full of metaphors taken from the sun and moon: this is ascribed by some to the bad taste of the *Asiaticks; the works of the Persians*, says *M. de Voltaire, are like the titles of their kings, in which the sun and moon are often introduced:* but they do not r eflect, that every nation has a set of images, and expressions, peculiar to itself, which arise from the difference of its climate, manners, and history. There seems to be another reason for the frequent allusions of the *Persians* to the sun, which may, perhaps, be traced from the old language and popular religion of their country: thus *Mihridâd*, or Mithridates, signifies *the gift of the sun*, and answers to the *Theodorus* and *Diodati* of other nations. As to the titles of the *Eastern* monarchs, which seem, indeed, very extravagant to our ears, they are merely formal, and no less void of meaning than those of *European* princes, in which *serenity* and *highness* are often attributed to the most *gloomy* and *low-minded* of men.

The midland provinces of *Persia* abound in fruits and flowers of almost every kind, and, with proper culture, might be made the garden of Asia: they are not watered, indeed, by any considerable river, since the *Tigris* and *Euphrates*, the *Cyrus* and *Araxes*, the *Oxus*, and the five branches of the *Indus*, are at the farthest limits of the kingdom; but the natives, who have a turn for agriculture, supply that defect by artificial canals, which sufficiently temper the dryness of the soil; but in saying they *supply* that defect, I am falling into a common error, and representing the country, not as it *is* at present, but as it *was a* century ago; for a long series of civil wars and massacres have now destroyed the chief beauties of *Persia*, by stripping it of its most industrious inhabitants.

The same difference of climate, that affects the air and soil of this extensive country, gives a variety also to the persons and temper of its natives: in some provinces they have dark complexions, and harsh features; in others they are exquisitely fair, and well made; in some others, nervous and robust: but, the general character of the nation is that *softness*, and *love of pleasure*, that *indolence*, and *effeminacy*, which have made them an easy prey to all the western and northern swarms, that have from time to time invaded them. Yet they are not wholly void of martial spirit; and, if they are not naturally brave, they are at least extremely docile, and might, with proper discipline, be made excellent soldiers: but the greater part of them, in the short intervals of peace that they happen to enjoy, constantly sink into a state of inactivity, and pass their lives in a pleasurable, yet studious retirement; and this may be one reason, why *Persia* has produced more writers of every kind, and chiefly *poets*, than all *Europe* together, since their way of life gives them leisure to pursue those arts, which cannot be cultivated to advantage, without the greatest calmness and serenity of mind. There is a manuscript at *Oxford*,[1] containing *the lives of an hundred and thirty-five of the finest Persian poets*, most of whom left very ample collections of their poems behind them: but the versifiers, and *moderate poets*, if *Horace*[2] will allow any such men to exist, are without number in *Persia*.

This delicacy of their lives and sentiments has insensibly affected their language, and rendered it the softest, as it is one of the richest, in the world: it is not possible to convince the reader of this truth, by quoting a passage from a *Persian* poet *in European* characters; since the sweetness of sound cannot be determined by the sight, and many words, which are soft and musical in the mouth of a *Persian*, may appear harsh to our eyes, with a number of consonants and guturals: it may not, however, be absurd to set down in this place, an Ode of the poet *Hafez*, which, if it be not sufficient to prove the delicacy of his language, will at least show the liveliness of his poetry.

> *Ai bad nesîmi yârdari,*
> *Zan nefheï mushcbâr dari:*
> *Zinhar mecun diraz-desti!*
> *Ba turreï o che câr dari?*
> *Ai gul, to cujá wa ruyi zeibash.*
> *O taza, wa to kharbâr dari.*
> *Nerkes, to cujâ wa cheshmi mestesh?*
> *O serkhosh, wa to khumâr dari.*
> *Ai seru, to ba kaddi bulendesh,*
> *Der bagh che iytebâr dari?*
> *Ai akl, to ba wujûdi ishkesh*
> *Der dest che ikhtiyâr dari?*
> *Rihan, to cujâ wa khatti sebzesh?*
> *O mushc, wa to ghubâr dari.*
> *Ruzi bures bewasli Hafiz,*
> *Gher takati yntizâr dari.*

---

1   In Hyperoo Bodl. 128. There is a prefatory discourse to this curious work, which comprises the lives of ten *Arabian* poets. (Author's note)

2   Quintus Horatius Flaccus, (65-68 BCE), known in the English-speaking world as Horace, was the leading Roman lyric poet during the time of Augustus. Translations of his *Ars Poetica* were particularly important for theories of poetic taste in the eighteenth century.

That is, word for word, *O sweet gale, thou bearest the fragrant scent of my beloved; thence it is that thou hast this musky odour. Beware! do not steal: what hast thou to do with her tresses? O rose, what art thou, to be compared with her bright face? She is fresh, and thou art rough with thorns. O narcissus, what art thou in comparison of her languishing eye? Her eye is only sleepy, but thou art sick and faint. O pine, compared with her graceful stature, what honour hast thou in the garden? O wisdom, what wouldst thou choose, if to choose were in thy power, in perference to her love? O sweet basil, what art thou, to be compared with her fresh cheeks? They are perfect musk, but thou art soon withered. Come, my beloved, and charm Hafez with thy presence, if thou canst but stay with him for a single day.* This little song is not unlike a sonnet ascribed to Shakespeare, which deserves to be cited here, as a proof that the Eastern imagery is not so different from the *European* as we are apt to imagine.

> *The forward violet thus did I chide:*
> *"Sweet thief! whence didst thou steal thy sweet that smells,*
> *If not from my love's breath? The purple pride,*
> *Which on thy soft cheek for complexion dwells,*
> *In my love's veins thou hast too grossly dyed."*
> *The lily I condemned for thy hand,*
> *And buds of marjoram had stol'n thy hair;*
> *The roses fearfully on thorns did stand,*
> *One blushing shame, another white despair;*
> *A third, nor red nor white, had stol'n of both,*
> *And to his robb'ry had annex'd thy breath;*
> *But for his theft, in pride of all his growth,*
> *A vengeful canker eat him up to death.*
> *More flow'rs I noted, yet I none could see,*
> *But scent or colour it had stol'n from thee.*
> *Shakespeare's Poems*, p. 207[1]

The Persian style is said to be ridiculously bombast, and this fault is imputed to the slavish spirit of the nation, which is ever apt to magnify the objects that are placed above it: there are bad writers, to be sure, in every country, and as many in *Asia* as elsewhere; but if we take the pains to learn the *Persian* language, we shall find that those authors, who are generally esteemed in *Persia*, are neither slavish in their sentiments, nor ridiculous in their expressions: of which the following passage in a moral

---

1 Jones cites Shakespeare's Sonnet 99 in its entirety.

work of *Sadi*, entitled *Bostàn*, or, *The Garden*, will be a sufficient proof.[1]

[Here Jones cites Sadi in the original and renders it as follows:]

That is, I have heard that king Nushirvan, just before his death, spoke thus to his son Hormuz: Be a guardian, my son, to the poor and helpless; and be not confined in the chains of thy own indolence. No one can be at ease in thy dominion, while thou seekest only thy private rest, and sayest, It is enough. A wise man will not approve the shepherd, who sleeps, while the wolf is in the fold. Go, my son, protect thy weak and indigent people; since through them is a king raised to the diadem. The people are the root, and the king is the tree that grows from it; and the tree, O my son, derives its strength from the root.

Are these mean sentiments, delivered in pompous language? Are they not rather worthy of our most spirited writers? And do they not convey a fine lesson for a young king? Yet *Sadi's* poems are highly esteemed at *Constantinople*, and at *Ispahan;* though, a century or two ago, they would have been suppressed in *Europe*, for spreading with too strong a glare the light of liberty and reason.

As to the great Epick poem of *Ferdusi*, which was composed in the tenth century, it would require a very long treatise, to explain all its beauties with a minute exactness.[2] The whole collecion of that poet's works is called *Shahnâma*, and contains the history of *Persia*, from the earliest times to the invasion of the *Arabs*, in a series of very noble poems; the longest and most regular of which is an heroick poem of one great and interesting action, namely, *the delivery of Persia by Cyrus* from the oppressions of *Afrasiab*, king of the *Transoxan Tartary*, who being assisted by the emperors of *India* and *China*, together with all the dæmons, giants and enchanters of *Asia*, had carried his conquests very far, and become exceedingly formidable to the *Persians*. This poem is longer than the *Iliad*; the characters in it are various and striking; the figures bold and animated; and the diction every where sonorous, yet noble; polished, yet full of fire. A great profusion of learning has been thrown away by some cricks, in comparing

---

1 *The Gulistan* or *The Garden of Roses* was a major work by the Persian poet and Sufi thinker Sadi (1184-1291).

2 Ferdosi (935-1020) was the author of the *Shahnameh*, a highly revered epic based on ancient sources that interweaves Persian myths, legends, and historical events. It relates the history of Iran from the creation of the world to the Arab conquest in the seventh century.

Homer with the heroick poets, who have succeeded him; but it requires very little judgment to see, that no succeeding poet whatever can with any propriety be compared with *Homer:* that great father of the *Grecian* poetry and literature, had a genius too fruitful and comprehensive to let any of the striking parts of nature escape his observation; and the poets, who have followed him, have done little more than transcribe his images, and give a new dress to his thoughts. Whatever elegance and refinements, therefore, may have been introduced into the works of the moderns, the spirit and invention of *Homer* have ever continued without a rival: for which reasons I am far from pretending to assert that the poet *of Persia* is equal to that of *Greece;* but there is certainly a very great resemblance between the works of those extraordinary men: both drew their images from nature herself, without catching them only by reflection, and painting, in the manner of the modern poets, *the likeness of a likeness;* and both possessed, in an eminent degree, *that rich and creative invention, which is the very soul of poetry.*

3. From John Nott, *Select Odes from the Persian Poet Hafez, translated into English verse, with notes critical and explanatory* (London: T. Cadell, 1787)

[Nott's preface gives a useful summary of the guiding formal principles of the ghazal, the primary verse form practiced by both Hafiz and Abu Talib, and the difficulties they pose for the translator. Two samples of Nott's translations are provided not only as comparison texts for Jones's translation, but also as examples of what Nott styles their "philosophic voluptuousness."]

From the "Preface"

It was from this grammar [William Jones's *Persian Grammar*], studded with Oriental gems, that I was encouraged to enter seriously with my *munshi* on my scholastic exercises. Mr. Richardson, and the Count Reviski gave an ardour to the undertaking. And the very Odes I now venture to hold up for the instruction of others, are those by which I endeavoured to instruct myself, writing them over in the Taleek character.[1]

---

1   The *Taleek,* or depending character, in the Persian, is the common manuscript hand.... (Author's note)

I once thought of a greater regularity in my choice of the *Gazel*; and of compleating the second class of the *Divan* in English, in the same manner, and, were it possible, with the same spirit, as the Count Reviski[1] has compleated the first class in the Latin: but this I declined, from a belief that the present collection would be of more service to the studious beginner than the other. For instead of resting solely on my authority, he will now find (except in one or two instances, where there has been no other translation) how each *Gazel* has been understood, and managed by others. He will compare different ideas; and perceiving the progress of taste in each, he will at last insensibly acquire a taste and judgement of his own. The foundation will then be laid. The great difficulty is then over: and according as he has abilities or opportunity, he will add to the general stock of Oriental improvement.

I have just made use of two expressions, the *Gazel*, and the *Divan*, which come in this place necessarily to be explained; but it is an explanation that will not detain us long.

> *Bonas in partes, lector, accipias velim;*
> *Sic ista tibi rependet brevitas gratiam.*[2]

And here we will first observe, that the *Gazel* or Persian Ode, may be divided into its subject, and its construction.

Its subject is generally of a festive nature; "dropping odours, dropping wine!" The tenets it inculcates are those of the philosophic voluptuary: and it concludes, from the shortness of human life, that we should not let a flower of it steal by us unnoticed and unenjoyed.

Whether Anacreon[3] borrowed the gaiety of his Odes from the Persian *Gazel*, or whether Hafez enriched his native language by an imitation of the Teian bard, I will not venture to determine. The similarity of sentiment is oftentimes wonderful. And perhaps

---

1 The Hungarian orientalist and diplomat Count Károly Reviczky (1736–93) was a leading authority on Hafiz. His *Traité sur la poësie orientale* (1770) was a key text for both John Nott and Sir William Jones and contained French verse translations of ten of Hafiz's poems.

2 Nott is misquoting Phaedrus, *Fables* II.11–12. P.F. Widdows translates these lines as "I count on you, Reader, for your kind indulgence/And may conciseness compensate for the license you allow me." In *The Fables of Phaedrus* (Austin: U of Texas P, 1992), 39.

3 Anacreon (570–488 BCE), a Greek lyric poet, who like Hafiz was famous for his drinking songs and hymns.

it may be said of both; that they wrote not so much to the under-standing as to the heart.

With respect to the construction of the *Gazel*, it is altogether unique. Its first rule is, that it must be composed of distichs. Its second, that the lines of the first distich must not only rhyme, but that the same rhymes shall be continued in the last line of every succeeding distich; the first line of each standing alone, and seemingly independent of the versification.

As to the number of distichs which are necessary to compleat a true *Gazel*, it is on all hands agreed, that there should be not fewer than five. Meninski[1] extends them to eleven, Reviski to thirteen, and Herbelot[2] to eighteen; adding that whenever a poem has more distichs than these it becomes the *Kessideh* or Elegy.

The last distich of the *Gazel* is called the royal distich: in which, it is observable, that the bard constantly introduces himself, not without some flattery or compliment. The Greek, and especially the Roman poets, delighted in the same kind of self applause. But it was left for Hafez to praise with delicacy, and to commend without exaggeration. The Italians, who have a strange mixture of ancient literature with modern tinsel and conceit, do also con-clude most of their amatory verses in a similar manner. I need but mention the Canzoni of Petrarch;[3] which, in this instance at least, is an exact imitation of the Persian *Gazel*.

It must be confessed there is one circumstance in the *Gazel*, which I had much rather attempt to account for, than to excuse; and that is, its apparent incongruity, or want of union.

The progress of learning, especially in our nation, has been such, that there are few who read, who are not masters likewise of the first principles of criticism. Perspicuity and method are as essential to the art of pleasing in these days as wit and sentiment. But the *Gazel* is totally unconnected; and its distichs are an assemblage of bold and scattered images, which appear

---

1 Francois Meninski à Mesgnien (1623-89), Polish orientalist and author of *Thesaurus Linguarum Orientalium* (1680).

2 Barthélemy d'Herbelot de Molainville (1625-95), French orientalist who compiled the *Bibliothèque orientale* (1697), one of the most compre-hensive works on Asian languages.

3 Francesco Petrarca (1304-74), known in English as Petrarch, was an Italian scholar, poet, and one of the earliest Renaissance humanists. His collection of lyrics addressed to Laura, *Il Canzoniere*, became the model for much European love poetry.

"Like Orient pearls at random strung."[1]

I have no doubt but this may arise, in some measure, from the peculiar disadvantage under which the *Gazel* labours. For when one rhyme is necessarily to be continued throughout each distich; so that in a *Gazel* of eighteen distichs you will necessarily have nineteen similar terminations; the fettered bard, instead of "darting from heaven to earth, from earth to heaven," must be content to set down a patient selector of mere words; and I confess neither French poetry, nor French criticism have yet convinced me that there is any merit in taking up a burden, which is as unwieldy as it is unnatural. But beside this, I am still to be informed of the language, which is rich and copious enough to afford sufficient variations for only five distichs upon every separate letter of its alphabet.

This is so evidently the case, and so difficult is it, allowing every thing for national modes and customs, to reconcile it to common sense, that I am apt to think our knowledge of the *Gazel* is still very incompleat. How happy shall I esteem myself if some future inquirer, led by these remarks, shall at length rescue Persian taste from that cloud of doubt which here evidently rests upon it.

To these observations on the *Gazel*, I beg leave briefly to subjoin that it is a collection of such *Gazels* duly terminating, as above-mentioned, in some one letter, that is called a *Divan*. But the great and more perfect *Divan* is, when the poet, as Hafez did, shall have regularly gone through each letter of the Persian alphabet. It may not be amiss to add, for further information to the learner, that any set of poems, and even prose collections, have now and then been styled *Divans*: but this is founded on no good authority whatever: nor can I agree with a learned Orientalist, who tells us, that a *Divan* was properly applied to such a collection of an author's works as were published after his death.....

[Nott goes on to explain that his translations do not attempt to follow exact metrical scansion or to replicate the sound of the Persian language.]

In compliance with Oriental usage, I have given to my book one of those sportive titles, of which the Persians are so fond; calling it out of compliment to my favourite bard, who particularly mentions this gay child of summer's velvet breeze, *Laléhzar*, or *The Bed of Tulips*.

---

1 Nott is quoting Sir William Jones, "A Persian Song of Hafiz," 1.51.

A poet of our own has likewise noticed the same flower with that minute elegance, which is the leading feature of his descriptive abilities.

> Then comes the Tulip race: where beauty plays
> Her idle freaks; from family diffused
> To family, as flies the father-dust,
> The varied colours run: and while they break
> On the charmed eye, th'exulting florist marks
> With secret pride the wonders of his hand.
> Thompson's "Spring"[1]

I am aware that no authority will be of itself sufficient to extort approbation from the English reader. He must be convinced from his own reflections. And if, with more solid judgement than vivacity, he has not suffered himself to be caught by a poetic wildness of words, it is in vain that I shall endeavour to defend one fanciful expression by another; it will little avail to inform him, that almost all Persian productions are named after some beautiful or striking subject....

He will call this Oriental rhapsody and conceit. Be it so. It is a playfulness, not only into which the chaster Greeks have also fallen; but let him remember, that we have even in our own language a collection of verses named the *Garland*; and another compilation, which I recollect somewhere to have seen, under the title of the *Amaranth*.

I should not have so much pressed this little circumstance, if it did not lead to a necessary observation on Eastern poetry in general; which is, that we should make all liberal allowance for that singularity of expression, which every nation justly claims to itself as its distinguishing privilege; and not judging of the glow of Eastern dialogue by the standard of our colder feelings and ideas, that we should suppose it possible for their phrases and metaphors to be highly just and beautiful, however they may differ from the more exact rules of English criticism and taste.

---

1   James Thomson's (1700-48) *The Seasons* was published in its entirety in 1730 and quickly became one of the most widely admired poems of the eighteenth century. Throughout the poem he adapted Milton's style to a meditation on the forces of nature. The quoted lines are from "Spring," ll. 539-44.

Ode I

Unless my fair-one's cheek be near
To tinge thee with superior red,
How vain, O rose, thy boasted bloom!
Unless, prime season of the year,
The grape's rich streams be round thee shed,
Alike how vain is thy perfume!

In shrubs which skirt the scented mead,
Or garden's walk embroider'd gay,
Can the sweet voice of joy be found—
Unless, to harmonize the shade,
The nightingale's soft-warbled lay
Pour melting melody around?

Thou flow'ret trembling to the gale,
And thou, O cypress! waving slow
Thy green head in the summer air;
Say—What will all your charms avail,
If the dear maid, whose blushes glow
Like living tulips, be not there?

The nymph who tempts with honied lip,
With cheeks that shame the vernal rose,
In rapture we can ne'er behold;
Unless with kisses fond we sip
The luscious balm that lip bestows—
Unless our arms that nymph enfold.

Sweet is the rose-empurpled bow'r,
And sweet the juice distilling bright
In rills of crimson from the vine:
But are they sweet, or have they pow'r
To bathe the senses in delight,
Where beauty's presence does not shine?

Ode II[1]

Hither, boy, a goblet bring,
Be it of wine's ruby spring!
Bring me one, bring me two;
Nought but purest wine will do!

It is wine, boy, that can save
Even lovers from the grave;
Old, and young alike will say—
'Tis the balm that makes us gay.

Wine's the sun:[2] the moon, sweet soul!
We will call the waning bowl:
Bring the sun,[3] and bring him soon,
To the bosom of the moon!

Dash us with this liquid fire,
It will thoughts divine inspire;
And, by nature taught to glow,
Let it like the waters flow!

If the rose should fade, do you
Bid it chearfully adieu:

---

1 In this ode, which is truly bacchanalian, and might alone entitle our
   poet to the appellation of the Anacreon of Persia, Hafez concludes each
   distich in the original by calling for wine: but this poetical burden, so
   peculiar to the genius of the Persian distich, I have not ventured to
   translate. (Original note)
2 If the elegant author of the following stanza had not Hafez in view, when
   it was written, he was at least animated with a truly Hafezian spirit:

   > This bottle's the sun of our table
   > His beams are rosy wine:
   > We, planets who are not able,
   > Without his light, to shine.
   > Songs, in Sheridan's *Duenna* (Original note)

   Nott is referring to the opening "Glee and Chorus" from Act III, scene
   5 of Richard Brinsley Sheridan's ballad opera *The Duenna* (1775).
3 The original only says: "in the midst of the moon place the sun." This
   Oriental metaphor, when simplified, means nothing more than, pour the
   wine into the cup." (Original note)

Like rose-water to each guest
Bring thy wine, and make us blest.

If the nightingale's rich throat
Cease the music of its note;
It is fit, boy, thou shouldst bring
Cups that will with musick ring.

Be not sad, whatever change
O'er the busy world may range;
Harp and lute together bring,
Sweetly mingling string with string!

My bright maid,[1] unless it be
In some dream, I cannot see:
Bring the draught, that will disclose
Whence it was sleep first arose!

---

1 *My bright maid, &c.*] By the words *wesel o* the poet certainly implies the
possession of his mistress, and not the pleasures of wine, as some commentators imagine. Be this as it may: the occurrence of the word *wesel*,
which signifies *enjoyment*, I believe, in almost all its senses, but more particularly in an amatorial one, induces me to make a criticism, which
although not pertinent to this ode in particular, is yet highly so to the
asiatic languages in general. Doctor Johnson, in his *Miscellaneous Observations on Mackbeth*, is at great pains to derive the old English words *was-
sailer*, and *wassail*, from *was-heiler*, or a *wisher of health*; and the liquor
(says he) was termed *was-heil*, because *health* was so often *wished over it*:
whereas, the words appear to me of a far different, and more evident der-
ivation. So, in his Dictionary, he supposes *gules*, the colour *red* in her-
aldry, to be derived from a French word, *geule*, the *throat*; perhaps
because the *throats* of most animals are red withinside; not knowing, I
imagine, that *gul*, in the Persian, implied a *rose*; which clearly proves the
origin of the heraldic term *gules*: for doubtless many of our words are
deduced from the Persian and Arabic; the Crusades communicating to
the Western world much of the language, and fiction of the East. The
liquour we call *shrub*, is most probably from *shrab*, *wine*: but it is needless
to enumerate the various examples of this kind that may be exhibited.
    I trust, none will construe these observations as invidious, or as dero-
gating from the merits of a scholar, whom his country shall long revere;
he gave stability to the language, he adorned it with exemplary virtues;
they only strengthen that regret I expressed in my preface, that the study
of the oriental languages is not more generally, and more liberally prosecuted. Mr. Warton, in his ingenious *History of English Poetry*, throws great
light on the introduction of Eastern learning into Europe. (Original note)

Should it chance o'erpow'r my mind,
Where's the remedy I find?
'Tis in wine: then, boy, supply
Wine, till all my senses die!

Unto Hafez, boy, do you
Instant bring a cup or two:
Bring them; for the wine shall flow[1]
Whether it be law, or no!

4. Sir William Jones, "The Sixth Discourse; on the Persians, delivered 19 February, 1789," *Asiatick Researches; or, transactions of the Society, instituted in Bengal, for inquiring into the history and antiquities, the arts, sciences and literature of Asia* vol. II (Calcutta: Manuel Cantopher, 1790) 43–66

[This address extrapolates from and consolidates Jones's monumental Indo-European thesis first articulated in "The Third Anniversary Discourse, on the Hindus" (1786) in which he argued that the classical languages of Europe, the Near East, and India derived from a common linguistic source. The method is deeply antiquarian, yet its historical, comparative, and structural focus had a deep impact on modern comparative philology. Recent scholarship has also demonstrated the degree to which Jones's Indo-European thesis was indebted to Parsi scholars such as Bahman Yazdi and Mir Muhammad Husain Isfahani. The former worked with Jones in the mid-1780s on the translation of key legal documents and the latter, like Abu Talib, actually travelled to England and France in 1775. It is worth considering how Jones deploys Bahman Yazdi's knowledge in this essay in light of Abu Talib's scepticism regarding Jones's scholarship.]

Gentlemen,

I turn with delight from the vast mountains and barren deserts of *Túràn*, over which we travelled last year with no perfect knowl-

---

1 *For the wine shall flow, &c.*] How far the doctrine of Mahomet may be infringed by these expressions, let the friends of our poet determine, who counted for his being a good mussulman: it is certain they add a beauty to his poetry, for which the bon-vivant will always express himself his debtor. (Original Note)

edge of our course, and request you now to accompany me on a literary journey through one of the most celebrated and most beautiful countries in the world; a country, the history and languages of which, both ancient and modern, I have long attentively studied, and on which I may without arrogance promise you more positive information, than I could possibly procure on a nation so disunited and so unlettered as the *Tartars*: I mean that, which *Europeans* improperly call *Persia*, the name of a single province being applied to the whole Empire of *Iràn*, as it is correctly denominated by the present natives of it, and by all the learned *Muselmans*, who reside in these *British* territories.[1] To give you an idea of its largest boundaries, agreeably to my former mode of describing *India, Arabia*, and *Tartary*, between which it lies, let us begin with the source of the great *Assyrian* stream, *Euphrates*, (as the *Greeks*, according to their custom, were pleased to miscall the *Foràt*) and thence descend to its mouth in the Green Sea, or *Persian* Gulf, including in our line some considerable districts and towns on both sides the river; then coasting *Persia*, properly so named, and other *Iranian* provinces, we come to the delta of the *Sindhu* or *Indus;* whence ascending to the mountains of *Cashghar*, we discover its fountains and those of the *Faihùn*, down which we are conducted to the *Caspian*, which formerly perhaps it entered, though it lose itself now in the sands and lakes of *Khwárezm:* we next are led from the sea of *Khozar*, by the banks of the *Cur*, or *Cyrus*, and along the *Caucasean* ridges, to the shore of the *Euxine*, and thence, by the several *Grecian* seas, to the point, whence we took our departure, at no considerable distance from the *Mediterranean*.....

It may seem strange, that the ancient history of so distinguished an Empire should be yet so imperfectly known; but very satisfactory reasons may be assigned for our ignorance of it: the principal of them are the superficial knowledge of the *Greeks* and *Jews*, and the loss of *Persian* archives or historical compositions. That the *Grecian* writers, before XENOPHON, had *no* acquaintance with *Persia*, and that *all* their accounts of it are *wholly* fabulous, is a paradox too extravagant to be seriously maintained;[2] but their connection with it in war or peace had, indeed, been

---

1 Jones is referring to Muslims residing in Bengal.
2 In a characteristic gesture, Jones takes the Greek historian Xenophon's account of Cyrus's expedition against the Persian empire in his landmark history the *Anabasis* and collates it with similar events and personages in Ferdosi's epic poem of Iranian history, the *Shahnameh*.

generally confined to bordering kingdoms under feudatory princes; and the first *Persian* Emperor, whose life and character they seem to have known with tolerable accuracy, was the great CYRUS,[1] whom I call, without fear of contradiction, CATKHOSRAU; for I shall then only doubt that the KHOSRAU of FIRDAUSI[2] was the CYRUS of the first *Greek* historian, and the Hero of the oldest political and moral romance, when I doubt that Louis *Quatorze* and LEWIS *the Four-teenth* were one and the same *French* King: it is utterly incredible, that two different princes of Persia should each have been born in a foreign and hostile territory; should each have been doomed to death in his infancy by his maternal grandfather in conse-quence of portentous dreams, real or invented; should each have been saved by the remorse of his destined murderer, and should each, after a similar education among herdsmen, as the son of a herdsman, have found means to revisit his paternal kingdom, and having delivered it, after a long and triumphant war, from the tyrant, who had invaded it, should have restored it to the summit of power and magnificence. Whether so romantick a story, which is the subject of an Epick Poem,[3] as majestick and entire as the *Iliad*, be historically true, we may feel perhaps an inclination to doubt; but it cannot with reason be denied, that the outline of it related to a single Hero, whom the *Asiaticks*, conversing with the father of *European* history, described according to their popular traditions by his true name, which the *Greek* alphabet could not express: nor will a difference of names affect the question; since the *Greeks* had little regard for truth, which they *sacrificed* will-ingly *to the Graces* of their language, and the nicety of their ears; and, if they could render foreign words melodious, they were never solicitous to make them exact; hence they probably formed CAMBYSES from CA'MBAKHSH, or *Granting desires*, a title rather than a name, and XERXES from SHI'RU'YI, a Prince and warriour in the *Sháhnámah*, or from SHI'RSHA'H, which might also have been a title; for the *Asiatick* Princes have con-stantly assumed new titles or epithets at different periods of their lives, or on different occasions; a custom, which we have seen

---

1 Cyrus II of Persia (c. 590 BCE or 576-August 529 BCE or 530 BCE) was the founder of the Persian Empire under the Achaemenid dynasty.
2 Hakim Abu l-Qasim Firdawsi Tusi, or Ferdowsi, (935-1020) was a highly revered Persian poet. He was the author of the *Shahnameh*, the national epic of the Persian-speaking world.
3 The *Shahnameh* by Ferdowsi.

prevalent in our own times both in *Iràn* and *Hindustán,* and which has been a source of great confusion even in the scriptural accounts of *Babylonian* occurrences: both *Greeks* and *Jews* have in fact accommodated *Persian* names to their own articulation; and both seem to have disregarded the native literature of *Iràn,* without which they could at most attain a general and imperfect knowledge of the country. As to the *Persians* themselves, who were contemporary with the *Jews* and *Greeks,* they must have been acquainted with the history of their own times, and with the traditional accounts of past ages; but for a reason, which will presently appear, they chose to consider CAYU'MERS as the founder of the empire; and, in the numerous distractions, which followed the overthrow of DA'RA', especially in the great revolution on the defeat of YEZDEGIRD,[1] their civil histories were lost, as those of *India* have unhappily been, from the solicitude of the priests, the only depositaries of their learning, to preserve their books of law and religion at the expense of all others: hence it has happened, that nothing remains of genuine *Persian* history before the dynasty of SA'SA'N,[2] except a few rustick traditions and fables, which furnished materials for the *Sháhnámah,* and which are still supposed to exist in the *Pahlaví* language. The annals of the *Píshdádi,* or *Assyrian,* race must be considered as dark and fabulous; and those of the *Cayáni* family, or the *Medes* and *Persians,* as heroick and poetical; though the lunar eclipses, said to be mentioned by PTOLEMY,[3] fix the time of GUSH-TASP, the prince, by whom ZERA'TUSHT[4] was protected: of the *Parthian* kings descended from ARSHAC or ARSACES, we know little more than the names; but the *Sásáni's* had so long an

---

1 See n. 2.
2 The Sassanid Empire or Sassanian Empire is the name used for the fourth Iranian dynasty, and the second Persian Empire (226-651). The Sassanid dynasty was founded by Ardashir I after defeating the last Arsacid king, Artabanus IV and ended when the last Sassanid Shahan-shah (King of Kings), Yazdegerd III (632-651), lost a 14-year struggle to drive out the early Caliphate, the first of the Islamic empires. In many ways the Sassanid period witnessed the highest achievement of Persian civilization, and constituted the last great Iranian Empire before the Muslim conquest and the ensuing adoption of Islam.
3 Ptolemy (c. 90-c. 168) was a geographer, astronomer, and astrologer who lived in the Hellenized culture of Roman Egypt.
4 Zarathustra or Zoroaster was an ancient Iranian prophet and the founder of Zoroastrianism, the religion of the Sassanid empire.

intercourse with the Emperors of *Rome* and *Byzantium*, that the period of their dominion may be called an historical age. In attempting to ascertain the beginning of the *Assyrian* empire, we are deluded, as in a thousand instances, by names arbitrarily imposed: it had been *settled* by chronologers, that the first monarchy established in Persia was the *Assyrian*; and NEWTON,[1] finding some of opinion, that it rose in the first century after the Flood, but unable by his own calculations to extend it farther back than *seven hundred and ninety* years before CHRIST, rejected part of the old system and adopted the rest of it; concluding, that the *Assyrian* Monarchs began to reign about two hundred years after SOLOMON, and that, in all preceding ages, the government of *Iràn* had been divided into several petty states and principalities. Of this opinion I confess myself to have been; when, disregarding the wild chronology of the *Muselmàns* and *Gabrs*, I had allowed the utmost natural duration to the reigns of eleven *Pishdádi* kings, without being able to add more than a hundred years to NEWTON'S computation. It seemed, indeed, unaccountably strange, that, although ABRAHAM had found a regular monarchy in *Egypt*, although the kingdom of *Yemen* had just pretensions to very high antiquity, although the *Chinese*, in the twelfth century before our era, had made approaches at least to the present form of their extensive dominion, and although we can hardly suppose the first *Indian* monarchs to have reigned less than three thousand years ago, yet *Persia*, the most delightful, the most compact, the most desirable country of them all, should have remained for so many ages unsettled and disunited. A fortunate discovery, for which I was first indebted to *Mir* MUHAMMED HUSAIN,[2] one of the most intelligent *Muselmàns* in India, has at once dissipated the cloud, and cast a gleam of light on the primeval history of *Iràn* and of the human race, of which I had long despaired, and which could hardly have dawned from any other quarter.

---

1 Jones is referring to Isaac Newton's (1642-1727) largely heretical theological tracts. The most likely source here is *Chronology of Ancient Kingdoms Amended* which was published shortly after Newton's death.

2 Mir Muhammad Husain (d. 1790) travelled to England and France from 1775 to 1778 largely in search of scientific knowledge. After his return from Europe he circulated in the same scholarly circles as Abu Talib and socialized with British orientalists and administrators of the East India Company. At the behest of Warren Hastings, he collaborated with other local scholars on the translation of the *Hidayah*, the book of Muslim jurisprudence, from Arabic into Persian.

The rare and interesting tract *on twelve different religions*, entitled the *Dabistàn*,[1] and composed by a *Mohammedan* traveller, a native of *Cashmìr*, named MOHSAN, but distinguished by the assumed surname of FA'NI', or *Perishable*, begins with a wonderfully curious chapter on the religion of HU'SHANG, which was long anterior to that of ZERA'TUSHT, but had continued to be secretly professed by many learned *Persians* even to the author's time; and several of the most eminent of them, dissenting in many points from the *Gabrs*, and persecuted by the ruling powers of their country, had retired to *India*; where they compiled a number of books, now extremely scarce, which MOHSAN had perused, and with the writers of which, or with many of them, he had contracted an intimate friendship: from them he learned, that a powerful monarchy had been established for ages in *Iràn* before the accession of CAYU'MERS, that it was called the *Mahábádian* dynasty, for a reason which will soon be mentioned, and that many princes, of whom seven or eight only are named in the *Dabistàn*, and among them MAHBUL, or MAHA'BELI, had raised their empire to the zenith of human glory. If we can rely on this evidence, which to me appears unexceptionable, the *Iranian* monarchy must have been the oldest in the world; but it will remain dubious, to which of the three stocks, *Hindu, Arabian*, or *Tartar*, the first Kings of *Iràn* belonged, or whether they sprang from a *fourth* race distinct from any of the others; and these are questions, which we shall be able, I imagine, to answer precisely, when we have carefully inquired into the *languages* and *letters*, *religion* and *philosophy*, and incidentally into the *arts* and *sciences*, of the ancient Persians.

I. In the new and important remarks, which I am going to offer, on the ancient *languages* and *characters* of *Iràn*, I am sensible, that you must give me credit for many assertions, which on this occasion it is impossible to prove; for I should ill deserve your indulgent attention, if I were to abuse it by repeating a dry

---

1   According to Mohamad Tavakoli-Targhi, Jones was introduced to the *Dabistan-i Mazahib* by Mir Muhammad Husayn Isfahani: "Dabistan and other 'dasatiri texts' provided a mythistorical narrative inaugurated by the pre-Adamite Mahabad, who was supposed to have initiated a great cycle of human existence well before Adam.... This proto-nationalist historical imagination provided Jones with necessary 'evidence' for establishing the origins of languages and nations.... The historical narrative of *Dabistan* ... enabled Jones ... to imagine both linguistic and racial diversification of human societies." (28-29)

list of detached words, and presenting you with a vocabulary instead of a dissertation; but, since I have no system to maintain, and have not suffered imagination to delude my judgement; since I have habituated myself to form opinions of men and things from *evidence*, which is the only solid basis of *civil*, as *experiment* is of *natural*, knowledge; and since I have maturely considered the questions which I mean to discuss; you will not, I am persuaded, suspect my testimony, or think that I go too far, when I assure you, that I will assert nothing positively, which I am not able satisfactorily to demonstrate. When MUHAMMED was born, and ANUSHI'RAVA'N, whom he calls *the Just King*, sat on the throne of *Persia*, two languages appear to have been generally prevalent in the great empire of *Iràn;* that of the *Court*, thence named *Derì*, which was only a refined and elegant dialect of the *Pàrsì*, so called from the province, of which *Shìràz* is now the capital, and that of the learned, in which most books were composed, and which had the name of *Pahlavì*, either from the *heroes*, who spoke it in former times, or from *Pahlu*, a tract of land, which included, we are told, some considerable cities of *Iràk*: the ruder dialects of both were, and, I believe, still are, spoken by the rusticks in several provinces; and in many of them, as *Heràt, Zàbul, Sifuàn* and others, distinct idioms were vernacular, as it happens in every kingdom of great extent. Besides the *Pàrsì* and *Pahlavì*, a very ancient and abstruse tongue was known to the priests and philosophers, called *the language of the Zend*, because a book on religious and moral duties, which they held sacred, and which bore that name, had been written in it; while the *Pàzend, or* comment on that work, was composed in *Pahlavì*, as a more popular idiom; but a learned follower of ZERA'-TUSHT, named BAHMAN,[1] who lately died at *Calcutta*, where he had lived with me as a *Persian* reader about three years, assured me, that the *letters* of his prophet's book were properly called *Zend*, and the *language, Avestà*, as the words of the *Védas* are *Sanscrit*, and the characters, *Nàgarì;* or as the old *Saga's* and poems of *Iseland* were expressed in *Runick* letters; let us however, in compliance with custom, give the name of *Zend* to the sacred language of *Persia*, until we can find, as we shall very soon, a

---

1 Bahman Yazdi was one of a large number of scholars who assisted Jones in his studies and whose contributions to orientalist learning have been consistently downplayed or ignored. For an extremely important discussion of these forgotten figures and of Jones's claim to philological originality see Tavakoli-Targhi, 18-34.

fitter appellation for it. The *Zend* and the old *Pahlavì* are almost extinct in *Iràn;* for among six or seven thousand *Gabrs*, who reside chiefly at *Yezd*, and in *Cirmàn*, there are very few, who can read *Pahlavì*, and scarce any, who even boast of knowing the *Zend;* while the *Pársì*, which remains almost pure in the *Sháh-námah*, has now become by the intermixture of numberless *Arabick* words, and many imperceptible changes, a new language exquisitely polished by a series of fine writers in prose and verse, and analogous to the different idioms gradually formed in *Europe* after the subversion of the Roman empire: but with modern *Persian* we have no concern in our present inquiry, which I confine to the ages, that preceded the *Mohammedan* conquest. Having twice read the works of FIRDAUSI with great attention, since I applied myself to the study of old *Indian* literature, I can assure you with confidence, that hundreds of *Pársì* nouns are pure *Sanscrit*, with no other change than such as may be observed in the numerous *bháshà's* or vernacular dialects, of *India;* that very many *Persian* imperatives are the roots of *Sanscrit* verbs; and that even the moods and tenses of the *Persian* verb substantive, which is the model of all the rest, are deducible from the *Sanscrit* by an easy and clear analogy: we may hence conclude, that the *Pársì* was derived, like the various *Indian* dialects, from the language of the *Bráhmans;* and I must add, that in the pure *Persian* I find no trace of any *Arabian* tongue, except what proceeded from the known intercourse between the *Persians* and *Arabs*, especially in the time of BAHRA'M, who was educated in *Arabia*, and whose *Arabick* verses are still extant, together with his heroick line in *Deri*, which many suppose to be the first attempt at *Persian* versification in *Arabian* metre: but, without having recourse to other arguments, *the composition of words*, in which the genius of the *Persian* delights, and which that of the *Arabick* abhors, is a decisive proof, that the *Pársì* sprang from an *Indian*, and not from an *Arabian*, stock. Considering languages as mere instruments of knowledge, and having strong reasons to doubt the existence of genuine books in *Zend* or *Pahlavì* (especially since the well-informed author of the *Dabistàn* affirms the work of ZERA'TUSHT to have been lost, and its place supplied by a recent compilation) I had no inducement, though I had an opportunity, to learn what remains of those ancient languages; but I often conversed on them with my friend BAHMAN, and both of us were convinced after full consideration, that the *Zend* bore a strong resemblance to *Sanscrit*, and the *Pahlavì* to *Arabick*. He had at my request translated into *Pahlavì* the fine inscription, exhibited in the *Gulistàn,*[1] on the diadem of Cyrus; and I had the patience to read the list of words from the *Pázend* in the appendix to the *Farhangi Jehángìrì*: this examination gave me perfect conviction, that the *Pahlavì* was a dialect of the Chaldaick; and of this curious fact I will exhibit a short proof. By the nature of the *Chaldean* tongue most words ended in the first long vowel like, *sbemiá,* heaven; and that very word, unaltered in a single letter, we find in the *Pàzend,* together with *lailià,* night, *meyà,* water, *nirà,* fire, *matrà,* rain, and a multitude of others, all *Arabick* or *Hebrew* with a *Chaldean* termination: so *zamar,* by a beautiful metaphor from *pruning trees,* means in *Hebrew* to *compose verses,* and thence, by an easy transition, to *sing* them; and in *Pahlavì* we see the verb *zamrúniten,* to *sing,* with its forms *zamrúnemi,* I *sing,* and *zamrúníd,* he *sang;* the verbal terminations of the *Persian* being added to the *Chaldaick* root. Now all those words are integral parts of the language, not adventitious to it like the *Arabick* nouns and verbals engrafted on modern *Persian;* and this distinction convinces me, that the dialect of the *Gabrs,* which they pretend to be that of ZERA'TUSHT, and of which BAHMAN gave me a variety of written specimens, is a late invention of their priests, or subsequent at least to the *Muselman* invasion; for, although it may be possible, that a few of their sacred books were preserved, as he used to assert, in sheets of lead or copper at the bottom of wells near *Yezd,* yet as the conquerors had not only a spiritual, but a political, interest in persecuting a warlike, robust, and indignant race of irreconcilable conquered subjects, a long time must have elapsed, before the hidden scriptures could have been safely brought to light, and few, who could perfectly understand them, must have remained; but, as they continued to profess among themselves the religion of their forefathers, it became expedient for the *Múbeds* to supply the lost or mutilated works of their legislator by new compositions, partly from their imperfect recollection, and partly from such moral and religious knowledge, as they gleaned, most probably, among the *Christians,* with whom they had an intercourse. One rule we may fairly establish in deciding the question, whether the books of the modern *Gabrs* were anterior to the invasion of the *Arabs*: when an *Arabick* noun occurs in them changed only by the spirit of the *Chaldean* idiom, as *wertà,* for

---

1   *The Gulistan* or *The Garden of Roses* was a major work by the Persian poet and Sufi thinker Sadi (1184-1291).

werd, a rose, *dabà*, for *dbahab*, gold, or *demàn*, for *zemàn*, time, we may allow it to have been ancient *Pahlaví;* but, when we meet with verbal nouns or infinitives, evidently formed by the rules of *Arabian* grammar, we may be sure, that the phrases, in which they occur, are comparatively modern; and not a single passage, which BAHMAN produced from the books of his religion, would abide this test.

We come now to the language of the *Zend;* and here I must impart a discovery, which I lately made, and from which we may draw the most interesting consequences. M. ANQUETIL,[1] who had the merit of undertaking a voyage to *India,* in his earliest youth, with no other view than to recover the writings of ZERA'-TUSHT, and who would have acquired a brilliant reputation in *France,* if he had not sullied it by his immoderate vanity and virulence of temper, which alienated the good will even of his own countrymen, has exhibited in his work, entitled *Zendávestà,* two vocabularies in *Zend* and *Pahlaví,* which he had found in an approved collection of *Rawáyát,* or *Traditional Pieces,* in modern *Persian:* of his *Pahlaví* no more needs be said, than that it strongly confirms my opinion concerning the *Chaldaick* origin of that language; but, when I perused the *Zend* glossary, I was inexpressibly surprized to find, that six or seven words in ten were pure *Sanscrit,* and even some of their inflexions formed by the rules of the *Vyácaran;* as *yushmácam,* the genitive plural of *yushmad.* Now M. ANQUETIL most certainly, and the *Persian* compiler most probably, had no knowledge of *Sanscrit;* and could not, therefore, have invented a list of *Sanscrit* words: it is, therefore, an authentick list

---

1   From as early as 1771, Jones had been involved in a controversy with the French orientalist scholar Abraham-Hyacinth Anquetil-Du Perron (1731-1805) regarding the origins of the Persian language. While in India Anquetil-Du Perron was tutored by Parsi priests who translated the *Avesta,* the sacred texts of Zoroastrianism, from the Avestan language into Persian for him. In 1771, the same year that Jones brought out his *A Grammar of the Persian Language,* he in turn published the *Avesta* in a French translation which marked the introduction of Zoroastrian thought into Europe. Because Jones's text appeared not to be aware of either the Avestan or the Pahlavi languages, Jones and other scholars attempted to discredit Anquetil-Du Perron. In this essay, Jones attempts to subsume the controversy into his thesis regarding the foundational status of Sanskrit. For a brief account of the controversy see Arthur D. Waley, "Anquetil Duperron and Sir William Jones," *History Today* 2 (January 1952): 23-33.

of Zend words, which had been preserved in books or by tradition; and it follows, that the language of the *Zend* was at least a dialect of the *Sanscrit*, approaching perhaps as nearly to it as the *Prácrit*, or other popular idioms, which we know to have been spoken in *India* two thousand years ago. From all these facts it is a necessary consequence, that the oldest discoverable languages of *Persia* were *Chaldaick* and *Sanscrit;* and that, when they had ceased to be vernacular, the *Pahlavi* and *Zend* were deduced from them respectively, and the *Pársì* either from the *Zend,* or immediately from the dialect of the *Bráhmans;* but all had perhaps a mixture of *Tartarian;* for the best lexicographers assert, that numberless words in ancient *Persian* are taken from the language of the *Cimmerians*, or the *Tartars* of *Kipchák;* so that the *three* families, whose lineage we have examined in former discourses, had left visible traces of themselves in *Irán,* long before the *Tartars* and *Arabs* had rushed from their deserts, and returned to that very country, from which in all probability they originally proceeded, and which the *Hindus* had abandoned in an earlier age, with positive commands from their legislators to revisit it no more. I close this head with observing, that no supposition of a mere political or commercial intercourse between the different nations will account for the *Sanscrit* and *Chaldaick* words, which we find in the old *Persian* tongues; because they are, in the first place, too numerous to have been introduced by such means, and, secondly, are not the names of exotick animals, commodities, or arts, but those of material elements, parts of the body, natural objects and relations, affections of the mind, and other ideas common to the whole race of man.

If a nation of *Hindus,* it may be urged, ever possessed and governed the country of *Iràn,* we should find on the very ancient ruins of the temple or palace, now called *the throne* of JEMSHI'D, some inscriptions in *Dévanágarì,* or at least in the characters on the stones at *Elephanta,* where the sculpture is unquestionably *Indian,* or in those on the *Staff of* FI'RU'Z SHA'H, which exist in the heart of *India;* and such inscriptions we probably should have found, if that edifice had not been erected after the migration of the *Bráhmans* from *Iràn,* and the violent schism in the *Persian* religion, of which we shall presently speak; for, although the popular name of the building at *Istakhr,* or *Persepolis,* be no certain proof that it was raised in the time of JEMSHI'D, yet such a fact might easily have been preserved by tradition, and we shall soon have abundant evidence, that the temple was posteriour to the reign of the Hindu monarchs: the cypresses indeed, which are represented with the figures in procession, might induce a reader of the *Sháhnámah* to believe, that the sculptures related to the new faith introduced by ZERA'TUSHT; but, as a cypress is a beautiful ornament, and as many of the figures appear inconsistent with the reformed adoration of fire, we must have recourse to stronger proofs, that the *Takhti* JEMSHI'D was erected after CAYU'MERS. The building has lately been visited, and the characters on it examined, by Mr. FRANCKLIN;[1] from whom we learn, that NIEBUHR[2] has delineated them with great accuracy: but without such testimony I should have suspected the correctness of the delineation; because the *Danish* traveller has exhibited two inscriptions in modern *Persian*, and one of them from the same place, which cannot have been exactly transcribed: they are very elegant verses of NIZA'MI[3] and SADI[4] *on the instability of human greatness*, but so ill engraved or so ill copied, that, if I had not had them nearly by heart, I should not have been able to read them; and M. ROUSSEAU of *Isfahàn*, who translated them with shameful inaccuracy, must have been deceived by the badness of the copy; or he never would have created a new king WAKAM, by forming one word of JEM and the particle prefixed to it. Assuming, however, that we may reason as conclusively on the characters published by NIEBUHR, as we might on the monuments themselves, were they now before us, we may begin with observing, as CHARDIN[5] had observed on the very spot, that they bear no resemblance whatever to the letters used by the

---

1 William Francklin (1763-1839) was a career soldier with the British East India Company, who, like Jones, was a noted orientalist. His *Observations Made on a Tour from Bengal to Persia* (Calcutta, 1788) not only established his scholarly reputation, but also constituted one of the richest accounts of Persian society available in a European language.

2 Carsten Niebuhr (1733-1815) was a German traveler who, under the aegis of Frederick V of Denmark, was part of an ill-fated scientific expedition to Egypt, Arabia, and Syria. He eventually made his way to Bombay and upon his return published *Beschreibung von Arabien*, a heavily illustrated and highly descriptive account of his travels in Arabia, at Copenhagen in 1772.

3 Nezami Ganjavi (1141-1209) brought a colloquial and realistic style to the Persian epic.

4 Sadi (1184-1291) renowned Persian poet and practitioner of Sufism.

5 Jean Chardin (1643-1713) was a French merchant and traveler. His *Voyages de monsieur le chevalier Chardin en Perse et autres lieux de l'orient* (1711), or *Sir John Chardin's Travels in Persia* (1720) was and remains a standard scholarly work on Persia.

Gabrs in their copies of the *Vendidàd:* this I once urged, in an ami-
cable debate with BAHMAN, as a proof, that the *Zend* letters
were a modern invention; but he seemed to hear me without sur-
prize, and insisted, that the letters, to which I alluded, and which
he had often seen, were monumental characters never used in
books, and intended either to conceal some religious mysteries
from the vulgar, or to display the art of the sculptor, like the
embellished *Cúfick* and *Nágarì* on several *Arabian* and *India*
monuments. He wondered, that any man could seriously doubt
the antiquity of the *Pahlavì* letters; and in truth the inscription
behind the horse of *Rustam*, which NIEBUHR has also given us,
is apparently *Pahlavì*, and might with some pains be decyphered:
that character was extremely rude, and seems to have been
written, like the *Roman* and the *Arabick*, in a variety of hands; for
I remember to have examined a rare collection of old *Persian*
coins in the Museum of the great Anatomist, WILLIAM
HUNTER,[1] and, though I believed the legends to be *Pahlavì*,
and had no doubt, that they were coins of *Parthian* kings, yet I
could not read the inscriptions without wasting more time, than
I had then at command, in comparing the letters and ascertain-
ing the proportions, in which they severally occurred. The gross
Pahlavì was improved by ZERA'TUSHT or his disciples into an
elegant and perspicuous character, in which the *Zendávestà* was
copied; and both were written from the right hand to the left like
other *Chaldaick* alphabets; for they are manifestly both of
Chaldean origin; but the *Zend* has the singular advantage of
expressing all the long and short vowels, by distinct marks, in the
body of each word, and all the words are distinguished by full
points between them; so that, if modern *Persian* were unmixed
with *Arabick*, it might be written in *Zend* with the greatest convenience, as any one may perceive by copying in that character a
few pages of the *Sháhnámah*. As to the unknown inscriptions in
the palace of JEMSHI'D, it may reasonably be doubted, whether
they contain a system of letters, which any nation ever adopted:
in *five* of them the letters, which are separated by points, may be

---

1 William Hunter (1718-83) was an anatomist, physician, and man-
   midwife. Late in his illustrious career he amassed an extraordinary collection of coins, anatomical preparations, insects, shells, corals, and
   materials collected during Cook's expeditions, which were put on
   display in a private museum in Great Windmill Street, London. According to Helen Brock in the *Oxford Dictionary of National Biography*, "His
   collection of coins was second only to that of the King of France."

reduced to forty, at least I can distinguish no more essentially different; and they all seem to be regular variations and compositions of a straight line and an angular figure like the head of a javelin, or a leaf (to use the language of botanists) *hearted and lanced.* Many of the *Runick* letters appear to have been formed of similar elements; and it has been observed, that the writing at *Persepolis* bears a strong resemblance to that, which the *Irish* call *Ogham:* the word *Agam* in *Sanscrit* means *mysterious knowledge;* but I dare not affirm, that the two words had a common origin, and only mean to suggest, that, if the characters in question be really alphabetical, they were probably secret and sacerdotal, or a mere cypher, perhaps, of which the priests only had the key. They might, I imagine, be decyphered, if the language were certainly known; but, in all the other inscriptions of the same sort, the characters are too complex, and the variations of them too numerous, to admit an opinion, that they could be symbols of articulate sounds; for even the *Nágarì* system, which has more distinct letters than any known alphabet, consists only of forty-nine simple characters, two of which are mere substitutions, and four of little use in *Sanscrit* or in any other language; while the more complicated figures, exhibited by NIEBUHR, must be as numerous at least as the *Chinese* keys, which are the signs of *ideas* only, and some of which resemble the old *Persian* letters at *Istakhr:* the *Danish* traveller was convinced from his own observation, that they were written from the left hand, like all the characters used by *Hindu* nations; but I must leave this dark subject, which I cannot illuminate, with a remark formerly made by myself, that the square *Chaldaick* letters, a few of which are found on the *Persian* ruins, appear to have been originally the same with the *Dévanágarì*, before the latter were enclosed, as we now see them, in angular frames....

[Jones moves from linguistic matters to make a similar argument through the history of ancient Persian religion. He then indicates that he has little to say about Persian arts or sciences and concludes as follows:]

Thus has it been proved by clear evidence and plain reasoning, that a powerful monarchy was established in *Iràn* long before the *Assyrian*, or *Pìshdádi*, government; that it was in truth a *Hindu* monarchy, though, if any chuse to call it *Cusian*, *Casdean*, or *Scythian*, we shall not enter into a debate on mere names; that it subsisted many centuries, and that its history has been ingrafted on that of the *Hindus*, who founded the monarchies of *Ayódhyà* and *Indraprestha;* that the language of the first *Perisan* empire was the mother of the *Sanscrit*, and consequently of the *Zend*, and *Parsi*, as well as of *Greek*, *Latin*, and *Gothick*; that the language of the *Assyrians* was the parent of *Chaldaick* and *Pahlavì*, and that the primary *Tartarian* language also had been current in the same empire; although, as the *Tartars* had no books or even letters, we cannot with certainty trace their unpolished and variable idioms. We discover, therefore, in *Persia*, at the earliest dawn of history, the *three* distinct races of men, whom we described on former occasions as possessors of *India*, *Arabia*, *Tartary*; and, whether they were collected in *Iràn* from distant regions, or diverged from it, as from a common centre, we shall easily determine by the following considerations. Let us observe in the first place the central position of *Iràn*, which is bounded by *Arabia*, by *Tartary*, and by *India;* whilst *Arabia* lies contiguous to *Iràn* only, but is remote from *Tartary*, and divided even from the skirts of *India* by a considerable gulf; no country, therefore, but *Persia* seems likely to have sent forth its colonies to all the kingdoms of *Asia:* the *Bráhmans* could never have migrated from *India* to *Iràn*, because they are expressly forbidden by their oldest existing laws to leave the region, which they inhabit at this day; the *Arabs* have not even a tradition of an emigration into *Persia* before MOHAMMED, nor had they indeed any inducement to quit their beautiful and extensive domains; and, as to the *Tartars*, we have no trace in history of their departure from their plains and forests, till the invasion of the *Medes*, who, according to etymologists, were the sons of MADAI, and even they were conducted by princes of an *Assyrian* family. The *three* races, therefore, whom we have already mentioned, (and more than three we have not yet found) migrated from *Iràn*, as from their common country; and thus the *Saxon* chronicle, I presume from good authority, brings the first inhabitants of *Britain* from *Armenia;* while a late very learned writer concludes, after all his laborious researches, that the *Goths* or *Scythians* came from *Persia;* and another contends with great force, that both the *Irish* and old *Britons* proceeded severally from the borders of the *Caspian;* a coincidence of conclusions from different media by persons wholly unconnected, which could scarce have happened, if they were not grounded on solid principles. We may therefore hold this proposition firmly established, that *Iràn*, or *Persia* in its largest sense, was the true centre of population, of knowledge, of languages, and of arts; which, instead of travelling westward only, as it has been fancifully supposed, or eastward, as might with equal reason have been asserted, were expanded in all directions to all the regions of the world, in which the *Hindu* race had settled under various denominations: but, whether *Asia* has not produced other races of men, distinct from the *Hindus*, the *Arabs*, or the *Tartars*, or whether any apparent diversity may not have sprung from an intermixture of those three in different proportions, must be the subject of a future inquiry. There is another question of more immediate importance, which you, gentlemen, only can decide: namely, "by what means we can preserve our Society from dying gradually away, as it has advanced gradually to its present (shall I say flourishing or languishing?) state." It has subsisted five years without any expense to the members of it, until the first volume of our Transactions was published; and the price of that large volume, if we compare the different values of money in *Bengal* and in *England*, is not more than equal to the *annual* contribution towards the charges of the Royal Society by each of its fellows, who may not have chosen to compound for it on his admission: this I mention, not from an idea that any of us could object to the purchase of one copy at least, but from a wish to inculcate the necessity of our common exertions in promoting the sale of the work both here and in *London*. In vain shall we meet, as a literary body, if our meetings shall cease to be supplied with original dissertations and memorials; and in vain shall we collect the most interesting papers, if we cannot publish them occasionally without exposing the Superintendents of the Company's press, who undertake to print them at their own hazard, to the danger of a considerable loss: by united efforts the *French* have compiled their stupendous repositories of universal knowledge; and by united efforts only can we hope to rival them, or to diffuse over our own country and the rest of *Europe* the lights attainable by our *Asiatick Researches*.

Appendix D: Comparative Ethnographies

1. From Montesquieu, Charles de Secondat, baron de. *Persian Letters. By M. de Montesquieu. Translated from the French, by Mr. Flloyd. In two volumes. ...* The fourth edition. With several new letters and notes. Vol. 1. London, 1762

[This extract is from the most widely available English translation of Montesquieu's seminal epistolary novel/treatise *Lettres Persanes* (1721). In this work, Montesquieu uses the contrivance of a small group of Persian travelers to detail the follies of French society and to advocate for various elements of enlightenment reform. In addition, its representation of Persian manners, society and culture was deeply influential on later European representations of the Orient. This is especially the case with regard to its representation of Asiatic women. The description of the Parisian theatre in Letter XXVIII makes for an illuminating comparison with Abu Talib's representation of theatres in Dublin, London, and Paris. Minor textual errors have been silently corrected.]

LETTER XXIV.

Rica to Ibben, at Smyrna.

We have been this month at Paris, and all the while in a continual motion. There is a good deal to be done before one can be settled, meet with all the persons one has business with, and procure every thing necessary, all which are wanted at once. Paris is as large as Ispahan. One would imagine the houses were only inhabited by astrologers, they are so lofty. Thou wilt easily judge, that a city built in the air, which has six or seven houses one on another, must be extremely populous, and that, when all this world of people are come down into the streets, there must be a fine bustle. Thou wilt not, perhaps, believe, that during the month I have been here, I have not yet seen one person a walking. There is no people in the world who make better use of their machine than the French; they run; they fly; the slow carriages of Asia, the regular pace of our camels, would make them fall asleep. As for my own part, who am not made for such expedition, and who often go on foot, without altering my pace, I am sometimes as mad as a Christian; for passing over them splashing me from head to foot, I cannot pardon the punches of elbows, which I receive regularly and periodically. A man comes behind me, and passes me, turns me half round, and another who crosses me on the other side, in an instant returns me back again into my first place; and I am more bruised before I have walked a hundred paces than if I had travelled ten leagues. Thou must not expect that I can as yet give thee a perfect account of the European manners and customs; I have myself only a faint idea of them, and have scarcely had more than time to wonder. The king of France is the most puissant prince in Europe. He has not, like his neighbour the king of Spain, mines of gold; but his riches are greater than his; for he supplies them from the vanity of his subjects, more inexhaustible than those mines. He has engaged in, and supported, great wars without any other fund than the sale of titles of honour, and his troops have been paid, his towns fortified, and his fleets fitted out, by a prodigy of human pride. This prince is, besides, a great magician; he exercises his empire even over the minds of his subjects, and makes them think as he pleases. If he has but only a thousand crowns in his treasury, and has occasion for two, he needs only tell them that one crown is worth two, and they believe it. If he has a difficult war to maintain, and has no money, he has only to put it into their heads that a piece of paper is money, and they are presently convinced of the truth of it. He even goes so far as to make them believe that he can cure them of all kinds of evils by touching them; so great is the power and influence which he has over their minds. Thou needest not be astonished at what I tell thee of this prince; there is another magician more powerful than him, who is no less master of his mind than he is of those of others. This magician is called the Pope: sometimes he makes him believe, that the bread which he eats is not bread, or that the wine which he drinks is not wine, and a thousand other things of the same nature. And, to keep him always in breath, and that he may not lose the habit of believing, he gives him, from time to time, to exercise him, certain articles of faith. It is two years since he sent him a large scroll, which he called, *constitution*, and would needs oblige, under great penalties, this prince and all, his subjects, to believe every thing it contained. He succeeded with the king, who instantly submitted, and set an example to his subjects; but some among them revolted, and declared they would believe nothing of all that was contained in the scroll. The women are the movers of this rebellion, which divides the whole court, all the kingdom, and every family in it. This *constitution* prohibits the women reading a book, which all the Christians say was brought down from heaven which is properly their Koran. The women, enraged at this affront offered to their sex, raise all their force against the constitution; they have gained the men to their party, who, on this occasion, will not receive their privilege. The Mufti, it must be owned, does not reason amiss; and, by the great Hali,[1] it must be, that he has been instructed in the principles of our holy faith; for, since the women are an inferior creation to ours, and that our prophets inform us, that they will not enter into Paradise, for what end should they concern themselves in reading a book, which is only designed to teach the way to Paradise? Some miraculous things; I have heard related of the king, which I doubt not but you will hesitate to believe. It is said, that whilst he made war against his neighbours, who were all leagued against him, he had, in his kingdom, an infinite number of enemies, who surrounded him. They add, that he searched for them, above thirty years, and that, notwithstanding the unwearied pains of some dervishes, who have his confidence, he could never discover one. They live with him; are in his court, in his capital, in his troops, in his tribunals; yet it is said, he will have the mortification to die without finding one of them. They may be said to have a general existence, and to have nothing of individuality; it is a body, but without members. Doubtless it is heaven, that would punish this prince, for not having been sufficiently moderate towards his conquered enemies, since it hath raised up against him invisible ones, whose genius and appointment are superior to his own. I shall continue to write to you, and to acquaint you with things extremely remote from the character and genius of the Persians. It is indeed the same earth that bears us both; yet the men of the country in which I live, and those of that which thou inhabitest, are very different kinds of men.

Paris, the 4th of the moon of the 2d Rebiab, 1712.

---

1   Ali ibn Abu Talib (599 or 600-661) was the cousin, son-in-law of the Islamic prophet Muhammad. Sunni Muslims consider Ali as the fourth and final Rashidun (Rightly Guided Caliph). Shia Muslims regard Ali as the first infallible Imam and consider him and his descendants as the rightful successors to Muhammad. This disagreement split the Muslim community into the Sunni and Shi'a branches.

LETTER XXVI.

Usbek to Roxana, at the Seraglio at Ispahan.

How happy art thou, Roxana, to be in the delightful country of Persia, and not in these poisoned climes, where neither virtue nor modesty are known! How happy art thou! Thou livest in my seraglio, as in the abode of innocence, secure from the attempts of all mankind; you, with pleasure, experience a happy inability to go astray; never did man pollute you with his lascivious looks; during the freedom of festivities even your father-in-law never saw your fine mouth; you never neglected to cover it with a holy veil. Happy Roxana! whenever you have gone into the country, you have always had eunuchs to march before, to punish with death the temerity of those who did not fly from your sight. Even I myself, to whom heaven gave you to make me happy, how much trouble have I had to render myself master of that treasure, which with so much constancy you defended! How distressing to me, during the first days of our marriage, not to see you! And how impatient when I had beheld you! Yet you would not satisfy it; on the contrary you increased it, by the obstinate refusals of your bashful alarms; you did not distinguish me from all other men, from whom you are always concealed. Do you recollect the day I lost you among your slaves, who betrayed me, and hid you from my searches? Do you remember another time, when finding your tears insufficient, you engaged the authority of your mother, to stop the eagerness of my love? Do you remember, when every other resource failed you, those you found in your own courage? You took a dagger, and threatened to sacrifice a husband, who loved you, if he persisted in requiring of you what you prized more than your husband himself. Two months passed in the struggle between love and modesty. You carried your modest scruples too far; you did not even submit after you were conquered. You defended to the last moment a dying virginity; you regarded me as an enemy who had done you a wrong, not as a husband who had loved you; you were above three month before you could look at me without a blush; your bashful looks seemed to reproach me with the advantage I had taken. I did not enjoy even a quiet possession; you deprived me of all those charms and graces that you could; and without having obtained the least favours, I was ravished with the greatest. If your education had been in this country, here, you would not have been so troublesome. The women here have lost all modesty; they present themselves before the men with their faces uncovered, as though they would demand of them their defeat; they watch for their looks; they see them in their mosques, their public walks, and even by themselves; the service of eunuchs is unknown to them. In the room of that noble simplicity, and that amiable modesty which reigns amongst you, a brutal impudence prevails, to which it is impossible to be accustomed. Yes, if thou wert here, Roxana, you would be enraged at the wretched shamefulness to which your sex is degenerated; you would fly these polluted places, and sigh for that sweet retreat, where you find innocence, and yourself secure, and where no dangers terrify you: in a word, where you can love me without fear of ever losing that love for me which is my due. When you heighten your beautiful complexion with the finest colours; when you perfume your whole body with the most precious essences, when you deck yourself with the richest dresses, when you endeavour to distinguish yourself from your companions by your graceful motions in dancing, and when, by the sweetness of your voice, you pleasingly dispute with them charms, affability, and gaiety, I cannot imagine you have any other object to please but myself ; and, when I see your modest blush, that your eyes seek mine, that you insinuate yourself into my heart by your soft alluring speeches, I cannot, Roxana, suspect your love. But what can I think of the European women? The art which forms their complexion, the ornaments they use in dress, the pains which they take with their persons, the constant desire to please that possesses them, are blemishes in their virtue and affronts to their husbands. It is not, Roxana, that I suspect they carry their encroachments upon virtue to such a length as their conduct might lead one to believe; or that they carry their defection to such a horrid excess, that makes one tremble, as really to violate the conjugal vow. There are few women abandoned enough to go this length; they all bear in their hearts, a certain impression of virtue, naturally engraved on them, which though their education may weaken, it cannot destroy. Though they may decline the external duties which modesty exacts; yet, when about to take the last step, nature returns to their help. Thus when we shut you up closely, when we make you be guarded by so many slaves, when we so strongly restrain your desires, when they would range too far; it is not that we fear the least infidelity; but because we know that purity cannot be too great, and that by the least stain it may be polluted. I pity you, Roxana; your chastity, so long tried, merited a husband who would never have left you, and who might himself have satisfied those desires which can be subdued by your virtue alone.

Paris, the 7th day of the moon Regeb, 1712.

LETTER XXVIII.

Rica to ***

Yesterday I saw a very extraordinary thing, though it happens every day at Paris. After dinner, towards evening, all the people assemble to act a kind of mimickry, which I heard called a play. The performance is in a place called a theatre, on each side are little nooks, called boxes, in which the men and women act together dumb scenes; something like those in use in Persia. Here you see a languishing love sick lady; another more animated eagerly ogling her lover, whose returns are as ardent; all the passions are painted in their faces, and expressed by an eloquence which though dumb is not the less lively. Here, the actresses expose but half their bodies, and commonly, out of modesty, wear muffs to conceal their arms. In the lower part of the theatre, is a troop of people standing, who ridicule those who are above, and they, in their turn, laugh at those below. But those who put themselves to the greatest trouble, are some who take the advantage of their youth to support the fatigue of it. They are forced to be every where, they go through passages known only to themselves, they mount, with extraordinary activity, from story to story; they are above, below, and in every box; they dive, if I may so speak; they are lost this moment, and appear again the next; they often leave the place of the scene, and go to play in another. Now there are others, though such a prodigy is not to be expected, seeing they use crutches, who walk and move about like the others. You come, at length, to some rooms where they act a private comedy, This commences with low bows, continued by embraces; the slightest acquaintance, they say, gives a man a right to squeeze another to death. This place seems to inspire tenderness; in fact, they say, that the princesses who reign here are not cruel, and excepting two, or three, hours a day, in which they are hard hearted enough, one must allow that they are very tractable, and that the other humour is a kind of drunkenness which they easily quit.

All that I have been relating to you, is pretty nearly transacted in another place, called the Opera house; all the difference is, that they speak at the one, and sing at the other. A friend of mine, the other day, took me into a room where one of the principal actresses was undressing; we became so intimate, that the next day I received, from her, the following epistle.

Sir,

I am the most unhappy woman in the world. I have been always the most virtuous woman in the whole opera. Seven, or eight, months ago, as I was dressing myself for a priestess of Diana, in the same room you saw me in yesterday, a young abbot came in, and regardless of my white habit, my veil, or my frontlet, deprived me of my innocence. I have in vain remonstrated to him the sacrifice I made to him, he only laughs, and maintains he found me a very profane woman. In the mean time I dare not come upon the stage I am so big; for I am, with respect to honour, inconceivably delicate, and I always insist, that to a woman well born it is more easy to lose her virtue than her modesty. With this delicacy, you may readily judge, that the young abbot had never succeeded, if he had not made to me a promise of marriage; such a lawful motive induced me to pass over those little usual formalities, and to begin where I ought to have concluded. But since his infidelity has dishonoured me, I will no longer continue at the opera, where, between you and me, they scarcely give me sufficient for my support for, at present, that I advance in years, and lose the advantage of charms, my salary, though the same, seems to diminish daily. I have learned from one of your attendants, that in your country a good dancer is highly esteemed, and that if I was at Ispahan, my fortune would be quickly made. If you would take me under your protection, you would have the praise of doing good to a woman, who by her virtue and prudent conduct, would not render herself unworthy of your generosity.
I am, &c.

From Paris, the 2d of the moon of Chalval, 1712.

LETTER XXX.

Rica to the Same [Ibben], at Smyrna.

The people of Paris are curious to an extravagant degree. When I came here I was stared at as if I had been sent from heaven; old and young, men, women and children, all must have a peep at me. If I went out, everybody was at their windows; if I walked in the Tuilleries,[1] I was presently surrounded by a circle; the women formed a rainbow about me, variegated with a thousand colours; if I attended the public shows, my strange figure attracted a hundred spying glasses; in short, never was a man so much looked at as myself. I smiled sometimes at hearing persons, who but scarcely ever stirred from their chamber, whispering to each other; it must be allowed he has much of the air of a Persian. But what is very wonderful, I met with my own picture everywhere, saw myself multiplied in every shop, upon every chimney-piece; so fearful were they of not seeing me sufficiently. All these honours however are only burdensome; I did not imagine I was so curious, or so extraordinary, a person; and though I think very well of myself, I never imagined I should have disturbed the quiet of a great city where I was wholly unknown. This determined me to quit my Persian dress, and put on that of an European, to try if my physiognomy would yet retain any of the wonderful. This experiment convinced me of what I really was; divested of these foreign ornaments I found myself properly rated. I had occasion enough to be displeased with my tailor for making me lose all public regard and attention, for I at once sunk into a contemptible nothingness. I was sometimes an hour in company without being the least noticed, and without any body's giving me occasion to speak. But if by chance any one informed the company that I was a Persian, there was a buzz around me; ha! ha! the gentleman a Persian, very strange! that any one should be a Persian!

Paris, the 6th of the moon Chalval, 1712.

---

1 Famous gardens on the banks of the Seine.

LETTER XXXIII.

Usbek to Rhedi, at Venice.

At Paris wine is so extremely dear, on account of the duties laid on it, that it seems as if it was designed to fulfil the commands of the divine Koran, which prohibits the drinking of it. When I think upon the melancholy, fatal effects of this liquor, I cannot avoid considering it as the most dreadful present that nature hath made to mankind. If anything ever disgraced the lives and characters of our monarchs, it hath been their intemperance; it hath been the most empoisoned spring from whence have issued all their injustice and cruelty. I must needs say to the disgrace of these men, the law prohibits our Princes the use of wine, and yet they drink it to an excess that degrades them of humanity; this custom on the contrary is indulged to the Christian princes, and never observed to lead them into any crime. The mind of man is a contradiction to itself. During a licentious debauch they transgress the precepts, and the law made to render us just, serves only to render us more culpable. Yet when I disapprove of the use of this liquor which destroys our reason, I do not at the same time condemn those beverages which exhilarate the mind. The Orientals are so wise as to inquire after remedies against melancholy, with the same solicitude as for more dangerous disorders. When any misfortune happens to an European, he hath no other resource but to read a philosopher called Seneca:[1] but the Asiatics, more sensible than them, and in this case better naturalists, drink a liquor capable of cheering the heart, and of charming away the remembrance of its sufferings. There is nothing so distressing as the consolations drawn from the necessity of evil, the inefficacy of medicines, the irreversibleness of fatality, the decrees of providence,[2] and the miserable condition of humanity. It is mockery to attempt to soften evils by the consideration, that it is the consequence of our being born; it is much better to divert the mind from its reflexions, and to treat man as a being susceptible of sensation, rather than reason. The soul united to a body is con-

---

1 Lucius Annaeus Seneca (c. 4 BCE-CE 65) was a Roman Stoic philosopher, statesman, and dramatist. Seneca wrote numerous dialogues of consolation.

2 This may be true according to the absurd ideas of them which Mahometism teaches; but by no means so with respect to that idea which the Christian revelation gives of them. (Original note)

tinually under its tyrannical power. If the blood moves too slowly, if the spirits are not sufficiently pure, if they are not enough in quantity, we become dejected and melancholy; but if we make use of such liquors that can change the disposition of our bodies, our soul again becomes capable of receiving pleasing ideas, and is sensible of a secret pleasure in perceiving its machine recover, as it were its life and motion.

Paris, the 25th of the moon Zilcade, 1713.

LETTER XXXIV.

Usbek to Ibben, at Smyrna.

The women of Persia are finer than those of France; but those of this country are prettier. It is difficult not to love the first, and not to be pleased with the latter; the ones are more delicate and modest, and the others more gay and airy. What in Persia renders the blood so pure, is the regular life the women observe, they neither game nor sit up late, they drink no wine, and do not expose themselves to the open air. It must be allowed that the seraglio is better adapted for health than for pleasure; it is a dull uniform kind of life, where every thing turns upon subjection and duty; their very pleasures are grave, and their pastimes solemn, and they seldom taste them but as so many tokens of authority and dependance. The men themselves in Persia are not so gay as the French; there is not that freedom of mind and that appearance of content which I meet with here in persons of all estates and ranks. It is still worse in Turkey, where there are families in which from father to son, not one of them ever laughed from the foundation of the monarchy. The gravity of the Asiatics arises from the little conversation there is among them, who never see each other but when obliged by ceremony. Friendship, that sweet engagement of the heart, which constitutes here the pleasure of life, is there almost unknown. They retire within their own house, where they constantly find the same company; insomuch that each family may be considered as living in an island detached from all others. Discoursing one time on this subject with a person of this country, he said to me, that which gives me most offence among all your customs is the necessity you are under of living with slaves, whose minds and inclinations always savour of the meanness of their condition. Those sentiments of virtue which you have in you from nature are enfeebled and destroyed by these base wretches who surround you from your infancy. For, in short, divest yourself of prejudice, and what can you expect from an education received from such a wretch, who places his whole merit in being a jailer to the wives of another man, and takes a pride in the vilest employment in society? who is despicable for that very fidelity which is his only virtue, to which he is prompted, by envy, jealousy, and despair? who inflamed with a desire of revenging himself on both sexes, of which he is an outcast, submitting to the tyranny of the stronger sex, provided he may distress the weaker; a wretch who, deriving from his imperfection, ugliness and deformity, the whole lustre of his condition, is valued only because he is unworthy to be so; who, in short, riveted for ever to the gate where he is placed, and harder than the hinges and bolts which secure it, boasts of having spent a life of fifty years in so ignoble a nation, where, commissioned by his master's jealousy, he exercises all his cruelties.

Paris, the 14th of the moon Zilhade, 1713.

LETTER XXXV.

Usbek to Gimchid, his cousin, Dervise of the shining Monastery of Tauris.

What dost thou think, sublime dervise, of the Christians? Dost thou believe, that at the day of judgment it will be with them as with the unbelieving Turks, who will serve the Jews for asses, and to carry them in a high trot to hell? I well know that their abode will not be with the prophets, and that the great Haly is not come for their sakes. But dost thou believe they will be sentenced to eternal punishment, because they have been so unhappy as to find no mosques in their country? and that God will punish them for not praising a religion that he never made known to them? I can assure thee I have frequently examined these Christians; I have questioned them, to see if they had any idea of the great Haly, who was the most excellent of mankind, and have found that they have never so much as heard him mentioned. They are not like those infidels whom our holy prophet put to the sword, for refusing to believe in the miracles of heaven; but rather like those unhappy people who lived under the darkness of idolatry, before the divine light illuminated the face of our great prophet.

Again, if you search their religion closely, you will find some seeds of our doctrines. I have often admired the secret dispositions of providence, which seems thereby willing to prepare them for a general conversion. I have heard speak of a book of their doctors, called *Polygamy Triumphant*, in which is proved, that polygamy is enjoined to Christians. Their baptism is an emblem of our legal washings; and the Christians only mistake in the efficacy that they ascribe to this primary ablution, which they believe sufficient for every other. Their priests and monks, like us, pray seven times in a day. They hope to enjoy a paradise, where they shall taste a thousand delights, by the means of the resurrection of their bodies. They have, as well as we, set fasts, and mortifications, by which they hope to incline the divine mercy. They worship good angels, and fear the evil. They pay a holy credulity to the miracles which God works by the ministry of his servants. They acknowledge, as we do, the insufficiency of their own merits, and the need they have of an intercessor with God. I see Mahometism throughout the whole, though I do not there find Mahomet. Do all we can, truth will prevail and shine through the cloud that surrounds it. A day will come, when the eternal will see none upon the earth but true believers. Time, which consumes all things, will destroy even errors themselves. All mankind will be astonished to find themselves under the same standard. All things, even to the law itself, shall be done away; the divine exemplars will be taken up from the earth, and carried to the celestial archives.

Paris, the 20th of the moon Zilhage, 1713.

LETTER XXXVI.

Usbek to Rhedi, at Venice.

Coffee is very much used at Paris; here are a great many public houses where they sell it. In some of these houses they talk of news, in others they play at draughts. There is one where they prepare the coffee in such a manner, that it inspires the drinkers of it with wit; at least, of all those who frequent it, there is not one person in four who does not think he has more wit after he has entered that house. But what offends me in these wits is, that they do not make themselves useful to their country, and that they trifle away their talents on childish things. For instance, at my arrival in Paris, I found them very warm about the most trifling controversy imaginable; they were disputing about the character of an old Greek poet, of whose country, and the time of his death, they have been ignorant these two thousand years. Both parties allowed he was an excellent poet; the question was only whether he had more or less merit, ascribed to him than he deserved. Each was for settling the value, but amidst these distributors of reputation, some made better weight than others; such was the quarrel. It has been very fierce, for they so heartily abused each other, and were so bitter in their raillery, that I did not less admire the manner of their dispute, than the subject of it. If any one, said I to myself, should be giddy-headed enough in the company of these defenders of this Greek poet, to attack the reputation of an honest citizen, he would be but badly received! and surely this zeal, so delicate for the reputation of the dead, would be inflamed in defense of that of the living! But however that may be, added I, may I ever be defended from the censors of this poet, whose abode of two thousand years in the grave, has not defended him from so implacable an hatred! They now do but beat the air, but how would it be, if their fury was animated by the pretense of an enemy? These I have been speaking of, dispute in the vulgar tongue, and must be distinguished from another kind of disputants, who make use of a barbarous language, which seems to augment the fury and obstinacy of the combatants. There are particular quarters of the town where these people engage as in a battle, night and day; they, as it were, feed themselves with distinctions, and live upon obscure reasonings, and false consequences. This trade, by which it should seem no bread could be got, yet does not fail answering. A whole nation, expelled from their own country, hath been seen to pass the seas, to settle in France, bringing nothing with them to ward off the necessities of life, but a formidable talent for disputation. Farewell.

Paris, the last day of the moon of Zilhage, 1713.

2. **From Lady Mary Wortley Montagu,** *Letters of the Right Honourable Lady M—y W—y M—e: written during her travels in Europe, Asia and Africa, to persons of distinction, men of letters, &c in different parts of Europe. Which contain, among other curious relations, accounts of the policy and manners of the Turks.* **3 vols. (London: Becket and De Hondt, 1763)**

[This letter, written in 1717 while Lady Mary was stationed in Constantinople with her husband was not published in Britain until 1763. The entire set of letters is fascinating, but this letter in particular bears comparison with Abu Talib's "Vindication of the Liberties of the Asiatic Women" in his final appendix to the *Travels* (361).]

Letter XXIX
To the Countess of _____   Adrianople, April 1, O.S. 1717

I wish to God, dear sister, that you were as regular in letting me have the pleasure of knowing what passes on your side of the globe as I am careful in endeavouring to amuse you by the account of all I see that I think you care to hear of. You content yourself with telling me over and over that the town is very dull. It may possibly be dull to you when every day does not present you with something new, but for me that am in arrear at least two months news, all that seems very stale with you would be fresh and sweet here. Pray let me into more particulars. I will try to awaken your gratitude by giving you a full and true relation of the novelties of this place, none of which would surprise you more than a sight of my person, as I am now in my Turkish habit, though I believe you would be of my opinion that 'tis admirably becoming. I intend to send you my picture. In the meantime accept of it here.

The first piece of my dress is a pair of drawers, very full, that reach to my shoes, and conceal the legs more modestly than your petticoats. They are of a thin rose colour damask, brocaded with silver flowers, my shoes of white kid leather embroidered with gold. Over this hangs my smock of a fine white silk gauze, edged with embroidery. This smock has wide sleeves hanging half way down the arm and is closed at the neck with a diamond button; but the shape and colour of the bosom is very well to be distinguished through it. The *entari* is a waistcoat made close to the shape, of white and gold damask with very long sleeves falling back and fringed with deep gold fringe, and should have diamond or pearl buttons. My caftan of the same stuff with my drawers, is a robe exactly fitted to my shape and reaching to my feet, with very long straight-falling sleeves. Over this is the girdle of about four fingers broad which all that can afford have entirely of diamonds or other precious stones; those that will not be at that expense have it of exquisite embroidery in satin, but it must be fastened before with a clasp of diamonds. The cüppe is a loose robe they throw off, or put on, according to the weather, being of a rich brocade (mine is green and gold) either lined with ermine or sables. The sleeves reach very little below the shoulders. The headdress is composed of a cap, called kalpak which is in the winter of fine velvet embroidered with pearls or diamonds and in summer of a light shining silver stuff. This is fixed on one side of the head, hanging a little way down with a gold tassel, and bound on either side with a circle of diamonds (as I have seen several) or a rich embroidered handkerchief. On the other side of the head the hair is laid flat and here ladies are at liberty to show their fancies, some putting flowers, others a plume of heron's feathers and, in short, what they please; but the most general fashion is a large bouquet of jewels made like natural flowers; that is, the buds of pearl, the roses of different coloured rubies, the jessamines of diamonds, the jonquils of topazes, etc, so well set and enamelled 'tis hard to imagine anything of that kind so beautiful. The hair hangs at its full length behind, divided into tresses braided with pearl or ribbon, which is always in great quantity.

I never saw in my life so many fine heads of hair. I have counted a hundred and ten of these tresses of one lady, all natural. But, it must be owned that every beauty is more common here than with us. 'Tis surprising to see a young woman that is not very handsome. They have naturally the most beautiful complexions in the world and generally large black eyes. I can assure you with great truth the court of England, though I believe it the fairest in Christendom, cannot show so many beauties as are under our protection here. They generally shape their eyebrows and both the Greeks and Turks have a custom of putting round their eyes on the inside a black tincture that, at a distance, or by candlelight, adds very much to the blackness of them. I fancy many of our ladies would be overjoyed to know this secret, but 'tis too visible by day. They dye their nails rose colour; I own I cannot enough accustom myself to this fashion to find any beauty in it.

As to their morality or good conduct, I can say, like Harlequin, that 'tis just as 'tis with you, and the Turkish ladies don't commit one sin less for not being Christians. Now that I am a little acquainted with their ways I cannot forbear admiring either the exemplary discretion or extreme stupidity of all the writers that have given accounts of them. 'Tis very easy to see they have more liberty than we have, no woman, of what rank so ever permitted to go in the streets without two muslins, one that covers her face all but her eyes and another that hides the whole dress of her head, and hangs half way down her back and their shapes are also wholly concealed by a thing they call a *ferace* which no woman of any sort appears without. This has straight sleeves that reaches to their fingers ends and it laps all round them, not unlike a riding hood. In winter 'tis of cloth and in summer plain stuff or silk. You may guess then how effectually this disguises them, that there is no distinguishing the great lady from her slave and 'tis impossible for the most jealous husband to know his wife when he meets her, and no man dare either touch or follow a woman in the street.

This perpetual masquerade gives them entire liberty of following their inclinations without danger of discovery. The most usual method of intrigue is to send an appointment to the lover to meet the lady at a Jew's shop, which are as notoriously convenient as our Indian houses, and yet, even those that don't make use of them do not scruple to go to buy pennyworths and tumble over rich goods, which are chiefly to be found amongst that sort of people. The great ladies seldom let their gallants know who they are, and 'tis so difficult to find it out that they can very seldom guess at her name they have corresponded with above half a year together. You may easily imagine the number of faithful wives very small in a country where they have nothing to fear from their lovers' indiscretion, since we see so many that have the courage to expose themselves to that in this world, and all the threatened punishment of the next, which is never preached to the Turkish damsels. Neither have they much to apprehend from the resentment of their husbands, those ladies that are rich having all their money in their own hands, which they take with them upon a divorce with an addition which he is obliged to give them. Upon the whole, I look upon the Turkish women as the only free people in the empire. The very Divan pays respect to them and the Grand Signor himself, when a pasha is executed, never violates the privileges of the harem (or women's apartment) which remains unsearched entire to the widow. They are queens of their slaves, which the husband has no permission so much as to look upon, except it be an old woman or two that his lady chooses. 'Tis true their law permits them four wives, but there is no instance of a man of quality that makes use of this liberty, or of a woman of rank that would suffer it. When a husband happens to be inconstant, as those things will happen, he keeps his mistress in a house apart and visits her as privately as he can, just as 'tis with you. Amongst all the great men here, I only know the *tefterdar* (ie treasurer) that keeps a number of she-slaves for his own use (that is, on his own side of the house, for a slave once given to serve a lady is entirely at her disposal) and he is spoke of as a libertine, or what we should call a rake, and his wife won't see him, though she continues to live in his house.

Thus you see, dear sister, the manners of mankind do not differ so widely as our voyage writers would make us believe. Perhaps it would be more entertaining to add a few surprising customs of my own invention, but nothing seems to me so agreeable as truth, and I believe nothing so acceptable to you. I conclude with repeating the great truth of my being, dear sister etc.

3. From Charles Grant, "Observations on the State of Society among the Asiatic Subjects of Great Britain, particularly with respect to Morals; and on the means of improving it.—Written chiefly in the Year 1792," from a much larger text, dated 15 June 1813, prepared and printed for Parliament to influence Indian policy

[As Abu Talib states, Grant was a member of the board of directors of the East India Company in the 1790s and spent considerable time in the Company's service both in India and in London. Grant's efforts were crucial in guaranteeing missionaries access to India—something previously prohibited by the Company—and this document stands as a key document of British imperial ethnocentricism.]

Chapter II

It has suited the views of some philosophers to represent [the people of Hindostan] as amiable and respectable; and a few late travellers have chosen to place some softer traits of their characters in an engaging light, than to give a just delineation of the whole. The generality however of those who have written concerning Hindostan, appear to have concurred in affirming what foreign residents there have as generally thought, nay, what the natives themselves freely acknowledge of each other, that they are a people exceedingly depraved.

In proportion as we have become better acquainted with them, we have found this description applicable, in a sense beyond the conception even of former travellers. The writer of this paper, after spending many years in India ... is obliged to add his testimony to all preceding evidence, and to avow that they exhibit human nature in a very degraded humiliating state, and are at once, objects of disesteem and of commiseration....

Of the Bengaleze then, it is true most generally that they are destitute, to a wonderful degree, of those qualities which are requisite to the security and comfort of society. They want truth, honesty, and good faith, in the extreme, of which European society furnishes no example. In Europe those principles are the standard of character and credit; men who have them not are still solicitous to maintain reputation of them, and those who are known to be devoid of them sink into contempt. It is not so in Bengal. The qualities themselves are so generally gone, that men do not found their pretension in society upon them; they take no pains to acquire or to keep up the credit of possessing them....

In the worst parts of Europe, there are no doubt great numbers of men who are sincere, upright, and conscientious. In Bengal, a man of real veracity and integrity is a great phenomenon; *one conscientious in the whole of his conduct*, it is to be feared is an unknown character. Every where in this quarter of the globe, there is still much generous trust and confidence, and men are surprised when they find themselves deceived. In Bengal, distrust is awake in all transactions; bargains and agreements are made with mutual apprehensions of breach of faith, conditions and securities are multiplied, and failure in them excites little or no surprise.

[After animadverting on their general want of honesty, Grant argues further that the Hindu population is prone to selfishness, banditry, cruelty and want of benevolence. His rhetoric reaches its climax when he turns to domestic society.]

The domestic state of the better ranks is more concealed from general view; but from the knowledge which is acquired, and from the peculiar usages by which marriage is governed among the Hindoos, we have no reason to believe that it is often sweetened by generous attachment or rational enjoyment. The parties betrothed by their parents whilst mere children, transplanted, with minds uncultivated and inexperienced, from the maternal zenana[1] into one of their own, united whilst reason is still in its infancy, can give little more account of the situation in which they find themselves than animals of a lower species. Affection and choice have had no influence in this connection, nor does it often happen that the former is studied and improved. The parties continue passive under that law which first brought them together. According to the despotic manners of the East, the husband is lord, and the wife a servant; seldom does he think of making her a companion or a friend. Polygamy, which is tolerated among the Hindoos, tends still more to destroy all rational domestic society. The honour of the family, and the preservation of its caste, the most awful of its concerns, depends on the reputation of the wife. She is secluded from all eyes but those of her nearest relations, and the most terrifying and disgraceful punishments are held out against misconduct. From so early an union, and such subsequent care, Europeans may suppose that order and decorum reign in the Hindoo zenanas; but the conclusion is founded on conjecture, rather than upon actual knowledge. The profound reserve and caution observed by the men in their conduct, and even in their conversation, respecting their family connections, keep all foreigners at a distance; and it is to honour of the English, that there is perhaps no instance of their attempting an invasion of the domestic recesses of the Hindoos. But those who have an opportunity of living among the natives in the interior of the country, see reasons for apprehending that the purity of the female character is not always so well preserved in reality, as in appearance.

In a residence of several years entirely among the natives, the present writer heard so many charges of irregularity, and saw so many disorders among the inferior ranks, that he could not but believe the existence of a gross laxity of behaviour and principle in this great branch of morals, in some degree at least reaching the better classes. But the disgrace and loss which follow to the family from the proof of dishonour in the wife are such as to induce the parties concerned to hush up all matters of that sort, and to take their revenge some secret way; they will seldom seek redress openly unless the affair has already become notorious.... Imperious dominion, seclusion and terror, are the means afterwards used, to enforce the fidelity of the wife. But opportunities of guilt are not wanting. In the hours of business, men are gener-

---

1 The private apartments of the women. (Original note)

ally at a distance from the retirements of the women; they are often, and for considerable periods, far from home; females who are the great instruments of corrupting their own sex are permitted access to the zenanas; besides the Hindoo law allows women to converse with Soneassees, a set of vagrant devotees, some of them most indecent in their appearance. The consequences are such as might be expected.

It is not however asserted or believed, that the infection of depravity has overspread the whole mass of females, many of whom, doomed to joyless confinement through life, and a violent premature death, are perhaps among the most inoffensive and suffering of the Hindoo race. As to the men, they are under little restraint from moral considerations. The laws of caste impose restrictions and fines for offences of the nature in question, so far as *that distinction* is concerned, but leave great scope for new connections, and for promiscuous intercourse, which is matter of little scruple or observation. Receptacles for women of infamous character are every where licensed, and the women themselves have a place in society. The female dancers, who are of this order, make the principal figure in the entertainments of ceremony given by the great. Indecency is the basis of their exhibitions; yet children and young persons of both sexes are permitted to be present at these shows, which have admittance even to the principal zenanas.[1] Licentious connections are therefore most common, though subsisting apparently without that intoxication of passion which hurries on the mind against conviction, and carried on without much concealment, nay almost with insensibility of brutes. On such points, the Hindoos seem to advert to no rule except what the law enjoins; there is no sentiment, diffused at large through society, which attaches shame to criminality. Wide and fatal are the corruption of manners; a corruption not stopping here, but extending even to the unnatural practices of the ancient Heathens, though in these the Mahomedans are still more abandoned....

It will not however be understood, that what is here advanced generally, is to be applied to the utmost extent to every individual, and every transaction; it is the universality of great depravity that is here insisted on,—a general moral hue, between which,

---

1 Lord Cornwallis, soon after his arrival in Bengal, refused to be present at an entertainment of this sort, to which he was invited by the Nabob. (Original note)

and the European moral complexion, there is a difference, analogous to the difference of the natural colour of the two races.

[Grant proceeds to give quotations from various East India Company officials which ostensibly substantiate his argument before turning to the Muslim population.]

Of the Mahomedans, who mix in considerable numbers with the former inhabitants of all the countries subdued by their arms in Hindostan, it is necessary also to say a few words. Originally of the Tartar race, proud, fierce, and lawless; attached also to their superstition, which cherished their native propensities; they were rendered by success yet more proud, sanguinary, sensual, and bigoted. Their government, though meliorated under the house of Timour,[1] was undoubtedly a violent despotism, and the delegated administration of it too often a severe oppression. Breaking through all the restraints of morals which obstructed their way to power, they afterwards abandoned themselves to the most vicious indulgences, and the most atrocious cruelties. Perfidy in them, was more signal than in the Hindoos. Successive treacheries, assassinations, and usurpations, mark their history more perhaps than that of any other people. The profession of arms was studied by them, and they cultivated the Persian learning. They introduced Arabic laws, formed for rude and ignorant tribes, and in the administration of them ... were most corrupt.

Every worldly profession, indeed every course of secular business, was in their avowed opinion (an opinion which they still hold) irreconcilable with strict virtue. Commerce, and the details of the finances, they left chiefly to the Hindoos, whom they despised and insulted. Where their government still prevails, the character resulting from their original temper, and superstition, aggravated by the enjoyment of power, remains in force. In our provinces, where their authority is subverted, and where many of them fall into the lower lines of life, that character becomes less obvious: but with more knowledge, and more pretensions to integrity, they are as unprincipled as the Hindoos. Their perfidy, however, and licentiousness, are the perfidy and licentiousness of a bolder people.

---

1   Timur (1336-1405) conqueror of much of Western and Central Asia, and founder of the Timurid Empire (1370-1405) in Central Asia and of the Timurid dynasty, which survived in some form until 1857. He conquered India at the end of the fourteenth century.

From the government and intermixture of the Mahomedans, the Hindoos have certainly derived no improvement of character. The invaders, may fairly be supposed to have contributed their share to the general evils, and even to have increased them. But they did not produce those evils, nor could they have perpetuated them in opposition to the genius and spirit of the Hindoos, who are in number probably as eight to one. They may therefore be considered, rather as constituting an accession, than as giving a character to the mass. The vices however of the Mahomedans, and Hindoos, are so homogeneous, that in stating their effects, it is not inaccurate to speak of both classes under the description of the one collective body into which they are now formed.

Upon the whole, then, we cannot avoid recognizing in the people of Hindostan, a race of men lamentably degenerate and base; retaining but a feeble sense of moral obligation; yet obstinate in their disregard of what they know to be right, governed by malevolent and licentious passions, strongly exemplifying the effects produced on society by great and general corruption of manners, and sunk in misery by their vices, in a country peculiarly calculated by its natural advantages, to promote the happiness of its inhabitants. The delineation from which this conclusion is to be formed, has been a task so painful, that nothing except the consciousness of meaning to do good could have induced the author to proceed in it. He trusts he has an affecting sense of the general imperfection of human nature, and would abhor the idea of needlessly or contemptuously exposing the defects of any man, or set of men. If he has given an unfavourable description, his wish is not to excite detestation, but to engage compassion, and to make it apparent, that what speculation may have ascribed to physical and unchangeable causes, springs from moral sources capable of correction.

[In subsequent chapters Grant argues that the moral depravity of the subject populations of India is due to a slavish adherence to superstition. After an extended attack on Hinduism, he argues that it is incumbent upon the British government to inculcate Christianity among Hindus and Muslims alike through widespread training in the English language. This is all couched in the language of enlightenment and compassion for a benighted people. In subsequent legislation, Britain would proceed to enact precisely these dicta.]

Select Bibliography

Ballaster, Ros. *Fabulous Orients: Fictions of the East in England 1662-1785*. Oxford: Oxford UP, 2006.

Bayly, C.A. *Imperial Meridian: The British Empire and the World, 1780-1830*. Cambridge: Cambridge UP, 1989.

Das, Sisir Kumar. *Shahibs and Munshis: An Account of the College of Fort William*. Calcutta: Orion, 1978.

Fisher, Michael H. *Counterflows to Colonialism: Indian Travellers and Settlers in Britain, 1600-1857*. Delhi: Permanent Black, 2004.

———. "Representing 'His' Women: Mirza Abu Talib Khan's 1801 'Vindication of the Liberties of Asiatic Women'." *Indian Economic and Social History Review*, 37.2 (2000): 215-37.

Jones, Sir William. *Selected Poetical and Prose Works*. Ed. Michael J. Franklin. Cardiff: U of Wales P, 1995.

Joseph, Betty. *Reading the East India Company, 1720-1840: Colonial Currencies of Gender*. Chicago: U of Chicago P, 2004.

Khair, Tabish. "Remembering to Forget Abu Taleb." *Wasifiri*, 34 (Autumn 2001): 34-38.

Khan, Gulfishan. *Indian Muslim Perceptions of the West During the Eighteenth Century*. Oxford: Oxford UP, 1998.

Leask, Nigel. "'Travelling the Other Way': *The Travels of Mirza Abu Taleb Khan* and Romantic Orientalism." *Romantic Representations of British India*. Ed. Michael J. Franklin. London: Routledge, 2006, 220-37.

Mahomet, Sake Deen. *The Travels of Dean Mahomet: An Eighteenth-Century Journey Through India*. Ed. Michael H. Fisher. Berkeley: U of California P, 1997.

Said, Edward. *Orientalism*. New York: Vintage, 1978.

Tavakoli-Targhi, Mohamad. *Refashioning Iran: Orientalism, Occidentalism and Historiography*. Houndmills: Palgrave, 2001.

Teltscher, Kate. *India Inscribed: European and British Writing on India 1600-1800*. Delhi: Oxford UP, 1995.

———. "The Shampooing Surgeon and the Persian Prince." *interventions*, 2.3 (2000): 409-23.

Visram, Rozina. *Asians in Britain: 400 Years of History*. London: Pluto Press, 2002.

———. *Ayahs, Lascars and Princes: Indians in Britain, 1700-1747*. London: Pluto Press, 1998.

Viswanathan, Gauri. *Masks of Conquest: Literary Study and British Rule in India*. New York: Columbia UP, 1989.